PENSIONS
POCKET BOOK
2014

GW00493846

ECONOMIC AND FINANCIAL PUBLISHING

IN ASSOCIATION WITH

PENSIONS POCKET BOOK
2014 EDITION

ISBN: 978-0-9567104-3-7

Produced and published by:

Economic and Financial Publishing Ltd ● 1, Ivory Square
● Plantation Wharf ● London SW11 3UE ● United Kingdom
Tel: (020) 7326 8350 ● Fax: (020) 7326 8351

Comments and suggestions for future editions of this pocket book are welcomed. Please contact: Editor, Pensions Pocket Book, Economic and Financial Publishing Ltd at the above address.

Whilst every effort has been made in the preparation of this book to ensure accuracy of the statistical and other contents, the publishers and data suppliers cannot accept any liability in respect of errors or omissions or for any losses or consequential losses arising from such errors or omissions. Readers will appreciate that the data contents are only as up-to-date as their availability and compilation, and printing schedules, will allow and are subject to change during the natural course of events.

Printed and bound in Great Britain by Shore Books and Design
www.shore-books.co.uk

NOTES

(i)   Symbols used:
      '–' *or* 'n/a' = data not available or not available on a comparable basis.
(ii) Constituent figures in the tables may not add up to the totals, due to rounding.
(iii) For full definitions readers are referred to the sources given at the foot of the tables.
(iv) Some topics are mentioned in more than one place but the information is not necessarily from the same source. Any differences are likely to be due to difference in definition, method of calculation or periods covered.

ACKNOWLEDGEMENTS

The publishers would like to thank all those who have contributed to this compilation of pensions data, in particular Aon Hewitt – co-producers of the book – whose contribution and support have been invaluable.

Other contributors, including government departments, whose help is gratefully acknowledged, include:

Association of Consulting Actuaries

Barclays plc

Financial Conduct Authority (FCA)

General Register Office for Scotland

International Social Security Association

The National Association of Pension Funds Ltd

Northern Ireland Statistics and Research Agency

Office for National Statistics (ONS)

Organisation for Economic Co-operation and Development (OECD)

The Pension Protection Fund

The Pensions Management Institute

The Pensions Regulator

Population Research Bureau

TradingEconomics.com

US Social Security Administration

Wilmington Publishing & Information

The World Bank

WorldEconomics.com

The WM Company

AON HEWITT

Aon Hewitt is the global leader in human resource solutions. The company partners with organizations to solve their most complex benefits, talent and related financial challenges, and improve business performance. Aon Hewitt designs, implements, communicates and administers a wide range of human capital, retirement, investment management, health care, compensation and talent management strategies. With more than 29,000 professionals in 90 countries, Aon Hewitt makes the world a better place to work for clients and their employees. For more information on Aon Hewitt, please visit *www.aonhewitt.com*.

ECONOMIC AND FINANCIAL PUBLISHING LIMITED

Economic and Financial Publishing Ltd, formerly known as NTC Publications, is a specialist provider of information to pensions professionals and economists working in industry, government and public bodies, education and research institutions.

CONTENTS

Section 28: SIGNIFICANT PENSION DATES (continued)

Section 29: UK PENSIONS CASE LAW

Section 30: INTERNATIONAL

High Level Overview:
  Economy and Government; Labour Relations; Cost of Employment;
  Employment Terms and Conditions; Social Security and other
  Required Benefits; Healthcare System; Taxation of Compensation and
  Benefits; Recent Developments,
for the following countries:

Reference Section 1: ECONOMIC & DEMOGRAPHIC DATA

Reference Section 2: INVESTMENT DATA

Reference Section 3: PENSION STATISTICS

Reference Section 4: SOCIAL SECURITY BENEFITS AND TAX RATES

APPENDICES

Expert focus for your fund. Wise choice.

Managing pension fund risk and investments has become increasingly more demanding and complex. A successful scheme needs a focused eye and dedicated investment expertise to deliver performance. That's why experienced trustees are turning to fiduciary management as the solution

We believe our delegated consulting service is one of the most transparent and independent fiduciary management offerings in the industry. We dev bespoke solutions, based on a clear understanding of your scheme and your needs. By managing your day-to-day investment decisions, we use expertise to deliver the performance and funding stability you want to ac

Make a wise choice and talk to one of the UK's leading providers of fiduciary services. Call us on 0800 279 5588 or email enquiries@aonhewitt.com

aonhewitt.co.uk/delegatedconsulting

Follow us on **twitter** @aonhewittuk

FOREWORD

The year 2013 saw continued progress in two areas that are expected to form the foundation of UK pension provision for many years into the future. Firstly, the proposed structure of the new single-tier State pension from 2016 was incorporated into the Pensions Bill which is expected to receive Royal Assent early in 2014. Secondly, many medium-sized and all large employers have automatically enrolled employees into schemes providing at least a minimum level of benefits – and the majority of these employees have remained members rather than opting out.

It remains unclear whether the revised State pension together with automatic enrolment will result in adequate levels of pension provision for future generations. A single-tier State pension will be easier for individuals to understand and will mean that they can more easily assess their need for additional retirement income, but the end of contracting out from 2016 – as a result of the Pensions Bill proposals for the single-tier pension – will lead to employers with contracted-out schemes reviewing their benefit structure. If such employers were to move to defined contribution arrangements with the minimum level of contribution required under auto-enrolment, this would result in much lower benefit expectations for their employees. The Government's plans to reinvigorate workplace pensions may diminish this impact, but its proposals are in the early stages of development.

There was welcome news for employers on funding defined benefit schemes. The whole industry breathed a collective sigh of relief when it was announced that changes to the EU's pensions Directive would not cover the solvency of pension funds, but would instead at this stage focus on governance and transparency. In addition, the Pensions Bill gives the Pensions Regulator a new objective, requiring it to minimise any adverse impact on employer growth when exercising its powers in respect of scheme funding. This is likely to lead to a more balanced approach, when applied in conjunction with the objectives of protecting members and reducing PPF risk.

At a more detailed level, there were many new developments for trustees and employers to address. The tax allowances for lifetime and annual pension savings are to be reduced once again. The lower allowances will apply from April 2014 with a new range of transitional protections for individuals. The Regulator has also focused its attention on DC governance issues and produced a significant amount of material which trustees need to consider.

Looking ahead, there are further potential complexities on the horizon such as amendments to the automatic enrolment requirements and legislation requiring automatic transfers of pots below £10,000.

The Pensions Pocket Book covers all of the above issues and more. We are sure you will find it a valuable source of information over the coming year.

Michael Clare
UK Country Director, Aon Hewitt

THE UK STATE PENSION SCHEME

There are currently two tiers of State pension provision: the Basic State Pension (BSP) and the State Second Pension (S2P), the latter replacing the State Earnings Related Pension (SERPS) from April 2002. The current Pensions Bill sets out details of the proposed new single-tier pension, which will apply for those reaching State Pension Age from 6 April 2016 *(see below)*.

State Pension Age

State Pension Age (SPA) is currently 65 for men. For women it was to be gradually increased from 60 to 65 over the ten years to April 2020. Having equalised SPA, from 2024 to 2046 it was to have gradually increased from 65 to 68. The Pensions Act 2011 accelerates the increase to 66. It provides for SPA to be equalised at 65 by December 2018 and then to increase to 66 by October 2020. The SPA varies by month of birth; SPAs for sample dates of birth are set out in the table below:

Date of birth in tax month commencing	State Pension Date
6 March 1950 or earlier	60th birthday (65th birthday for men)
6 September 1950	6 March 2011 (65th birthday for men)
6 March 1951	6 March 2012 (65th birthday for men)
6 September 1951	6 March 2013 (65th birthday for men)
6 March 1952	6 March 2014 (65th birthday for men)
6 September 1952	6 March 2015 (65th birthday for men)
6 March 1953	6 March 2016 (65th birthday for men)
6 July 1953	6 July 2017 (65th birthday for men)
6 November 1953	6 November 2018 (65th birthday for men)
6 December 1953	6 March 2019
6 February 1954	6 July 2019
6 April 1954	6 November 2019
6 June 1954	6 March 2020
6 August 1954	6 July 2020
From 6 October 1954	66th birthday

The Pensions Bill will bring forward the increase from 66 to 67 so that it takes place between 2026 and 2028. The Bill also introduces a regular review of the State Pension Age to take into account factors such as increases in longevity – it proposes that a report in relation to this is published at least every six years.

Basic State Pension

This is a flat-rate pension that is payable to any individual who has sufficient 'qualifying years'. Qualifying years are years in which the individual has received earnings at least equal to the Lower Earnings Limit (LEL), or is credited as earning the LEL because, for example, they receive certain benefits, or because they care, or receive child benefit, for a child under 12. Under changes made from 6 April 2010 by the Pensions Act 2007, the number of qualifying years needed for a full BSP is 30 for both men and women. Individuals without sufficient qualifying years (either from earnings or credits) receive a proportion of the full amount.

The BSP is increased in April each year. The Pensions Act 2007 includes a legislative provision to increase the BSP in line with earnings. However, from April 2012 annual increases have been in line with the higher of earnings increases, price increases (based on the Consumer Prices Index measure, rather than RPI) and 2.5%.

State Earnings Related Pension

SERPS accrued between 1978 and 2002 and is paid in addition to the BSP. It forms part of the Category A pension (and on the pensioner's death it forms part of their survivor's category B pension). It is based on a person's earnings throughout their career. When it was replaced in 2002, SERPS was targeting a pension of approximately 20% of the employee's Middle Band Earnings (i.e. earnings between the Lower and Upper Earnings Limits) at SPA.

The State Second Pension

S2P came into effect on 6 April 2002 and is currently an earnings-related scheme like SERPS, which it replaced. Any SERPS entitlement earned up until April 2002 will remain. S2P has salary bands which build up benefits at different rates *(see below)*. Certain non-earners (or low earners), such as those caring for the sick or disabled, also build up a S2P entitlement.

The salary bands used to calculate S2P take into account the Low Earnings Threshold (LET) and initially also a figure which approximated to 3 × LET – 2 × LEL. This figure is referred to below as the Middle Earnings Threshold (MET).

There were originally three bands:

Band 1 – LEL to LET: Target pension 40% of earnings
Band 2 – LET to MET: Target pension 10% of earnings
Band 3 – MET to UAP:*   Target pension 20% of earnings

(* Up to 5 April 2009 this upper limit was the Upper Earnings Limit (UEL). The Upper Accrual Point (UAP) was introduced at 6 April 2009, at a fixed amount equal to the 2008/09 UEL.)

Bands 2 and 3 merged from 6 April 2010 and now accrue pension at a target rate of 10% of earnings.

From 2012, the lower band was replaced by a flat rate per year for each year of accrual (£91.00 for 2013/14). From the same date, the Band 2 and 3 accrual was also changed from a target rate of 10% over an individual's working life to 1/440th for each year. As the UAP is frozen, the government's intention was that this upper band would gradually disappear, so that, from around 2030, S2P would become a flat-rate top-up to the BSP. These plans will now be replaced by the single-tier pension *(see below)*.

S2P is increased in April each year in line with prices (based on the Consumer Prices Index measure).

Categories of pension

There are three main categories of pension. Category A pension (including BSP and S2P) is based on the individual's own National Insurance contribution record. Category B pension is based on the National Insurance contribution record of the individual's spouse or civil partner. It may supplement or replace the individual's own Category A pension. Category D pension is paid to individuals aged at least 80 whose own basic pension (Category A or B) is less than the Category D rate. A fourth category – C – is only available, under certain conditions, to someone who was over SPA on 5th July 1948 or to the widow of such a man.

Contracting out

The ability to contract out of the additional State pension *(see Section 2)* was introduced alongside SERPS in 1978. Contracting out is now only possible on a salary-related basis. (Between 1988 and 2012, it was possible to contract out on a money purchase basis.) The single-tier pension will mean that contracting out will be abolished from April 2016 *(see below)*.

Payment and deferral of State pension

The basic pension for a Category A pensioner is payable from SPA. It is not paid automatically, and must generally be claimed. A Category B pension is payable from the individual's SPA, but the contributor (i.e. the individual's spouse or civil partner) must also have reached SPA and be entitled to their Category A pension.

Since April 2005, individuals who defer their State pension have had the choice of either:

- a lump sum based on pension foregone plus interest (providing they have deferred for at least 12 months), *or*
- an increased State pension.

Under the Pensions Bill *(see below)*, the lump sum option will be removed. From April 2011, an individual is not eligible for any enhancement on deferral of State benefits while they are in receipt of State pension credit, or while their partner is in receipt of State pension credit or certain other allowances.

Information on State pensions

Individuals are able to obtain a statement of their State pension entitlement from *www.gov.uk/state-pension-statement*. The State pension statement gives estimates based on the National Insurance record as it stands when the statement is produced, but does not give any projected amounts. Trustees are also able to obtain State pension information from the DWP for their scheme members, so that they can provide benefit statements combining both State and scheme pension entitlements.

State pension credits

State pension credits are tax-free weekly entitlements for individuals aged 60 and over and resident in Great Britain, and are targeted at pensioners on low and modest incomes. There are two elements of pension credit: the guarantee credit and the savings credit. They can be claimed by one member of a couple, but not both:

- *guarantee credit* – this brings recipients' incomes to a guaranteed level and is payable to both men and women at or over the current minimum qualifying age for women to receive the BSP, *and*

- *savings credit* – this allows a claimant to receive a cash addition of £0.60 a week for every £1 of pension and income from savings they have above the level of the savings credit threshold. However, for every £1 of income a pensioner has above the level of guarantee credit, the pensioner's saving credit is reduced by £0.40. Savings credit is payable to claimants over age 65, or if a spouse or civil partner is over age 65.

The single-tier State pension will remove the need for the guarantee credit for those entitled to the full amount, as it will be set above the pension credit standard minimum guarantee. Savings credit will be abolished for those reaching State Pension Age from 6 April 2016.

Single-tier pension

The Pensions Bill, which is currently proceeding through Parliament and expected to receive Royal Assent in April or May 2014, sets out the provisions for the new single-tier pension to apply to those who reach State Pension Age on or after 6 April 2016.

The full rate of single-tier pension will be payable to individuals with 35 or more 'qualifying years' (defined as above for the current BSP). This pension will be reduced (to 1/35th of the full rate for each qualifying year) for those who have fewer than 35 but at least a minimum number of qualifying years. (This minimum will be specified in regulations, but will be no more than 10 years).

The White Paper released in January 2013 assumed a starting rate of single-tier pension of £144 per week (with the intention that the eventual starting amount would be set above the level of the pension credit standard minimum guarantee – *see* 'State pension credits' *above*). The Bill provides for the single-tier pension to be increased in line with earnings, although illustrations in the White Paper assumed that the 'triple lock', based on the higher of annual increases in earnings and prices and 2.5%, currently applying to the BSP would also apply to the single-tier pension.

Transitional arrangements will apply for those with qualifying years before 6 April 2016. For these people, the BSP and S2P entitlement earned up to that date will be compared to the single-tier pension that would have accrued by then on the new rules (in both calculations, deducting an amount to reflect contracted-out employment under the current scheme). The greater of the two figures will be used as the starting amount: a 'foundation amount'. If the foundation amount is lower than the full rate of single-tier pension, the individual can use further qualifying years to add to their entitlement up to the level of the full rate of single-tier pension. If it exceeds the full rate of single-tier pension the excess will be protected, although it will not be increased in the same way as the single-tier pension; the legislation provides for increases only in line with prices.

Entitlement to the new State pension will be based only on the individual's own National Insurance (NI) record, with two exceptions: someone who married or entered a civil partnership before April 2016 may still inherit pension based on their late spouse's or civil partner's pre-2016 NI record; and some women who have elected to pay 'reduced-rate' NI contributions will be entitled to a pension equal to their current Category B rate of BSP, plus any entitlement from their own post-2016 qualifying years.

As at present, an increased weekly amount will be available to individuals choosing to defer their State pension, but the option of a lump sum will be removed.

The new single-tier pension will mean that contracting out will no longer be possible and the Bill provides for the abolition of salary-related contracting out, from April 2016 *(see Section 2)*.

CONTRACTING OUT

The ability to contract out of the additional State pension was introduced alongside SERPS *(see Section 1)* in 1978.

Between 1988 and 2012, it was possible to contract out on either a salary-related (COSR) basis or a money purchase (COMP) basis. However, contracting out on a money purchase basis was abolished from April 2012. In addition, the introduction of a single-tier State pension will involve the abolition of all contracting out; this is due to take place in April 2016 *(see below)*.

Where a COSR is no longer actively contracting out, legal requirements relating to those contracted-out rights that have already accrued continue to apply. However, certain restrictions are expected to be removed for schemes that cease to contract out in April 2016.

What does contracting out involve?

When earners are contracted out, their State additional pension (SERPS between April 1978 and April 2002; State Second Pension (S2P) thereafter – *see Section 1*) becomes subject to a contracted-out deduction in respect of the periods of contracted-out service.

Under a COSR, the employee and employer pay reduced rates of National Insurance (NI) contributions. For schemes contracted out on a COMP basis before April 2012, the position was as follows:

- the HMRC National Insurance Contributions Office (NICO) made payments directly to the scheme in respect of its contracted-out members (Appropriate Personal Pension, or APP), *or*
- reduced rates of NI contributions were paid by the employee and employer, and the employer paid the level contracting-out rebates into the scheme with top-up, age-related payments made to the scheme by NICO (Contracted-out Money Purchase scheme, or COMP).

In order to protect contracted-out members' pensions, extra requirements and restrictions apply to COSRs. NICO has responsibility for contracting-out procedures and supervision, with some aspects being handled by the HMRC Pension Schemes Services office.

Contracted-out deductions from State additional pension

Where an employee was contracted out prior to 6 April 1997, the accrual of SERPS pension up to that date is subject to a contracted-out deduction broadly equal to the guaranteed minimum pension (GMP) (or the 'notional' GMP in the case of a member of a contracted-out scheme other than a COSR).

Between April 1997 and April 2002, the contracted-out deduction for members of all types of contracted-out scheme was equal to the full SERPS pension, and so they accrued no SERPS benefit.

Following the introduction of S2P in April 2002, members of contracted-out occupational schemes continue to have a contracted-out deduction based on the SERPS level of benefit with earnings limits changed as for S2P *(see Section 1)*. A top-up pension, payable by the State, accrues to such members, equal to the amount (if any) by which the member's S2P would have exceeded the SERPS level of benefit adjusted as for S2P *(see Section 1)*. The same applied up to 5 April 2012 for members of COMPs. In contrast, the contracted-out deduction for members of APPs until April 2012 was equal to the full S2P and so they did not accrue a top-up pension from the State (except for members earning below the Low Earnings Threshold – *see Section 1)*. These differences were reflected in the rebates available between 2002 and 2012.

BASIS OF CONTRACTING OUT

Salary-related contracting out

Guaranteed Minimum Pensions (GMPs)

Before 6 April 1997, COSRs had to promise to pay at least a minimum pension (the GMP) to each participating employee; this reduced the employee's SERPS pension from the State and, in return, both the employer and the employee paid lower-rate NI contributions. COSRs still need to provide GMPs accrued before 6 April 1997.

These are subject to strict regulatory requirements, including revaluation for early leavers, as described in *Section 12*. Tables of revaluation rates are included *on pages 11 and 12*.

The total NI rebates for contracted-out schemes are split between employee and employer. The split has varied over time, *and components can be found on page 12*.

Legislation that allows schemes the option of converting GMPs to 'normal' scheme benefits of equal value came into effect on 6 April 2009. To use this option, trustees must have employer consent and have consulted affected members.

The Government believes that equalising occupational scheme benefits to reflect the different GMPs between men and women is necessary *(see Section 15)*, and consulted in 2012 on draft regulations. It is expected to publish statutory guidance in due course, covering both conversion to 'normal' scheme benefits and equalisation.

The Reference Scheme Test (RST)

From 6 April 1997, no further GMPs accrued and, in order to contract out, the scheme has to pass a 'Reference Scheme Test'.

The scheme's actuary is required to certify that the pensions provided by the scheme are 'broadly equivalent to' or 'better than' the pensions under a Reference Scheme which is specified in legislation. The test is applied 'collectively' for employees and separately for their widows, widowers or surviving civil partners. The RST is failed if benefits for more than 10% of individual employees or their survivors are not broadly equivalent to, or better than, pensions under the Reference Scheme. The RST must be carried out separately for each separate benefit scale (if relevant) within a scheme, which must satisfy the test in its own right before the members to whom it applies can be contracted out on a salary-related basis. If separate contracting-out certificates are required for individual employers participating in a scheme, then the test must be carried out separately for each employer. The main features of the Reference Scheme from 6 April 2009 are:

Pension age	65
Pension accrual rate	1/80
Pensionable salary	average qualifying earnings in the last three tax years
Qualifying earnings	90% of earnings between the Lower Earnings Limit (×52) and the Upper Accrual Point (×53)
Service	if limited to a maximum, this must not be less than 40 years
Spouse's or surviving civil partner's pension	50% of the member's pension (based on completed service for members who die before age 65)

Frequency of testing

Legislation requires the actuary to consider, at least every three years, whether there are any changes in the scheme's membership profile that might prevent the scheme from continuing to satisfy the test. A scheme's ability to pass the test must also be reconsidered whenever the actuary is informed of any changes which might affect that ability, such as:

- a change to the terms affecting ongoing accrual in the scheme (e.g. the definition of pensionable pay), *or*
- a significant change to the scheme's active membership profile, including remuneration patterns.

Money purchase contracting out

COMP scheme

Occupational money purchase schemes could contract out if contributions equal to the flat-rate contracted-out rebates were paid to the scheme by the employer. Part of this was recoverable from the employee, *as discussed below*. COMP NI rebates were age-related between April 1997 and April 2012. The age-related rebates were capped at 7.4% of Upper Band Earnings from April 2007.

The flat-rate part of the rebate (3% from April 2007) was paid by the employer to the trustees. Of this, 1.6% was attributed to, and could be recovered from, the employee. For members whose age-related rebate exceeded the flat-rate part, the balance was paid to the trustees in the following tax year by NICO. All rebates paid into the COMP, and any investment return on them, were known as Protected Rights and had to be used to provide benefits as set out in legislation, prior to 6 April 2012.

Appropriate Personal Pension (APP)

Employees could take out an APP contract in order to contract out. Employers and employees continued to pay full-rate NI contributions and, following the end of the tax year, NICO then rebated part of these NI contributions by making so-called 'minimum contributions' directly into the APP. A basic rate 'tax rebate' on that part of these minimum contributions deemed to be in respect of employee NI contributions was also paid into the scheme by NICO. These payments, and any investment return on them, were Protected Rights under an APP.

From April 1997, minimum contributions were age-related, again subject to a cap. From April 2010, earnings between the Lower Earnings Limit and Upper Accrual Point were divided into two bands and different rebate rates applied to earnings falling within each band.

Contracted-out Mixed Benefit (COMB) scheme

Between 6 April 1997 and 5 April 2012, two sections of a single scheme were permitted to contract out concurrently on the two different bases.

STATE SCHEME PREMIUMS

Before 6 April 1997, contracted-out schemes were able to buy their members back into SERPS by payment of a State scheme premium in a number of circumstances, thereby extinguishing the scheme's liability to provide the member with contracted-out benefits. Only the Contributions Equivalent Premium (CEP) now remains, which COSRs may pay in respect of members with less than two years' qualifying service when either scheme membership ceases or the scheme ceases to contract out.

CONTRACTING BACK IN

COMPs and APPs were automatically contracted back in from 6 April 2012. COSRS are due to be automatically contracted back in from 6 April 2016 (see below).

Before 6 April 2016 a COSR can decide to cease to contract out (and in some cases must do so). In order to do so the trustees or managers must notify Pension Schemes Services and will, in turn, receive a notice from them setting out the date from which the contracting-out certificate is cancelled. From this date all affected members will be contracted back in and the trustees or managers will then have two years to either discharge the rights or determine to preserve them within the scheme, in which case the scheme will need to continue to comply with the relevant requirements. (If no action is taken HMRC may issue a notice giving the scheme six months to discharge the liabilities outside the scheme.) The following methods may be used to secure the liabilities:

- transfer to another scheme (see Section 13) — member consent will currently be required unless this is part of a bulk transfer exercise to another COSR or former COSR and prescribed conditions are met
- the purchase of an annuity or deferred annuity contract, or

- provision of benefits within the scheme that satisfy HMRC requirements.

The scheme does not need to use the same method for all members.

ABOLITION OF CONTRACTING OUT

COMP schemes

Contracting out on a money purchase basis *(as set out above)* was abolished from 6 April 2012. Contracting-out certificates were automatically cancelled and all affected schemes automatically contracted back in.

During a three-year transitional period, existing arrangements for the payment and recovery of age-related rebates will continue. After April 2015, any outstanding payments will be made directly to members.

Contracted-out rights (known as 'Protected Rights' – *see above*) ceased to exist from April 2012 and will be treated in exactly the same way as any other money purchase benefits, subject to any restrictions written into scheme rules. This applies to contingent spouses' rights as well as to members' rights. Some occupational pension schemes needed to change their rules to remove the Protected Rights requirements: regulations allow any such change to be made by resolution during a six-year transitional period.

Those schemes that switched instead to contracting out on a salary-related basis have to meet the normal requirements for contracting out on a COSR basis *(see above)*, including satisfying the Reference Scheme Test.

COSR schemes

The basis of contracting out on a salary-related basis is explained above. However, this option is due also to be abolished, from April 2016, as a result of the Government's proposals to move to a single-tier State pension combining the BSP and S2P *(see Section 1)*.

To reflect the removal of NI rebates, employers are expected to be given an overriding power to amend the rules of contracted-out schemes, which would apply in addition to any amendment powers under scheme rules. This power will last for five years from April 2016, and may be used to increase employee contributions or to alter future accrual of benefit (or a combination of the two).

Restrictions on GMPs are due to be maintained, requiring them to be revalued and not to be 'franked' against excess pension. However, the requirement for a 'Protection Rule' to be added to the rules of a scheme that has ceased to contract out *(see Section 21)* is expected to be removed for schemes ceasing to contract out on 6 April 2016.

For members with periods of contracted-out service before April 2016, their calculated 'foundation amount' of single-tier State pension will be reduced, reflecting the deduction that would have applied to their SERPS/S2P entitlement.

FIXED RATE GMP REVALUATION FACTORS

Number of Years	Terminations on or after:						
	6.4.1978 8.5%	6.4.1988 7.5%	6.4.1993 7.0%	6.4.1997 6.25%	6.4.2002 4.5%	6.4.2007 4.0%	6.4.2012 4.75%
1	1.085	1.075	1.070	1.0625	1.045	1.040	1.0475
2	1.177	1.156	1.145	1.1289	1.092	1.082	1.0973
3	1.277	1.242	1.225	1.1995	1.141	1.125	1.1494
4	1.386	1.335	1.311	1.2744	1.193	1.170	1.2040
5	1.504	1.436	1.403	1.3541	1.246	1.217	1.2612
6	1.631	1.543	1.501	1.4387	1.302	1.265	1.3211
7	1.770	1.659	1.606	1.5286	1.361	1.316	1.3838
8	1.921	1.783	1.718	1.6242	1.422	1.369	1.4495
9	2.084	1.917	1.838	1.7257	1.486	1.423	1.5184
10	2.261	2.061	1.967	1.8335	1.553	1.480	1.5905
11	2.453	2.216	2.105	1.9481	1.623	1.539	1.6661
12	2.662	2.382	2.252	2.0699	1.696	1.601	1.7452
13	2.888	2.560	2.410	2.1993	1.772	1.665	1.8281
14	3.133	2.752	2.579	2.3367	1.852	1.732	1.9149
15	3.400	2.959	2.759	2.4828	1.935	1.801	2.0059
16	3.689	3.181	2.952	2.6379	2.022	1.873	2.1012
17	4.002	3.419	3.159	2.8028	2.113	1.948	2.2010
18	4.342	3.676	3.380	2.9780	2.208	2.026	2.3055
19	4.712	3.951	3.617	3.1641	2.308	2.107	2.4151
20	5.112	4.248	3.870	3.3619	2.412	2.191	2.5298
21	5.547	4.566	4.141	3.5720	2.520	2.279	2.6499
22	6.018	4.909	4.430	3.7952	2.634	2.370	2.7758
23	6.530	5.277	4.741	4.0324	2.752	2.465	2.9077
24	7.085	5.673	5.072	4.2844	2.876	2.563	3.0458
25	7.687	6.098	5.427	4.5522	3.005	2.666	3.1904
26	8.340	6.556	5.807	4.8367	3.141	2.772	3.3420
27	9.049	7.047	6.214	5.1390	3.282	2.883	3.5007
28	9.818	7.576	6.649	5.4602	3.430	2.999	3.6670
29	10.653	8.144	7.114	5.8015	3.584	3.119	3.8412
30	11.558	8.755	7.612	6.1641	3.745	3.243	4.0237
31	12.541	9.412	8.145	6.5493	3.914	3.373	4.2148
32	13.607	10.117	8.715	6.9587	4.090	3.508	4.4150
33	14.763	10.876	9.325	7.3936	4.274	3.648	4.6247
34	16.018	11.692	9.978	7.8557	4.466	3.794	4.8444
35	17.380	12.569	10.677	8.3467	4.667	3.946	5.0745
36	18.857	13.512	11.424	8.8683	4.877	4.104	5.3155
37	20.460	14.525	12.224	9.4226	5.097	4.268	5.5680
38	22.199	15.614	13.079	10.0115	5.326	4.439	5.8325
39	24.086	16.785	13.995	10.6372	5.566	4.616	6.1095
40	26.133	18.044	14.974	11.3021	5.816	4.801	6.3997
41	28.354	19.398	16.023	12.0084	6.078	4.993	6.7037
42	30.764	20.852	17.144	12.7590	6.352	5.193	7.0221
43	33.379	22.416	18.344	13.5564	6.637	5.400	7.3557
44	36.217	24.098	19.628	14.4037	6.936	5.617	7.7051
45	39.295	25.905	21.002	15.3039	7.248	5.841	8.0711
46	42.635	27.848	22.473	16.2604	7.574	6.075	8.4545

Source: Aon Hewitt.

SECTION 148 ORDERS:
REVALUATION OF EARNINGS FACTORS

				Tax Year of Termination				
Tax Year of Earnings	2013/14 (%)	2012/13 (%)	2011/12 (%)	2010/11 (%)	2009/10 (%)	2008/09 (%)	2007/08 (%)	2006/07 (%)	2005/06 (%)
1978/79	734.2	719.5	705.0	686.9	677.6	654.2	623.8	595.3	572.4
1979/80	636.3	623.3	610.5	594.5	586.3	565.7	538.8	513.7	493.5
1980/81	515.1	504.3	493.6	480.2	473.3	456.1	433.7	412.7	395.8
1981/82	415.2	406.1	397.1	385.9	380.2	365.7	347.0	329.4	315.3
1982/83	367.9	359.6	351.5	341.4	336.1	323.0	306.0	290.0	277.2
1983/84	334.5	326.8	319.2	309.8	305.0	292.8	276.9	262.1	250.2
1984/85	302.3	295.2	288.2	279.5	275.0	263.7	249.0	235.3	224.3
1985/86	277.4	270.7	264.2	256.0	251.7	241.2	227.4	214.5	204.2
1986/87	246.5	240.4	234.4	226.9	223.0	213.3	200.7	188.8	179.3
1987/88	222.7	217.0	211.3	204.3	200.7	191.7	179.9	168.9	160.1
1988/89	196.8	191.6	186.4	180.0	176.7	168.4	157.5	147.4	139.3
1989/90	167.9	163.2	158.5	152.7	149.7	142.2	132.4	123.3	115.9
1990/91	149.7	145.3	140.9	135.5	132.7	125.7	116.6	108.1	101.2
1991/92	126.8	122.8	118.8	113.9	111.4	105.0	96.7	89.0	82.8
1992/93	112.9	109.2	105.5	100.8	98.5	92.5	84.7	77.5	71.6
1993/94	102.8	99.2	95.7	91.3	89.0	83.3	75.9	69.0	63.5
1994/95	96.7	93.2	89.8	85.5	83.3	77.8	70.7	63.9	58.5
1995/96	88.4	85.1	81.8	77.7	75.6	70.3	63.5	57.0	51.9
1996/97	83.3	80.0	76.8	72.9	70.8	65.7	59.0	52.7	47.7
1997/98	74.5	71.5	68.4	64.6	62.7	57.8	51.4	45.5	40.7
1998/99	66.9	63.9	61.0	57.4	55.5	50.9	44.8	39.1	34.5
1999/00	60.1	57.3	54.5	51.1	49.3	44.8	38.9	33.5	29.1
2000/01	50.7	48.0	45.4	42.1	40.4	36.2	30.7	25.6	21.4
2001/02	44.9	42.3	39.8	36.6	35.0	31.0	25.7	20.7	16.8
2002/03	38.9	36.4	34.0	31.0	29.5	25.6	20.5	15.8	11.9
2003/04	34.1	31.7	29.4	26.5	25.0	21.2	16.3	11.7	8.1
2004/05	29.2	26.9	24.6	21.8	20.4	16.8	12.1	7.6	4.1
2005/06	24.1	21.9	19.7	17.0	15.6	12.2	7.6	3.4	
2006/07	20.0	17.9	15.8	13.2	11.8	8.5	4.1		
2007/08	15.3	13.2	11.2	8.7	7.4	4.2			
2008/09	10.6	8.7	6.7	4.3	3.1				
2009/10	7.3	5.4	3.5	1.2					
2010/11	6.0	4.1	2.3						
2011/12	3.6	1.8							
2012/13	1.8								

Source: Aon Hewitt, compiled from government information.

CONTRACTING-OUT REBATES

	Employee	Employer	
Tax Years	(% Upper Band Earnings)	COSR (% UBE)	COMP[1] (% UBE)
2002/03 to 2006/07	1.60	3.50	1.00
2007/08 to 2011/12	1.60	3.70	1.40
2012/13 to 2015/16[2]	1.40	3.40	n/a

Notes: 1. For COMPs, in addition to the flat-rate rebates shown in the table above for tax years up to 2011/12, a further age-related payment was due from NICO.
2. Contracting out on a salary-related basis is due to be abolished from April 2016.

Source: Aon Hewitt, compiled from government information.

SCHEME DESIGN AND BENEFITS

This section gives a brief explanation of the different types of benefit commonly provided by occupational pension schemes in the UK, and some of the factors that affect the design of those benefits.

Pension schemes are often classified as defined benefit (DB) or defined contribution (DC). Over the past ten years or so, many employers have closed traditional DB final salary pension schemes because of the significant risks, and associated costs, that they have to bear. In many cases employers have replaced these with DC schemes where individual members bear most of the risks.

However, employers are also looking for other solutions that fall somewhere between these two extremes, retaining the risks they want to manage, whilst providing benefits which are still attractive to employees from a recruitment and retention perspective. These newer designs incorporate features of both DB and DC schemes. Further, hybrid schemes also exist which provide different types of benefit in different circumstances. The Government is also exploring the scope for new types of risk-sharing ('defined ambition') schemes, and has published a paper outlining possible options.

The classification of certain benefits as either money purchase (DC) or non-money purchase (DB) has been the subject of legal debate over recent years, and the judgment in the *Imperial Home Decor* case brought this to the attention of the Government. The Pensions Act 2011, once brought into effect, will clarify the legislative definition of money purchase benefits. In some cases, this will mean that benefits may have been regarded as DC but may now be considered DB.

The key characteristics of the various scheme designs are covered below.

TYPES OF PENSION BENEFIT – DEFINED CONTRIBUTION

DC schemes provide benefits which depend on the amount of the contributions paid into the scheme, the investment return credited to those contributions, any expenses deducted and the financial conditions at the time benefits are converted into a future retirement income. There are a number of types of arrangement that can be used to provide DC benefits which are described below.

Trust-based occupational pension schemes

Employer-sponsored occupational DC pension schemes and NEST *(see Section 7)* are operated as trusts *(see Section 8)*. In many cases the scheme may contain separate DC and DB sections within the same trust. Most DB schemes offer additional voluntary contributions on a DC basis and many that accept transfers into the scheme will offer DC benefits in respect of the transfer payment received even if other benefits are accruing on a DB basis.

Personal pensions and retirement annuity contracts

Personal pensions in their present form have been available since July 1988. They were introduced with the intention of extending pension choice and encouraging individuals not in occupational schemes to save for retirement. All personal pensions are DC and are provided as a contract with an insurer or other provider, rather than being trust-based. Personal pensions replaced retirement annuity contracts (RACs), often referred to as s226 contracts. Those who already had RACs prior to July 1988 were allowed to continue to contribute to them.

Group personal pensions

Group personal pensions (GPPs) are personal pensions arranged by an employer for the benefit of its employees. These are often seen as a low-cost (to the employer) alternative to a trust-based, occupational DC scheme, as most administration is handled by the insurance company running the GPP and is usually included in the annual management charge deducted from the members' funds.

Self-invested personal pensions

A self-invested personal pension (SIPP) is an arrangement under a personal pension scheme which allows the member to choose the investments. As the members may select the investments, SIPPs are classed as 'investment-regulated pension schemes'. As such, SIPPs are subject to prohibitive tax charges if they invest in residential property or most tangible moveable assets.

Stakeholder pensions

Stakeholder pension schemes were introduced by the government in 2001 as a way of encouraging private pension provision. Various special requirements and restrictions apply to stakeholder schemes, including that the scheme must

- be formally registered as a stakeholder scheme with the Pensions Regulator
- meet certain 'minimum standards', including in relation to the level of charges, flexibility of contribution payments, acceptance of transfer payments and provision of information, *and*
- provide a default 'lifestyle' investment option so that members do not need to make a choice about how their money is invested, although other investment choices can be offered.

The requirement for employers with five or more employees to provide access to a stakeholder scheme for employees not already covered by a suitable pension scheme was removed from 1 October 2012, to coincide with the introduction of automatic enrolment *(see Sections 4 to 6)*. However, the requirement to deduct contributions and pay them to the scheme will continue for existing arrangements.

TYPES OF PENSION BENEFIT – DEFINED BENEFIT

Final Salary

The traditional form of DB scheme was the final salary scheme, under which the pension paid is equal to the number of years worked, multiplied by the member's salary at or near to retirement, multiplied by a factor known as the accrual rate (commonly 1/80 or 1/60). After a career of 40 years, this would give a pension of one-half or two-thirds of the member's 'final salary'.

Members generally pay a fixed rate of contributions (or no contribution in some cases), with the employer funding the balance of the costs – and therefore bearing all the funding risks.

CARE

Career Average Revalued Earnings (CARE) schemes are DB in nature, but are a variation of the traditional final salary design. Rather than the pension retirement being based on earnings close to retirement, it is based on the average earnings throughout the member's entire career. These earnings are usually revalued up to retirement in line with price inflation.

If the revaluation rate is lower than the average earnings increases received by the member (which has tended to be the case), then the pension at retirement will be less than for an otherwise identical final salary scheme. From an employer's perspective, this means that a CARE scheme would usually cost less to fund.

TYPES OF PENSION BENEFIT – OTHER

Cash Balance and Retirement Balance

Under these arrangements, members build up lump sum benefits on either a final salary or a CARE basis. For example, the lump sum accrual rate could be 20% of salary per annum, giving a lump sum after 40 years of 8 times either final or career average earnings. Another way of thinking of these schemes is as a DC benefit with the investment return guaranteed at the outset. For example, the return could be defined as the increase in RPI plus 2% per annum.

Up to retirement, the scheme is considered as DB. At retirement, part of the lump sum can be taken as cash with the balance turned into pension. The conversion to pension is usually carried out by purchasing an annuity with an insurance company, in the same way as for a DC scheme. However, in some cases preferential conversion terms are offered through the scheme itself.

Hybrid schemes

There are many forms of hybrid scheme which incorporate features of the above designs. The two most common types are:

- a better of two (or more) different types of benefit, for example a DC scheme with a minimum level of benefit calculated on a DB basis, *and*
- a combination of different types of benefit, for example benefits might accrue on a final salary basis up to a certain level of earnings, but on a DC basis above that level.

Other forms of risk sharing

In recent years some schemes have started to incorporate alternative risk-sharing features into their benefit design. For example, longevity-adjusted schemes adjust future benefit accrual to take account of changes in life expectancy.

The Government is exploring the possibility of new models of scheme which would allow greater risk sharing. In a paper published in November 2012, it outlined various options for 'defined ambition' schemes, which include more flexible forms of DB such as:

- simplified/core DB schemes, which would provide a guaranteed 'core' level of benefit, with additional ('ambition') benefits being given on a discretionary basis and subject to lighter regulation; schemes would not need to offer escalation or spouse's benefits, or could make escalation conditional on the funding target being met
- converting benefits at retirement from DB to a DC fund of equivalent value
- allowing pensions in payment to fluctuate to an extent, depending on a scheme's funding position *and*

- linking retirement age to State Pension Age (for both past and future service benefits)

as well as variations on DC which would provide greater certainty than the basic DC design. These include:

- mutualised guarantees and risk-sharing, including money-back guarantees on contributions and sharing longevity risk between the guarantee provider and the provider of the retirement income
- insured guarantees and risk sharing, such as guaranteed returns for a fixed period, or an underpin on retirement income
- employer-financed 'smoothing fund', which would be used to manage targeted retirement outcomes *and*
- collective defined contribution (CDC) schemes, in which risk is spread across members of the scheme. This idea was explored and rejected by the previous government, but is reconsidered in this paper.

The ideas are at an early stage and new legislation would be needed to enable many of the designs above. A further paper on the proposals for defined ambition was due to be published in summer 2013.

OTHER ISSUES AFFECTING SCHEME DESIGN

Automatic enrolment

From 2012 onwards employers have been required to automatically enrol eligible jobholders into a qualifying pension scheme and to make minimum contributions on behalf of their workers *(see Sections 4 to 6)*. The employer may use its own scheme if that meets minimum quality requirements, NEST (the government-funded nationwide scheme for automatic-enrolment – *see Section 7)*, or one of the privately funded nationwide schemes that have been established

Registered Pension Schemes

To obtain tax concessions, the majority of UK pension schemes are registered with HMRC. Registered schemes are subject to requirements that impact on the type and level of benefits that they can provide. *These requirements as described in Section 10. Section 11 describes arrangements outside the tax privileged environment.*

Options at retirement

Members can usually choose to take some of their benefits as a lump sum currently tax free within certain limits *(see Section 10)*. In a DB scheme this usually achieved by the member giving up some of their pension, although some schemes provide a lump sum as a separate benefit.

In a DC scheme members can usually take one-quarter of their retirement fund as a lump sum and use the remainder to purchase pension benefits. DC schemes have greater flexibility than DB schemes when it comes to the form of pension benefits, which may be paid as a lifetime annuity, drawdown pension or a scheme pension (DB schemes may only pay a scheme pension. Drawdown pension is generally subject to strict limits, although under certain conditions a member can apply for flexible drawdown, which removes the limits. *See Section 10 for further details on all the types of pension and lump sum benefits payable from registered pension schemes.*

In addition to the standard options, new forms of 'at retirement options' are being introduced, typically by employers, in an effort to manage their defined benefit liabilities. These include pension increase conversion exercises (subject to the requirements below for increases in payment), flexible retirement options and flexible drawdown *(see Section 20 for further details).*

Interaction with State Benefits

Many schemes are designed to target an overall level of pension at retirement, including State pensions. DB schemes can also contract out of the State Second Pension (S2P), and previously SERPS. However, contracting out for DB schemes will be abolished from April 2016, to coincide with the introduction of the single-tier State pension *(see Section 1).* Contracting out on a money purchase basis was abolished from April 2012. *For information on contracting out, see Section 2.*

Many schemes are therefore reviewing their design to reflect the forthcoming changes in the State system *(see Section 1).* Where scheme rules do not permit such adjustments, draft regulations will give employers overriding powers – for a period of five years – to amend the rules of contracted-out schemes to increase member contributions or alter future accrual of benefit (or a combination of the two).

Some schemes also provide bridging pensions between retirement and subsequent State Pension Age to smooth the change in a member's total income from State and scheme combined. Increases in State Pension Age *(see Section 1)* will impact such arrangements or options.

AVCs

From 6 April 1988, all occupational pension schemes had to allow members to make Additional Voluntary Contributions (AVCs). Free-standing Additional Voluntary Contributions (FSAVCs) were introduced in 1987 to allow members to pay AVCs outside their occupational scheme in order to benefit from greater flexibility in investment choice and portability should they leave service. Under the current tax regime, FSAVCs are virtually indistinguishable from personal pensions.

With effect from 6 April 2006, the requirement for trustees to provide members with access to an AVC arrangement was removed. However, this does not stop such a facility being offered.

Pension increases in payment

The Pensions Act 1995 made it compulsory for approved occupational pension schemes to provide at least Limited Price Indexation (LPI) of pensions accrued after 5 April 1997 once in payment. However, the scope of this requirement was reduced from 6 April 2005 when the Pensions Act 2004 removed it for pensions arising from DC benefits coming into payment on or after that date.

For pensions that remain subject to the LPI requirement, the minimum annual increase required is the lower of price inflation and 5% for service between 6 April 1997 and 5 April 2005, and the lower of price inflation and 2.5% for service after 5 April 2005.

In 2010, the Government moved from using RPI to using CPI as the basis for determining price inflation for future statutory minimum increases to pensions in payment and revaluations in deferment. The Pensions Act 2011 included provisions to allow schemes to continue to use RPI as the basis for such increases, in certain circumstances.

Salary sacrifice

A salary sacrifice is an arrangement whereby an employee waives entitlement to part of their salary (or bonus), in exchange for the employer paying a pension contribution of an equivalent amount.

An advantage of salary sacrifice is that savings in National Insurance contributions (NICs) can be generated. Employee contributions are paid out of salary which is subject to NICs (both employer and employee), whereas employer contributions are not.

Historically, salary sacrifice was used almost exclusively for higher earners However the concept is now commonplace through the growth of flexible remuneration plans, under which employees have a flex fund which they can use to select from a range of benefits, and receive the remaining money as salary.

Scheme modifications

Legislation sets out conditions for making 'regulated modifications' of accrued rights or entitlements to pension scheme benefits. Essentially, modifications of an occupational pension scheme are 'voidable' unless for each member or survivor:

- *either* informed consent has been given in writing by the member or survivor *or* (where permitted) the actuarial equivalence requirements involving certification by the scheme actuary, have been met, *and*
- the trustees have formally determined to make (or have consented to the modification and, before it takes effect, have notified the affected members and survivors.

Informed consent is always required in relation to a special category of major changes called protected modifications. Members must be given a reasonable opportunity to make representations, and the modification must take effect within a reasonable period of the consent being given.

The Pensions Regulator may make an order declaring the modification void if the requirements have not been met. It also has the power to levy fines on trustees and others exercising a power to modify a scheme, where voidable modifications have been made or the requirements specified in an order by the Regulator have not been met. The Regulator has issued a Code of Practice to help trustees comply with the legislation and to provide guidance on what the Regulator considers to be reasonable periods for the various stages of the process.

Consultation by employers

Legislation (applying to businesses that employ 50 or more staff) gives employees the right – in certain circumstances – to be informed and consulted about the business they work for, including:

- the prospects for employment, *and*
- substantial changes in work organisation (e.g. proposed redundancies or changes in working hours) or contractual relationships.

The requirement for employers to have an agreement to inform and consult is not automatic but can be triggered in various ways, for example by a formal request from a minimum number of employees. If an employer fails to initiate negotiations for an agreement to inform and consult employees when required to do so, or when negotiations fail, 'standard provisions' apply.

In addition, the Pensions Act 2004 also requires employers to consult with members before they can make certain listed changes to a pension scheme. Listed changes include increasing normal pension age, closing a scheme, changing from DB to DC, ceasing or reducing DB accrual, changing what elements of pay constitute pensionable earnings, reducing an employer's contribution to a DC scheme or changing the rates of indexation to pensions in payment or revaluation of pensions in deferment where that change would be less generous. The Department for Work and Pensions published guidance on the regulations, in order to help employers comply with the legislation.

Inalienability of occupational pension

With certain exceptions, entitlements or rights under occupational pension schemes may not be forfeited, assigned, surrendered, subjected to a charge or lien, or set off, and an agreement to do any of these things is unenforceable. These exceptions include allowing trustees to reduce future benefits to recover a previous payment made in error or as a result of fraud, or to meet the annual allowance charge from scheme benefits *(see Section 10)*.

Cross-border activities

The Pensions Act 2004 introduced a number of provisions relating to cross-border activities under the EU Pensions Directive. A UK scheme that wishes to accept contributions from employers elsewhere in the EU (which employ members of the scheme who work elsewhere in the EU) must receive a general authorisation from the Pensions Regulator. It must also apply for and receive approval from the Regulator in respect of each EU employer. Based on information passed on about the social and labour laws of the host member state (i.e. the other EU country), the UK scheme has the responsibility for ensuring compliance, with the Regulator being able to monitor such compliance and impose sanctions for non-compliance. Where the cross-border activity is the other way round (i.e. the UK is the host state and the scheme is established elsewhere), the Regulator has the role of notifying the other country's authority of relevant UK law and monitoring compliance with it. The EU Directive requires that non-money purchase cross-border schemes are fully funded at all times. UK law interprets this as meeting the statutory funding objective introduced by the Pensions Act 2004 *(see Section 17)*. In addition, in order to be authorised, cross-border schemes must obtain annual actuarial valuations, with any deficit against the statutory funding objective being removed within 24 months of the valuation's effective date.

There are concerns that, if Scotland were to vote for independence and remain in the EU, pension schemes operating between Scotland and the remainder of the UK would be classed as 'cross-border'. The complexity and burden created by cross-border issues could result in the splitting of existing UK-wide pension schemes into separate schemes covering Scotland and the rest of the UK.

AUTOMATIC ENROLMENT – EMPLOYERS' OBLIGATIONS

The Government first announced in 2006 that it intended to introduce a system of automatic pension scheme enrolment. The Pensions Act 2008 implemented the framework for the regime and subsequent regulations have set out the detail of the requirements. It came into force in 2012, requiring employers, under a phased implementation first applying to larger employers, to automatically enrol workers who satisfy earnings and age criteria in a qualifying scheme. The scheme can be the employer's own scheme or an alternative arrangement such as NEST, *which is described in Section 7.* Employers' qualifying schemes *are covered in Section 5.*

In 2013, the Government consulted on a number of simplifications to the automatic enrolment requirements. Some of the resulting amending regulations came into force on 1 November 2013, and others will do so on 1 April 2014. The revised requirements are covered below.

WHEN DO THE OBLIGATIONS START?

Automatic enrolment is being phased in between 1 October 2012 and 1 April 2017. Larger employers became subject to the new employer requirements in 2012, and smaller employers have 'staging dates' *as set out in the schedule at the end of this section.* Each employer has its own staging date that is based on the size of its PAYE scheme as at 1 April 2012, which in some cases includes pensioners. For employers that participate in more than one PAYE scheme, it is based on the size of the largest PAYE scheme in which they have workers. New employers setting up between April 2012 and September 2017 have staging dates between 1 May 2017 and 1 February 2018. The Pensions Regulator is writing to employers to remind them of their staging dates.

Employers can bring their staging date forward.

An employer cannot delay its staging date, although it can postpone automatic enrolment of a worker for up to three months, if it provides the appropriate notification to the worker. *(See below for more on postponement.*

WHO DO THE DUTIES APPLY TO?

The new duties apply to employers in respect of 'workers'. A worker is an individual who has a contract of employment with the employer, or a contract of service with the employer to do work or provide services personally and not as part of their own business. The distinction between personal service workers and those who provide services as part of their own business may be hard to determine, and the Regulator includes a list of considerations in its Detailed Guidance no. 1.

The duties apply in respect of individuals working in the UK or ordinarily working in the UK. This is another aspect that may be hard to determine, and the Regulator has provided examples in its Detailed Guidance no. 3.

WORKFORCE CATEGORISATION

Employer duties vary according to a worker's age and earnings. The level of earnings is determined for a *pay reference period*. The employer can now choose to determine the pay reference period of a worker as either the period over which the worker is paid (e.g. monthly, weekly) or (under an alternative definition in force from 1 November 2013) using 'tax months' (or 'tax weeks'). The table below sets out the different categories of worker and the following sub-sections set out the requirements for each type of worker.

Earnings (2013/14)	Age		
	16–21	22–State Pension Age	State Pension Age–74
Up to £5,668	**Entitled worker** (has the right to join a scheme)		
Between £5,668 and £9,440	**Non-eligible jobholder** (can choose to opt into a qualifying scheme)		
Over £9,440	**Non-eligible jobholder**	**Eligible jobholder** (must be auto-enrolled into a qualifying scheme)	**Non-eligible jobholder**

The earnings levels shown in the table above are those that apply for a worker who is paid annually. The corresponding levels for pay reference periods of different lengths are set out in the table below. For the purpose of assessing a worker, earnings are gross earnings, including sick pay and statutory maternity, paternity and adoption pay – regardless of whether an employer is using its own occupational pension scheme with its own definition of pensionable earnings.

Qualifying earnings (2013/14)	Pay reference period						
	1 week	2 weeks	4 weeks	1 month	3 months	6 months	12 months
earnings trigger	£182	£364	£727	£787	£2,360	£4,720	£9,440
lower threshold	£109	£218	£436	£473	£1,417	£2,834	£5,668
upper limit	£797	£1,594	£3,188	£3,454	£10,363	£20,725	£41,450

The earnings trigger for eligible jobholders and the qualifying earnings limits will be reviewed annually by the government.

CONTRIBUTION REQUIREMENTS

When using a defined contribution qualifying scheme, the minimum level of contributions is 8% of qualifying earnings, with the employer paying at least 3% and the employee making up any shortfall. These contribution rates are being phased in over six years to October 2018. Under alternative requirements, defined contribution schemes can use certain other definitions of pensionable earnings. *Further detail on contribution requirements is set out in Section 5.*

For NEST or personal pensions, the 'relief at source' method will provide basic rate tax relief, with the relief paid directly into the scheme and counting towards the 8% minimum. Higher-rate taxpayers need to claim additional relief from HMRC via self-assessment. The employer must deduct any contributions payable by workers from remuneration and pay them to the scheme.

AUTOMATIC ENROLMENT PROCESS

From its staging date an employer is required to automatically enrol eligible jobholders into an automatic enrolment scheme. Existing members of a qualifying scheme of the employer do not need to be automatically enrolled. The requirement to automatically enrol a worker into a pension scheme normally applies from the first day the worker becomes an eligible jobholder (unless the employer is operating postponement; *see below*) and must be completed within one month (or within six weeks, with effect from 1 April 2014) of this 'automatic enrolment date'.

Contributions must be deducted in line with the scheme rules. With effect from 1 November 2013, the period during which initial contributions deducted must be paid by the employer to the scheme was extended further – all contributions deducted during the first three months of membership must reach the scheme by the 22nd of the fourth month, where paid electronically (or by the 19th if paid by another means). Extended contribution payment deadlines for new joiners were intended to allow employers to hold the money until such time as it is known whether or not the jobholder has opted out. The amendments effective from 1 November 2013 also widened the scope of the extended deadlines, applying to all new joiners of a qualifying scheme regardless of how they join, as well to entitled workers who join a registered scheme under the Pensions Act 2008.

The employer must provide the scheme with specified 'jobholder information' no later than one month (or six weeks with effect from 1 April 2014) after the automatic enrolment date. Specified 'enrolment information' must be provided by the employer to the jobholder, also no later than one month (or six weeks with effect from 1 April 2014) after the automatic enrolment date. For workplace personal pension schemes, 'terms and conditions' information must be provided by the scheme provider to the jobholder. *Further detail on information requirements is set out in Section 6.*

Postponement

Employers are able to postpone the automatic enrolment date by up to three months – from staging date, the date on which a worker is employed or the date on which an existing worker becomes an eligible jobholder. The employer must notify the worker within one month (or six weeks with effect from 1 April 2014) of when they would otherwise have been automatically enrolled that their enrolment has been postponed. *The requirements for 'postponement notices' are covered in Section 6.*

Transitional arrangements for defined benefit and hybrid schemes

Employers providing qualifying defined benefit and hybrid schemes are able to defer automatic enrolment for certain existing employees who continue to be eligible to join their scheme, until 1 October 2017, provided those employees can opt in during the period between the employer's staging date and 30 September 2017. During this period, any new employees who satisfy the eligibility criteria must be automatically enrolled in the normal way.

TUPE

Where a TUPE transfer occurs, the automatic enrolment requirements apply to the new employer following the transfer. This means that the new employer will need to assess the workers and, where appropriate, automatically enrol them. *The TUPE requirements are covered in Section 24.*

Corporate restructuring

Where the employer of a worker changes as a result of a corporate restructure, the automatic enrolment duties apply afresh to the new employer, even if the old and new employers belong to the same group of companies. The new employer must satisfy its obligations in respect of the employee in the same way as for any other new employee.

OPTING OUT

An employee who has been automatically enrolled can subsequently opt out by giving notice within a one-month period, in which case any member and employer contributions paid must be returned. The opt-out period starts from the later of the following dates for an occupational pension scheme:

- the date the jobholder is given the enrolment information *(see Section 6) and*
- the date on which the employer made arrangements for the jobholder to become an active member.

For a personal pension, it commences at the later of:

- the date the jobholder is given the enrolment information *and*
- the date the jobholder is given the terms and conditions information.

In order to opt out, the jobholder must request an opt-out notice, generally from the scheme and not the employer. It is the employer's duty, not the scheme's, to refund any employee contributions that have been made; this is not dependent on the employer recouping the money from the scheme.

The jobholder can usually then give notice to opt in although an employer not obliged to act on the request if it is less than twelve months since the worker gave a previous opt-in notice.

The Regulator has powers to issue a compliance notice to any employer that offers a worker an inducement, the main purpose of which is to encourage the worker to opt out of, or cease, membership of a qualifying scheme.

AUTOMATIC RE-ENROLMENT

Automatic re-enrolment is required every three years (within a six-month window centred initially on the third anniversary of the employer's staging date and subsequently of the previous re-enrolment date) unless the employee has opted out within the previous twelve months.

OPTING IN

Jobholders can give their employer an opt-in notice, requiring the employer to arrange for them to be enrolled in an automatic enrolment scheme.

Entitled workers can give their employer a joining notice, requiring the employer to enter them into a registered pension scheme, which need not be an automatic enrolment scheme. The employer has no obligation to make employer contributions for an entitled worker.

MAINTAINING ACTIVE MEMBERSHIP

In addition to the automatic enrolment requirements, employers must ensure that jobholders remain active members of a qualifying scheme, unless the employee chooses to end their membership. An employer must not stop a scheme from qualifying, eject a jobholder from the qualifying scheme or force an employee to cease active membership of the scheme. Where an employer is changing its pension scheme, membership of the new scheme must be arranged within a month, and have effect from the day after membership of the old scheme ends.

CONTRACTUAL ENROLMENT

Some employers make arrangements for their employees to join their pension scheme upon commencement of employment. They may do this for all workers, not just those who are required to be automatically enrolled under the Pensions Act 2008. The Regulator describes this as contractual enrolment, as it is usually included in the contract of employment with the worker. Where this is the case, the corresponding opt-out provisions (that apply when a worker is automatically enrolled under the Pensions Act 2008) are not available. However, a similar opt-out may be possible by cancellation of a personal pension contract, or where an occupational scheme's rules allow for the employee to be treated as never having been a member. More information about the considerations for employers that are using contractual enrolment is in the Regulator's Detailed Guidance no. 6.

COMPLIANCE BY EMPLOYERS

The monitoring of employers' compliance with the automatic enrolment and contribution requirements is a function of the Regulator. Employers must keep records and provide the Regulator with certain information, via a process of registration. During implementation, employers are required to register within four months (or five months with effect from 1 April 2014) of their staging date

Employers are required to keep records relating to the pension arrangements they have made, the enrolment of jobholders, postponement, opt-out and opt-in notices, and the pension contributions they have made. The Regulator can use these records where needed to check that employers have undertaken enrolment and opt-out correctly.

Occupational pension schemes and pension providers are required to keep records of enrolments, opt-ins and opt-outs in respect of each employer. The Regulator will use these records to confirm enrolment and payment of contributions with the pension scheme or provider, and to help identify prohibited behaviour such as employers inducing workers to opt out of pension saving.

All employers are required to re-register every three years, within one month (or two months with effect from 1 April 2014) of the automatic re-enrolment date, which includes the provision of information about the re-enrolment arrangements that have been made.

A penalty regime for employers that do not comply with the requirements is administered by the Regulator, which can issue compliance notices and unpaid contribution notices. Employers that contravene the automatic enrolment requirements may be required to take remedial action and fines may be imposed where things are not put right. In particular, workers may have to be put in the same position as if the contravention had not occurred.

A fixed penalty of £400 may be issued to employers that fail to engage with the reforms, or fail to keep records or supply information to the Regulator. Entrenched employer non-compliance may attract further penalties, rising to £10,000 per day for employers with 500 or more workers. Employers that try to screen out job applicants who might want to save in a qualifying scheme may receive a fixed fine, rising to £5,000 for employers with 250 or more workers.

Protection of employment rights

The Pensions Act 2008 includes provision to protect employees who do not opt out after automatic enrolment from suffering detrimental treatment by employers compared with those who do opt out. It includes statutory rights, building on the existing framework of employment rights, so that those individuals who wish to save should be protected from being unfairly dismissed and from other detrimental treatment (including in relation to recruitment).

STAKEHOLDER PENSIONS: ACCESS REQUIREMENTS

Since October 2001, most employers have had to 'designate' a stakeholder scheme *(see Section 3 for details)*. From 1 October 2012, the requirements for access to stakeholder schemes were removed, although the requirements to deduct contributions and pay them to the scheme remain for continuing members. Also, on receipt of a request by an employee to cease making contributions, the employer must notify the employee of the consequences of doing so.

AUTOMATIC ENROLMENT STAGING DATES

In this table 'Fewer than 30, with PAYE ref' is used to mean the last two characters in the PAYE reference number of employers with fewer than 30 workers in their PAYE scheme.

Employer (by PAYE scheme size or other description)	Staging date	Employer (by PAYE scheme size or other description)	Staging date
120,000 or more	1 October 2012	Fewer than 30, with PAYE ref:	
50,000–119,999	1 November 2012	– 12–16, 3A–3Z,	
30,000–49,999	1 January 2013	H1–H9 or HA–HZ	1 April 2016
20,000–29,999	1 February 2013	– I1–I9 or IA–IZ	1 May 2016
10,000–19,999	1 March 2013	– 17–22, 4A–4Z,	
6,000–9,999	1 April 2013	J1–J9 or JA–JZ	1 June 2016
4,100–5,999	1 May 2013	– 23–29, 5A–5Z,	
4,000–4,099	1 June 2013	K1–K9 or KA–KZ	1 July 2016
3,000–3,999	1 July 2013	– 30–37, 6A–6Z,	
2,000–2,999	1 August 2013	L1–L9 or LA–LZ	1 August 2016
1,250–1,999	1 September 2013	– N1–N9 or NA–NZ	1 September 2016
800–1,249	1 October 2013	– 38–46, 7A–7Z,	
500–799	1 November 2013	O1–O9 or OA–OZ	1 October 2016
350–499	1 January 2014	– 47–57, 8A–8Z,	
250–349	1 February 2014	Q1–Q9, R1–R9,	
160–249	1 April 2014	S1–S9, T1–T9,	
90–159	1 May 2014	QA–QZ, RA–RZ,	
62–89	1 July 2014	SA–SZ or TA–TZ	1 November 2016
61	1 August 2014	– 58–69, 9A–9Z,	
60	1 October 2014	U1–U9, V1–V9,	
59	1 November 2014	W1–W9, UA–UZ,	
58	1 January 2015	VA–VZ or WA–WZ	1 January 2017
54–57	1 March 2015	– 70–83, X1–X9,	
50–53	1 April 2015	Y1–Y9, XA–XZ	
Fewer than 30, with PAYE ref:		or YA–YZ	1 February 2017
– 92, A1–A9, B1–B9,		– P1–P9 or PA–PZ	1 March 2017
AA–AZ, BA–BW,		– 84–91 or 93–99	1 April 2017
M1–M9, MA–MZ,			
Z1–Z9, ZA–ZZ,		Fewer than 30 persons in the PAYE scheme, not meeting any other description in this table	1 April 2017
0A–0Z, 1A–1Z or			
2A–2Z	1 June 2015		
– BX	1 July 2015		
40–49	1 August 2015	Employer does not have a PAYE scheme	1 April 2017
Fewer than 30, with PAYE ref:		New employer: PAYE income first payable between:	
– BY	1 September 2015		
30–39	1 October 2015	– 1.4.12 and 31.3.13	1 May 2017
Fewer than 30, with PAYE ref:		– 1.4.13 and 31.3.14	1 July 2017
– BZ	1 November 2015	– 1.4.14 and 31.3.15	1 August 2017
– 02–04, C1–C9,		– 1.4.15 and 31.12.15	1 October 2017
D1–D9, CA–CZ		– 1.1.16 and 30.9.16	1 November 2017
or DA–DZ	1 January 2016	– 1.10.16 and 30.6.17	1 January 2018
– 00, 05–07, E1–E9 or		– 1.7.17 and 30.9.17	1 February 2018
EA–EZ	1 February 2016		
– 01, 08–11, F1–F9,			
G1–G9, FA–FZ or			
GA–GZ	1 March 2016		

AUTOMATIC ENROLMENT – QUALIFYING SCHEMES

The automatic enrolment regime requires employers to auto-enrol workers who satisfy earnings and age criteria in an 'automatic enrolment scheme'; *see Section 4*. This can be an employer's own pension scheme, a personal pension scheme or an alternative arrangement such as NEST, *which is described in Section 7*.

An automatic enrolment scheme is a 'qualifying scheme' that contains no provisions that might prevent the employer from making the required arrangements to automatically enrol or re-enrol a jobholder, or enrol one who opts in, and does not require the worker to express a choice or provide any information in order to remain an active member – for example, a defined contribution scheme must have a default investment option. Additional criteria apply for non-UK schemes *(see below)*.

A qualifying scheme is an occupational scheme or personal pension scheme that satisfies the 'quality requirement' for that jobholder, and is registered under Finance Act 2004 or is an overseas scheme that satisfies specified requirements. The quality requirement differs for defined contribution, defined benefit and hybrid schemes *(see below)*. In addition, a scheme that provides average salary benefits must revalue those benefits during pensionable service at a minimum rate *(see below)*.

Active members of a qualifying scheme do not need to be automatically enrolled, and the scheme does not need to meet the additional requirements to be an automatic enrolment scheme in respect of those members.

DEFINED CONTRIBUTION SCHEMES

An occupational defined contribution scheme or personal pension scheme will meet the quality requirement if a minimum level of contributions is paid to the scheme for all relevant jobholders.

Subject to transitional provisions *(see below)*, the minimum contributions required are a total of 8% of qualifying earnings, with the employer paying at least 3% and the employee making up any shortfall. For this purpose, qualifying earnings are gross earnings, including sick pay and statutory maternity, paternity and adoption pay, between £5,668 and £41,450 p.a. (for 2013/14). This qualifying earnings band is reviewed annually.

Instead of meeting this quality requirement, schemes can meet an 'alternative quality requirement' for each relevant jobholder where the scheme satisfies minimum contribution conditions under one of three tiers based on different definitions of pensionable pay. This may make it easier for schemes to be used for automatic enrolment where the definition of pensionable pay is not consistent with qualifying earnings. It is not necessary for all jobholders in a scheme to satisfy the same test. Subject to transitional provisions *(see below)* the three tiers are as follows:

- Tier 1 – 9% total (with 4% employer) where pensionable pay is subject to a minimum of basic pay
- Tier 2 – 8% total (with 3% employer) where pensionable pay is subject to a minimum of basic pay and constitutes at least 85% of total pay across all relevant jobholders, *or*
- Tier 3 – 7% total (with 3% employer) where all earnings are pensionable.

(For this purpose basic pay is those elements of pay, before deductions, that do not vary, but excluding certain elements specifically set out in legislation. These exclusions relate to commission, bonuses, overtime, shift premiums, car allowance and certain other allowances.)

There are further requirements for a personal pension scheme to be a qualifying scheme. Broadly, these require agreements to be in place between the provider, employer and employee to ensure that the employer and employee each pay the required contributions, and the provider monitors compliance with the agreed payments.

Contribution requirements during transitional periods

Minimum contributions will be phased in over six years. This will occur in three steps:

From	Employer minimum contribution	Total minimum contribution (including tax relief)
October 2012	1%	2%
October 2017	2%	5%
October 2018	Full (as above)	Full (as above)

Higher rates will apply under 'Tier 1' of the alternative quality requirements:

From	Employer minimum contribution	Total minimum contribution (including tax relief)
October 2012	2%	3%
October 2017	3%	6%
October 2018	Full (as above)	Full (as above)

DEFINED BENEFIT AND HYBRID SCHEMES

The following table sets out the quality requirements for defined benefit and hybrid pension schemes, which must be met if a scheme is to be used as a qualifying scheme for automatic enrolment. Employers offering defined benefit and hybrid schemes can also take advantage of transitional provisions *(see Section 4)*.

Scheme type	Conditions to meet quality test
Contracted-out schemes	The scheme satisfies the quality requirement by virtue of the jobholder being in contracted-out employment *(see*

Scheme type	Conditions to meet quality test
Contracted-out schemes *(continued)*	*Section 2).* For jobholders who are not in contracted-out employment, such as those over State pension age, the scheme must meet the requirement for the relevant type of contracted-in scheme below *(but see Certification below).* In addition, a career average scheme cannot be a qualifying scheme unless revaluation of benefits during pensionable service is at least 2.5% p.a. (or price inflation if lower) and is guaranteed and/or funded for.
Contracted-in final salary schemes and career average schemes providing a pension at retirement	The scheme satisfies the 'test scheme standard', which requires benefits at least as valuable as a pension paid: • at an annual rate of 1/120ths of average qualifying earnings in the last three tax years prior to exit multiplied by the number of years of pensionable service (up to a maximum of 40) • commencing at the higher of age 65 and the member's State pension age, and continuing for life, *and* • including at least the statutory minimum levels of revaluation in deferment (on the final salary basis) and of indexation in payment. In addition, a career average scheme cannot be a qualifying scheme unless revaluation of benefits during pensionable service is at least 2.5% p.a. (or price inflation if lower) and is guaranteed and/or funded for.
Contracted-in cash balance schemes, under which a sum of money is made available for the provision of benefits at retirement	The scheme satisfies the 'test scheme standard', which requires benefits at least as valuable as a lump sum: *EITHER* • accrued at an annual rate of 16% of average qualifying earnings in the last three tax years prior to exit multiplied

Scheme type	Conditions to meet quality test
Contracted-in cash balance schemes, under which a sum of money is made available for the provision of benefits at retirement *(continued)*	by the number of years of pensionable service (up to a maximum of 40) *and* • including at least the statutory minimum levels of revaluation in deferment (on the final salary basis); *OR* • accrued at an annual rate of 16% of average qualifying earnings multiplied by the number of years of pensionable service (up to a maximum of 40), *and* • where average qualifying earnings are calculated on the basis that each year's qualifying earnings are revalued during pensionable service by the lower of 2.5% and price inflation each year, *and* • including at least the statutory minimum levels of revaluation in deferment (on the final salary or average salary basis); *OR* • accrued at an annual rate of 8% of average qualifying earnings multiplied by the number of years of pensionable service (up to a maximum of 40), *and* • where average qualifying earnings are calculated on the basis that each year's qualifying earnings are revalued during pensionable service by 3.5% p.a. *plus* the lower of 2.5% and price inflation each year, *and* • including revaluation in deferment of at least 3.5% p.a. above the statutory minimum level (on the final salary or average salary basis). In all cases, the lump sum must be used to provide benefits commencing at the higher of age 65 and the member's State pension age, and continuing for life. In addition, a career average scheme cannot be a qualifying scheme unless

Scheme type	Conditions to meet quality test
Contracted-in cash balance schemes, under which a sum of money is made available for the provision of benefits at retirement *(continued)*	revaluation of benefits during pensionable service is at least 2.5% p.a. (or price inflation if lower) and is guaranteed and/or funded for. (This separate requirement will usually be met by a scheme that meets the second or third set of requirements above.)
Contracted-in hybrid schemes	The quality test applicable depends on the benefit structure of the scheme. In general, the scheme needs to satisfy the applicable 'test scheme standard' for members accruing defined benefits and meet the quality requirement (or an alternative quality requirement) for members accruing defined contribution benefits. For a 'combination' hybrid scheme, in which the test scheme standard or defined contribution quality requirements cannot be satisfied in full, the scheme needs to satisfy a test that modifies and combines those requirements.

CERTIFICATION

Defined contribution schemes

Certification can be used to confirm that a defined contribution scheme meets the quality requirement. It is required to confirm that a defined contribution scheme meets an alternative quality requirement. Certification is the responsibility of the employer, but can be delegated (e.g. to an adviser), and is carried out in relation to its jobholders and the scheme. Separate tests can be carried out for different groups of jobholders. The key requirement is that either the quality requirement is met or a valid certificate (or certificates) are in place for all relevant jobholders of the employer.

The certificate can be in force for up to 18 months, although employers may find it convenient to choose a shorter period. It must be reviewed if there is a significant change in circumstances. The review might lead to the certificate being terminated early.

At the end of a certification period, and before a new certificate can be given, the employer must assess whether the quality requirement (or an alternative quality requirement) was met during that period. If an element of the relevant requirement is not met, the employer needs to consider what action is to be taken to rectify this, and then take that action. However, no retrospective calculation of shortfalls in the contributions is required unless the Pensions Regulator determines that the scheme has been mis-certified (i.e. that there were not reasonable grounds for the employer to have certified).

The DWP has issued detailed guidance on this certification requirement.

Defined benefit and hybrid schemes

For contracted-in defined benefit and hybrid schemes, a certification process also exists, but the certificate must be given by *either*:

- an actuary, generally the scheme actuary, *or*
- the employer, but only where no actuarial calculations are required.

It is not necessary to re-certify routinely. However, the employer should keep the scheme's ability to satisfy the test scheme standard under review and, as a minimum, the scheme should be fully reviewed every three years. Significant changes should prompt an early review.

The DWP has issued detailed guidance for employers and for actuaries on certifying defined benefit and hybrid schemes. In particular, the guidance provides a simplification: for jobholders who are members of a contracted-out scheme but are not in contracted-out employment, the test scheme standard is met if benefits for those jobholders are calculated in the same way as for those who are contracted-out, rather than meeting the detailed requirements set out above.

NON-UK SCHEMES

A pension scheme with its main administration in an EEA state outside the UK can be an automatic enrolment scheme provided it is a qualifying scheme *(see below)* and it is:

- an IORP (institution for occupational retirement provision) as defined in the IORP Directive, or a personal pension scheme that is regulated by the relevant competent authority in its home state and operated by a person authorised by that authority, in relation to that activity, *and*
- subject to the following regulatory requirements:
  - at least 70% of the defined contribution benefits (or sum of money available for the provision of benefits under a defined benefit scheme) must be used to provide the jobholder with an income for life *and*
  - benefits must be paid no earlier than age 55 (unless on grounds of ill health).

A pension scheme with its main administration outside the EEA cannot be used for automatic enrolment, although it can be used for eligible jobholders who are existing members at the automatic enrolment date if it is a qualifying scheme.

A non-UK scheme can be a qualifying scheme if it:

- is an occupational or personal pension scheme and, in the country where it has its main administration or is established, there is a body that regulates such schemes and providers, and which regulates that scheme/provider

- is subject to regulatory requirements that provide that some of the benefits may be used to provide the jobholder with an income for life
- is registered with HMRC under Finance Act 2004 for tax purposes as a qualifying overseas pension scheme (or other specified conditions are met), *and*
- meets the quality requirements as outlined for UK schemes (other than in specified circumstances).

DEFAULT OPTIONS FOR DEFINED CONTRIBUTION SCHEMES

The DWP issued guidance in 2011 that set out standards for default options in defined contribution automatic enrolment schemes. It believes that the vast majority of individuals will not move from the default option. The guidance is aimed at providers, advisers, employers and governance committees, and was developed with the support of the FSA and after consultation with the Pensions Regulator.

The DWP will review the guidance periodically. If there is strong evidence to suggest that the guidance is being wilfully ignored or that it is not having the desired effect of promoting good practice, the DWP may consider issuing legislation to protect members' interests.

AUTOMATIC ENROLMENT – INFORMATION REQUIREMENTS

The Pensions Act 2008 requires an employer to provide certain information to its workers and to the pension scheme it has chosen to fulfil its automatic enrolment duties. There are extensive provisions, most of which are set out in the Occupational and Personal Pension Schemes (Automatic Enrolment) Regulations 2010.

The content of the information varies depending on the type of worker and whether the employer is postponing auto-enrolment, or using the transitional period for existing workers who were eligible to join a defined benefit or hybrid scheme at the employer's staging date.

This section summarises the main requirements. It does not cover the employer's duty to report and provide information to the Pensions Regulator, nor the need to keep records, *which are summarised in Section 4*. Normal scheme disclosure rules will also apply; *the disclosure requirements for occupational pension schemes are in Section 14*.

For an explanation of the types of worker described below, *see Section 4*.

It is the employer's duty to provide the right information to the right individual at the right time. In all cases, the information must be provided in writing, which includes being sent by email. It is not sufficient to signpost the employee (by email or otherwise) to a website, intranet site or poster within the workplace.

The Department for Work and Pensions has released a letter template tool with accompanying guidance, along with other material to help employers communicate effectively with their workers regarding automatic enrolment. The communication material is all available on the Pensions Regulator's website.

In 2013, the government consulted on technical changes to automatic enrolment. Some amendments have now been set out in amending regulations and other provisions are included in the current Pensions Bill.

INFORMATION TO BE PROVIDED IN RELATION TO ELIGIBLE JOBHOLDERS WHO ARE NOT SCHEME MEMBERS AND TO OPT-INS

Eligible jobholders must be automatically enrolled in the pension scheme *(see Section 4)*.

As part of this enrolment process, the employer must provide *enrolment information* to the jobholder being automatically enrolled and *jobholder information* to the pension scheme. If a contract-based scheme (e.g. a personal pension) is being used as the automatic enrolment scheme, the provider must also give the jobholder information about the *terms and conditions* of the arrangement.

When the automatic enrolment requirements first apply, there is no need to provide enrolment information to those who are already active members of a qualifying scheme, but they must be given a separate notice about their scheme membership *(see below)*, even if they have been told about the scheme in the past.

Broadly, the same information requirements apply on re-enrolment and when a non-eligible jobholder opts in.

Enrolment information to be provided to the jobholder

Enrolment information must be provided by the employer to the jobholder.

To Be Provided To	Time Frame	Summary Of Information Required
• **Eligible jobholders** who are being automatically enrolled (or re-enrolled). • **Non-eligible jobholders** who opt in. • **Eligible jobholders** who opt in during postponement or during the transitional period for a defined benefit or hybrid scheme.	No later than **one month*** after the jobholder's automatic enrolment date (or re-enrolment date, or opt-in enrolment date).	• That the jobholder has been or will be automatically enrolled and the automatic enrolment date (or equivalent). • The scheme contact details. • Details of the contributions payable and whether tax relief will be given through net pay or relief at source. • Details about the right to opt out, what it means and when and how to do this. • The right to opt back in. • That a jobholder will normally be automatically re-enrolled by the employer in accordance with regulations. • That any written notice from the jobholder must be signed (or, if given electronically, state that the jobholder personally submitted it). • A statement that if the jobholder ceases to be an active member of the scheme through no fault of their own while still working for that employer, arrangements will be made for the jobholder to join another automatic enrolment scheme. • Where to obtain further information about pensions and saving for retirement.

* With effect from 1 April 2014, this period will be extended from one month to six weeks.

Jobholder information to be provided to the pension scheme

Jobholder information must be provided by the employer to the trustees or managers of the occupational or personal pension scheme.

To Be Provided To	Time Frame	Summary Of Information Required
The pension scheme, in relation to **jobholders** who are being provided with **enrolment information** as above. Also applies in relation to **entitled workers** who exercise the right to join (see below)	No later than **one month*** after the jobholder's automatic enrolment date (or equivalent).	• Jobholder's name, sex, date of birth and postal residential address. • The automatic enrolment date (or equivalent). • National Insurance number (if this is not immediately available, the employer must provide it within one month of receiving it. If required, the following must also be provided: • Gross earnings in any pay reference period. • Value of contributions (expressed as a fixed amount or as a percentage of earnings). • Postal work address and individual's work email address. • Personal email address, where the employer holds this information.

* With effect from 1 April 2014, this period will be extended from one month to six weeks.

Terms and conditions information to be provided to the jobholder

The employer must make arrangements for the provider of the personal pension scheme to provide the jobholder with information on the terms and conditions of the scheme. This can form part of the key features information that the provider must issue under Financial Conduct Authority rules.

TO BE PROVIDED TO	TIME FRAME	SUMMARY OF INFORMATION REQUIRED
Jobholders who are being provided with **enrolment information** as above.	No later than **one month*** after the jobholder's automatic enrolment date (or equivalent).	• The purpose of the scheme, including information about the default fund(s). • The services to be provided by the provider. • The value of any contributions payable by the jobholder, where the provider has this information. • The charges that may be payable.

* With effect from 1 April 2014, this period will be extended from one month to six weeks.

INFORMATION FOR EXISTING SCHEME MEMBERS BECOMING JOBHOLDERS

Existing scheme members need to be told that their current pension arrangements meet the new requirements, no later than two months after the employer's staging date, or the member first becoming a jobholder.

The employer is only required to provide this information once – when the worker first meets the criteria to be a jobholder on or after the employer's staging date. This information need not be issued if it has previously been provided under the postponement requirements *(see below)*.

TO BE PROVIDED TO	TIME FRAME	SUMMARY OF INFORMATION REQUIRED
Jobholders who are already active members of a qualifying scheme when first becoming a jobholder.	No later than **two months** after the employer's staging date or the member first becoming a jobholder.	• Confirmation that the jobholder is an active member of a qualifying scheme. • A statement that if the jobholder ceases to be an active member of the scheme through no fault of their own while still working for that employer, arrangements will be made for the jobholder to join another automatic enrolment scheme. • Where to obtain further information about pensions and saving for retirement.

INFORMATION TO BE PROVIDED TO NON-ELIGIBLE JOBHOLDERS

An employer must inform a non-eligible jobholder who is not an active member of a qualifying scheme of the right to opt into an automatic enrolment scheme and be eligible for employer contributions.

There is no need to provide this information if the jobholder has previously opted out under the automatic enrolment legislation, or if it has previously been issued to a jobholder under the postponement requirements, or where the transitional period for defined benefit and hybrid schemes is used *(see below)*.

To Be Provided To	Time Frame	Summary Of Information Required
Non-eligible jobholders.	No later than **one month*** after the right to opt in first applies.	• That the jobholder may require the employer to make arrangements for them to become an active member of an automatic enrolment scheme and that the jobholder will be entitled to employer's contributions. • That the opt-in notice must be in writing and signed by the jobholder (or, if given electronically, state that the jobholder personally submitted it). • Where to obtain further information about pensions and saving for retirement.

* With effect from 1 April 2014, this period will be extended from one month to six weeks.

INFORMATION TO BE PROVIDED TO ENTITLED WORKERS

The employer must inform entitled workers who are not active members of a pension scheme of the right to join a registered pension scheme.

This information need not be issued if it has previously been provided under the postponement requirements *(see below)*.

To Be Provided To	Time Frame	Summary Of Information Required
Entitled workers.	No later than **one month*** after the right to join first applies to the entitled worker.	• That the worker may require the employer to make arrangements for them to become an active member of a pension scheme. • That the joining notice must be in writing and signed by the worker (or, if given electronically, state that the worker personally submitted it). • Where to obtain further information about pensions and saving for retirement.

* With effect from 1 April 2014, this period will be extended from one month to six weeks.

If a joining notice is received from the entitled worker, information about the worker must be provided to the pension scheme. This is the same information that is provided in respect of jobholders *(see* 'Jobholder information to be provided to the pension scheme' *above)*.

INFORMATION WHEN USING POSTPONEMENT

An employer may postpone automatic enrolment by up to three months for one, some or all of its workers. The employer can use postponement:

- at its staging date
- after using the transitional period for a defined benefit or hybrid scheme
- on the worker's first day of employment, *or*
- when a worker first meets the criteria to become an eligible jobholder.

Postponement is explained further *in Section 4*.

If the employer chooses to use postponement it must provide a notification no later than one month (six weeks, from 1 April 2014) after what would have been the automatic enrolment date.

There are four types of postponement notice that can be used, with varying levels of detail. The Pensions Regulator refers to these as General notice A, General notice B, tailored notice for a jobholder and tailored notice for an entitled worker.

Each employee must receive their own notice, even if the information on it is generic. **All** notices must explain:

- that automatic enrolment has been postponed until the deferral date (this is the last day of the postponement period and the date must be given)
- that if on the deferral date they meet the criteria to be an eligible jobholder, and are not already an active member of a qualifying scheme, they will be automatically enrolled
- that any notice from the worker must be in writing and signed by the worker (or if submitted electronically state that the worker has personally submitted the statement) *and*
- where to obtain further information about pensions and saving for retirement.

There are additional information requirements depending on the type of postponement notice that is used:

Type of Notice	Can be provided to	Summary Of Information Required
General notice A.	**All workers**, at the employer's staging date or the first day of employment.	A generic notice, explaining the right of jobholders to opt in and receive employer contributions, the right of entitled workers to join a registered pension scheme and certain rights relating to jobholders who are already active members of a qualifying scheme.
General notice B.	**All workers**, at the employer's staging date or the first day of employment, **who are not active members of a qualifying scheme**.	Similar to General notice A, but without the rights relating to active members. If this notice is used, the employer will need to provide separate notices for active members of the pension scheme *(see 'Information for existing scheme members becoming jobholders' above)*.
Tailored notice for a jobholder.	Eligible and non-eligible jobholders who are not active members of a qualifying scheme.	The notice is tailored to the circumstances of the jobholder. It explains the right to opt in and receive employer contributions.
Tailored notice for an entitled worker.	Workers other than jobholders who are not active members of a qualifying scheme.	The notice is tailored to the circumstances of the worker. It explains the right to join a registered pension scheme.

NOTICE OF DEFERRAL UNDER A TRANSITIONAL PERIOD FOR DEFINED BENEFIT AND HYBRID SCHEMES

An employer may choose to use the transitional period for defined benefit and hybrid schemes that would delay automatic enrolment until 2017. Transitional periods are usually applied at the employer's staging date *and they are explained further in Section 4*. If the employer decides to do this, it must notify eligible jobholders of its decision. Eligible jobholders may choose to opt in.

To Be Provided To	Time Frame	Summary Of Information Required
Eligible jobholders.	No later than **one month*** after the employer's first enrolment date.	• That the employer intends to defer automatic enrolment until the end of the transitional period for defined benefit and hybrid schemes. • The right to opt in to an automatic enrolment scheme and be entitled to employer's contributions. • That any notice must be in writing and signed by the jobholder (or, if given electronically, state that the jobholder personally submitted it). • Where to obtain further information about pensions and saving for retirement.

* With effect from 1 April 2014, this period will be extended from one month to six weeks.

OPT-OUT NOTICE

A jobholder who does not wish to become an active member of a pension scheme must provide an opt-out notice to the employer within the opt-out period. The notice must normally be obtained from the scheme, not the employer.

To Be Provided By	Time Frame	Summary Of Information Required
Eligible jobholders who wish to opt out after they have been automatically enrolled or re-enrolled; and **non-eligible jobholders** who wish to opt out having opted into the scheme	The opt-out period is **one month** from the later of the date the jobholder: • becomes an active member, *or* • is provided with the enrolment information above. It may be extended to six weeks if an invalid opt-out notice is submitted initially.	• Full name of jobholder. • Name of the employer. • National Insurance number, or date of birth. • That the jobholder wishes to opt out and understands the implications. • Signature or, if submitted electronically, a statement confirming that the jobholder personally submitted the notice. • Date the jobholder completed the form.

NEST

The automatic enrolment regime *is described in Sections 4 to 6*. Employers are required to auto-enrol employees into a qualifying scheme. The scheme can be the employer's own qualifying scheme *(the requirements of which are described in Section 5)* or the National Employment Savings Trust (NEST). Some providers have established master trusts, similar to NEST, to provide a further option for meeting employers' auto-enrolment obligations.

Employers can auto-enrol their workers into NEST and make the required contributions to it. NEST operates as a trust-based money purchase occupational pension scheme and is subject to most of the legislation applying to such schemes. The scheme is governed by the NEST Corporation. This section describes how NEST operates.

Maximum contributions

There is currently a maximum annual contribution to NEST – of £4,500 for 2013/14, to be increased in line with average earnings each year. The Government has announced that this contribution limit will be removed from April 2017.

Whilst the limit remains in place, NEST will cease to accept member contributions once the annual limit is exceeded. However, it will continue to accept statutory minimum employer contributions. After the end of the tax year, any excess contributions will be refunded, without interest or investment gain. Generally, employee contributions will be refunded prior to employer contributions. There is also a facility to offset excess contributions against contributions that are due in the following year.

Transfers

There is a general ban on transfer payments to or from NEST. However, the scheme will accept cash transfer sums in respect of leavers with less than two years' service *(see Section 12)*. In addition, transfers out are allowed for members who are over the normal minimum pension age (55) and members suffering from incapacity who have become entitled to benefits. This will allow members to consolidate their pension savings before an annuity purchase.

Transfers out are also permitted to comply with a pension sharing order and NEST will accept pension credits on divorce for existing members of the scheme *(see Section 16)*.

The Government has announced that the ban on individual transfers will be lifted when automatic transfers are introduced for defined contribution schemes *(see Section 13)* and the ban will be lifted in respect of bulk transfers from April 2017.

Benefits

NEST is subject to the same rules as other registered pension schemes with regard to the payment of benefits. For example, pension income cannot be brought into payment before normal minimum pension age, other than in cases of ill-health, and no more than 25% of a fund can be taken as a pension commencement lump sum.

Members are able to purchase a lifetime annuity under the open market option. NEST also provides members with access to its Retirement Panel, which offers a limited range of annuities from selected providers, at competitive prices, for members unwilling or unable to pursue the open market option. Each provider has given a commitment to provide annuities on pots from £1,500 upwards.

Members with NEST funds of under £2,000 are able to take a *de minimis* lump sum. Members are also able to convert small pension pots into cash lump sums under the trivial commutation provisions *(see Section 10)*.

Charges

Responsibility for setting the appropriate charges for NEST lies with the NEST Corporation. The Government stated that the Corporation is best placed to make decisions relating to the charging structure, the level of charges and any additional charges for particular services. In particular, trust law will provide an incentive for the Corporation to set a charging structure that is fair and to keep charges down.

The intention is that NEST will be self-financing through member charges 'in the long term' and that state support should not provide the scheme with an unfair competitive advantage.

The stated aim is to provide 'a low-cost, good value way to save'. NEST's annual management charge (AMC) is 0.3%. An additional charge is made on contributions going into the scheme of 1.8%, which will continue until initial setting-up costs are recovered. It is not known when the 1.8% charge will be removed.

Investment options

The NEST Corporation is responsible for investment decisions. The NEST Order and Rules *(see below)* provide the trustee with broad powers to invest funds and require the trustee to provide a default investment fund for all members who do not make an active investment choice.

NEST has a published Statement of Investment Principles. NEST's default options are 'Retirement Date Funds' – one for each expected retirement year – invested in a broad and diversified set of asset classes. The investment objectives for these funds include the achievement of performance in excess of inflation, using a benchmark of CPI.

In addition to the default funds, NEST provides a range of other fund choices:

- Higher Risk Fund – targeting high returns through taking more investment risk
- Lower Growth Fund – taking very little investment risk
- Ethical Fund – only investing in companies that meet ethical criteria and government bonds

- Sharia Fund – only investing in companies that are compliant with Sharia principles, *and*
- Pre-retirement Fund – for members who, in NEST's early years, want to buy an annuity rather than target a cash lump sum.

Governance

NEST is run as a trust-based occupational pension scheme:

- a trustee board – the NEST Corporation – is the governing body, with wide-ranging powers to manage the scheme in the interests of its members, *and*
- the NEST Corporation must comply with general pensions legislation although regulations modify certain aspects of pension legislation when applied to NEST.

The trustee takes the key strategic decisions, but delegates all executive and operational functions to a management board. The first members and their 'chair' were Government-appointed but subsequent appointments will be made by the Corporation itself. Appointments will be for no more than four years. The trustee will consult a Members' Panel on key decisions. There is also an Employers' Panel which may be consulted when the trustee reviews the Statement of Investment Principles. It is possible that a modified version of the member-nominated directors requirements of the Pensions Act 2004 could be applied in future.

The NEST Order, which established the scheme, and the initial Rules of NEST were published in 2010. The Order and Rules were most recently amended with effect from 1 April 2013. Further provisions about the scheme will be made by rules, which may only be made either by the trustee or with the consent of the trustee. Any proposed rules must be published in draft for comment by interested persons, and the members' and employers' panels must be consulted. Changes to the Order may only be made by the Secretary of State, with trustee consent and consultation.

The main areas covered in the Order and Rules are:

- the composition and function of the members' and employers' panels
- the situations where data may be shared with the government
- trustee indemnity
- promoting awareness of the scheme
- employer and member participation in the scheme
- contributions to and refunds from the scheme
- the powers to invest scheme assets and the requirement to establish a default investment fund
- the ban on most transfers into and out of the scheme, *and*
- the types of benefit permitted.

AON Hewitt

hedding
ght on
C pensions

e UK workers than ever are saving for retirement via Defined
:ribution pension plans. But many face a significant shortfall in their
ired retirement income due to inadequate retirement savings, poor
stment choices and growing retirement income needs.

cusing on improving member outcomes through a new governance
ework, employers and trustees can help address these issues. Shedding
 on the key challenges, Aon Hewitt's Achieving better member
omes – a practical guide to DC pensions, helps you identify what you
rying to achieve for your DC members and to deliver a positive impact
eir outcomes.

ting in higher retirement savings, smarter investment options and
 effective retirement support for your members.

 copy of the guide please visit aonhewitt.co.uk/dcpensions,
l enquiries@aonhewitt.com, or call us on 0800 279 5588.

v us on **twitter** @aonhewittuk

TRUSTEES AND SCHEME GOVERNANCE

This section deals with the role of trustees within the legal framework governing pensions in the UK and with scheme governance in general. References to the legal system are to the system which in general applies in the UK. However, some differences exist under Scottish law. The existing legal framework includes trust law, tax law, social security law (in particular, specific DWP pensions legislation), financial services legislation and European Union law.

Trust law, on which private sector occupational pension provision in the UK is traditionally based, is considered in more detail below. Tax law is dealt with in *Section 10*. Various aspects of DWP pensions legislation (including provisions which transpose EU requirements into UK law) are also discussed in this and other sections. The Financial Services and Markets Act 2000 is dealt with in more detail in *Section 26*.

TRUSTS AND TRUSTEES

Trust law

The principles of trust law have mainly been established, over the years, by court precedents. However, over time some of these principles have been incorporated in legislation, for example in the Trustee Act 2000.

What is a trust?

One definition is that 'a trust is an equitable obligation binding a person (who is called a trustee) to deal with property over which he has control (which is called the trust property) for the benefit of persons (who are called the beneficiaries) of whom he may himself be one, and any of whom may enforce the obligation'.

In the case of a pension scheme, the trustees hold the pension fund assets for the benefit of the members, and their first duty is to them – not to their employer, their trade union, or any outside body. Members include not just those currently employed and paying into the scheme, but also people with deferred pensions, those who are drawing benefits and those who are potentially eligible for benefits, such as spouses and other dependants.

Why use a trust?

The vast majority of UK occupational pension schemes are set up under trust. The three main reasons why trusts have been used are:

- to provide security for the members by keeping the scheme's assets separate from those of the employer
- to ensure third-party beneficiaries, such as spouses and dependants of members, have legal rights, *and*
- because the Pensions Act 2004 requires funded occupational schemes to be established under irrevocable trusts and to have effective written rules specifying the benefits and the conditions on which they are payable. This reflects the requirements of the EU Pensions Directive.

Historically, schemes were set up under trust to enable them to be approved by the Revenue as exempt approved schemes, and thereby qualify for valuable tax reliefs on contributions, investment income and some of the benefits paid.

Who can be a trustee?

The trustees of a scheme can be either individuals (so long as they are over 18 and not insane) or corporations, or a combination of both.

Neither the scheme actuary nor the scheme auditor can be a trustee, and certain people are automatically disqualified (e.g. undischarged bankrupts or people who have been convicted of an offence involving dishonesty). The Pensions Regulator has power to prohibit a person from acting as trustee of a particular scheme, a particular type of scheme, or schemes in general, where it is satisfied that he or she is not a fit and proper person to be a trustee. It may suspend a person from acting as a trustee where the outcome of legal proceedings is awaited. It may also appoint an independent trustee where an employer becomes insolvent or where it believes the appointment is in the best interest of the members *(see* Conflicts of interest, *below)*.

Legislation requires all schemes to have a minimum proportion of member-nominated trustees. Such trustees must be nominated as the result of a process involving (as a minimum) all the active and pensioner members of the scheme (or organisations representing them), and then selected as a result of a further process. The Pensions Regulator has issued a code of practice on this requirement. The minimum proportion was initially and remains one-third, but the government has given itself the power to increase this to one-half at some time in the future.

In autumn 2013, the European Commission is due to present proposals for a revised Pensions Directive, which could include requirements for those who run schemes or have key functions to be 'fit and proper'. It is not clear at this stage how onerous the measures might be and how they fit with the existing provisions, for example in relation to Trustee Knowledge and Understanding *(see below)*.

The trust deed and rules

A scheme's definitive documentation usually has two main parts: the trust deed and the rules. The trust deed defines the powers and duties of the trustees and employer, and the duties of trustees to the members.

The rules state who is eligible to be a scheme member and cover details of the benefits promised, the areas where the trustees have discretion, the arrangements for determining the employer's contributions, and the level of members' contributions.

The trust documents govern the trustees' actions. Generally speaking, only when the deed and rules do not deal with a point is it necessary to apply the principles of trust law. However, it should be noted that Acts of Parliament can override provisions contained in trust deeds, for example the Marriage (Same Sex Couples) Act 2013.

Scheme documentation can be altered in various ways: for example, a supplemental deed extends the definitive documentation, perhaps by introducing new powers. An amending deed changes it. Trustees may have to refer to several different documents, if amendments have not been incorporated into the main deed. It is therefore good practice to try to keep a single consolidated deed which is amended as necessary. Many trustees will now have a working copy of their rules which, whilst not a formally signed set of rules, incorporates changes into a single document.

Duties, responsibilities and rights of a trustee

The fundamental duty of a trustee is to give effect to the provisions of the trust deed. A trustee who fails to do this is in breach of trust. Other duties are many and varied, and include:

- paying out the right benefits at the right time
- keeping accurate records of members and their dependants
- keeping proper accounts, *and*
- ensuring that scheme assets are properly and prudently invested.

Under the provisions of the Employment Rights Act 1996, employee trustees (or employee directors of trustee companies) of an occupational scheme of their employer have statutory rights to time off work for the performance of their trustee duties and training, payment for this time off and rights not to suffer detriment or dismissal related principally to the performance of their trustee functions.

Legislation places a number of particular responsibilities on trustees. Exceptions apply in certain cases but, in general, these responsibilities include:

Appointment of professional advisers

The trustees must appoint an individual actuary (except for pure money purchase schemes) and an auditor (known respectively as the scheme actuary and the scheme auditor) and, where investments covered by the Financial Services and Markets Act 2000 are held, a fund manager, to carry out certain specified functions. Another actuary may also be appointed to provide actuarial advice which is not required to be given by the scheme actuary. Any person having custody of scheme assets must be appointed by the trustees, except where they are sub-custodians appointed by a main custodian or other adviser who has been specifically authorised by the trustees. A legal adviser must also be appointed by the trustees if such advice is required.

Investment of the scheme's assets

Trustees have complete power to invest scheme assets as if they were their own, subject to their duty of care, the taking of proper advice from qualified advisers, any scheme restrictions (except that any requirement for the direct or indirect consent of the employer is void) and the statutory restriction that not more than five per cent of the market value of the resources of a scheme may at any time be invested in employer-related investments. Their decision-making powers may be delegated to an external fund manager. The trustees remain responsible for any actions taken, but they are not liable for the fund manager's actions so long as they have taken steps to ensure that he has appropriate knowledge and experience, and is acting competently and in accordance with the written statement of investment principles *(see below)*.

Regulations introduced to comply with the EU Pensions Directive require the trustees (amongst other things) to invest predominantly in regulated markets and to ensure proper diversification.

Statement of investment principles

The trustees must prepare (and maintain) this statement, after taking advice from an experienced investment adviser and after consulting the employer (but without any requirement to agree it with the employer). Amongst other things it must cover:

- the kinds of investment to be held and the balance between them
- risk and expected return
- realisation of assets, *and*
- the trustees' policy (if any) on socially responsible investment, including the exercise of voting rights.

The statement must be reviewed at least every three years and immediately after any significant change in investment policy.

Compliance with scheme funding legislation
Scheme-specific funding was introduced under the Pensions Act 2004. Under this regime, trustees are responsible for setting the funding strategy as well as monitoring the funding level and payment of contributions. *See Section 17 for further details.*

Disclosure of pension scheme information
Under UK pensions law, scheme trustees are required to make a substantial range of information available to scheme members and others. *See Section 14 for further details.*

Compliance with the Data Protection Act 1998
For the purposes of the Data Protection Act 1998, pension scheme trustees are generally classified as data controllers. As such, they are required to ensure the adequacy of their own data security arrangements and of those who process data on their behalf; for example the scheme administrators. They are responsible for keeping the Information Commissioner up to date with details of their security measures. Trustees must obtain explicit member consent before holding or processing sensitive data, such as data relating to physical/ mental health or sexual life. They must also ensure they have suitable procedures in place for complying with requests by scheme members exercising their statutory right to see a copy of personal data held about them within 40 days.

Additional powers for the Information Commissioner's Office were announced on 6 April 2010. These allow it to fine data controllers, including trustees, up to £500,000 for serious breaches of the Data Protection Act. Trustees therefore need to understand how third parties use their scheme's data. They should ensure that they hold copies of all of their advisers' data security policies. Each adviser should be able to present their policy on request. Guidance from the Information Commissioner's Office now suggests that scheme actuaries are joint data controllers with the trustees of the schemes they advise, rather than data processors. It is not clear what impact this will have on the respective roles although trustees will still have data controller responsibilities.

EU data protection laws are being overhauled in a bid to modernise the existing rules, but it is not clear at this stage when they might be introduced and what the implications will be.

Whistle-blowing and Notifiable Events
Under the Pensions Act 2004, scheme trustees (and others) are responsible for reporting breaches (whistle-blowing), and trustees must notify the Regulator of certain events. *See Section 9 for further details.*

Scheme governance

Scheme governance encompasses the different aspects of operating a pension scheme. The Pensions Regulator is keen to ensure the highest standards of governance and administration, and better management of pension scheme risks. Trustees' core responsibilities include safeguarding and investing scheme assets, monitoring funding levels, ensuring members receive the correct benefits when they fall due, and ensuring compliance with the law and the scheme's own trust deed and rules. Meeting these responsibilities requires carefully developed procedures covering aspects such as:

- the constitution of the trustee body, appointment and removal of trustees, formation of sub-committees, the process of decision taking
- skills assessment, induction, training and performance evaluation
- risk assessment and management, and internal controls *(see below)*
- dealing with conflicts of interest *(see below)*, *and*
- relations with the sponsoring employer, exchange of information (and confidentiality agreements, where appropriate) and mutual understanding of objectives.

The seventh annual Pensions Regulator survey on occupational pension scheme governance, released in May 2013, found that 97% of schemes believed that their trustee boards were governing effectively overall. Evidence has shown that larger schemes tend to be associated with higher levels of governance activity. There tend to be lower perceived standards of governance in smaller DC schemes.

To support scheme governance, the Regulator has released a number of codes of practice, guidance notes and other publications, nearly all of which are directed at trustees. *See Section 9 for further details.*

Internal controls

A formal requirement (imposed by the EU Pensions Directive) for schemes to establish internal controls to ensure compliance with the law and their own rules was introduced into UK law by the Pensions Act 2004. The Pensions Regulator has issued a code of practice, accompanying guidance which was updated in 2010, and a set of e-learning modules covering internal controls. The code stresses the need for trustees to set up internal controls to enable them to react to significant operational, financial, funding, regulatory and compliance risks. These controls should be proportionate, based on an assessment of the risks to which the scheme is exposed, having regard to its particular circumstances and to their likelihood of materialising and potential impact. Internal controls should be reviewed at least annually and more frequently if substantial changes take place or inadequacies are revealed. It is suggested that a statement confirming that key risks have been considered and effective controls established could be incorporated in the scheme's annual report to demonstrate good practice.

Where trustees delegate their responsibilities (e.g. to third-party administrators or investment managers and custodians), they should take care to examine the internal control assurance reports produced by their agents.

Conflicts of interest

Conflicts of interest can pose a serious risk to good governance and, as such, are subject to some very complex legal considerations. In 2008, the Pensions Regulator published guidance relating to conflicts of interest. The guidance covers five broad principles, which relate to: understanding the importance of conflicts of interest; identifying conflicts of interest; evaluation, management or avoidance of conflicts; managing adviser conflicts; and conflicts of interest policy. The principles are supported by practical guidance on matters relating to the governance of each. The Internal Controls guidance describes behaviours the Pensions Regulator expects to see in identifying and resolving conflicts of interest.

Conflicts of interest do not generally invalidate trustees' decisions, so long as they are properly managed.

The importance of being able to control potential conflicts of interest was highlighted in the *Telent* case. In November 2007, Pensions Corporation bought Telent. The trustees of the Telent pension scheme asked the Pensions Regulator to intervene. It temporarily put in place three independent trustee directors with sole power over the scheme, as it was felt that a clear conflict of interest had arisen which had not been managed appropriately. In April 2008, Pensions Corporation and the Regulator came to an agreement on the future governance of the scheme – the three independent trustee directors would remain on the trustee board and measures would be put in place to identify and manage conflicts of interest on the board. Trustee conflicts of interest have also featured in other Regulator determinations such as the Hugh Mackay and Bonas schemes.

Adviser conflicts

The Pensions Regulator has published guidance that sets out some key issues for trustees to consider in their relations with advisers. It covers general issues as well as those specific to the scheme actuary, scheme auditor, legal adviser, scheme administrator, independent financial adviser and benefit consultant. The guidance also raises issues, provides hints on questions that trustees should be asking their advisers and urges trustees to obtain a written statement from the advisers on how conflicts of interest are avoided and/or managed.

On 1 July 2013 new professional standards for pension scheme actuaries took effect. Version 2 of Actuarial Standard APS P1 forms part of a package of conflicts of interest material, which includes a guide for actuaries and a note for pension scheme trustees. The standard now includes a presumption that a scheme actuary who advises the sponsoring employer on the funding of the scheme or on any matter relating to the benefits payable would be faced with an irreconcilable conflict of interest, although in exceptional circumstances the actuary can depart from that presumption provided they record the decision and can justify it.

The Bribery Act 2010

This Act came into force on 1 July 2011. Trustees are exposed to some of the offences under the Act. As part of good governance, trustees should establish and maintain suitable prevention procedures. The trustees' conflicts of interest policy should also be reviewed in line with these procedures.

Good scheme administration

The Pensions Regulator's guidance on monitoring and improving the quality of member data includes a framework for testing and measuring data. Specific events are noted which give rise to an urgent need to review record keeping: wind-up, entry to PPF assessment, change of administrator or buy-out.

The guidance initially introduced a deadline of December 2012 for schemes to meet specific targets for data standards. In addition, the Regulator reminded trustees that a failure to keep basic records would be wholly inconsistent with their obligations to operate internal controls and that it can use its statutory powers against schemes in these circumstances. In February 2013, the Regulator started a process of checks to establish whether schemes had met the targets and how they had addressed its guidance.

The recommended good practice approach is continuous improvement, with regular reports of progress. After completion of any plans to improve records, the data should be measured annually as evidence that controls are continuing to operate effectively.

The Regulator continuously highlights the importance of administration in enabling good member outcomes from pensions saving. As well as the risk to members' benefits, inaccurate and missing data can have serious cost implications for pension schemes. The Regulator is seeking to increase understanding amongst trustees and administrators of their accountabilities and responsibilities for achieving high standards. A number of documents have been issued to support this initiative, including its series of annual surveys.

Wednesbury principles
These define the process by which trustees should approach decision making in order to minimise the risk of legal challenge:

- the trustees must ask themselves the correct questions
- they must direct themselves correctly in law; in particular, they must adopt a correct construction of the trust deed and rules
- they must not arrive at a perverse decision, i.e. a decision at which no reasonable body of trustees would have arrived, *and*
- they must take into account all relevant and no irrelevant facts.

If the trustees can demonstrate that they followed this process when exercising discretionary powers, it is unlikely that their decision will be overturned by the Pensions Ombudsman or the courts. Recent Ombudsman determinations have highlighted the need for scheme minutes to include a clear record of the steps taken in reaching a decision. However, care should be taken if reasons are given, as these could be challenged.

Internal Dispute Resolution Procedure
Trustees are required to put in place, and disclose via the scheme's explanatory booklet, an internal scheme dispute resolution procedure under which scheme members may bring written complaints. This was initially set up as a two-stage procedure with an individual appointed by the trustees to rule in the first stage. If dissatisfied with the decision the complainant could then appeal to the trustees as a second stage. Since April 2008 schemes have had the option of replacing the two-stage procedure with a single-stage process under which all decisions are taken by the trustees. At that time the prescribed time limits were

replaced by the requirement to make a decision within a reasonable period. Having exhausted the scheme's internal dispute resolution procedure, a complainant may take his complaint to the Pensions Ombudsman.

Governance of defined contribution schemes

As part of its strategy to improve the standards of defined contribution (DC) provision, in 2011 the Pensions Regulator outlined six principles for the good design and governance of workplace DC schemes. The principles, which are intended to span the lifecycle of a scheme from the set-up stages through to the ongoing management, are:

(1) Schemes are designed to be durable, fair and deliver good outcomes for members.

(2) A comprehensive scheme governance framework is established at set-up, with clear accountabilities and responsibilities agreed and made transparent.

(3) Those who are accountable for scheme decisions and activity understand their duties and are fit and proper to carry them out.

(4) Schemes benefit from effective governance and monitoring through their full lifecycle.

(5) Schemes are well-administered with timely, accurate and comprehensive processes and records.

(6) Communication to members is designed and delivered to ensure members are able to make informed decisions about their retirement savings.

The principles have no legal standing, but they form the basis of its regulatory approach to DC schemes.

In 2013 the Regulator consulted on a package of measures to support the market in achieving good member outcomes in DC schemes, which included:

- New code of practice no. 13 on the governance and administration of occupational DC trust-based schemes. This provides practical guidance on meeting legislative requirements and sets out quality features that represent the standards and behaviours the Regulator expects to see. Each feature sits beneath one of the six principles.

- Regulatory guidance, setting out good practice in areas that do not relate directly to legal duties, such as value for money, transparency of charges and member communications. It includes quality features that are not addressed in the code.

- A regulatory approach document, including explanation of how the Regulator will work with the Financial Conduct Authority to ensure that the same standards apply to contract-based schemes. A DC compliance and enforcement policy is due in late 2013.

Trustee Knowledge and Understanding

The Pensions Act 2004 introduced a formal requirement for trustees to have knowledge and understanding about the law relating to pensions and trusts and the principles of funding and investment. In addition, they are required to be conversant with the scheme's trust deed and rules, statements of investment and (where applicable) funding principles and other relevant scheme documents. This means that they are expected to have a working knowledge of the documents, so as to be able to use them effectively.

The Pensions Regulator has issued and updated a code of practice and scope guidance on these requirements. The level of knowledge and understanding expected is that necessary for the individual concerned to exercise his or her own trustee function (so more is expected of the chair of the trustee board, or a significant sub-committee). Trustees should carry out a review of their training needs at least annually and when required in response to internal and external scheme changes or new responsibilities. Records should be kept of learning activities undertaken.

Newly appointed trustees generally have a six-month period of grace before the requirements apply to them.

The Regulator maintains a web-based trustee toolkit which trustees are recommended to complete. The Regulator provides regular updates for specific events and holds webinars on topical issues.

Investment governance

The Myners Principles set out guidelines for investment governance in pension schemes and cover:

- effective decision making
- clear objectives
- risk and liabilities
- performance assessment
- responsible ownership, *and*
- transparency and reporting.

The principles are voluntary with a comply or explain approach to reporting, although the government has suggested that legislation will be introduced i pension schemes do not comply with the principles.

The government established the Investment Governance Group to oversee the principles and provide further guidance, where necessary. In particular, the Group has published investment governance principles and best practice guidance for work-based DC pension schemes, both contract-based and trust based. The principles are:

- clear roles and responsibilities for investment decision making and governance
- effective decision making
- appropriate investment options
- appropriate default strategy
- effective performance assessment, *and*
- clear and relevant communication with members.

Reporting on these principles is also on a comply or explain basis.

In July 2010 the Financial Reporting Council (FRC) published Stewardship Code that sets out good practice to which the FRC believe institutional investors should aspire when engaging with the UK listed companies in which they invest. It is acknowledged that trustees of pension funds may not wish to become directly involved in engagement with companies in which they invest, but they are encouraged to set mandates for their investment managers that require them to act in line with the Code.

THE ROLE OF THE EMPLOYER

The employer is a party to the trust and retains certain duties and powers which may be specified in the trust deed. The employer normally carries a substantial burden of the cost of the scheme benefits, or its administration, or both, and would therefore expect to retain certain powers, especially in areas where there is a cost element, for example the power to augment benefits or to amend the scheme. The employer generally has the ultimate power to cease contributions to the scheme, which will lead to the scheme either winding up or ceasing to provide any further benefit accrual, according to the provisions of the trust deed. In normal circumstances, the employer should act in a reasonable manner to ensure that the trustees can operate the scheme satisfactorily; this includes providing information on members, paying contributions when due, and meeting any obligations imposed on them by the trust deed or by legislation.

Although the Pensions Act 2004 extended the trustees' statutory powers in relation to scheme funding, the method and assumptions, statement of funding principles, any recovery plan and the schedule of contributions are all, generally, subject to the agreement of the employer. *See Section 17 for further details.*

The employer is also required to consult with scheme members about proposed changes to scheme rules, if these fall within prescribed categories. *See Section 3.*

Since May 2013, companies planning a takeover have been required to provide information to the trustees of the target's pension scheme, who are then able to express their views about the impact for the scheme *(see Section 24).*

In July 2011 the Regulator published a statement to help trustees of defined benefit schemes understand the importance of identifying their statutory employer(s) and how they should do this. A statutory employer for this purpose is the employer who is responsible for scheme-specific funding, section 75 debts or triggering entry to the Pension Protection Fund. For their Scheme Return, schemes must identify the statutory employer(s). Where trustees conclude that the scheme has no statutory employer, they should contact the Regulator.

THE ROLE OF THE ACTUARY

Responsibilities of the scheme actuary

The scheme actuary appointed by the trustees has a number of statutory responsibilities. These include:

- advising the trustees on various aspects of scheme funding, as required by the Pensions Act 2004 *(see Section 17)*
- producing actuarial valuations for funding purposes *(see Section 17)*
- certifying the technical provisions and schedule of contributions as required by the scheme funding legislation *(see Section 17)*

- completing required certification for contracted-out salary-related schemes *(see Section 2)*
- along with other parties who are involved in running the scheme, reporting material breaches of statutory responsibilities by the employer or trustees to the Pensions Regulator *(see Section 9)*
- advising the trustees on various matters in relation to the calculation of individual transfer values *(see Section 13)*
- certifying bulk transfers of members without their consent *(see Section 24), and*
- certifying qualifying schemes for automatic enrolment *(see Section 5).*

Other actuarial advice

Most schemes require the trustees to take actuarial advice before taking decisions, on such matters as augmentations and bulk transfers, which will affect the finances of the scheme (and this is encouraged by the notifiable events framework – *see Section 9*). Actuaries also provide expert advice in benefit design and implementation, and assist both employers and trustees, subject to any conflict of interest restrictions, in ensuring that the pension provision offered to employees is both appropriate and soundly based. They also assess the pension cost to be disclosed in the company's accounts *(see Section 25)*.

THE ROLE OF THE AUDITOR

The statutory duties of the scheme auditor include the following:

- producing a report stating whether or not in his opinion the scheme accounts have been prepared in accordance with regulations
- producing an auditor's statement as to whether or not in his opinion the required contributions have been paid to the scheme
- if the auditor's statement is negative or qualified, giving a statement of the reasons, *and*
- along with other parties who are involved in running the scheme reporting material breaches of statutory responsibilities by the employer or trustees to the Pensions Regulator *(see Section 9)*.

THE ROLE OF THE ADMINISTRATOR

The scheme administrator has many duties. Some of these are imposed by statute and regulations. Others are set out under a contract with the trustees.

HMRC requires every registered pension scheme to appoint a Scheme Administrator to be responsible for providing information including scheme returns and event reports, accounting for tax and monitoring benefits against the lifetime allowance.

Day-to-day administrative responsibilities are very varied, ranging from organising the payment of benefits to individual beneficiaries in accordance with the scheme rules, to tasks such as organising the submission of information required by the Pensions Regulator. These may be carried out by someone other than the formal Scheme Administrator.

THE PENSIONS REGULATORY SYSTEM

The Pensions Regulator is the regulator of work-based pension schemes in the UK. This section covers its role, in particular in relation to trust-based schemes, and the roles of other bodies involved in the regulation of UK pension schemes.

THE ROLE OF THE PENSIONS REGULATOR

The Regulator's powers fall into three broad categories: investigating schemes, acting against avoidance and putting things right.

The Regulator has statutory objectives to protect members' benefits, to reduce the risk of calls on the Pension Protection Fund (PPF), to promote good administration and to maximise employers' compliance with their new duties in relation to automatic enrolment *(see Sections 4 to 6 for details)*. The current Pensions Bill will add another objective: 'to minimise any adverse impact on the sustainable growth of an employer' when exercising its functions under the scheme funding legislation *(see Section 17)*.

In May 2013, the Regulator published its corporate plan setting out five strategic themes (linked to its statutory objectives) for the next three years (2013–16):

- reducing risks to DB scheme members
- improving outcomes for DC scheme members
- improving governance and administration
- maximising employer compliance with automatic enrolment, *and*
- delivering operational efficiency and effectiveness.

Scheme returns

The Regulator requires all schemes to complete a regular scheme return. This provides a wide range of information about schemes, including details of membership, sponsoring employers, trustees, advisers, administration, funding and investment. These returns include the information required by the PPF to determine its annual levies *(see Section 19)*. A return is required only when the Regulator issues a scheme return notice. The Regulator issues scheme return notices annually for all but the smallest schemes.

It is the trustees' legal duty to complete the scheme return online by the completion date notified on the form. The online Exchange system also allows trustees and administrators to update scheme details during the year.

Codes of practice and guidance

The Regulator is required to publish codes of practice giving practical guidance on implementing certain parts of the legislation, and setting out the standards of conduct and practice expected. These codes are updated periodically. The codes are not law but nevertheless would be taken into account by a court in deciding whether or not legislation had been complied with. The following codes are in effect:

- Reporting breaches of the law *(see below)*
- Notifiable events *(see below)*

- Funding defined benefits *(see Section 17)*
- Early leavers – reasonable periods *(see Section 12)*
- Reporting late payment of contributions to occupational money purchase schemes *(see below)*
- Reporting late payment of contributions to personal pensions *(see below)*
- Trustee knowledge and understanding *(see Section 8)*
- Member-nominated trustees and directors – putting in place and implementing arrangements *(see Section 8)*
- Internal controls *(see Section 8)*
- Modification of subsisting rights *(see Section 3)*
- Dispute resolution – reasonable periods *(see Section 8)*
- Circumstances in relation to the material detriment test *(see below)*, *and*
- Governance and administration of occupational defined contribution trust-based pension schemes *(see Section 8 –* draft laid July 2013, expected to take effect November 2013).

In addition to publishing codes of practice (often with related guidance) the Regulator has also issued regulatory guidance for trustees and employers on a number of subjects including automatic enrolment, clearance, abandonment of defined benefit pension schemes, defined contribution schemes (various guides), member record-keeping, cash equivalent transfer values, winding up and conflicts of interest. Statements or warnings have also been issued on subjects such as defined contribution schemes, incentive exercises, scheme funding, pension liberation, the implications of its financial support directions for insolvency practitioners and prohibition orders.

Notifiable and reportable events

As noted above, the Regulator has issued codes of practice relating to notifiable events and reporting breaches of the law.

Trustees and/or employers are required to notify the Regulator in writing of certain notifiable events. Notification is only required for schemes that are eligible for the PPF. The purpose of notification is to reduce the risk of circumstances occurring that might lead to compensation being payable from the PPF, by providing an early warning of possible insolvency or underfunding. The events to be notified, including those under employer debt legislation, are set out below. (Where a withdrawal arrangement or approved withdrawal arrangement *(see Section 24)* is in force, each guarantor must notify the Regulator if it becomes aware that any of the events requiring notification by the employer occur in relation to it, and also if it becomes insolvent.)

Notifiable events – all cases	
Trustees	A decision by the trustees or managers to grant benefits, or a right to benefits, on more favourable terms than those provided for by the scheme rules, without either seeking advice from the actuary or securing additional funding where such funding was advised by the actuary.

	Notifiable events – all cases
Trustees	A decision to take action that will, or is intended to, result in entering into a scheme apportionment arrangement on or after the employer debt arose.
	A decision to take action that will, or is intended to, result in a flexible apportionment arrangement taking effect *(see Section 24)*.
Employer	Any decision by the employer to take action that will, or is intended to, result in a debt that is, or may become, due to the scheme not being paid in full.
	Ceasing to (or deciding to cease to) carry on business in the United Kingdom.
	Where applicable, receipt by the employer of advice that it is trading wrongfully, or circumstances being reached in which a director or former director of the company knows that there is no reasonable prospect that the company will avoid going into insolvent liquidation.
	The conviction of an individual for an offence involving dishonesty, if the offence was committed while the individual was a director or partner of the employer.
	Additional notifiable events – where scheme was under-funded at last s179 valuation or there has been a reportable breach of the schedule of contributions in previous 12 months
Trustees	Any decision by the trustees or managers to take action that will, or is intended to, result in any debt (above a *de minimis* threshold) that is, or may become, due to the scheme not being paid in full.
	Making (or deciding to make) a transfer payment to, or accepting (or deciding to accept) a transfer payment from, another scheme in excess of £1,500,000 (or 5% of scheme assets if lower).
	Granting (or deciding to grant) benefits, or a right to benefits, to a member in excess of £1,500,000 (or 5% of scheme assets if lower).
Employer	Any breach by the employer of a covenant in an agreement between the employer and a bank or other institution providing banking services, other than where the bank or other institution agrees with the employer not to enforce the covenant.
	Where the employer is a company, a controlling company relinquishing, or deciding to relinquish, control of the employer company.

Under separate legislation, there is a duty to report significant breaches that are 'likely to be of material significance to the Regulator'. These reportable events are not restricted to schemes eligible for the PPF. The duty to blow the whistle applies to a wide range of people, including trustees, employers, scheme administrators and professional advisers. Criteria for deciding whether or not a breach is likely to be of material significance are set out in the code of practice and guidance and cover the cause and effect of the breach, the reaction to it and any wider implications.

For both notifiable and reportable events, notification should be made in writing and where possible the standard form available from the Regulator's website should be used.

Late payments by employers

The Regulator issued two codes of practice about the reporting of late payments by employers, one relating to occupational money purchase pension schemes and the other to personal pension schemes. In 2013, these codes were expanded to cover setting up payment schedules (for occupational schemes) and direct payment arrangements (for personal pensions), providing information to members so that they can check what contributions are due, and carrying out a risk-based monitoring process including chasing outstanding payments. The revised codes are now accompanied by guidance, and a separate guide for employers has been released.

The codes set out reasonable periods within which trustees/managers must report late payments of contributions to the Regulator (within ten working days of identifying that a late payment is material) and to members/employees (no later than 30 days after the report to the Regulator, although trustees/managers are encouraged to do so earlier). A late payment must be reported if the trustees/managers have reasonable cause to believe that it is material. The code includes a guide to which circumstances would be considered material, such as where a contribution remains unpaid 90 days after the due date or where the trustees/managers have reasonable cause to believe that the employer is not willing to pay. Requirements regarding late payments to defined benefit occupational pension schemes are included in the code of practice covering scheme funding (see Section 17).

Acting against avoidance

The Regulator has powers to act where it believes that an employer is attempting to avoid its pension obligations (deliberately or otherwise), leaving the PPF to pick up the pension liabilities. These powers can be used under what the pensions industry refers to as the 'moral hazard' provisions. These provisions were extended in 2009 to cover situations, in particular 'non-insured buy-out' business models (see Section 23), where the previous powers were insufficient or difficult to implement. They allow the Regulator to issue any of the following:

(a) *Contribution notices*. If the Regulator determines that a company or individual has taken action with the main purpose of avoiding an obligation to meet a debt on the employer under section 75 of the Pensions Act 1995, it may direct that those involved pay a contribution to the scheme.

The Pensions Act 2008 introduced the ability for the Regulator to issue a contribution notice if the material detriment test is met. This is met if, in the Regulator's opinion, 'the act, or failure to act, has been materially detrimental to the likelihood of accrued scheme benefits being received'. The Regulator has issued a code of practice and guidance relating to the test.

The Regulator issued a contribution notice in June 2010, in connection with the pre-pack administration of the sponsor of the Bonas Group Pension Scheme, against the Belgian holding company, Michel Van De Wiele. However, the original contribution notice, for over £5m, was appealed and an out-of-court settlement reached; a contribution notice for £60,000 was issued in June 2011. In 2012, the Regulator published details of its determination (in 2010) to issue a contribution notice in relation to the Desmond and Sons Limited 1975 Pension and Life Assurance Scheme.

(b) *Financial support directions (FSDs)*. These are intended to apply in cases where corporate structures exist for legitimate business reasons but where the effect is that the employer in relation to a scheme is insufficiently resourced to deal with a potential section 75 obligation. Here the Regulator can require the company group to put in place financial support arrangements.

The Regulator issued its first two FSDs in February 2008, both against Sea Containers Limited.

In 2010, the Regulator determined that it would issue an FSD against a number of companies in the Nortel Group in relation to its UK pension scheme, and another against six companies in the Lehman Brothers Group (although, subsequently, the trustees of the Lehman Brothers Pension Scheme successfully applied for further companies within the group to come within the scope of an FSD). Nortel and Lehman Brothers brought a joint claim in the High Court challenging the Regulator's ability to issue an FSD while they are in administration. The judge ruled that an FSD can be issued in such circumstances and that the liabilities created are payable as an expense of the administration, thereby ranking above unsecured creditors, although, on appeal, in July 2013 the Supreme Court decided that an FSD should rank alongside unsecured creditors.

(c) *Restoration orders*. If there has been a transaction at an undervalue involving the scheme's assets, these allow the Regulator to take action to have the assets (or their equivalent value) restored to the scheme.

Companies considering corporate transactions where there is an underfunded defined benefit pension scheme can apply to the Regulator for a clearance statement. This gives assurance that the Regulator will not use its anti-avoidance powers in relation to the transaction once it is completed. The decision is binding on the Regulator unless the circumstances differ materially from what was disclosed in the clearance application.

The Regulator has also issued reports under section 89 of the Pensions Act 2004, setting out its considerations in relation to some schemes. These include situations in which it has intervened but where clearance has been provided.

Intervention

When the Regulator decides action must be taken to protect the security of members' benefits, there is a range of options available. These include:

- issuing an improvement notice to one or more persons
- taking action to recover unpaid contributions from the employer
- disqualifying trustees, or issuing prohibition or suspension orders to trustees
- appointing trustees, including independent trustees in certain circumstances, *and*
- imposing fines (maximum: £5,000 for individuals or £50,000 in other cases).

In 2012, the Regulator published details of its investigation in the *GP Noble Trustees Limited* case, which addressed fraud and the misappropriation of various schemes' funds. It issued determination notices to prohibit the directors from acting as trustees of trust schemes in general.

THE ROLE OF THE DWP

The Department for Work & Pensions (DWP) provides the overarching regulatory and legal framework governing the Regulator and the PPF. It has no responsibility for the day-to-day running of the Regulator and the PPF, but expects to be informed by them of potentially significant problems.

A tripartite Memorandum of Understanding between the DWP, the Regulator and the PPF establishes the framework for cooperation between them, including discussion forums, and sets out the role and responsibilities of each body.

THE ROLE OF HMRC

Since pension benefits are often costly, employers (and employees) will generally wish to take advantage of the tax reliefs that are available to schemes that meet certain criteria. This is monitored by Pension Schemes Service (PSS) within HM Revenue & Customs (HMRC). Schemes that wish to benefit from these tax reliefs must be registered (*see Section 10 for details*).

Following registration, PSS monitors schemes to ensure that they continue to meet their requirements. Scheme administrators are required to supply HMRC with the information necessary to enable its monitoring to be effective. This includes an Event Report, which must be completed annually, giving details of specified events (such as large benefit payments or payment of benefits to members with primary, enhanced or fixed protection) that have occurred during the tax year to which the report relates. HMRC also requires quarterly income tax returns to be completed and may require a copy of the audited annual accounts to be submitted.

THE PENSIONS ADVISORY SERVICE (TPAS)

TPAS (The Pensions Advisory Service) is a non-profit, independent and voluntary organisation giving free help and advice to members of the public who have problems concerning State, occupational or personal pensions. The service is available to anyone who believes he or she has pension rights: this includes working members of pension schemes, pensioners, deferred pensioners and dependants. TPAS is grant-aided by the DWP.

TPAS has no statutory powers and any decisions it reaches are subject to the agreement of the parties involved. Where no agreement can be reached, cases may be referred to the Pensions Ombudsman (*see below*).

THE ROLE OF THE FINANCIAL CONDUCT AUTHORITY

The Financial Conduct Authority (FCA) is responsible for regulating the standards of conduct in financial markets and for supervising the infrastructure that supports those markets, so that the markets function well (*see Section 26*).

A Memorandum of Understanding between the FCA and the Regulator sets out the arrangements for cooperation and coordination between the two in carrying out their respective regulatory responsibilities under the Financial Services and Markets Act 2000, the Pensions Acts of 2004 and 2008, and other relevant legislation.

THE PENSIONS OMBUDSMAN

The Pensions Ombudsman's role is to investigate disputes and complaints concerning occupational and personal pension schemes. Complaints may be made by actual or potential beneficiaries against the trustees, employer or anyone involved in the administration of a scheme. The Ombudsman's jurisdiction also covers complaints made by the trustees against the employer, and vice versa, and disputes between trustees of either the same scheme or different schemes.

During an investigation, the trustees of the scheme involved, and anyone else against whom a complaint has been made, are given a chance to explain their position, and the Ombudsman can require any necessary information or documentation to be provided to him.

Unlike TPAS, the Pensions Ombudsman has statutory authority with regard to the complaints brought to him. In particular:

- he has the same powers as the court in respect of the examination and attendance of witnesses
- anyone obstructing an investigation, for example by refusing to give certain information, can be taken to court and, following representations by either or both sides, be dealt with as if he or she had been in contempt of that court, *and*
- the Ombudsman's decision, and any directions he gives, are final and binding, and are enforceable in a county court as if they were judgments of that court. An appeal can be made to the High Court on any points of law involved in the case.

The Pensions Ombudsman is able to appoint one or more Deputy Ombudsmen who have the power to carry out any of the Ombudsman's duties.

The Pensions Ombudsman works closely with the Financial Ombudsman Service in cases where their remits overlap.

LEVIES

Occupational pension schemes are generally required to pay the following levies:
- the General Levy (which also applies to personal pension schemes)
- the Fraud Compensation Levy, *and*
- the Financial Reporting Council Levy.

Schemes that are eligible for future entry into the PPF are also required to pay levies to the PPF *(see Section 19)*.

General Levy

The General Levy covers the cost of the Regulator, the Pensions Ombudsman, the PPF Ombudsman and any grants to support TPAS.

The current levy rates, which were revised for 2012/13 onwards, are set out below:

Band	Number of members:	Occupational schemes: General Levy (per member):	Min. payment (per scheme):	Personal pension schemes: General Levy (per member):	Min. payment (per scheme):
1	2–11	–	£29	–	£12
2	12–99	£2.88	–	£1.15	–
3	100–999	£2.08	£290	£0.81	£120
4	1,000–4,999	£1.62	£2,080	£0.69	£810
5	5,000–9,999	£1.23	£8,100	£0.46	£3,450
6	10,000+	£0.86	£12,300	£0.35	£4,600

Fraud Compensation Levy

The PPF is responsible for operating the Fraud Compensation Fund *(see Section 19)*.

This is funded by a Fraud Compensation Levy on all schemes eligible for this compensation at a rate determined by the PPF. Regulations cap the levy at 75 pence per member per year (23 pence prior to 31 March 2011). The levy is only charged as and when needed. Levies were raised in 1997/98, 2004/05 and 2010/11, all at the rate of 23 pence per member, and in 2011/12 and 2012/13 at the rate of 25 pence per member, but for 2013/14 no levy will be raised.

Financial Reporting Council Levy

Since April 2006, the Financial Reporting Council has had responsibility for actuarial standards and regulation. The cost is met by an annual levy. For 2013/14 this is £2.3m and is collected:
- 10% from the Actuarial Profession
- 45% from life and general insurance companies, *and*
- 45% from pension schemes with 1,000 or more members (at the rate of £2.55 per 100 members).

PENSIONS TAXATION – REGISTERED PENSION SCHEMES

The taxation regime for registered pension schemes allows individuals to receive tax-advantaged benefits subject to two allowances:

- the *lifetime allowance* – an overall limit on an individual's tax-privileged retirement savings, *and*
- the *annual allowance* – a limit on an individual's retirement savings during the year.

This regime of annual and lifetime allowances for registered pension schemes came into force on 6 April 2006 under the Finance Act 2004, and replaced the previous tax regimes for all types of pension scheme. This regime applies to all members of all arrangements in registered pension schemes. It can also impact certain overseas schemes where the member is deemed to have benefited from UK income tax relief. Retirement and death benefits can be provided outside a registered scheme by an 'Employer-financed Retirement Benefits Scheme' (EFRBS) – *see Section 11* – and by 'Excepted Group Life Assurance' policies.

The lifetime and annual allowances had been increased annually but recent Finance Acts have made two significant reductions *(see below)*. There is no commitment to increase either allowance in future years, although the legislation allows for future increases by Treasury Order.

Tax Year	Lifetime Allowance	Annual Allowance
2006/07	£1,500,000	£215,000
2007/08	£1,600,000	£225,000
2008/09	£1,650,000	£235,000
2009/10	£1,750,000	£245,000
2010/11	£1,800,000	£255,000
2011/12	£1,800,000	£50,000
2012/13	£1,500,000	£50,000
2013/14	£1,500,000	£50,000
2014/15–	£1,250,000	£40,000

The Finance Act 2011 also made a number of changes to the authorised benefits permitted to be paid by registered schemes, including removing the requirement to annuitise members' money purchase funds by age 75.

For the purpose of specifying the benefits that may be paid and testing against the above limits, the regime distinguishes between three main types of pension 'arrangement'. These are the two familiar ones, 'defined benefit' and 'money purchase', and an additional one, 'cash balance', which is expressed as a sub-category of money purchase. The type of arrangement determines how the 'pension input amount' is calculated for assessing the value of any increase in accrued rights against the annual allowance and the nature of the benefits that may be paid as authorised payments.

This section sets out the main features of the current regime. At the end of this section is a brief summary of the pre-6 April 2006 regimes, parts of which are still relevant under transitional provisions.

LIFETIME ALLOWANCE CHARGE

The value of benefits must be tested against the lifetime allowance (or the part of it that remains after any previous 'crystallisations') on each occasion that benefits come into payment, or otherwise 'crystallise'. On crystallisation, up to 25% of the value of benefits crystallised (or their cost, under money purchase arrangements) within the lifetime allowance is available as a tax-free lump sum.

A single factor (for all ages) of 20:1 is used for valuing *scheme pensions (see below)* on crystallisation. The valuation of annuities provided under money purchase arrangements is based on their cost.

A lifetime allowance charge is payable if the value of the benefits being crystallised exceeds the balance of any lifetime allowance available. The rate is

- 25% if the benefits being crystallised are taken in pension form, *or*
- 55% (equivalent to the payment of a 25% charge plus income tax at an assumed rate of 40% – irrespective of the individual's actual marginal rate) if taken as a lump sum.

If the charge is met by the administrator (and the member's benefits under the scheme are not reduced to reflect this), the tax payment is itself treated as part of the excess benefit value on which tax is calculated.

ANNUAL ALLOWANCE CHARGE

Member contributions

In any one tax year member contributions of up to 100% of relevant UK earnings (or £3,600 if higher where the scheme is operating on a 'Relief at Source' basis attract income tax relief. Further contributions may be paid, but attract no tax relief. As well as taxable benefits in kind, 'relevant UK earnings' includes taxable income arising from share schemes and taxable severance payments.

Annual allowance charge

Where the 'total pension input amount' – the aggregate of *pension input amount (see below)* arising under schemes of which the individual is a member – exceeds the annual allowance, the individual is normally liable for a charge at their higher tax rate(s) on amounts above the annual allowance; prior to 6 April 2011, the charge was a flat-rate 40%. 'Unused annual allowance' can be carried forward for up to three years, permitting an annual allowance charge to be reduced or not be payable.

There are exemptions from the charge in the tax year in which a member

- dies
- has their benefits commuted as a *serious ill-health lump sum (see below)*, or
- becomes entitled to an ill-health pension where he/she is unlikely to be able to work in any capacity (other than to an insignificant extent) before reaching pensionable age.

These replaced a general exemption, prior to 6 April 2011, which applied in any tax year in which an individual's benefits under the arrangement were taken in full.

Pension input amount

Under a defined benefit or cash balance arrangement, the pension input amount for the purposes of the annual allowance is the amount of any increase in the value of the member's rights under the arrangement. This is calculated as the difference between the opening and closing values of the member's rights, with an adjustment to the opening value to allow for the increase in the Consumer Prices Index (CPI). Under a defined benefit arrangement, accrued pension is valued by multiplying the annual pension by 16; prior to 6 April 2011, a factor of 10:1 was used.

Under a money purchase arrangement (other than a cash balance arrangement), the pension input amount is the total of the contributions paid by, or in respect of, the individual.

Scheme pays

Individuals facing significant charges following the reduction in the annual allowance from 6 April 2011 are generally able to require their scheme to pay the annual allowance charge on their behalf. Broadly, where a member's liability to the charge in a particular tax year exceeds £2,000, schemes may be required to pay the charge but have the power to make a corresponding adjustment to the member's benefits. The legislation sets out deadlines for the scheme and the member to provide information in order to elect for the scheme to pay the charge.

Special annual allowance charge

The special annual allowance charge was introduced under the anti-forestalling measures that applied for the tax years 2009/10 and 2010/11 only, and affected certain individuals with annual incomes in excess of £150,000 (later, £130,000). The anti-forestalling measures are set out in a summary available at *www.pensionspocketbook.com*.

OTHER TAX CHARGES

Other tax charges that may arise in particular circumstances *are discussed below*. The Finance Acts allow these charges to be varied by order. This gives the government the scope to vary them to reflect changes in the rate of income tax.

Unauthorised payments charge

If a benefit paid from a registered scheme is not *authorised (see below)* the member (or other recipient in the case of a death benefit) is liable for an unauthorised payments charge, at a rate of 40%. A 15% surcharge (resulting in an overall charge of 55%) applies if the unauthorised payment exceeds 25% of the value of the member's benefits. A payment subject to an unauthorised payments charge is, however, exempt from any income tax charge.

Scheme sanction charge

The scheme administrator is potentially subject to a scheme sanction charge at a rate of 40% in respect of most unauthorised payments. If the member has paid an unauthorised payments charge, the scheme sanction charge is reduced by the lesser of 25% and the actual amount of the unauthorised payments charge paid. The administrator can apply to be excused the charge if it could not reasonably have known that the payment was unauthorised at the time it was made.

TRANSITIONAL ARRANGEMENTS

Transitional arrangements were put in place at 6 April 2006, and subsequently at 6 April 2012 (and will be at 2014), to protect benefits accrued prior to these dates, including:

- *primary protection*, whereby individuals with benefits accrued in excess of £1.5m at 5 April 2006 could register for an enhancement to their lifetime allowance
- *enhanced protection*, for individuals to have existing benefits at 5 April 2006 (whether or not already in excess of £1.5m) ring-fenced by opting out of any future 'accrual',
- *fixed protection* from 6 April 2012, whereby the lifetime allowance is underpinned by £1.8m, provided no accrual is deemed to occur in any year from that date
- *fixed protection 2014*, from 6 April 2014, whereby the lifetime allowance is underpinned by £1.5m, provided no accrual is deemed to occur in any year from that date, *and*
- *individual protection 2014* (to be included within Finance Act 2014), where individuals with benefits accrued in excess of £1.25m at 5 April 2014 will be able to register for an enhancement to their lifetime allowance.

Transitional provisions also allow individuals to receive higher tax-free lump sums than they would otherwise under the current regime, by protecting lump sum rights at 5 April 2006.

Primary protection (6 April 2006)

This applies where total relevant pension rights in approved pension schemes as at 5 April 2006 were valued in excess of £1.5m and were registered by 5 April 2009. In exceptional circumstances, registration can be made after the April 2009 deadline. Errors in the details registered can also be corrected after this deadline.

The value of the accrued rights at 5 April 2006 was determined in a similar manner to values at crystallisation. However, pensions that were already in payment on 5 April 2006 were valued as 25 times the annual rate of pension in payment, to allow for the lump sum that was presumed to have been taken. If the member was taking drawdown, the maximum possible pension under the relevant drawdown provisions had to be used.

There was an overriding limit on the benefits that could be registered for protection corresponding to the maximum permitted on leaving service at 5 April 2006 under whichever of the previous tax regimes was applicable at this date.

Under primary protection, the individual is granted a personal lifetime allowance, based on the total value calculated as above, in place of the standard lifetime allowance. The personal lifetime allowance is increased annually in line with the standard lifetime allowance, but taking the latter to be at least equal to £1.8m for tax years following 5 April 2012. It is subject to adjustment if a pension debit arises as a result of a pension sharing order implemented on or after 6 April 2006.

Enhanced protection (6 April 2006)

Enhanced protection was available to all individuals with benefits in schemes that became registered pension schemes on 6 April 2006, as an alternative to primary protection. Where this applies, there are no lifetime allowance charges in respect of the individual and, prior to 6 April 2011, there were no annual allowance charges. This means that, broadly speaking:

- accrued defined benefit rights at 6 April 2006 can continue to be linked to salary (although any pre-6 April 2006 restriction due to the earnings cap will still apply), *and*
- money purchase funds accrued at 6 April 2006 can be increased by the full investment return achieved subsequently.

To retain enhanced protection, no further 'relevant benefit accrual' (or money purchase contributions) are permitted under any registered scheme after 5 April 2006. Other than in exceptional circumstances, registration by 5 April 2009 was required. Any errors in the registration details can be corrected after this date.

In a defined benefit arrangement, continuation of contributions or of pensionable service does not in itself count as relevant benefit accrual. Instead, for enhanced protection not to be lost, the resulting benefits must not breach the member's 'appropriate limit' at the first or a subsequent crystallisation date (or where there is a permitted transfer out of the scheme). This, in effect, means that, if the pre-6 April 2006 service benefits turn out to be lower than expected (e.g. because a reduction applies for early retirement), it may be possible to provide post-5 April 2006 service benefits without enhanced protection being lost.

As under primary protection, there was an overriding limit on the benefits that could be registered, corresponding to the maximum permitted immediately before 6 April 2006. Where enhanced protection applied, any benefits in excess of this maximum had to be surrendered (or refunded in the case of surplus AVCs).

Individuals could apply for both primary and enhanced protection – this means that if enhanced protection is lost, either because the conditions for its retention are breached or because it is given up voluntarily, the individual can then rely on primary protection. Primary protection cannot be lost or given up.

Fixed protection (6 April 2012)

Fixed protection is available to all individuals with benefits in registered schemes who do not have primary or enhanced protection and who registered for it before 6 April 2012. Where this applies, the tax legislation will be applied as if the individual's lifetime allowance is the greater of:

- the standard lifetime allowance, *and*
- £1.8m.

To retain fixed protection, 'benefit accrual' (or money purchase contributions) are not permitted under any registered scheme after 5 April 2012. Unlike under enhanced protection, where relevant benefit accrual in a defined benefit scheme can only occur when benefits are crystallised, under fixed protection benefit accrual can occur at any time.

Fixed protection 2014 (6 April 2014)

This will be similar to the fixed protection regime introduced from April 2012, but in place of the £1.8m figure, an underpin of £1.5m will be applied to the individual's lifetime allowance. Similarly to fixed protection, fixed protection 2014 will be lost if 'benefit accrual' occurs after the cut-off date (in this case 6 April 2014).

Fixed protection 2014 will not be available to those individuals who retain any of the forms of protection introduced in 2006 or 2012; however it can be used in conjunction with individual protection 2014 *(see below)*.

Individual protection 2014 (from 6 April 2014)

Under the proposals for individual protection 2014, a member's benefits would be valued at 5 April 2014 using methods similar to those used for primary and enhanced protection at 5 April 2006 *(see above)*, and taking account of any benefits that have crystallised after 5 April 2006. Where this value exceeds £1.25m the individual's lifetime allowance would effectively be set equal to this higher amount (but capped at £1.5m).

Applications for individual protection 2014 are expected to be allowed up to 5 April 2017.

Protection of lump sum rights that exceeded £375,000

Existing lump sum rights of more than £375,000 at 5 April 2006 are protected if the individual registered for primary or enhanced protection. If an individual with primary or enhanced protection does not have this lump sum protection the maximum *pension commencement lump sum (see below)* is restricted to 25% of the standard lifetime allowance.

If the lump sum rights were over both £375,000 and 25% of the value of the benefits but the individual did not register for primary or enhanced protection, lump sum protection is available *as set out below*.

Protection of lump sum rights that exceed 25% of the value placed on total benefit rights under a scheme

Existing rights to a lump sum of more than 25% can be protected if the individual has not registered for either primary protection or enhanced protection, or their lump sum rights at 5 April 2006 were valued at less than £375,000. This is subject to the condition that all benefits under the scheme (that had not already been taken on or before 5 April 2006) are taken on the same date. Special provision apply in some cases where there has been a transfer value paid into or out of the scheme in which the protected entitlement resides.

Additional protections

Further protections under the Finance Act 2004, or introduced in subsequent legislation, extend the scope for paying benefits arising under pre-6 April 2006 scheme rules without incurring unauthorised payments or lifetime allowance charges. These include:

- it is permissible to take benefits as authorised payments before *normal minimum pension age* in certain cases where such a right existed before 6 April 2006
- individuals granted a pension credit before 6 April 2006 were able to register for a form of protection which provides an enhanced lifetime allowance in a similar way to primary protection
- pensions may in some circumstances be paid to children who are over age 23 and are still in full-time education or vocational training, are suffering from serious physical or mental deterioration, or were financially dependent on the member
- benefits accrued in 'lump sum only' schemes at 5 April 2006 can be taken as tax-free lump sums on and after 6 April 2006 provided no 'relevant benefit accrual' (as for enhanced protection) has occurred, *and*
- lump sum death benefits that exceed the protected amounts under primary or enhanced protection may be protected.

Overrides during a transitional period

Until 5 April 2011, regulations overrode the rules of some registered schemes where previous scheme benefits would not be *authorised* under the 2006 pensions tax regime, or where the removal of the earnings cap that applied in the previous regime could have resulted in unplanned increases to benefit entitlements.

AUTHORISED PENSIONS PAYABLE TO MEMBER

A defined benefit arrangement may pay an authorised member pension only in the form of a *scheme pension*, as described below.

For a money purchase arrangement, there are essentially three options as to the type of authorised member pension that may be provided:

- a *scheme pension* as for defined benefit arrangements, provided the member had been offered an open market option
- a *lifetime annuity*, or
- a *drawdown pension*, consisting of income withdrawal and/or a short-term annuity. The rate of annual drawdown is generally subject to strict limits and referred to as *capped drawdown*. However, a member can apply for *flexible drawdown*, which removes these limits, provided they meet certain conditions *described below*.

All pensions payable from registered schemes are subject to income tax at the recipient's marginal rate and they must be paid under PAYE, where applicable.

Minimum age from which pension may be paid

Member pensions (including drawdown pension) must not commence before *normal minimum pension age*, except on ill-health retirement. Normal minimum pension age is 55; prior to 6 April 2010, it was 50. Under transitional provisions, members may be able to receive an authorised pension before age 55 if such a right existed at 6 April 2006.

Scheme pension

Scheme pensions must be payable at least annually and may not be reduced from one 12-month period to the next, except in specified circumstances. These include the cessation of an ill-health pension, a bridging pension ceasing between ages 60 and 65 (or State Pension Age if greater), as a consequence of a pension sharing order, where reductions are applied to all scheme pensions, when a scheme in deficit is winding up, or where the pension scheme has satisfied the individual's liability for an *annual allowance charge* and a commensurate reduction is made to the scheme pension as a consequence.

Lifetime annuity

A lifetime annuity must be payable by an insurance company, with the member having had the opportunity to select the insurance company – the 'open market option'. The annuity may be level, increasing or investment/index-linked.

Period of payment

Lifetime annuities and scheme pensions must generally be payable for life and may, additionally, carry a guarantee of up to ten years payable (to any person) in the form of continued pension instalments.

Capped drawdown

The maximum annual drawdown pension is currently 120% of the amount of the 'relevant annuity' that could be provided from the member's drawdown fund, where this amount is determined by reference to tables published by the Government Actuary's Department. There is no minimum level of drawdown pension.

Flexible drawdown

Flexible drawdown allows a member to gain access to the whole of their drawdown fund without an annual cap on withdrawals. To be eligible, the member must declare that the following three conditions are met:

- the member has a secure lifetime pension income, which may include state pensions, of at least £20,000 a year
- no relievable member or employer contributions have been paid to any money purchase arrangement of the member in the tax year in which the declaration is made, *and*
- at the time of the declaration, the member is not an active member of any defined benefit or cash balance arrangement.

Pension errors and arrears

The list of authorised payments was extended in 2009, with retrospective effect from 6 April 2006, to include the following payments:

- pensions paid in error or up to six months after the pensioner's death, including payments after the error is discovered, provided that a reasonable steps had been taken to prevent payment; this also applies to pension death benefits, *and*
- payment of arrears of pension from a defined benefit arrangement after the member's death; if he or she had died on or after 6 April 2006, it

required that the scheme could not reasonably have been expected to make the payment before his or her death.

These payments are taxable as pension in the tax year of payment.

AUTHORISED LUMP SUMS PAYABLE TO MEMBER

Apart from additional authorised payments prescribed under transitional provisions *(see above)*, the only authorised lump sum benefits that may be paid to a member of a registered pension scheme are set out below.

Pension commencement lump sum

A tax-free pension commencement lump sum (PCLS) of up to 25% of the value of the benefits crystallised *(see above)* may normally be paid in connection with a member becoming entitled to a *scheme pension*, a *lifetime annuity* or *income withdrawal*. The maximum pension commencement lump sum payable is also normally restricted to one-quarter of the unused portion of the standard lifetime allowance.

Under regulations made in 2009, the following may also be authorised payments, with retrospective effect from 6 April 2006, although not strictly PCLSs:

- a commencement lump sum based on an incorrect pension figure, annuity or scheme pension purchase price, *and*
- a commencement lump sum paid under a defined benefit arrangement, no more than a year after the scheme administrator first knew (or could reasonably have been expected to know) of the member's death, if entitlement was not established and payment could not reasonably have been expected before the member died.

Serious ill-health lump sum

Where a member is expected to live for less than one year, a serious ill-health lump sum may be paid in respect of uncrystallised benefits. Up to the available lifetime allowance, this is tax free.

Short service refund lump sum

A refund of the member's contributions (without interest) may be paid from an occupational pension scheme on leaving service, if the member has no right to preservation (although the Government is planning to abolish this facility for money purchase schemes, perhaps as early as 2014). The scheme administrator is able for tax on the first £20,000 of such refunds at 20% and on the remainder at 50%. Interest may be paid in addition to the short service refund lump sum as a scheme administration member payment' *(see below)* and is taxed as income.

Trivial commutation and other small lump sums

A trivial commutation lump sum is permitted only if all of a member's benefits under all pension arrangements are valued in aggregate at no more than £18,000 (or 1% of the standard lifetime allowance prior to 6 April 2012). The commutations must take place within a single 12-month window, chosen by the member, who must have reached age 60. A payment to a member that would be a trivial commutation lump sum but for the continued payment of a lifetime annuity under the same scheme is also permitted.

With effect from 1 December 2009, the range of authorised lump sum payments was significantly extended to include the following small payments, which must not exceed £2,000 and must extinguish the member's entitlement under the scheme:

- a payment from a public service or occupational pension scheme to a member who has reached the age of 60. All benefits including those in related schemes must be within the £2,000 limit
- a payment by a larger public service or occupational pension scheme (with at least 50 members) to a member who has reached the age of 60
- a payment after a 'relevant accretion', such as where a scheme passes on an unexpected additional allocation received after a member has transferred out or purchased an annuity
- a payment made by way of compensation under the Financial Services Compensation Scheme, *and*
- with effect from 6 April 2012, and on no more than two occasions, a payment from a personal pension to a member aged 60 or over.

If the member has uncrystallised rights immediately before the lump sum is paid, 25% of the value of such rights is tax free, with the balance taxed as income.

Winding-up lump sum

A winding-up lump sum, not exceeding £18,000 (or 1% of the standard lifetime allowance prior to 6 April 2012) may be paid, subject to certain conditions, to extinguish the member's entitlement to benefits under the pension scheme. If the member has uncrystallised rights immediately before the lump sum is paid, 25% of the value of such rights is tax free, with the balance taxed as income.

Lifetime allowance excess lump sum

Where none of a member's lifetime allowance is available, any remaining uncrystallised benefits may be taken as a lifetime allowance excess lump sum taxed at 55%. This may not be paid until *normal minimum pension age* (unless the member is in ill health), and cannot include s9(2B) rights or Guaranteed Minimum Pensions.

Refund of excess contributions lump sum

Where in any tax year a member's pension contributions exceed the maximum that qualifies for tax relief (relevant UK earnings or, where the scheme is operating on a 'relief at source' basis, £3,600 if greater), a refund of the excess may be paid without giving rise to liability for income tax. Any excess contributions that had been paid net of basic rate income tax under a 'relief at source' arrangement cannot be included in the refund. A 'scheme administration member payment' *(see below)*, taxable as income, may also be made in respect of interest or investment growth.

Scheme administration member payment

A scheme administration member payment is defined as 'a payment by a registered pension scheme to or in respect of... a member of the pension scheme which is made for the purposes of the administration or management of the pension scheme'. The legislation expressly states that payments of wages, salaries or fees to persons administering the scheme and payments made for the purchase of scheme assets are scheme administration payments, whereas a loan is not. A scheme administration payment may not exceed the amount that might be expected to be paid on arm's length terms. The taxation will vary depending on the nature of the payment.

AUTHORISED PENSIONS PAYABLE ON DEATH

A pension death benefit is a pension payable to an eligible dependant on the death of a member, other than continuing payments of member pension for a limited period under a permitted member pension. The forms of the dependant's pension that may be provided under the different types of arrangement correspond to those for members' pensions. An authorised *dependant's scheme pension* is restricted to 100% of the member's pension (plus an adjustment for any tax-free lump sum taken) if the member was over 75 years of age at the date of death. All dependants' pensions payable from registered schemes are subject to income tax at the recipient's marginal rate and must be taxed under PAYE, where applicable.

Eligible 'dependants' are:

- a member's spouse or civil partner at date of death
- a person who was married to, or a civil partner of, the member when the member first became entitled to the pension
- a child of the member who either has not reached age 23 (extended in some circumstances under transitional provisions) or who, in the opinion of the scheme administrator, was dependent on the member at the date of the member's death because of physical or mental impairment, *and/or*
- any other person who, in the opinion of the scheme administrator, at the date of the member's death:
  - was financially dependent on the member
  - had a financial relationship of mutual dependence with the member, *or*
  - was dependent on the member because of physical or mental impairment.

AUTHORISED LUMP SUMS PAYABLE ON DEATH

The only authorised lump sum death benefits that may be paid by a registered pension scheme are those described below (other than payments allowed for under transitional provisions – *see above*). Except where otherwise indicated, the legislation imposes no restrictions on the recipient of the benefit.

Defined benefits lump sum death benefit

On the death of a member a defined benefits lump sum death benefit of unrestricted amount can be paid. This is tax free up to the amount of the member's remaining lifetime allowance if the member died before age 75. If the member died after reaching age 75, the payment is taxable at 55%.

Uncrystallised funds lump sum death benefit

On the death of a member of a money purchase arrangement, a lump sum not exceeding the amount of the uncrystallised funds can be paid, tax free up to the amount of the member's remaining lifetime allowance if the member died before age 75. If the member died after reaching age 75, the payment is taxable at 55%.

Pension/annuity protection lump sum death benefit

On the death of a member whilst in receipt of a scheme pension or lifetime annuity, a lump sum can be paid, taxable at 55%. This benefit may not exceed the amount by which the instalments paid up to the date of death fall short of the amount originally crystallised.

Drawdown pension fund lump sum death benefit

On the death of a member of a money purchase arrangement, or of a dependant, who was entitled to income withdrawal at the time of death, a lump sum can be paid, taxable at 55%.

Charity lump sum death benefit

On the death, leaving no dependants, of a member of a money purchase arrangement (or of a dependant) who was in receipt of a drawdown pension, a charity lump sum death benefit may be paid to a charity nominated by the member or dependant as appropriate. A charity lump sum death benefit may also be paid on the death of a member who has reached age 75, leaving no dependants, in respect of uncrystallised funds.

Trivial commutation lump sum death benefit/ winding-up lump sum death benefit

In specified circumstances, a lump sum, not exceeding £18,000 (or 1% of the standard lifetime allowance prior to 6 April 2012) may be paid to a dependant taxable as income.

REGISTRATION AND REPORTING TO HMRC

Registration

'Registration' of a pension scheme replaced the previous 'HMRC approval' as the process by which schemes obtain tax-advantaged status from 6 April 2006. Pension schemes that had HMRC approval prior to 6 April 2006 automatically became 'registered schemes' on 6 April 2006 unless they explicitly opted out.

Reporting

Registered pension schemes have to comply with a number of administration requirements. These include providing HMRC with quarterly returns for tax accounting purposes, reports on the occurrence of certain events and, if requested, a *Pension Scheme Return*.

OVERSEAS ASPECTS

Scheme membership

There is no restriction on non-UK-resident individuals becoming members of registered pension schemes.

The annual and lifetime allowance charges, and unauthorised payment charges, apply whether or not the individual is resident, ordinarily resident or domiciled in the UK. However, the lifetime allowance may be enhanced to allow for overseas periods of membership falling after 5 April 2006 during which contributions to the scheme are not eligible for UK tax relief.

Transfers may be accepted by registered schemes from any overseas pension schemes. The lifetime allowance may be enhanced for transfers from *recognised overseas pension schemes (see Appendix 2, Glossary of Terms).*

Transfers may be made from registered schemes to *qualifying recognised overseas pension schemes ('QROPS'),* and count as benefit crystallisation events for lifetime allowance purposes. If it transpires that the scheme does not satisfy the QROPS criteria, then the transfer will be unauthorised and the member subject to unauthorised payment charges and surcharges.

Following a transfer to a QROPS, various member payment charges could apply in relation to payments made from funds which had their source in a UK registered scheme. These include charges on unauthorised payments, short service refunds and commutation of pensions.

In recent years there has been a progressive tightening of the requirements relating to transfers to QROPS with the aim of ensuring better operation of the regime and deterring misuse.

Migrant member relief

Migrant member relief allows UK tax relief on contributions paid to overseas schemes where a *relevant migrant member* comes to the UK, and was a member of a qualifying tax-relieved overseas pension scheme at any time in the ten previous ten years. The manager of that scheme must provide HMRC with details of any relevant benefit crystallisation events that occur. Contributions and benefits accruing after 5 April 2006 would normally count towards the annual and lifetime allowances, although from 2008 this excludes benefits and contributions in respect of earnings that are not subject to UK taxation.

OTHER MATTERS

Investment

There is one set of tax rules covering investments for almost all registered pension schemes. These allow schemes to invest in any type of investment where this is held for the purpose of the scheme, and generally exempt them from income and capital gains tax. However, other non-tax regulations do limit or prohibit certain types of investment. These rules allow 'authorised employer loans' subject to conditions. However, occupational schemes are still prevented from making such loans by the 'employer-related investment' provisions under the Pensions Act 1995 *(see Section 8).* Special rules apply to schemes where members can direct the investment policy (such as SIPPs). In such cases tax rules make it unattractive to invest in 'taxable property'. This includes tangible moveable property and residential property that is held directly as opposed to indirectly through for example a Real Estate Investment Trust).

Surplus

A repayment of surplus funds to the employer is only authorised in limited circumstances and is taxed at 35%. For instance, a refund cannot reduce the assets of the scheme below the level required to buy out all members' benefits with an insurance company.

PRE-APRIL 2006 TAX REGIMES

Previous tax regimes limited benefits and/or contributions by reference to parameters such as earnings, company service and age in order for schemes to have a tax-advantaged status. Benefits outside these limits had to be provided in a separate, less tax-advantaged scheme (FURBS or UURBS – *see Section 11*).

The benefit structures of many occupational schemes still reflect the constraints imposed by previous tax regimes. The features of the main tax-approved regimes that existed prior to 6 April 2006 and applied to occupational schemes are summarised below.

'Revenue limits' set out maximum pensions and lump sums in three categories, according to the date the member joined the scheme ('pre-1987', '1987' and '1989'). The three categories are similar, and generally allow a member to be provided with a pension of 1/60 × final remuneration and, by commutation of this pension, a lump sum of 3/80 × final remuneration, for each year of service with the employer (up to a maximum of 40), regardless of retained benefits from previous employers' schemes or personal pensions. However, higher benefits could often be provided, with the maximum pension of $\frac{2}{3}$ × final remuneration (including retained benefits) payable after 10 or 20 years.

Ill-health and death benefits were based on a similar calculation but allowing for potential service up to the scheme's normal retirement age. Spouses' pensions were generally allowed to be up to $\frac{2}{3}$ of the member's pension, and an additional lump sum of 4 × final remuneration plus a refund of the member's own contributions could be provided on death in service. There was a limit on member contributions (including AVCs) of 15% of remuneration in any tax year.

The 1989 limits introduced the 'earnings cap' – a limit on the amount of final remuneration that could be used in calculating benefits under that regime. The 1987 limits included a monetary cap on lump sum retirement benefits but not on pension benefits.

Further detail on the previous tax regimes (including those applicable to personal pensions) is available at *www.pensionspocketbook.com*.

EMPLOYER-FINANCED RETIREMENT BENEFIT SCHEMES

DISGUISED REMUNERATION MEASURES

The Finance Act 2011 introduced measures aimed at reducing the attractiveness of vehicles used to 'disguise remuneration and avoid, reduce or defer payment of tax'. These measures had a significant impact on EFRBS.

BACKGROUND

There have always been limits on the extent to which any individual can benefit from the tax advantages offered by registered (or prior to April 2006, 'approved') pension schemes. As a consequence there has for many years been a demand for top-up arrangements of one sort or another outside the 'tax-privileged' pensions savings environment.

Before April 2006, the main top-up vehicles used were Funded Unapproved Retirement Benefit Schemes (FURBS) and Unfunded Unapproved Retirement Benefit Schemes (UURBS). The tax treatment of FURBS was broadly: *t*axed on contributions on the way in, *t*axed on investment returns but *e*xempt from tax on benefits paid out (TTE). There were certain tax and National Insurance advantages on contributions and investment returns, but these were progressively reduced over the years. UURBS were attractive to employers because of cash flow and National Insurance contribution (NIC) considerations. But from the employee's viewpoint, the absence of pre-funding often represented a significant risk. A compromise was the secured UURBS, a benefit promise that was unfunded but where security was given by the employer. Typically, if the employer experiences a change of control or insolvency event, this security is paid into a trust which subsequently pays a benefit to the employee.

From April 2006, FURBS and UURBS became known as Employer-Financed Retirement Benefit Schemes, or EFRBS. The taxation of funded EFRBS was changed from TTE to ETT (relief available on contributions paid in, but benefits ultimately paid out subject to tax – investment returns on the funds are taxed under both regimes). Thus the main attractions of funded EFRBS became the potential exemption from NICs and deferral of income tax. However, since corporation tax relief was also deferred until the benefits were paid, on balance funded EFRBS became unattractive and were rarely used for further contributions after April 2006. Unfunded EFRBS continued to be popular, particularly where security was available.

From December 2010 EFRBS became affected by new measures aimed at ensuring that 'disguised remuneration' provided through third parties would be no more attractive than other forms of remuneration.

TAXATION OF EFRBS

The disguised remuneration provisions contained in the Finance Act 2011 apply when a 'relevant third person' (meaning broadly someone other than the employer, connected company or employee, but including the employer or employee if they are acting as a trustee) makes provision in connection with the employee's employment. In this case, the money or assets set aside in connection with the benefit promise will be taxed (and NICs due) as employment income. Thus any contributions paid to a funded EFRBS after 5 April 2011 will result in an income tax and NI charge on the employee (although to avoid double counting, there is a deduction from the tax and any NI that would otherwise be due when the benefits are paid out).

The disguised remuneration provisions also apply where an employer earmarks, or starts to hold, assets (or otherwise provides security) in connection with a 'relevant undertaking' to provide retirement benefits to the employee via a relevant third person (such as an insurance company or trust). As a result, except where the benefits payable from a secured unfunded EFRBS will be paid direct by the employer, any new security provided after 5 April 2011 can result in an income tax and NI charge on the employee.

Unfunded EFRBS under which there is no undertaking to provide the benefit via a third person are currently unaffected by the Finance Act 2011 provisions. However the Government has said that it will continue to monitor changes in patterns of pension savings behaviour and will act if necessary to prevent loss of tax revenue.

The other main features of the taxation of EFRBS are as follows:

- benefits accrued under an EFRBS are not to be counted for the annual allowance or the special annual allowance, nor are they to be tested against the member's lifetime allowance when paid *(see Section 10)*
- the arrangement's investment income and capital gains are subject to tax
- lump sum and pension benefits are subject to income tax when received by the employee, *and*
- employers can deduct the costs of providing the benefits from taxable profits, but only when the benefits are paid from the scheme and chargeable to tax on the employee. (So corporation tax relief is not available until then.)

In addition, provided that the payments from the EFRBS meet specific conditions (including that the form of benefits would have been authorised if the scheme had been registered, and that employment has ceased and the member is not re-employed by the company), no NICs are payable.

However, if the EFRBS is set up so that provision of the benefits results in a reduction in the benefits payable to or in respect of the employee under a registered pension scheme, or its payment is triggered by a reduction in the benefits payable under a registered pension scheme, then corporation tax relief for the employer will generally not be available, and may be withheld in respect of contributions to the registered scheme.

UNFUNDED EFRBS AND SECURITY

The main drawback of an unfunded arrangement is its inherent lack of security. A number of ways of overcoming this drawback are considered below:

Charges over assets

The establishment of a charge over assets to provide the security for an unfunded retirement benefit promise might be considered. However, as discussed above, if this is done in conjunction with a trust (or other relevant third person) it is likely to give rise to income tax and NI charges.

Insolvency insurance

It may be possible to arrange insurance cover to pay the benefits if an employer becomes insolvent and unable to do so. Premiums paid to insure against the risk of default will be regarded as an employee benefit in kind and taxed accordingly.

Bank guarantees

Bank guarantees could be a source of external financial back-up for unfunded pensions, but are likely to be difficult to arrange and are available only for short-term cover.

ACCOUNTING

EFRBS, whether funded or unfunded, fall within the scope of FRS 17 and IAS 19 *(see Section 25)*.

DWP LEGISLATION

The Pension Schemes Act 1993, the Pensions Act 1995 and the Pensions Act 2004 are generally applicable to non-registered arrangements, although there are a large number of provisions from which such arrangements are exempt. For example, the protections against forfeiture of benefits do apply, but the scheme funding provisions do not and the disclosure requirements are limited.

Preservation and EFRBS

Preservation and transfer value rights for early leavers apply to funded EFRBS as to registered schemes. However, preservation does not apply to unfunded EFRBS unless it is explicitly written into the scheme documentation. If preservation does apply, then revaluation will also apply, and pension sharing on divorce will reflect the preserved benefit.

TAX TREATMENT OF EFRBS

A brief summary comparing the tax treatment of registered pension schemes and EFRBS is set out in this table.

| | Registered Pension Scheme | EFRBS[1] | |
| | | Disguised Remuneration Provisions | |
		do not Apply	Apply
Employer's contributions/ allocations to reserves:			
– corporation tax relief for employer	yes	no[2]	yes
– employer's NICs payable	no	no	yes
– income tax charge on employee	no[3]	no	yes
– employee's NICs payable	no	no	yes
Member's contributions:			
– income tax relief for employee	yes[3]	no	no
Investment returns/ growth in reserves:	no income tax or capital gains tax payable	income and capital gains taxable at trust rates	income and capital gains taxable at trust rates
Tax paid by beneficiary[4] on:			
– pension	income tax payable[5] (but no NICs)	income tax payable[5,8] (but no NICs)[6]	income tax payable[5,8,9] (but no NICs)[6]
– lump sum	tax-free (lump sum generally limited to 25%)	income tax payable[7,8] (but no NICs)[6]	income tax payable[7,8,9] (but no NICs)[6]

Notes:

1. The EFRBS is assumed to be established as an 'accumulation trust' with UK-resident trustees.
2. CT relief may generally be claimed when benefits are paid and chargeable to tax on the employee.
3. However, any 'pension input' in excess of the annual allowance may be subject to a tax charge – see *Section 10.*
4. The Finance Act 2007 amended ITEPA 2003 to include a power to make retrospective regulations extending the definition of benefits from an EFRBS that are excluded from taxation.
5. All pensions, regardless of the type of arrangement, are taxed at source via the PAYE system.
6. Provided that the payments from the EFRBS meet specific conditions, no NICs are payable.
7. The amount of the lump sum that is taxable is reduced by the amount of any contributions paid by the employee towards its provision. In addition, part of the lump sum will be tax-free if contributions, on which the employee was taxed, were paid to the FURBS before 6 April 2006; if no contributions have been made since then, the whole of the lump sum will be tax-free.
8. There is no exemption from inheritance tax for benefits payable from an EFRBS, except to the extent that they arose from contributions made to a FURBS before 6 April 2006.
9. The income tax charge will be reduced by the amount of the charge paid by the employee at the time the employer contributions were made.

LEAVING SERVICE BENEFITS

PRESERVATION

Since 1975, the preservation legislation has provided members of an occupational pension scheme with a legal right to short service benefit (SSB) if they leave pensionable service before normal pension age (NPA). The essential principle is that an early leaver's benefits should be calculated on a consistent basis with those of a member who remains in service up to NPA.

Entitlement to SSB is dependent *(but see below)* upon the member either having at least a minimum period of 'qualifying service' or having transferred benefits from a personal pension into the scheme. This minimum period was reduced in 1988 from five to two years; a requirement to be aged at least 26 was removed in 1986. 'Qualifying service' is the sum of all actual pensionable service under the scheme plus pensionable service in any scheme from which a transfer payment has been received. Members who do not satisfy the preservation conditions may nevertheless be granted deferred benefits if scheme rules so provide. Alternatively, the scheme may provide for them to receive a refund of their own contributions, if any, less tax and (for a COSR) less their share of any Contributions Equivalent Premium required to reinstate contracted-out service back into the State scheme.

Special provisions apply where a member is automatically enrolled before opting out under Pensions Act 2008 *(see Section 4)*.

Payment of short service benefits

Preserved benefits must normally be payable not later than the member's NPA. The preservation legislation defines NPA as the earliest age at which a member is entitled to receive benefits on retirement from the relevant employment, disregarding any special provisions for early retirement. Therefore, even if scheme rules define normal retirement age as (say) 63, NPA could be earlier if members have an unqualified right to retire on an unreduced pension from an earlier age.

However, if NPA is lower than 65, to satisfy the preservation requirements, SSB need only be payable from age 65. (Before 6 April 2005, the preservation legislation required SSB to be payable from the later of NPA and age 60.)

The Court of Appeal ruled in both *Cripps v TSL* and *Foster Wheeler v Hanley* that a member can have more than one normal retirement age (for example when he is entitled to part of his benefits from 60 and part from 65 following changes to scheme rules to comply with the *Barber* judgment). The question of whether a member can have more than one NPA was not considered, although the rulings do not prevent such a conclusion.

Leavers with three months' pensionable service

From 6 April 2006, pension scheme leavers must be given the option of a transfer value (the 'cash transfer sum') of their full accrued benefits, having completed between 3 and 24 months' pensionable service. Trustees must notify the member of this option, as an alternative to a refund of just the member's own contributions, if applicable, within a 'reasonable period' of leaving pensionable service. The Pensions Regulator's Code of Practice defines a reasonable period as normally within three months for this purpose. If the member does not reply within a further 'reasonable period' (which must have been specified and should be at least three months, although the Regulator considers a longer period may be necessary in some circumstances) a refund of contributions may be paid by default (but not before a further month has elapsed). Where the member opts for a cash transfer sum, this must be calculated in the same way as a cash equivalent transfer value under the scheme and paid 'without unjustifiable delay' (in any event, normally within three months). In contracted-out schemes, the overall timetable may need to be compressed to meet the six-month deadline for payment of a Contributions Equivalent Premium.

Automatic transfer of small DC pots

The current Pensions Bill is due to provide for the automatic transfer of small DC pots into a new employer's DC scheme. Detailed provisions will be set out in regulations, but it is proposed that pots under £10,000 will be affected and that members will be able to opt out of transferring.

When the Bill receives Royal Assent, expected in spring 2014, short service refunds from DC occupational pension schemes will be abolished. At the same time, the requirement for two years' qualifying service will also be removed for DC occupational schemes, and new members will have an immediate entitlement to the SSB deriving from contributions paid by or in respect of them.

REVALUATION

The position of early leavers from final salary occupational pension schemes improved significantly from 1986. Before then, with the exception of Guaranteed Minimum Pensions (GMPs), there was no legal requirement for preserved benefits to be increased during the period of deferment until the pension came into payment. Consequently, the purchasing power of the eventual pension could be seriously eroded by inflation. The Social Security Act 1985 introduced the requirement to increase (or 'revalue') in deferment the preserved pension in excess of GMP by at least the specified revaluation percentage. This requirement applied initially only to service completed on or after 1 January 1985, but was further extended to cover the whole of the member's pension in excess of GMP for members leaving pensionable service on or after 1 January 1991. The revaluation percentage (*see table on next page*) was the *lesser* of the increase in the general level of prices and 5% per annum compound over the whole period of deferment. The Pensions Act 2008 reduced the revaluation cap for pensionable service accrued after 5 April 2009 from 5% p.a. to 2.5% p.a.

The increase in the general level of prices is based on the opinion of the Secretary of State. From September 2010 onwards, the increase in prices is assessed using the Consumer Prices Index (CPI) instead of the Retail Prices Index (RPI) – periods of deferment which straddle 2010 are therefore revalued with a combination of RPI and CPI.

Deferred Pension Revaluation Percentages

Complete years since leaving	Calendar year of Normal Pension Age			Complete years since leaving	Calendar year of Normal Pension Age		
	2013 (%)	2012 (%)	2011 (%)		2013 (%)	2012 (%)	2011 (%)
Pensionable service before 6 April 2009							
1	2.2	5.0	3.1	14	45.2	46.7	44.4
2	7.5	8.5	1.7	15	49.9	51.9	47.5
3	10.8	6.9	6.7	16	55.3	55.1	53.2
4	9.3	12.3	10.9	17	58.5	61.2	56.6
5	14.8	16.7	14.9	18	64.7	64.7	59.4
6	19.2	20.9	18.0	19	68.4	67.7	65.1
7	23.5	24.1	21.7	20	71.4	73.7	71.9
8	26.9	28.0	25.1	21	77.6	80.9	90.7
9	30.8	31.6	27.2	22	84.8	100.6	105.1
10	34.5	33.8	29.3	23	105.0	115.8	116.8
11	36.7	36.1	33.6	24	120.6	128.1	125.9
12	39.1	40.6	35.1	25	133.1	137.7	132.9
13	43.7	42.1	39.4	26	142.9	145.1	
				27	150.4		
Pensionable service after 5 April 2009							
1	2.2	2.5	2.5	3	7.7	6.9	
2	5.1	5.1	1.7	4	9.3		

GMPs

In addition to the revaluation requirements on the excess of the member's pension over any GMP, members of contracted-out schemes must also have their GMP revalued between leaving service and age 65 for men and age 60 for women, either:

(1) in line with Average Earnings (Section 148 orders, *see Section 2*); *or*

(2) by fixed rate revaluation at the following rate per annum:
   - leavers after 5 April 2012   4.75%
   - leavers after 5 April 2007, but before 6 April 2012   4.0%
   - leavers after 5 April 2002, but before 6 April 2007   4.5%

– leavers after 5 April 1997, but before 6 April 2002	6.25%
– leavers after 5 April 1993, but before 6 April 1997	7.0%
– leavers after 5 April 1988, but before 6 April 1993	7.5%
– leavers before 6 April 1988	8.5%

For leavers before 6 April 1997, schemes could choose to apply limited revaluation, which provided the lesser of Section 148 orders and 5% p.a. revaluation. A Limited Revaluation Premium was payable to the State. This option was withdrawn from 6 April 1997.

For members who left pensionable service after 31 December 1984, the revaluations on the GMP cannot be 'franked' against the excess pension over the GMP, or against revaluations on the excess. GMP accrual ceased from April 1997, but GMPs earned prior to this date continue to be revalued as above on leaving service.

TRANSFER VALUES

Members of registered occupational pension schemes whose pensionable service has ended have the right to the cash equivalent of all or, in particular circumstances, part of their benefits to be paid as a transfer value to another registered scheme *(see Section 13 for further details of transfer values, including transfers of contracted-out benefits; restrictions imposed by HMRC; and overseas transfers)*.

TRANSFER VALUES

Pension scheme leavers have had the statutory right to a cash equivalent as an alternative to deferred benefits under a scheme since 1986 – *see Section 12*. Trustees are responsible for setting assumptions for the calculation of cash equivalent transfer values and may also need to consider whether it is appropriate to offer members more than the minimum required by legislation.

Individual transfers are considered in this Section; *Section 24* covers bulk transfer arrangements.

Right to a cash equivalent

Generally, members of occupational pension schemes whose pensionable service ended on or after 1 January 1986 have the right to the cash equivalent of all or, in particular circumstances, part of their benefits to be paid as a transfer value to another registered pension scheme. From 6 April 1997, this right was extended to most members whose pensionable service ended before 1 January 1986. This right is normally subject to there being a period of at least one year between the termination of the member's pensionable service and NPA, although, where NPA is earlier than 60, the right arises on termination of service at any time before NPA.

Members who opt out of pension schemes without leaving their jobs also have the right to transfer at least part of their benefits. This right only entitles the member to a 'partial' cash equivalent, related to service completed on or after 6 April 1988 (when members generally first had the right to opt out).

For defined benefit transfer values there is a three-month window from the date of calculation in which the cash equivalent is guaranteed and may be taken without being subject to recalculation. There are other time limits and disclosure requirements *(see Section 14)* imposed on the process of making a transfer.

The current Pensions Bill sets out a legal framework for the automatic transfer of money purchase benefits, unless a member opts out. This is expected to apply to pots of less than £10,000 that began to accrue after a certain date.

Calculation of transfer values

The trustees have responsibility for setting the basis for the calculation of defined benefit transfer values. The fundamental principle is that the initial cash equivalent transfer value (before any adjustment – *see below*) should be broadly equal to the expected cost of providing the benefit within the scheme. Trustees are required to set financial and demographic assumptions on a 'best estimate' basis, having regard to the scheme's investment strategy and having obtained advice from the actuary. (This contrasts with the scheme funding requirement to use 'prudent' assumptions.) The Regulator has issued guidance that outlines the advice on assumptions that the trustees must seek from their actuary. Nevertheless, the trustees are responsible for determining, amongst other things, the interest rate used for discounting future benefit payments and the expected longevity of members. Trustees also need to determine an appropriate allowance for member options and discretionary benefits. The Regulator's guidance makes it clear that only those options that increase the value of a member's benefits should be taken into account, although allowance can be made for the proportion of members likely to exercise such options. In deciding whether to make allowance for discretionary benefits, the guidance suggests that trustees should usually consult any person whose consent is needed, and consider past history and any allowance in scheme funding, amongst other things.

For members with defined contribution benefits, the cash equivalent transfer value is the realisable value at the date of calculation of any benefits to which the member is entitled.

Paying more or less

For underfunded defined benefit schemes, which would not have enough money to pay full transfer values for all members, the legislation permits the initial cash equivalent to be reduced in line with the extent of underfunding shown in an 'Insufficiency Report' commissioned from the actuary. The Regulator's guidance suggests that trustees should not normally make such a reduction where an employer's covenant is judged to be strong and any funding shortfall is being remedied over a reasonably short period.

The legislation also allows the trustees to pay transfer values at a level higher than best estimate. This may be appropriate if the scheme rules require it or where simpler calculations would make it cost-effective. Alternatively, the trustees may simply decide that it is appropriate to pay higher transfer values than the minimum required (perhaps following a request by, or in consultation with, the employer). Higher transfer values might encourage take-up, which, if transfer values remained below the prudent reserves required for funding the members' liabilities, could reduce a scheme's deficit (or increase its surplus). Indeed, a transfer incentive exercise may be undertaken – *see Section 20*.

Transfers of contracted-out benefits

Transfers of contracted-out benefits can be made freely between most arrangements contracted out on the salary-related basis *(see Section 2)*. GMPs remain as GMPs and post-97 COSR rights remain as post-97 COSR rights. Contracting out on a money purchase basis was abolished on 6 April 2012, so schemes that were COMPs no longer hold protected rights and the associated statutory restrictions on transfers do not apply. Transfers where there are no GMP or post-97 COSR rights can occur freely between salary-related or money purchase schemes, personal pensions and buy-out policies.

From 6 April 2012 it has been possible to transfer GMPs and post-97 COSR rights to a scheme that is not contracted out, provided:

- the member consents in writing
- the transfer payment in respect of any GMP is at least equal to the cash equivalent of the member's GMP

- the transfer payment in respect of any post-97 COSR rights is at least equal to the cash equivalent of the member's post-97 COSR rights, *and*

- the member has acknowledged in writing to the transferring scheme that he has received a statement from the receiving scheme showing the benefits to be awarded in respect of the transfer payment, and he accepts that:
  - ○ the benefits in the receiving scheme may be different in form and amount to those payable by the transferring scheme, *and*
  - ○ there is no statutory requirement for the receiving scheme to provide survivors' benefits out of the transfer payment.

Transferred benefits cease to be treated as contracted-out rights in the receiving scheme.

Disclosure and payment

Disclosure requirements, including those in respect of transfer values, are described in *Section 14*. A guaranteed cash equivalent may be accepted within the three-month 'guarantee period' without being subject to recalculation. Generally, the trustees are required to pay the transfer value within six months of the date of calculation where the cash equivalent is guaranteed and within six months of the original request where it is not (for example, where the benefits are money purchase in nature). Trustees are also required to inform members of salary-related schemes:

- that the Financial Conduct Authority, the Pensions Advisory Service and the Pensions Regulator provide information that may assist in their decision on whether to transfer

- of the existence of the PPF and that the scheme is eligible for it (eligible schemes only), *and*

- that it is recommended that they should take financial advice before making a decision.

Failure to follow the required process could result in liabilities not being discharged properly. This is particularly relevant in relation to recent warnings about pensions liberation *(see below)*: although trustees must act on a valid transfer application within the appropriate timescales, they must take all reasonable steps to ensure that the receiving scheme is acting in good faith in order for the statutory discharge to apply.

Restrictions imposed by HMRC

Since 6 April 2006, the majority of restrictions on pension transfers and the benefits that could be provided in respect of them under previous tax regimes have been removed. In general, under the Finance Act 2004 tax regime, transfers of 'uncrystallised' pension rights can be made between registered pension schemes (or to deferred annuity contracts or buy-out policies) without restriction, provided that scheme rules permit. Transfers can also be made to 'qualifying recognised overseas pension schemes' *(see below)*.

The previous restrictions on partial transfers were removed by the Finance Act 2004. However, members only have a *statutory* right to a 'partial cash equivalent' in limited circumstances (e.g. on opting out *(see above)* or where the receiving scheme will not accept transfers of COSR rights). Partial transfers will therefore generally be possible only where scheme rules permit.

Pensions already in payment can also be transferred, provided that scheme rules allow and certain conditions are met (e.g. the amount of the pension is not reduced except to the extent needed to meet the administrative cost of the transfer and any guarantee is no longer than that remaining before the transfer). Drawdown pension funds may be transferred to another such arrangement (which may not be used to hold any other funds).

Certain forms of transitional protection *(see Section 10)* may be lost on transfer, unless prescribed conditions are satisfied. In particular, enhanced protection, fixed protection or fixed protection 2014 will be lost unless the transfer is a 'permitted transfer' (requiring, *inter alia*, that the transfer is to a money purchase, but not cash balance, arrangement, or a bulk transfer that meets specified criteria).

Pensions liberation

Pensions liberation refers to the transfer of a member's pension savings to an arrangement that will allow them to access their funds before they are entitled to receive them, through early payment of pension and cash or through the payment of excessive cash.

The Regulator has encouraged trustees to ensure that members are aware of the risks. It notes that some arrangements may be illegal and even those that appear to operate within the law may result in the member facing unauthorised payment tax charges, in addition to high charges and high investment risks. The Regulator has produced material to assist trustees in communicating the issues to their members.

Overseas transfers

A transfer to an overseas arrangement would only be a 'recognised transfer' for tax purposes if that arrangement falls within the definition of a qualifying recognised overseas pension scheme *(see Appendix 2, Glossary of Terms)*. If such a transfer takes place, the scheme administrator of the registered pension scheme must ensure that certain information detailing the transfer is submitted to HMRC within 60 days of the transfer. Information may also be required by HMRC from the manager of the overseas scheme. Other transfers to overseas arrangements are likely to be treated as unauthorised payments for tax purposes *(see Section 10)* and the transferring member must acknowledge that tax charges may apply.

DISCLOSURE OF
PENSION SCHEME INFORMATION

Pensions legislation including the Pension Schemes Act 1993 and the Pensions Act 1995 requires the trustees of occupational pension schemes to disclose actuarial and accounting information, as well as individual benefit details for each member. These rules override any provisions in schemes' trust documents if the two are in conflict.

Details to be disclosed differ depending on whether the benefits are of a defined benefit or defined contribution nature. One difference is that disclosures relating to defined contributions must, for members who have not yet retired, be provided automatically at least once a year, whereas disclosures relating to defined benefits need only be provided on request. Disclosure requirements also may differ for schemes with fewer than 100 members.

The Government consulted in 2013 on new regulations that would consolidate the main disclosure requirements for occupational and personal pension schemes. The aim is to achieve consistency, where possible, across different types of scheme a well as extending the provisions for electronic communication. The changes cover only the core disclosure regulations and not the further disclosure provisions that sit within other sets of regulations. The new regulations are due to come in to force on 6 April 2014.

Information must also be disclosed to pension credit members and further disclosure requirements also arise at the time when pension sharing arrangements are being made. These are too extensive to describe in detail here, but an outline is included in *Section 16*.

The following pages set out the main disclosure requirements for occupational schemes. Disclosure requirements for personal pension and stakeholder schemes are discussed later in this section.

Disclosure rules relating to automatic enrolment are summarised in *Section 6*.

SUMMARY OF DISCLOSURE REQUIREMENTS
FOR OCCUPATIONAL PENSION SCHEMES

Information	To be Disclosed to	In What Circumstances	Time Limits/Other Details
Trust Deed and Rules or other documents constituting the scheme, including names and addresses of participating employers.	Members*, Prospective Members, their Spouses and Civil Partners. Beneficiaries. Recognised independent Trade Unions.	For inspection on request, free of charge. A copy to keep on request; any charge must be limited to the cost incurred in copying, posting and packaging.	Within two months of the request being made. Any documentation not relevant to the rights of the particular person does not need to be disclosed.

Note: * Throughout this summary 'members' includes pension credit members, as well as pensioners and deferred pensioners.

Information	To be Disclosed to	In What Circumstances	Time Limits/Other Details
Scheme Details including an address for enquiries.	**Members*, Prospective Members,** their **Spouses** and **Civil Partners.** **Beneficiaries.** Recognised independent **Trade Unions.**	**New members** must be given scheme details **automatically** (and in advance where practicable).	New members (other than those being automatically enrolled – *see Section 6*) must receive scheme details within two months of joining the scheme. For automatic enrolment schemes, trustees must normally provide this within one month of receiving jobholder information.
		On request, no more than **once a year.**	Within two months of the request being made.
			Any material change in the scheme details, and any change in the address for enquiries, must be notified to all members and beneficiaries, within three months.
Estimate of Cash Equivalent	**Active Members** of any scheme, and **Deferred Members** of schemes providing money purchase benefits.	**On request**, no more than **once a year.**	Within three months of the request.
Statement of Entitlement to Guaranteed Cash Equivalent	**Deferred** and **Pension Credit Members** of schemes providing final salary benefits.	**On request**, no more than **once a year.**	To be calculated within three months of the request and passed to the member within ten working days of calculation.
Statement of Prospective Transfer Credits	**Members** and **Prospective Members.**	**On request**, no more than **once a year.**	Within two months of the request.
Benefit Statements	**Members.** **Beneficiaries.**	**Automatically** when benefit is due, or changes other than as described in a previous statement. **To non-pensioner members of final salary schemes, on request**, no more than **once a year**, within two months of request. **To non-pensioner members of schemes with a money purchase element, automatically**	Where benefits become due or are changed other than as described in a previous statement within one month, or two months in cases of early retirement. Leavers must be told their rights and options within two months of the trustees being notified that the member has left service. Options under money purchase benefits are to be notified to members at

Information	To be Disclosed to	In What Circumstances	Time Limits/Other Details
Benefit Statements *(continued)*		within 12 months of the end of each scheme year in respect of money purchase benefits including Statutory Money Purchase Illustrations (SMPIs) *(see page 99)*.	least six months before normal pension age (normal benefit age for pension credit members) or earlier agreed date of retirement.
			Beneficiaries over age 18 must be notified of rights and options within two months of trustees being notified of death. Personal representatives of members who have died may request information, which must be provided within two months.
Pension savings statement	Members.	**Automatically** to those whose pension input exceeds the annual allowance for the pension input period.	Once each tax year, by 6 October. Figures must be given for the relevant tax year and for the previous three years.
		On request, if the individual will not get a statement automatically.	Within three months of the request, or by 6 October if later.
Information about Benefit Crystallisation Events (BCEs)	**Members** who have taken some or all of their benefits.	**Automatically**, following a BCE unless an annual pensioner statement will be supplied *(see below)*.	Within three months of the BCE, confirming the amount of lifetime allowance expended and details of any lifetime allowance charge.
Annual pensioner statements	Pensioners.	**Automatically** to those retiring with a scheme pension since 6 April 2006.	Once each tax year. A statement of the cumulative total percentage of lifetime allowance crystallised in respect of the scheme.
Summary Funding Statement	Members. Beneficiaries.	**Automatically**, annually, except where a member is entitled to only money purchase benefits. Must be issued within a **reasonable period** (generally three months) after the deadline for completion of actuarial valuation or actuarial report.	To include information on the funding and solvency positions of the scheme.

Information	To be Disclosed to	In What Circumstances	Time Limits/Other Details
Trustees' Annual Report including: · audited accounts · latest certification of schedule of contributions · investment report.	**Members, Prospective Members,** their **Spouses** and **Civil Partners.** **Beneficiaries.** Recognised independent **Trade Unions.**	Reports covering the previous five years must be available: · **for inspection,** free of charge · a copy of the most recent report on request, **to keep,** free of charge · copies of earlier reports on request, **to keep,** for which any charge must be limited to the cost of copying, posting and packaging.	Within two months of the request being made. The report must be available within seven months of the end of the scheme year. The report should contain a statement that other information is available and from where it may be obtained.
Actuarial Valuation or **Report, Schedule of Contributions, Payment Schedule, Recovery Plan,†** **Statements of Funding Principles†** and of **Investment Principles,** and outline **Winding-Up Procedure** (if applicable)	**Members, Prospective Members,** their **Spouses** and **Civil Partners.** **Beneficiaries.** Recognised independent **Trade Unions.**	**For inspection,** free of charge. **A copy to keep, on request,** for which any charge must be limited to the cost of copying, posting and packaging.	Within two months of the request being made.

Note: † *See Section 17.*

SCHEME DETAILS

Scheme details must include:

- eligibility and conditions for membership
- the period of notice which a member must give to leave pensionable servic
- whether re-entry to pensionable service is permitted and, if so, upon what conditions
- how employers' and members' normal contributions are calculated
- any arrangements made for members to pay Additional Voluntar Contributions (AVCs)
- taxation status
- contracted-out status
- normal pension age

- the benefits payable, and how they are calculated, including the definition of pensionable earnings, the accrual rate and whether any are payable only on discretion
- the conditions on which benefits, including survivors' benefits, and any pension increases in excess of statutory requirements, are payable and whether any are payable only on discretion
- whether the trustees accept transfers in to the scheme
- a summary of the method of calculating transfer values
- where cash equivalents do not take into account discretionary additional benefits, a statement to this effect
- the arrangements for providing refunds, preserved benefits, and estimated or guaranteed cash equivalents for early leavers
- a statement that the scheme annual report is available on request, except for public service pension schemes
- the procedure for internal resolution of disputes and the address and job title of the contact
- the functions and addresses of the Pensions Ombudsman, The Pensions Advisory Service and the Pensions Regulator, *and*
- a statement that further information is available and an address for enquiries.

BENEFIT STATEMENTS

Active and deferred members of salary-related schemes

On request, an active member must be given:

- a statement of accrued benefits, or benefits allowing for service up to normal pension age, based on current salary, *and*
- a statement of the benefits payable if the member were to die in service within one month of the date of receipt of the information.

The trustees need not comply with a request made within a year of providing the information, so if they provide benefit statements automatically once a year there is no need to respond to one-off requests.

Leaving service rights and options must be given automatically within two months of the trustees being notified that pensionable service has ceased.

On subsequent request, a deferred member must be given a statement of the date pensionable service ceased and the amount of his/her own benefits, and any survivors' benefits, payable from normal pension age or on death.

For both active and deferred members the information must include:

- the date on which pensionable service commenced and ceased
- the accrual rate or formula for calculating the member's own benefits and any survivors' benefits
- the amount of the member's pensionable earnings (at the date pensionable service ceased for a deferred member and at the current date for an active member), *and*

- details of how any deduction from benefits (e.g. offset for State pension or any pension debit) is calculated.

Pension credit members of salary-related schemes

On request, the member must be given a statement of the amount of his/her own benefits, and any survivors' benefits, payable from normal benefit age or on death. The information must include:

- the method or formula for calculating the member's own benefits and any survivors' benefits, *and*
- details of how any deduction from benefits is calculated.

All members of money purchase schemes (or schemes with a money purchase element)

Statements must be given automatically within 12 months of the end of each scheme year and must show, in relation to money purchase benefits:

- contributions credited to the member (before deductions) during the immediately preceding scheme year and, if the scheme was contracted out at any time in the past, until April 2015 the amount of those contributions that is attributable to:
  - (i) minimum payments made by the employer during the immediately preceding scheme year
  - (ii) age-related payments made to the trustees by the Department for Work and Pensions, *and*
  - (iii) the date of birth used to determine any age-related payment and a contact name and address if this is incorrect
- value of any accrued rights at a specified date
- cash equivalents of these rights at the specified dates, if they differ from the values, *and*
- statutory money purchase illustrations (SMPIs) of projected benefit are required in addition to the above information (*see below*).

In addition, a member with money purchase benefits must be provided with an explanation of the different annuities available, his/her right to an open market option and a statement that the member should consider taking advice. This information must be provided no less than six months before the member's normal retirement date, or within seven days if a retirement date is agreed which is less than six months in the future.

TRUSTEES' ANNUAL REPORT

The report must include:

- audited accounts, including auditor's statement
- latest actuarial certificate certifying the adequacy of the schedule of contributions

- names of trustees or directors of the trust company, and the rules for changing trustees; names of the professional advisers, custodians and banks acting for the trustees, indicating any changes during the year
- a copy of the statement which any auditor or actuary of the scheme has made on resignation or removal as auditor or actuary during the year
- numbers of active, deferred and pensioner members and beneficiaries at a date during the year
- except for money purchase schemes, percentage increases made during the year to pensions and deferred pensions, in excess of those required by law – the extent to which increases were discretionary is to be stated
- except for money purchase schemes which are wholly insured, if transfer values paid during the year were not calculated in accordance with the law, an explanation as to why they have differed; if any were less than the full value of the member's preserved or pension credit benefits, an explanation as to why and when full values are likely to be available; and a statement as to whether discretionary benefits are included in the calculation and, if so, how they are assessed
- name of investment manager, and the extent to which the trustees have delegated their responsibility to him
- whether the trustees have produced a statement of investment principles and, if so, that a copy is available on request, and information on investments made other than in accordance with the statement
- except for wholly insured schemes, a statement of the trustees' policy on the custody of scheme assets
- investment report including review of performance, over the year and over a period of between three and five years, and of the scheme's assets
- details and percentage of any employer-related investment and steps taken or proposed to reduce excessive employer-related investment
- address for enquiries, *and*
- an explanation, where applicable, of why the auditor's statement about scheme contributions is negative or qualified and a statement as to how the situation has been, or is likely to be, resolved.

AUTOMATIC DISCLOSURE IN SPECIAL CIRCUMSTANCES

Trustees must disclose information automatically, rather than on request, in the following circumstances.

(a) **If any contributions are not paid by the due date,** and the trustees believe that this will be of material significance to the Pensions Regulator, members (and the Regulator) must be informed within a reasonable period (generally 30 days). The amounts and the due dates are those set out in the scheme's schedule of contributions or payment schedule.

(b) **Details of any proposed transfer without the member's consent** *(see Section 24)*, including the value of the rights being transferred, must be provided at least one month before the proposed date of the transfer.

(c) **If a scheme is being wound up** *(see Section 22)*, all members and beneficiaries (except deferred pensioners and pension credit members who cannot be traced) must be given a notice within one month of the winding-up having commenced, and at least every 12 months thereafter. These notices must report on the action being taken to determine the scheme's assets and liabilities; give an indication of when final details are likely to be known; and indicate the extent to which the value of the member's accrued benefits is likely to be reduced (where the trustees have sufficient information to state this). In addition, the first notice must state that the scheme is winding up together with the reasons; supply a name and address for further enquiries; provide a statement where relevant that an independent trustee is required; and provide a statement to active members as to whether death in service benefits will continue to be provided.

Once the assets have been applied in accordance with the legislative requirements, members and beneficiaries (except deferred pensioner and pension credit members who cannot be traced) must be told their benefit entitlements within three months, together with detail as to who is responsible for paying the benefits, and the extent to which any benefits were reduced because the assets were insufficient. In addition the trustees must make periodic progress reports covering specified information to the Pensions Regulator. (A scheme for which a Recovery Plan is in place which commences to wind up must also prepare and provide to the Regulator a 'Winding Up Procedure'.) If requested, copies must be passed to members within two months.

(d) **Where a refund of surplus is proposed** *(see Section 17)* to be made to the employer from a scheme that *is not winding up*, all members of the scheme must be sent a notice containing the following:

- a statement that the trustees have decided to make a payment to the employer
- the amount and date of the payment (which must be in the period the relevant valuation certificate is valid for and at least three months after the date of the notice), *and*
- a statement that, on a request made within one month of the notice, a copy of the certificate will be made available.

For a scheme that *is winding up*, all members and beneficiaries must be given two written notices (the first running for at least two months and the second for at least three months) setting out the proposal and inviting representations.

(e) **Details of any independent trustee appointed on employer insolvency** *(see Section 22)* must be provided to all members and recognised independent trade unions within a reasonable period of the appointment being made. Details of the scale of fees chargeable to the scheme and of the actual fees charged by the independent trustee in the previous 12 months must be provided on request to members, recognised independent trade unions and prospective members within a reasonable period of the request.

(f) **In the appointment of member-nominated trustees or directors** *(see Section 8)*, active and pensioner members (or organisations that adequately represent them) have to be invited to participate in the nomination process, and the selection process must include some or all members of the scheme. Nominations and results of the selection process should be communicated appropriately to members.

(g) **Consultation by employers** *(see Section 3)* with members and prospective members of occupational pension and personal pension schemes is required before they can make certain 'listed changes' to the scheme. This is generally the employer's responsibility, but trustees are likely to have an interest in the process.

(h) **Modification of the accrued benefits provided by an occupational pension scheme** *(see Section 3)* requires notification to members. The Pensions Regulator's Code of Practice 'Modification of subsisting rights' provides guidance on the trustees' duties and responsibilities under the various stages of the requirements, including the process for communicating with and, where necessary, obtaining the consent of, members.

EXEMPTIONS FROM DISCLOSURE

- Schemes with fewer than two members.
- Schemes providing only death benefits.
- Schemes neither established in the UK nor with a trustee resident in the UK.
- Certain public service pension schemes are not required to obtain audited accounts or an actuarial valuation, or to publish an annual report.

ELECTRONIC PROVISION OF INFORMATION

Disclosure regulations that came into force on 1 December 2010 amended the requirement to give access to scheme documentation and certain other information on request to allow schemes to discharge their obligations by placing the information on a website.

Subject to certain safeguards, schemes may provide information by email they are satisfied that recipients are able to access and store or print the information. Trustees' obligations will not be met by means of email or website if the member requests otherwise in writing. If a scheme wishes to convert from paper to electronic communication, the member must be given written notification and the opportunity to opt for continued paper communication.

In 2013 the Government consulted on draft regulations intended to clarify the existing requirements and extend the availability of electronic disclosure. The Department for Work and Pensions has clarified that where existing regulations require information to be sent by post or in writing, this would include email but not making the information available on a website.

Where disclosure requirements state that information must be given, but do not specify the method, the regulations are due to be amended from April 2014 in order to provide certainty to pension schemes that they may use electronic communication if they wish.

DISCLOSURE REQUIREMENTS FOR PERSONAL PENSION AND STAKEHOLDER SCHEMES

The disclosure requirements relating to personal pensions and stakeholder schemes are generally the same as those for defined contribution (DC) occupational pensions. Also, as such schemes are provided by an insurer they must comply with additional disclosure requirements imposed by the Financial Conduct Authority (FCA). In 2013 the Government consulted on draft disclosure regulations that are expected to consolidate the requirements for occupational and personal pension schemes into one statutory instrument from 6 April 2014. The disclosure rules for stakeholder pension schemes are to remain separate.

CODES OF CONDUCT

The Pensions Regulator's strategy for DC schemes has seen an increasing focus on achieving good outcomes for savers. In line with this, in November 2012 the NAPF published a joint industry Code of Conduct on DC pension charges that is intended to help employers make informed choices about which scheme to use for automatic enrolment *(see Section 4)*. All types of DC scheme are expected to follow the code. It is not mandatory, but the Pensions Ombudsman and Financial Services Ombudsman may have regard to the code when dealing with complaints. The existing disclosure of information requirements remain. The code covers additional disclosures from providers and advisers to employers, not to members. It is expected that advisers and consultants will follow the code as a minimum, as well as providing information to employers about other factors for consideration when picking a pension scheme.

The Association of British Insurers (ABI) has released a Code of Conduct on retirement choices, to help customers understand their options, shop around and make informed decisions about their income in retirement. The code will see insurers doing more to explain annuity options and should help ensure that clear, timely information is provided to people approaching retirement. The ABI will consider how it can integrate the principles into trust-based occupational schemes, so that all pension scheme members can expect common standards.

STATUTORY MONEY PURCHASE ILLUSTRATIONS

The legislation requires schemes under which any money purchase benefits are provided to supply members with annual illustrations of such benefits on a prescribed statutory basis, referred to as Statutory Money Purchase Illustrations (SMPIs). This legal requirement applies to any arrangement which is already required to issue annual benefit statements and covers occupational pension schemes (even those which are primarily on a defined benefit basis), free-standing and other AVCs, personal pensions, stakeholder schemes, and benefits bought out in the name of scheme trustees rather than members. Retirement annuities and non-registered arrangements are excluded, as are members within two years of retirement and those with small benefits (generally less than £5,000).

The overall aim is to provide illustrations of the amount of pension at retirement (in today's terms) on a broadly consistent basis for the different types of money purchase arrangement.

In 2013 the Government consulted on draft regulations, now due to come into force in April 2014, that aim to be more closely aligned with projections provided to members of personal pension schemes, as required by the FCA, and that would allow for a more personalised approach.

SMPIs must be prepared in accordance with the methodology and assumptions specified in detail in the latest version of Technical Memorandum (TM1). Version 3.0 of TM1 applies for all statutory illustrations with an illustration date on or after 6 April 2013 (although Version 2.0 may continue to be used until 6 April 2014).

In particular, it must be assumed that the pension will be index-linked in payment and will generally include a 50% contingent spouse's pension (although the provider need not include this if the member is single). Any regular contributions are assumed to continue. These specific annuity requirements are due to be removed under the revised regulations.

For the period before retirement, providers must use an accumulation rate that is justifiable, taking account of the different asset classes in which the members' assets are invested and consistent with an assumed inflation rate of 2.5% p.a. The rationale for the chosen rate must be made available to members on request. Allowance for expenses must be based on actual experience. The assumed cost of purchasing annuities at retirement will be market-derived, based on conditions on 15 February in the previous tax year. No allowances are made for mortality before retirement. After retirement, blended unisex factors are adopted.

Specified information about the nature of the illustration and an overview of the assumptions must accompany the statement, together with other details listed in TM1. The value of the member's current fund may (but need not) also be included, as well as further illustrations on alternative bases, but it must be made clear which of the illustrations is on the statutory basis. Since December 2010 schemes have had flexibility in the way that SMPI statements can be delivered, so that some of the information may now be provided electronically.

EQUAL TREATMENT

Over several years, the UK government has incorporated into UK statute a number of provisions mostly designed to implement the various equal treatment requirements imposed by European law. Under EU law, there are a number of equal treatment principles that are of particular relevance to UK pensions.

The Equality Act 2010 sought to consolidate and harmonise previous legislation on equal treatment and strengthen the law to support progress on equality. The main provisions of the Act came into force on 1 October 2010. Most aspects of the Act, as they relate to pensions, are the same as or very similar to provisions under previous legislation. The Act requires a single 'non-discrimination' rule in respect of various 'protected characteristics' to be deemed to be included in the rules of occupational pension schemes, together with separate equality rules in respect of sex and maternity. These generally prohibit indirect discrimination unless it can be justified as a proportionate means of achieving a legitimate aim. Direct discrimination based on age and disability can also be justified on these grounds, but indirect discrimination or the grounds of pregnancy or maternity cannot be so justified.

Further details of the principles of equal treatment, and how the Equality Act and associated regulations seek to implement them, are given below.

GENERAL PRINCIPLES OF EQUAL TREATMENT BY SEX

The deemed 'sex equality rule' under the Equality Act 2010 covers both admission of members and benefits. This arises from Article 157 (originally Article 119) of the Treaty on the Functioning of the European Union ('the Treaty of Rome'), which requires men and women performing work of equal value to receive equal pay. Case law at the Court of Justice of the European Union (CJEU) has shown that occupational pensions (though not social security schemes) fall within the definition of pay.

Equal benefits

The Equality Act 2010, together with previous legislation, requires equality for benefits accrued in respect of service on or after 17 May 1990, except for claims initiated earlier. *(See* 'Pension age and benefit accrual' *below.)*

Equal access

Men and women must have equal rights to join their employer's pension scheme. The exclusion of part-timers may thus constitute 'indirect' sex discrimination if the exclusion affects a much greater number of one sex than the other, *unless* the employer shows that it may be explained by objectively justified factors unrelated to sex. There are time limits for bringing claims in relation to unequal access as well as to the extent to which membership can be backdated *(see below).*

Role of trustees, employers and the courts

Trustees must observe the principle of equal treatment in performing their duties. Both trustees and employers are bound to use all the means available under national laws in order to eliminate discrimination. National courts must apply the principle of Article 157 in the context of domestic laws, taking due account of the respective liabilities of employers and trustees. Article 157 may be relied on in claims against trustees as well as against employers.

APPLICATION OF PRINCIPLES OF EQUAL TREATMENT BY SEX TO OCCUPATIONAL AND STATE PENSIONS

Member contributions

The equal treatment principle of Article 157 applies to the whole benefit paid by an occupational pension scheme, and no distinction need be made between the parts derived from the employer's and from the employee's contractual contributions. However, benefits derived from members' additional voluntary contributions are not pay and so do not fall within the scope of Article 157.

Pension age and benefit accrual

Normal pension ages for men and women must not be discriminatory for benefits accrued since 17 May 1990. In respect of service from 17 May 1990 up to the date benefits are equalised (the equalisation date), the provisions applying to the less-favoured sex must be levelled up to those of the more-favoured sex. For periods of service after the equalisation date, Article 157 does not preclude equal treatment being achieved by levelling benefits down, e.g. by raising the lower pension age. If members have a right to retire early, this right must not be discriminatory for benefits accrued since 17 May 1990. This can result in members having different pension ages for different periods of service.

Benefit accrual for service since 17 May 1990 must be equalised not only for scheme members but also for their dependants. For benefits not linked to length of service, e.g. lump sum benefits on death in service, equal benefits must be provided for men and women when the event triggering payment of the benefit occurs on or after 17 May 1990.

Where the funds held by the trustees are insufficient, any decision on how equalisation of benefits should be achieved must be resolved on the basis of national law. In 2009 the Court of Appeal ruled in the *Foster Wheeler* case that any resolution should involve minimum interference with the scheme's provisions, and should not result in members receiving a windfall (for example, members with mixed pension ages should not be allowed to take all their benefits at the lowest age, without an actuarial reduction being applied to benefits accrued by reference to a higher pension age).

Bridging pensions and State pension offsets

Unequal bridging pensions (and State pension offsets) that allow for the difference between men's and women's State pension ages are permitted. The extra pension payable to a man may not exceed the total Category A State retirement pension (i.e. basic plus additional component) payable to a woman with the earnings history of the individual in question in respect of their period of pensionable service under the scheme. Furthermore, it may be paid only between the corresponding female and male State pension ages.

On 19 April 2002, the High Court ruled in the *Shillcock* case that, for the purposes of calculating contributions and benefits, the operation of a Lower

Earnings Limit (LEL) deduction from pensionable pay without pro-rating for part-timers did not constitute indirect sex discrimination and was, in any case, a reasonable method of implementing the legitimate objective of integration with State benefits and so was objectively justified.

Transfers

Schemes may, if they wish, calculate transfers out using actuarial factors which vary according to sex. The benefits to which the factors are applied are required to be equalised for service since 17 May 1990. Where a transfer value has in fact been based on unequal benefits for a period of service after 16 May 1990, the transfer value might be lower than it would have been if it had been based on equalised benefits. In such circumstances the *receiving* scheme must increase the benefits provided to those which could have been bought by the higher transfer value that should have been paid.

Actuarial factors and insurance premiums

Under current UK legislation, actuarial factors that vary according to sex may be used for commutation, early and late retirement, and surrender of pension for a dependant (as well as transfers out, *as above*). Emerging pension benefits from money purchase arrangements may also be calculated using sex dependent factors.

However, since 21 December 2012, the use of gender-based insurance premiums has been unlawful following the 2011 CJEU ruling in the *Test Achats* case. This affects Purchased Life Annuities and annuities purchased by individuals with individual personal pensions. It does not directly affect occupational pensions, nor group personal pensions 'arranged by employers although annuities purchased by members of such schemes as part of the normal open market option process are affected.

The case has no direct impact on actuarial factors used by occupational pension schemes. Unless existing legislation is amended there is no requirement for factors to be identical for males and females, and this is not expected in the near future.

Contracting-out problems

Contracted-out schemes have particular difficulties in equalising the benefits they provide because GMPs accrued at different rates and are required to come into payment at different ages for men and women. This issue was partly addressed by regulations, originally under the Pensions Act 1995, which give contracted-out schemes some scope to provide unequal pension increases that reflect sex-related differences in the ways in which the increase in members' State pensions are calculated. While this exemption might appear to ease the position for schemes with unequal post-16 May 1990 GMPs *when pensions are in payment*, it does not address the problems associated with differences under the anti-franking legislation (primarily concerning increases in deferment).

In January 2012, the DWP issued a consultation on equalising benefits to reflect unequal GMPs. The consultation was based on the assumption that schemes are under an obligation to equalise benefits to allow for inequalities in the calculation of GMPs, in respect of accruals from 17 May 1990 to 5 April 1997. Many experts have questioned whether this initial assumption is correct. In April 2013, the DWP published an interim response to the consultation which stated that the Government is still considering the responses to the consultation in detail, but is looking at whether the GMP conversion process (*see Section 2*) could be used to equalise scheme benefits for the effect of GMPs and may provide statutory guidance on this. A full response will be published at a later date.

The Pension Protection Fund (PPF) received legal advice that it is required to equalise compensation to allow for differences in GMPs, where schemes enter the PPF or the Financial Assistance Scheme. Total benefits earned on or after 17 May 1990 are equalised at the higher of the level for men and women at any point in time (*see Section 19*).

Time limits for bringing claims and backdating membership

The ECJ (now CJEU) ruling in the indirect sex discrimination part-timer case of *Preston v Wolverhampton*, and subsequent legal proceedings, have clarified that in the UK:

- claims for unlawful equal treatment must be brought to industrial tribunals within six months of leaving service, *and*
- individuals may claim backdated membership in respect of service back to 8 April 1976.

Maternity, adoption and paternity leave

The Equality Act 2010 (and previously the Employment Rights Act 1996) requires *all* benefits in kind, including pension accrual, to be maintained during *statutory* ordinary maternity leave (whether paid or unpaid). The Employment Act 2002 provisions, which generally took effect from April 2003, gave similar rights to adoptive parents with the introduction of statutory adoption leave, and also introduced new requirements for continued pension accrual during statutory paternity leave and statutory parental leave.

Legislation also requires all *paid* maternity, adoption and paternity absence to be treated as a period of normal service as far as an employer-related benefit scheme is concerned. When assessing benefits (or employer contributions to a defined contribution occupational scheme) it should be assumed that the normal pay for the job was received. However, the member is required to pay contributions based only on the remuneration actually received. For paid (but non-statutory) 'family leave' (other than maternity, adoption or paternity leave), legislation only requires benefits to be based on actual (not on normal) remuneration.

Provisions introduced in April 2011 for additional statutory paternity leave currently allow employed fathers to 'trade' unused statutory leave and pay with the child's mother or adopter. The Government has set out plans to allow more flexibility in terms of how this is shared between them. These proposals are intended to be introduced in 2015.

State pension ages

From November 2018, State pension age is planned to be equalised at 65 for men and women. The change is being phased in for women from April 2010 to November 2018 *(see Section 1)*.

EQUAL TREATMENT FOR PART-TIMERS

In 1997, the EU adopted a part-time work directive requiring member states to outlaw all discrimination against part-time workers, and not just in cases of indirect sex discrimination covered under the general 'equal pay' provisions. UK regulations implementing the directive came into force on 1 July 2000, and applied with immediate (although not retrospective) effect. The legislation is now incorporated in the Equality Act 2010. It is no longer possible to treat a part-timer less favourably than a 'comparable' full-timer, unless the less favourable treatment is justified on objective grounds. The regulations provide that, in determining whether or not treatment is unfavourable, a 'pro-rata' principle applies, 'unless it is inappropriate'. The extent to which it is legal to provide inferior (or no) benefits to part-timers (on grounds such as non-comparability with full-timers, 'objective justification' or inappropriateness of a pro rata principle) is only likely to become clear as case law is built up. Complaints by individuals under this legislation must generally be taken to an employment tribunal within three months of the last day on which they consider they were unfavourably treated.

EQUAL TREATMENT FOR FIXED-TERM WORKERS

UK regulations implementing the EU fixed-term worker directive came into force on 1 October 2002. The legislation is now incorporated in the Equality Act 2010. Direct discrimination against fixed-term workers in relation to terms and conditions including pensions is prohibited when compared to permanent employees, unless it is justified on objective grounds. The regulations specifically provide that less favourable treatment in relation to some contractual terms is objectively justified where the fixed-term employee' overall employment package is no less favourable than that of a comparable permanent employee. Complaints by individuals under this legislation must generally be taken to an employment tribunal within three months of the last day on which they consider they were unfavourably treated.

The EU Agency Workers Directive was finalised in November 2008. UK regulations implemented this directive with effect from 1 October 2011. These do not cover participation in occupational pension schemes but workers are eligible for the auto-enrolment provisions *(see Sections 4 and 5)*.

EQUAL TREATMENT AND SEXUAL ORIENTATION

The deemed non-discrimination rule under the Equality Act 2010 prevents trustees and employers from discriminating against, harassing or victimising members and prospective members, in carrying out their functions in relation to the scheme, on grounds of sexual orientation or gender reassignment. Previous legislation also applied from 1 December 2003. However, preventing or restricting access to a benefit by reference to marital status remains lawful (*but see below*), as do discriminatory benefits in respect of service before 1 December 2003.

The Civil Partnership Act took effect from 5 December 2005. It introduced a facility for same-sex partners to register civil partnerships and thereby receive increased legal recognition. It extended the divorce pension sharing and earmarking regulations and social security legislation in line with the principle that civil partners should be treated in the same way as married people. Under the Act, contracted-out schemes have to provide the same contracted-out benefits to civil partners as to spouses for all service after 5 April 1988. In addition, subsequent legislation requires all schemes to treat civil partners in the same way as spouses for service on or after 5 December 2005.

The Marriage (Same Sex Couples) Act 2013 will allow same-sex couples to marry, from a date in 2014. Its provisions currently require occupational pension schemes to provide benefits for most same-sex spouses only in the same way as for civil partners, rather than opposite-sex spouses. However, it also requires the Secretary of State to complete a report, before 1 July 2014, on differences in survivor benefits under occupational pension schemes and to make regulations to eliminate or reduce those differences if he thinks the law should be changed.

The Gender Recognition Act came into force on 4 April 2005. It is designed to give formal recognition to transsexuals who successfully register in their acquired gender.

EQUAL TREATMENT AND RACE, RELIGION OR BELIEF

The deemed non-discrimination rule under the Equality Act 2010 prevents trustees and employers from discriminating against, harassing or victimising members and prospective members, in carrying out their functions in relation to the scheme, on grounds of race, religion or belief. Previous legislation also applied in respect of rights accruing from 2 December 2003. The anti-discrimination requirements cover admission to schemes as well as treatment once admitted. Particularly in the realm of indirect discrimination, potential issues could possibly arise for pension schemes, for example where all investment funds offered under a DC arrangement are unacceptable to members of a particular religion.

EQUAL TREATMENT AND DISABILITY

The deemed non-discrimination rule under the Equality Act 2010 prevents trustees and employers from discriminating against, harassing or victimising members and prospective members, in carrying out their functions in relation to the scheme, on grounds of disability. Previous legislation also applied from October 2004. From this date, trustees also became subject to the requirement to make 'reasonable adjustments'. Both direct and indirect discrimination can potentially be objectively justified as a 'proportionate means of achieving a legitimate aim'. Although the legislation does not in general affect benefits earned before October 2004, it does extend to communications with members in relation to such rights.

EQUAL TREATMENT AND AGE

Regulations under the Equality Act 2010 replaced previous, identical, age discrimination legislation, which mostly took effect from 1 October 2006, although the provisions relating to pensions took effect from 1 December 2006.

Both direct and indirect discrimination by employers and by trustees of pension schemes are prohibited, unless such a practice can be objectively justified as a 'proportionate means of achieving a legitimate aim'. There are a number of occupational pension scheme practices that are specifically exempted from being age-discriminatory. These include:

- the use of a minimum or maximum age for admission to a scheme
- the use of age-based actuarial factors in benefit calculations
- the use of a maximum period of service for benefit calculations
- limiting the payment of benefits to a minimum age
- the application of age restrictions which would be required to ensure the scheme is eligible for taxation concessions under the Finance Act 2004
- the provision of age-related employer contributions to money purchase schemes, where the aim is to provide benefits that do not vary by age of member (or to provide 'more nearly equal' benefits) in respect of each year of pensionable service, *and*
- the payment of equal contributions to money purchase schemes irrespective of age, even though this will provide different levels of benefit to members of different ages.

Many previously common occupational pension scheme practices are, however, not exempt under the legislation. For example, benefit accrual may not generally cease at a fixed retirement age. In addition, there is a great deal of uncertainty concerning how much of the legislation will be interpreted, and clarification is expected to emerge only slowly as actual cases are considered by tribunals and courts.

The Equality Act 2010 retained a default retirement age of 65, but this was abolished with effect from 1 October 2011. Employers wishing to dismiss or retire an older employer will need to go through a 'fair procedure'. A compulsory retirement age will be permitted only if it can be objectively justified as a proportionate means of achieving a legitimate aim. There is an exemption, however, which allows group risk insured benefits provided by employers to cease at age 65.

Complaints by individuals under this legislation must generally be taken to an employment tribunal within three months of the last day on which they consider they were unfavourably treated. A number of court cases, both in the UK and in Europe (such as *Seldon* and *Rosenbladt – see Section 29*), have considered whether an employer can objectively justify maintaining a compulsory retirement age. These provide guidance on the factors that can be considered in determining whether compulsory retirement can be objectively justified.

PENSIONS AND DIVORCE

Courts are required to take benefits under pension schemes into account when considering financial provision on divorce. In many cases, this may be achieved by making a divorce settlement which distributes other marital assets in such a way as to keep pension rights intact. However, there are also two alternative approaches available for allowing one party to the divorce to benefit directly from the benefit entitlements under a pension scheme of the other party. The first alternative, earmarking, was introduced for petitions for divorce filed on or after 1 July 1996 (or 19 August 1996 in Scotland). It orders a specified portion of a scheme member's lump sum (all jurisdictions) and/or pension (England, Wales and Northern Ireland only) to be paid instead to his or her ex-spouse. The second alternative, pension sharing, was introduced for divorce proceedings beginning on or after 1 December 2000, and results in a 'clean break' between the divorcing parties.

A pension share may be triggered by a UK court order. However, where the divorce is governed by Scots law, a pension share might instead be triggered by a corresponding provision in a 'qualifying agreement' made between the divorcing parties. In the remainder of this Section, references to orders should be read to include provisions under qualifying agreements.

Since December 2005, the provisions for pension sharing and earmarking have been extended so that they also apply when civil partnerships are dissolved. In the remainder of this Section, 'divorce' should be read to include 'dissolution of civil partnership', 'ex-spouse' to include 'ex-civil partner' etc., as the context requires.

Since 6 April 2011, legislation has allowed the sharing and earmarking of Pension Protection Fund (PPF) compensation on divorce and on dissolution of a civil partnership.

Further details of the pension sharing regime are given below.

PENSION SHARING

Provision of information

If a benefit valuation is to be included, schemes have to supply basic information within three months of the request; or within six weeks, where the member has notified them that proceedings for financial provision on divorce have commenced; or within such shorter period as may be specified in a court order. If no benefit valuation is to be included the basic information must be provided within one month. Further information must be provided within 21 days of being notified that a pension sharing order may be made, unless the prescribed information has already been supplied. Additional information requirements arise subsequently if it is decided that a pension sharing order will be made.

What rights may be shared?

All rights under occupational and personal pensions and retirement annuity policies (including pensions in payment and annuities or insurance policies purchased to give effect to any such rights) may be shared. However, the regulations exclude survivors' pensions payable as a result of a previous marriage and Equivalent Pension Benefits (EPBs) where these are the only benefit under a scheme. SERPS/S2P rights are also included, but the State Graduated Scheme and the Basic State Pension are not. Since 6 April 2011, compensation payments under the PPF *(see Section 19)* may be shared on divorce.

What triggers pension sharing?

Any decision on sharing is triggered by a court order between the parties. The order is stayed until any appeals process has been completed. The order is expressed in terms of a transfer from one party to the other of a percentage of rights accrued prior to the date the order takes effect. In Scotland, these rights are restricted to those that accrued during the marriage and the transfer can alternatively be expressed as a fixed amount.

Rights to be provided to ex-spouse

The person receiving a share of his or her ex-spouse's rights usually has to be offered a transfer value in respect of those rights. Rights under unfunded schemes, including SERPS/S2P, are excluded from this requirement.

Schemes that are obliged to offer an external transfer to another suitable pension arrangement may, but do not have to, offer the ex-spouse the alternative option of a pension credit benefit within the scheme calculated on the scheme's normal transfer-in basis. Ex-spouse members of pension schemes are, essentially, treated like deferred pensioners. If the ex-spouse is also an employee member of the scheme that provides the pension credit benefit, the scheme can insist that, on taking a subsequent cash equivalent, both sets of rights are transferred.

Basis of calculation for sharing

Calculations for pension sharing are based on the scheme's current established cash equivalent basis, extended to cover cases (like pensions in payment) where a transfer value would not normally arise. There is a facility for transfer values for ex-spouses (along with other transfer values) to be reduced if the scheme is underfunded. However, the legislation provides that such a reduction is to be applied only if the ex-spouse has been offered (but has declined) the alternative of a pension credit benefit within the scheme based on the unreduced transfer value.

Pension credit benefits

Pension credit benefits, if offered under the scheme, should be determined on the incoming transfer value basis, with appropriate adjustments where added-year pensions are normally awarded and the ex-spouse is not himself or herself an active member of the scheme. Benefits are generally payable from normal benefit age but can be paid early where the member has attained normal minimum pension age or qualifies for an ill-health pension. Pension credit benefits can also be partially commuted for a pension commencement lump sum, or fully commuted in certain circumstances, in accordance with the Finance Act 2004 provisions. Except for pension credit benefits in money purchase form where the benefit had not come into payment before 6 April 2005, the regulations require

LPI indexation of benefits derived from post-97 rights (other than those derived from AVCs). For this purpose, LPI is capped at 5% if the pension credit benefit was awarded before 6 April 2005, or 2.5% if awarded after 5 April 2005. Schemes are not prevented from indexing the whole of the pension credit benefit, in order to simplify administration.

Pension debits

In defined benefit schemes, the member's benefit becomes subject to a debit, designed to be of equal value to the amount transferred to the ex-spouse. For non-pensioners, this is, essentially, a negative deferred pension. Each part of the member's vested benefit entitlement immediately prior to the date the pension sharing order takes effect is reduced in the same proportion (including contracted-out benefits). Defined contribution scheme debits are the stipulated proportion of the fund value or, if applicable, of the benefit already in payment.

Contracted-out rights

Until 6 April 2009, restrictions applied to pension credit benefits derived from contracted-out rights. These were known as 'safeguarded rights'. However, the restrictions were removed from that date and, subject to the scheme rules, these rights may be treated in the same manner as other pension credit benefits.

Timing of implementation

Schemes generally have four months, after the date the relevant court order takes effect or (if later) receipt of all relevant divorce documentation and personal information about the divorcing parties, to implement the pension share in accordance with the option chosen by the ex-spouse. If no valid instructions are given, the pension share can be implemented in accordance with the scheme's chosen default procedure. The Pensions Regulator may (on application) extend the implementation period, in circumstances broadly similar to those which apply for the late payment of 'normal' cash equivalents.

Expense charges

Schemes are allowed to charge the divorcing parties for costs reasonably incurred in providing information for and implementing the pension share, and are usually able to insist on receiving these before they have to provide the information or implement the share. However, most charges are allowable only to the extent that they were disclosed in a Schedule of Charges at the outset, and no charge may be made for information that would be available for free under the Disclosure requirements *(see Section 14)*. The trustees can require that the charges are paid in cash, with deduction from the benefits being an alternative. Only costs specifically relating to an individual divorce case can be charged, and therefore initial costs involved in setting up administrative procedures to deal with pension sharing may not be passed on.

Tax treatment

Under the tax regime introduced from 6 April 2006 *(see Section 10)*, the benefits tested against an individual's lifetime allowance are the actual benefits payable after taking account of a pension debit or credit. In most circumstances, an individual whose benefits have become subject to a debit will have scope within his or her lifetime allowance to rebuild lost rights. An ex-spouse who became entitled before 6 April 2006 to a pension credit had until 5 April 2009 to register for an increased lifetime allowance, so that he or she would not lose scope to build up further tax-privileged pension rights. The tax treatment of pension credits and debits for individuals whose benefits are 'protected' under transitional arrangements *(see Section 10)* will depend on the type of protection.

Under *primary protection*, a divorcing member with protection will see his or her lifetime allowance reduced to take account of a post-5 April 2006 pension debit. A pension credit received after 5 April 2006 gives rise to an increase in the personal lifetime allowance of an ex-spouse with primary protection only if it arises from pension that had come into payment between 6 April 2006 and the date of the share, and the increase is registered within the required timescale.

Under *enhanced protection*, for a divorcing member with protection, rights lost under a defined benefit or cash balance arrangement as a result of a post-5 April 2006 pension debit can – in general – be rebuilt, although this would not be possible under a money purchase arrangement. An ex-spouse would lose enhanced protection if a post-5 April 2006 pension credit paid to his or her defined benefit or cash balance arrangement caused the pension limits to be breached. However, enhanced protection is not lost if the pension credit is paid to a money purchase arrangement that is not a cash balance arrangement, provided that this arrangement existed at 5 April 2006.

Under *fixed protection* and under *fixed protection 2014*, which applies from 6 April 2014, there is limited scope under defined benefit and cash balance arrangements for a divorcing member to rebuild lost rights without losing protection. The value of members' rights is assessed every tax year and protection is lost if the increase over the year exceeds a certain limit, so any rebuilding would need to occur in the tax year in which the pension debit took effect. An ex-spouse's protection will not be lost if a pension credit is paid to a money purchase arrangement that is not a cash balance arrangement, provided that the arrangement existed at 5 April 2012 (or 5 April 2014 for fixed protection 2014). If it is paid into an existing defined benefit or cash balance arrangement, protection will be lost if the limit on the increase in benefits for the tax year is exceeded.

Under *individual protection 2014* (to be included within Finance Act 2014), it is proposed that, where a divorcing member with protection is subject to a pension debit after 5 April 2014, the lifetime allowance will be reduced to take account of the debit. There is no corresponding provision for increasing the personal lifetime allowance if a pension credit is received.

PENSION SCHEME FUNDING

ACTUARIAL VALUATIONS

Actuarial valuations are central to the process of funding defined benefit (DB) schemes. They are also used for other purposes, including accounting for pension costs *(see Section 25)*. Many different types of valuation may be called for in different circumstances. The basic principles of two of the main types, 'ongoing' and 'discontinuance' valuations, are described briefly below.

Ongoing valuation

When a DB scheme is established, the actuary's calculations of the amount of contributions to be paid have to be based on assumptions about how the scheme will evolve. However, events will invariably unfold differently from the original assumptions, and it is necessary to examine the scheme periodically to value the assets and liabilities and to revise the contribution rate.

To value the liabilities, the actuary receives individual details of the scheme's active, retired and deferred members. Data relating to changes in membership since the previous valuation may also be supplied to enable a reconciliation of the membership numbers to be carried out and to test actual experience against the assumptions of the last valuation.

Various assumptions need to be made; these are financial (e.g. the discount rate and rates of salary and pension increases) and demographic (e.g. rates of mortality, ill-health, early retirement and leaving service). The starting point for the financial assumptions is often the yields on fixed-interest and index-linked securities available in the market at the valuation date. Valuations may be based on a 'yield curve', reflecting the variation in market yields by term, or a single flat-rate approximation.

Various different valuation methods are used according to the individual needs of the scheme and the employer, and to meet statutory requirements. The differences only relate to the valuation of 'active members' – the most common method is the *Projected Unit Method*, which allows for expected salary increases to retirement, leaving service or death, as appropriate. An alternative is the *Current Unit Method* in which members are assumed to leave service at the end of a specified period.

The actuary also requires details of the assets held by the scheme. Assets are given at market value in the audited accounts, and this is the value that is used in actuarial valuations in conjunction with market-based yields for valuing liabilities. Some assets, such as insurance policies, may not have a market value, and the actuary will need to calculate a value that is consistent with the value applied to the corresponding liabilities.

Discontinuance valuation

The discontinuance, or solvency, valuation assesses whether the scheme's assets would be sufficient to cover the liabilities if the scheme were to be discontinued at the valuation date and no further contributions were received from the employer. The liability for active members is usually based on service to and salary at the valuation date. Future expenses should be allowed for.

This assessment can be made on various bases. However, the scheme funding legislation requires the actuary to disclose the extent to which the assets of the scheme would be sufficient, at the valuation date, to cover the liabilities assessed on an annuity buy-out basis, regardless of whether or not the scheme would be likely to secure benefits in this way if it were to discontinue. As an alternative to using the cost actually quoted by a suitable insurance company for buying out the benefits at the valuation date, the actuary may use an estimate of the buy-out cost based on the principles likely to be adopted by an insurance company. Liabilities must include a realistic allowance for expenses. Assets must be taken at market value.

Monitoring funding

Between formal valuations, approximate updates of a scheme's funding position can be produced on ongoing and solvency bases. Some scheme trustees have developed 'flight plans', which set out how they intend to achieve their ultimate objectives – perhaps de-risking the scheme or securing benefits with an insurance company. A flight plan might include agreed actions to take when scheme funding reaches certain levels. Regular monitoring helps to ensure appropriate actions are taken at the right time.

SCHEME FUNDING UNDER THE PENSIONS ACT 2004

Under the 'statutory funding objective', a DB scheme is required to 'have sufficient and appropriate assets to cover its technical provisions', i.e. 'the amount required, on an actuarial calculation, to make provision for the scheme's liabilities'. Regulations require the technical provisions to be determined on a (normally 'ongoing') scheme-specific basis. There is no legal requirement for schemes to fund at a prescribed level. Each valuation must, however, include an estimate by the actuary of the solvency of the scheme, *as described above*. The trustees have ultimate responsibility for the funding decisions, but are required to take advice from the scheme actuary and – normally – to obtain the employer's agreement. However, where the trustees have power under the scheme's rules to set contribution rates without the employer's agreement, that requirement is replaced by one for consultation (although agreement should be obtained if possible). If the rules provide for the actuary to determine the contributions, the trustees and employer must still agree the contributions payable, but in addition the contributions must be certified as being no lower than the actuary would have set had he or she retained this responsibility.

Actuarial valuations are required with effective dates no more than three years apart, with additional written 'actuarial reports', covering development since the last valuation, in each intervening year. There is a general exception from the scheme funding requirement for schemes in wind-up but, where this commenced on or after 30 December 2005, the exception is conditional upon the preparation of an annual solvency estimate by the scheme actuary (on a buy-out basis) and a winding-up procedure *(see Section 22).*

Cross-border schemes *(see Section 3)* are subject to more onerous requirements, including a specified deadline for meeting the statutory funding objective and full actuarial valuations every 12 months.

The current Pensions Bill includes an amendment to the Pensions Act 2004, creating a new objective for the Pensions Regulator 'to minimise any adverse impact on the sustainable growth of an employer', in relation to scheme funding.

Statement of funding principles

The trustees must have a written statement of funding principles (SFP) setting out their policy for securing that the statutory funding objective is met and recording decisions as to the basis for calculating the technical provisions and the period within which any shortfall is to be remedied. The SFP must be reviewed at each valuation and, if amended, finalised (along with the valuation report and schedule of contributions) within 15 months of the effective date of the valuation.

Calculation of technical provisions

The trustees must choose an 'accrued benefits' funding method, such as the projected unit method *(see above)*, for calculating the technical provisions.

It is also the trustees' responsibility (having received advice from the scheme actuary) to choose the assumptions to be adopted for the calculation of the scheme's technical provisions. The trustees should also agree the assumptions with the employer (unless there is only a requirement for consultation – *see above*).

Legislation requires the assumptions to be chosen 'prudently', taking account, if applicable, of an appropriate margin for adverse deviation. The Regulator's code of practice states that assessment of the employer's covenant *(see below)* is required, to inform decisions on both the technical provisions and the recovery plan.

Recovery plan

If an actuarial valuation shows that the statutory funding objective is not met, the trustees must prepare a 'recovery plan' setting out the steps to be taken (and over what period) to make up the shortfall. The current code of practice states that trustees should aim for the shortfall to be eliminated as quickly as the employer can 'reasonably afford', taking into account the employer's business plans and the likely effect of the potential recovery plan on the employer's viability. The code is expected to be updated in 2014 to reflect the new regulatory objective in the current Pensions Bill, under which the Regulator must consider the employer *(see above)*. A copy of the recovery plan must be sent to the Regulator.

Schedule of contributions

The trustees must have in place a schedule of contributions setting out the rates and due dates of contributions payable to the scheme, which will normally have been agreed with the employer (unless there is only a requirement for consultation – *see above*). The schedule must be certified by the actuary as being sufficient to ensure that the funding objective will continue to be met for the next five years, or will be met by the end of the recovery period. In the latter case, a copy of the schedule must be sent to the Regulator. If contributions are not paid or are paid late, the trustees (and actuary or auditor, if they become aware of this) must inform the Regulator (and must alert members) if they believe that the failure is likely to be 'of material significance'.

Regulator's approach

In May 2006, the Regulator issued a statement detailing how it will regulate the funding of DB schemes. This set out the circumstances and manner in which it may take action to intervene where it forms the opinion that the scheme's funding plan is not compliant with the legal requirements, and outlined steps it expected trustees to have taken to ensure compliance. This regulatory approach is expected to be revised in 2014.

The Regulator issued a number of other statements during the economic downturn in 2008/9. It commented that trustees should consider reviewing recovery plans where there is a significant change in circumstances. However, the Regulator also said that recovery plans should not suffer to enable the employer to continue to pay dividends, and that the trustees should consider themselves as unsecured creditors and therefore take priority over shareholders.

Since April 2012, the Regulator has published annual statements on scheme funding. It believes that if trustees and employers follow the guidance in these statements, they will be more likely to reach funding agreements that will avoid the need for regulatory involvement. Where an approach is not in line with the statement, the Regulator will consider the case in more depth. From 2012, the Regulator has also pro-actively engaged with a very small minority of schemes from an early stage of their valuation process.

In its spring 2013 statement, the Regulator encouraged trustees to adopt an integrated approach to risk management. It explained that it was moving away from setting triggers for intervention (as set out in its 2006 statement on its regulatory approach) and was in the process of developing a suite of risk indicators relating to recovery plans, investment risk and employer covenant. It will use these indicators to identify schemes that are out of line with its principles and intervene in such cases. The Regulator stated that, where it does engage with schemes, a key area of focus will be the link between the strength of the covenant, the scheme's investment strategy and the prudence in the discount rates compared to expected investment returns.

The Regulator also has powers to intervene in cases where agreement cannot be reached between the trustees and employer or where the actuary is unable to provide the necessary certification. In addition, the Regulator has powers to intervene if it views the technical provisions as insufficiently prudent, even if the trustees and employer are in agreement. Possible courses of action include imposing a funding basis, modifying future accrual and freezing or winding up the scheme. However, the Regulator has stated that it aims to use its formal powers sparingly, preferring to achieve its desired outcome by more informal means.

Disclosure to members

Schemes are required to send members an annual 'summary funding statement' including information about the funding and discontinuance positions of the scheme and an explanation of any changes since the previous statement.

Employer covenant

The Regulator has stated that it is essential for the trustees to form an objective assessment of 'the employer's financial position and prospects as well as his willingness to continue to fund the scheme's benefits'. This assessment should be used to inform the trustees' decisions on both the technical provisions and any recovery plan needed. The Regulator has published guidance on 'monitoring employer support' which sets out standard practice that trustees are expected to follow in assessing and monitoring the employer's covenant.

Particular considerations apply to multi-employer schemes and the Regulator has produced specific guidance on 'Multi-employer schemes and employer departures'. Trustees also need to identify the scheme's 'statutory employers' on their scheme returns. A statutory employer is responsible for some or all of: scheme funding, any debt on the employer *(see Section 24)* and triggering entry into the PPF *(see Section 19)*.

Trustees will need to understand each employer's legal obligations and financial position. This includes any obligations to, or support available from, other employers within a corporate group, and any industry-wide factors. Trustees should place more weight on estimates of future performance than on evidence of past performance.

In order to carry out this assessment, the trustees will need to obtain information about each employer, either directly from the employer or by using commercially available services such as credit specialist advisers. Employers are generally required to provide information to trustees and their advisers to help them assess the covenant. Trustees should be prepared to accept confidentiality agreements where any information is price-sensitive. They should consider using external advisers if they do not have the relevant expertise, once trustees with conflicts are excluded, to assess the information themselves.

Trustees should carry out a full covenant review before each valuation, and continue to monitor the employer's covenant between valuations. The strength of covenant can change rapidly and trustees need to be in a position to respond quickly. This may involve reviewing both funding and investment policies. The Regulator's spring 2013 statement on scheme funding *(see above)* encouraged an integrated approach, linking the strength of the covenant with investment and funding risks.

Alternative financing

A number of schemes have put in place funding mechanisms that do not involve cash being paid directly to the pension scheme. Some of these arrangements are treated as assets of the scheme, and those that are not aim to increase the strength of the employer covenant and the overall security of the pension scheme.

There are a number of different types of alternative financing that have been used to date, including:

- transferring company assets (e.g. property or brand names) to the scheme, an escrow account or to a Special Purpose Vehicle which the scheme owns fully or partially; the trustees might initially just have a right to an income stream from the assets, with final ownership to be determined at a later stage, possibly depending on the funding position of the scheme and other circumstances at that time
- contingent assets, such as group company guarantees, security over assets or bank letters of credit, which pay out to the scheme if a specified event occurs, such as employer insolvency or increased employer borrowing; certain forms of contingent asset can reduce a scheme's PPF levy *(see Section 19), and*
- market instruments such as credit default swaps, which pay out if a company defaults on its corporate bond payments.

Trustees will need to take specialist advice on the suitability of a proposed alternative financing arrangement, including any particular legal issues such as employer-related investment. Ongoing advice will be needed to ensure that it continues to be available if needed and is properly enforceable.

The Regulator's guidance on monitoring employer support sets out considerations for trustees in relation to such arrangements.

Refunds of surplus

A power to repay surplus from the scheme can only be exercised by the trustees (subject to the agreement of the employer, if it was originally conferred on him) and only if it is in the members' interests and they have been notified.

Furthermore, a payment of surplus from the scheme to the employer will only be permitted to the extent that the scheme's assets exceed the full buy-out cost of the accrued liabilities, as indicated by a valuation carried out under the Pensions Act 2004 funding regime or a special valuation carried out for this purpose.

EU PENSIONS DIRECTIVE

In May 2013, the European Commission announced that the proposed revision of the EU Pensions Directive will not cover the issue of solvency capital requirements, which are being applied to insurance companies (under 'Solvency II'). The European Insurance and Occupational Pensions Authority (EIOPA) study of the solvency of certain pension funds highlighted the need to deepen knowledge before taking decisions on any European initiative on solvency of pension funds.

LONGEVITY

Dramatic increases in life expectancy over the past decade – particularly for men – have received much publicity, and mean that pensions are expected to be paid for longer, increasing costs. The combination of increased longevity and lower interest rates means that longevity risk is considerably greater for pension schemes than it was in the past. Trustees of defined benefit schemes in particular need to understand the risks arising from changes in life expectancy and how they can manage them. For example, trustees can purchase bulk annuities or longevity swaps to reduce longevity risk .

LONGEVITY RISK

Different types of mortality-related risk can be identified. One such risk, commonly referred to as 'mortality risk', is the risk of dying sooner than expected. 'Longevity risk' refers to the risk of living longer than expected. This is typically more of an issue for pension schemes, given recent increases in life expectancy and uncertainty over how these will persist. We will concentrate on 'longevity risk' in the rest of this section.

Longevity risk has different elements. Past data may tell us fairly accurately the historic mortality rates for the general population. But for any given pension scheme there must be uncertainty over:

- how mortality rates for its members differ from those for the general population (because of factors like location, social class, diet and smoking)
- how mortality rates will change in the future — will past improvements continue? *and*
- whether there might be a 'jump' change in mortality rates in the future (e.g. caused by an epidemic or, in the other direction, a medical breakthrough).

Longevity risk can fall on different parties depending on what type of pension scheme we are considering. The risk under a traditional final salary scheme falls on the sponsoring employer (although members' future benefit accrual could be reduced if increases in life expectancy cause the scheme to become too expensive). The risk under a pure defined contribution scheme buying annuities for its pensioners falls partly on the scheme members (since they do not know how much pension their money will buy when they retire) and partly on the insurance company (since the annuity rates it sets may turn out to be wrong).

ASSUMPTIONS

To place a value on the liabilities of a defined benefit pension scheme, the trustees need to make assumptions about how long its members will live. An insurance company selling annuities needs to do the same thing in order to set its annuity rates.

Mortality rates

Life expectancies are usually calculated based on mortality rates. 'Mortality rate' in this context means the assumed probability that an individual of a given age will die in the next year. The lower the mortality rates are, the longer the life expectancy is. The assumptions needed are in two parts: the rates assumed to apply for the next 12 months (the 'base tables') and how these rates are expected to change in future years. Different rates are calculated for men and women.

Base tables

There are two approaches to determining base mortality rates using data for individual scheme members. The first is to measure the scheme's actual mortality experience. This approach is limited to larger schemes because the experience needs to be of sufficient size to be statistically credible. The second approach is to use a postcode mortality model. Such models are created using a very large set of mortality experience data derived from a variety of schemes. These models relate postcodes to mortality rates by assuming similar mortality either for individuals of similar socio-economic type (typically assessed using a third-party postcode marketing database) or for individuals living in the same area (by using postcodes to determine geographic locations). These approaches may be combined in practice (whereby a pension scheme's mortality experience, although not statistically credible in isolation, is credible when combined with a postcode model).

In most cases, published standard tables are used as a starting point. These are usually tables prepared by the Continuous Mortality Investigation (CMI), a limited company wholly owned by the Institute and Faculty of Actuaries, based on data collated from life insurance companies or from

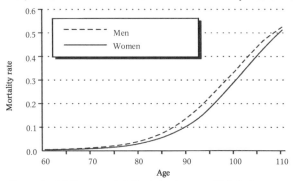

Mortality rate (probability that an individual of a given age will die in the next year)

Source: From the S1 series (pensioners, amounts), adjusted for use in 2014, allowing for default CMI_2012 projection factors and with a projected long-term improvement in mortality rates of 1.5% p.a.

self-administered pension schemes. The current pension scheme CMI tables are the 'S1' series (based on self-administered pension scheme experience from 2000 to 2006). At the time of writing, the CMI has consulted on and is shortly expected to publish the 'S2' series (based on self-administered pension scheme experience from 2004 to 2011).

The trustees and actuary may adjust the mortality rates from the standard tables to make them more appropriate for their own scheme's members (to reflect, for example, their locations and former occupations). Such adjustments may be based on an analysis of the scheme's own experience or, if this is not available or not large enough, on broad principles.

Future improvements

Longevity has improved dramatically in recent years, and it is now normal to make an explicit allowance for further improvements in the future. These are of course unknown. However, by 2002, it had become clear that longevity was improving at a faster rate than had previously been assumed, with the improvements being particularly marked for the generation (or 'cohort') of pensioners born between the two World Wars. In response to this, the CMI published sets of cohort improvement factors. In 2009, the CMI published a new projections model to allow for ongoing improvements in longevity, which is updated annually, superseding the cohort factors. At the time of writing, the current version of the model is 'CMI_2013', which reflects population data up to and including 2012. In 2013, the CMI consulted on its projections model. Although the structure of the model was unchanged for CMI_2013, it may be altered for CMI_2014 or possibly CMI_2015.

Another possibility is to adopt a stochastic approach. This involves assigning an assumed probability distribution for future mortality rates and then carrying out a large number of simulations to assess the range of outcomes. (A similar approach is often used to illustrate the effect on schemes' funding levels of different rates of future investment return.)

LOOKING AHEAD

Predicting future improvements in longevity is extremely difficult, not least because of the huge uncertainties surrounding the impact that future events may have. Medical advances, especially the availability of life-extending medical treatments, increases in obesity, changes in social behaviours and general prosperity will all have an impact.

In the past, it was not uncommon to hear the view that life expectancy would level off in the future (because it was difficult to foresee how future improvements would arise). However, estimates based on this view have consistently underestimated future life expectancy and, as a result, it is now common to assume that the rate of mortality improvement will continue at similar levels into the future indefinitely, albeit with variation along the way. The current debate around mortality improvement focuses on whether the rates of improvement (which are historically high at many ages) have peaked and will revert to their long-term average, the degree to which mortality improvement depends on birth year (or 'cohort') and how mortality improvement varies by socio-economic type.

This uncertainty makes it difficult for trustees and actuaries to decide what allowance to make for future improvements in longevity. However, the Pensions Regulator's guidance on mortality assumptions for scheme-specific funding *(see Section 17)* states that, in its view, these should be chosen prudently. For base tables, the Regulator views prudence as taking a margin below best estimate rates; for future mortality improvements, the Regulator views prudence as not assuming any rates lower than are reasonable based on up-to-date evidence.

MANAGING THE RISK

The requirement for prudence means that trustees need to consider carefully whether they remain comfortable with the assumptions made at previous funding valuations. For many schemes, significant changes have already been made to the mortality assumptions, leading to a significant increase in the calculated value of their liabilities.

There are a number of ways trustees and employers can reduce the longevity risk a scheme faces. Purchasing annuities with an insurance company removes the longevity risk entirely *(see Section 23)*. Some financial institutions are now offering longevity swaps, which can reduce longevity risk in pension schemes *(see Section 20)*.

For future service, the benefit structure could be changed, to:

- defined contribution
- cash balance, where a lump sum based on service and salary is used to purchase pension based on conversion terms that can change over time, *or*
- defined benefit, but where the normal retirement date is increased or a longevity adjustment factor is used to calculate pensions – for example, a factor based on a ratio of annuity values based on appropriate assumptions at the date of retirement and at a specified date in the past.

The Government is also exploring the possibility of facilitating new types of 'defined ambition' benefit structure which would allow greater sharing of risks between employers and employees, including longevity risk. *See Section 3 for further detail.*

THE PENSION PROTECTION FUND AND LEVIES

The Pension Protection Fund (PPF) was formally established under the Pensions Act 2004 and commenced on 6 April 2005, with the aim, in the words of the government, of 'guaranteeing members a specified minimum level of pension when the sponsoring employer becomes insolvent'.

The PPF covers eligible schemes where an insolvency event occurs to the employer on or after 6 April 2005. Schemes already in wind-up on that date are not covered by the PPF. The PPF is not underwritten by the government, but is funded by levies on eligible schemes *(see below)*. A separate Financial Assistance Scheme (FAS), which is funded by the government and managed by the PPF, provides assistance to members of schemes that went into wind-up on or after 1 January 1997 and are not eligible for the PPF *(see below)*. The Fraud Compensation Fund is also the responsibility of the PPF and covers claims from schemes that have lost assets as a result of an offence such as theft or fraud, where the employer is insolvent *(see below)*.

ADMISSION

The principle of the PPF is that it will 'assume responsibility' for 'eligible schemes' if their assets immediately before the insolvency event are insufficient to cover the 'protected liabilities' *(see below)*. 'Eligible schemes' excludes, in particular, pure money purchase schemes. 'Assuming responsibility' entails the PPF taking over the assets of the scheme and paying members the benefits provided under the 'pension compensation provisions' *(see below)*. The trustees are discharged from their obligations to pay benefits and administer the scheme.

The assessment period

During the 'assessment period', the PPF will determine whether or not the scheme is eligible. This period begins with the employer's insolvency (or, in certain circumstances, with either the trustees' application for the PPF to assume responsibility or a notification from the Pensions Regulator to the same effect). The legislation contains a lot of detail on the process for notifying insolvency events and confirming whether or not a 'scheme rescue' is possible (if, for example, the employer can continue as a going concern). Schemes must have a 'statutory employer' *(see Section 8)* in order to access the PPF; if a company supporting a pension scheme never employed any of those who have pension entitlements in the scheme, its insolvency would not trigger an assessment period.

The funding position of the scheme has to be determined, which may require an actuarial 'entry valuation' *(see below)* on a prescribed basis to be carried out. This assesses whether or not the scheme has sufficient assets to cover the 'protected liabilities' (i.e. the cost of securing the benefits provided for under the pension compensation provisions, together with any non-benefit-related liabilities and the estimated costs of wind-up). Once the PPF has determined the funding position of the scheme, normally either it will proceed to assume responsibility and issue a formal 'transfer notice' to the trustees, or (if there are sufficient assets to meet the protected liabilities) the trustees must proceed with winding up. In the latter case, the trustees can make an application to the PPF for reconsideration. Where winding up takes place, this may be subject to directions made by the PPF and/or the Regulator.

During an assessment period, lots of restrictions apply. Further benefits may not accrue and further contributions may not be made. Normally, transfers out are not permitted and a wind-up cannot be started. Benefit payments must be restricted to those payable under the pension compensation provisions. The PPF can also give directions to the trustees regarding, for example, scheme investment.

The assessment period ends when the 'transfer notice' is served, or when the PPF ceases to be involved with the scheme, or if the entry valuation indicates that the scheme has sufficient assets to cover its protected liabilities, normally *(but see below)* leaving it to be wound up outside the PPF. Reasons for the PPF ceasing to be involved include a scheme rescue and a refusal to assume responsibility for the scheme because it has been set up to exploit the PPF.

Closed schemes

Schemes that are too well funded to be taken on by the PPF but are too big to be able to find an insurer to buy out the liabilities must apply to the PPF to continue as 'closed schemes'. These closed schemes would then be subject to the same restrictions on contributions and accrual of benefits, and to directions from the PPF, that apply during an assessment period. Closed schemes are required to undertake regular valuations and, if at some point the assets have fallen below the value of the PPF liabilities, the PPF will then assume responsibility.

COMPENSATION

The admissible rules

The starting point for determining the benefits payable to members under the pension compensation provisions is the scheme's 'admissible rules'. Essentially, this means the rules as at the assessment date (i.e. the start of the assessment period), but disregarding rule changes within the previous three years that would increase the level of PPF compensation. Discretionary pension increases within the same period are also excluded to the extent that they exceed the increase in prices since the pension was last increased. Discretionary early retirement pensions that came into payment under a rule that is to be disregarded may have to cease, and the PPF can review – and, if necessary, adjust – ill-health pensions granted in the last three years.

Members' and dependants' benefits

Members over NPA at the assessment date and ill-health pensioners are entitled to 100% of the benefits under their scheme's admissible rules. Payments made by the scheme during the assessment period are offset against the PPF compensation. Members under NPA, including those already receiving pension, are entitled to 90% of accrued benefits under the admissible rules.

A future widow or widower is entitled to 50% of the pension payable to the member (unless the admissible rules had no provision for a survivor's pension). A 'relevant partner' (of either sex, living with the member as 'man and wife') has the same entitlement. Benefits for children are payable until age 18 (or 25 in some circumstances); their amount depends on the number of children and on whether or not there is a widow, widower or relevant partner.

Compensation can be shared or earmarked, on divorce or dissolution of a civil partnership, in a similar way to occupational pension scheme benefits *(see Section 16)*. The resulting pension credits are retained in the PPF and cannot be transferred elsewhere.

The compensation cap

For members whose compensation is subject to the 90% restriction, the initial rate of compensation is limited to a stipulated 'maximum permitted rate' at the date benefits come into payment. For 2013/14, a maximum pension of £31,380 p.a. at age 65 applies. The level of this 'cap' increases in line with earnings each year. The PPF has set adjustment factors to derive amounts applicable where benefits come into payment at ages above and below 65. In June 2013, the Government announced that the cap would be increased by 3% for every full year of service above 20 years, up to a maximum of double the standard cap, although full details and timescale had not been published at time of writing.

Revaluation and indexation

Benefits not in payment and accrued before 6 April 2009 are revalued between the assessment date and NPA (or earlier retirement) in line with CPI (RPI for periods up to 31 March 2011) up to a maximum of 5% p.a. The 5% p.a. limit is reduced to 2.5% p.a. in respect of benefits accrued from 6 April 2009.

Where the scheme provides no revaluation to any member in any circumstances, legislation provides that PPF compensation benefits are not revalued.

For deferred pensioners, revaluation between date of leaving and assessment date is based on the scheme rules.

Benefits in payment are increased annually in line with inflation up to a maximum of 2.5%. Increases apply only to benefits attributable to service from 6 April 1997. RPI was originally used as the measure of inflation but this was changed to CPI from 1 January 2012.

Options

Lump sum commutation, of up to 25% of benefits, is permitted using factors specified by the PPF. Early payment of benefits from age 55 (or from the later of age 50 and the 'protected' pension age, if any, that would have applied under the member's scheme) is permitted subject to actuarial reduction using factors specified by the PPF. Since 30 April 2013, late payment of benefits has been permitted under certain conditions, subject to actuarial increase using factors specified by the PPF. Trivial commutation and terminal ill-health lump sums are also available in certain circumstances.

Adjustments by the PPF

Where the scheme rules are such that the appropriate compensation benefits cannot be determined in accordance with the legislation, the PPF can decide the level of compensation that will apply to members.

The PPF received legal advice that it is required to equalise benefits to take account of differences in the way GMPs are calculated for men and women and has confirmed the approach to be adopted. Schemes transferring to the PPF since 1 June 2013 are required to adjust benefits during the assessment process in accordance with the PPF's guidance. For other schemes the PPF makes the necessary adjustments.

The PPF has the ability (after consultation) to adjust the rates of revaluation and increases in payment if necessary. If both of these have been reduced to zero they can recommend that the Secretary of State reduce the 90% and/or 100% levels of compensation. Such reductions would only apply in 'extreme circumstances'.

Money purchase benefits are excluded from the compensation provisions, so the PPF may direct the trustees to discharge these liabilities before entry. Alternatively, since 30 April 2013, the PPF has been able to pay a 'PPF money purchase lump sum' of up to £2,000 to a member, where it has assumed responsibility for money purchase benefits. Though not in effect at the time of writing, the definition of money purchase benefits, for this purpose, is to be amended under a provision of the Pensions Act 2011.

VALUATIONS

Two types of actuarial valuation are required by the PPF, each for a specific purpose – for levy calculations and to determine whether a scheme should enter the PPF.

Levy valuation

An eligible scheme must provide a 'section 179 valuation' to the PPF in order for it to determine the Pension Protection Levy payable by the scheme. These valuations must be carried out by the scheme actuary at intervals of no more than three years, and completed (and submitted via the Regulator's online 'Exchange' system) within fifteen months of the effective date.

For the purposes of the valuation, assets are generally taken at the value shown in the scheme's audited accounts.

Liabilities are valued, using assumptions set out in guidance issued by the PPF, to reflect the estimated cost of buying out the benefits with an insurance company. The benefits valued are broadly those provided under the scheme's rules, but allowing for members under NPA receiving 90% (not 100%) of benefits, the compensation cap, and the PPF levels of revaluation, indexation and spouse's pension.

Entry valuation

In most cases, a 'section 143 valuation' is required by the PPF to determine whether or not it should assume responsibility for a scheme that has entered an assessment period. The PPF will obtain this from the trustees, who will usually ask the scheme actuary to carry it out. It has to be obtained as soon as reasonably practicable after the insolvency event. Assets are generally taken at the value shown in the audited accounts. Liabilities are valued using assumptions set out in guidance issued by the PPF (which are similar to those for levy valuations but differ for some of the demographic assumptions to reflect the circumstances of the scheme), but the actual PPF compensation benefits are taken into account, rather than the broad approximations used in the section 179 valuation.

LEVIES

Schemes that are eligible for future entry to the PPF are required to pay two PPF-related levies, the Pension Protection Levy and the PPF Administration Levy. These are charged in respect of each levy year, which begins on 1 April.

Pension Protection Levy – general

The Pension Protection Levy consists of two parts: the risk-based levy (which must represent at least 80% of the total collected from all schemes) and the scheme-based levy. There are limits each year on the total estimated levy and the amount by which it can increase. These limits can only be changed by the Secretary of State following consultation and with the approval of the Treasury. Legislation allows the PPF to charge interest (at 5% above base rate) on any Pension Protection Levy that has not been paid within 28 days of the invoice date, although the PPF does have discretion to waive interest in certain circumstances.

Pension Protection Levy – up to 2011/12

Up to 2011/12, the risk-based levy was based on two elements: the assumed probability of insolvency of the employer (or a weighted average probability for multi-employer schemes), and an underfunding risk calculated as a specified percentage of the scheme's estimated PPF liabilities. This percentage depended on the funding level revealed by the levy valuation *(see above)* adjusted for market conditions on the day before the beginning of the previous levy year.

A scaling factor equated the proposed levy estimate with the estimated risk exposure across all schemes. The risk-based levy was capped in order to protect the weakest levy payers.

The scheme-based levy was based on a percentage of the scheme's estimated PPF liabilities, calculated by the application of a scheme-based multiplier.

Pension Protection Levy – 2012/13 onwards

For levy years from 2012/13, a new approach has applied to the levy calculation. The overall intention is to make a scheme's levy more stable and predictable as it is related to changes in the scheme's own risk profile, and less affected by the changes of other schemes (through the scaling factor) and short-term market movements.

The risk-based levy formula (including the scaling factor, levy cap and scheme-based levy multiplier) will normally be fixed for three years, except in certain 'extreme' circumstances. The scheme-based levy is set explicitly to cover any deficit within the PPF and any cross-subsidy from the cap on the risk-based levy, which applies to protect the weakest levy payers.

For 2013/14, the total levy estimate was £630m. At the time of writing, the PPF had announced that for 2014/15 the proposed total levy estimate is £695m. The proposed estimate will mean that most schemes will see a higher levy bill in 2014/15 than that in 2013/14. The PPF notes that the proposed 2014/15 estimate is in line with the change in risks faced by the PPF.

Risk-based levy

The risk-based levy formula is based on:

(a) The *assumed probability of insolvency of the employer* (or a weighted average probability for multi-employer schemes), using the average Dun & Bradstreet (D&B) failure score over the year prior to the levy year and then assigned to one of ten bands.

(b) *Underfunding risk*. This is calculated as a specified percentage of the scheme's estimated PPF liabilities, averaged over the previous five years (i.e. up to the last day of the previous levy year) and also adjusted to reflect the risk posed by a scheme's investment strategy in adverse market conditions (so schemes with a riskier strategy pay a higher levy). The PPF calculates the investment risk for most schemes, but schemes with liabilities of £1.5 billion or more must carry out their own more detailed test (and smaller schemes can choose to) which takes account of a wider range of asset classes, including derivatives. Any such test must be submitted via Exchange in the same way as the valuation.

For 2013/14, the risk-based levy scaling factor is 0.73 and the risk-based levy cap is 0.75% of a scheme's estimated PPF liabilities. At the time of writing the PPF had announced that, subject to consultation, for 2014/15 these figures would remain unchanged. This is in line with the PPF's intention to fix the parameters for three years, although for 2013/14 the PPF reduced factors from 2012/13 levels, so that the limit on how much the total levy estimate can increase from year to year was not breached.

There are several actions that may be taken to manage a scheme's risk-based levy, including:

- *monitor the D&B failure score* – D&B scores are based on factors such as the number of directors and the promptness of paying invoices, as well as the financial position of the company, so employers may be able to take relatively simple actions to improve their scores or ensure they do not fall into a worse risk band. (The PPF has confirmed that Experian will replace D&B as its provider of insolvency risk measure from 2014, with effect for levies from the 2015/16 levy year. At the time of writing, the implications for monitoring processes and levy calculations were unknown)

- *carry out the more detailed investment risk test* – schemes with liabilities of less than £1.5 billion have the option of doing this rather than relying on the PPF's default calculations

- submitting an *out-of-cycle s179 valuation* to reflect action taken to improve the scheme's funding position

- submitting details of *deficit reduction contributions* made since the relevant valuation date, over and above the cost of accruing scheme benefits, and as certified by the scheme actuary in accordance with guidance published by the PPF – this reduces the underfunding risk, *and*

- putting in place *contingent assets* (if in a standard form and legally binding) that produce cash for the scheme when an insolvency event occurs in relation to the employer – these can be in the form of a guarantee from another group company, a charge over assets of the employer, or a letter of credit, and they reduce the underfunding risk or the assumed insolvency probability, depending on the type of contingent asset. For a group company guarantee, the scheme must certify that it has no reason to believe that the guarantor could not meet its full financial commitment under the agreement; otherwise a lower amount can be certified. The PPF carries out its own analysis of the guarantor's strength and may ask a scheme to justify its assessment. From 2013/14, it has taken a stricter view on the appropriateness of such guarantees for use as contingent assets, considering the effect on the guarantor of the sponsoring employer's insolvency.

Scheme-based levy

For 2013/14, the scheme-based levy is calculated as 0.0056% of a scheme's estimated PPF liabilities. At the time of writing, the PPF had announced that, subject to consultation, for 2014/15 the scheme-based levy would remain at 0.0056% of a scheme's estimated PPF liabilities.

PPF Administration Levy

This is charged to meet the costs of establishing and running the PPF (other than the cost of paying compensation). It is based on the number of members on the last day of the scheme year which ended before the beginning of the previous levy year, and from 2012/13 ranges from £3.20 per member (for schemes with 12 to 99 members) to £0.95 per member (for schemes with 10,000 or more members but subject to a minimum of £13,600). It is invoiced with the General Levy *(see Section 9)* and not with the Pension Protection Levy.

FINANCIAL ASSISTANCE SCHEME

The Financial Assistance Scheme (FAS) provides government-funded support for members of underfunded pension schemes which began to be wound up between 1 January 1997 and 22 December 2008 and in limited other circumstances, where the scheme is not eligible to enter the PPF but meets other eligibility criteria. In response to the requirement for there to be a 'statutory employer' *(see Section 8)* if a scheme is to enter the PPF, new regulations will enable certain pension schemes that do not have a 'statutory employer' to become qualifying schemes for FAS where the connection between the scheme and the last statutory employer was severed before 10 June 2011.

The FAS provides a top-up to a member's benefits so that the total benefits received by the member are broadly the same as those provided by the PPF. Members who would receive higher benefits from the scheme's assets under the statutory priority order maintain that higher level of benefit.

When the FAS was set up, it did not cover all schemes described above, and was restricted to pensioners and members near retirement. The level of FAS benefits has also been increased over time, as the original benefits were much lower than those provided by the PPF.

The FAS initially provided top-up payments, after the scheme had been wound up and members' benefits had been bought out with an insurance company. (Schemes dealt with in this way are now referred to as 'FAS1 schemes.) However, with effect from 26 September 2007, schemes eligible for FAS support have been prohibited from purchasing annuities where they have not already done so. Since April 2010, the government has started to take on the assets of these 'FAS2' schemes and make combined payments of scheme and FAS benefits to members. The PPF now manages the FAS and is aiming to have transferred all FAS1 schemes, and the majority of FAS2 schemes, to the government by 31 March 2014. FAS compensation is subject to an equalisation process in respect of GMPs, similar to that for the PPF *(see above)*.

FRAUD COMPENSATION FUND

An occupational pension scheme that has lost assets as a result of an offence (such as theft or fraud) committed after 6 April 1997 may be eligible for compensation if the employer is insolvent. The amount of any compensation payment is determined by the PPF, and is limited to the amount of any loss that cannot reasonably be recovered. Applications for compensation may be made by the trustees, administrators or scheme members.

The Fund is financed by a Fraud Compensation Levy, potentially payable by all schemes eligible for this compensation (a wider group than for the PPF). For the amount of the Fraud Compensation Levy *see Section 9*.

LIABILITY MANAGEMENT EXERCISES

In recent years, employers have looked at a number of ways of managing defined benefit liabilities. A common theme is the reduction of risk and, in some cases, possible improvement in the financial position of the scheme for funding or accounting purposes. Some of the approaches which have been considered are outlined below.

TRANSFER INCENTIVE EXERCISES

Under transfer incentive exercises (sometimes referred to as transfer inducement exercises), members are actively encouraged to transfer their defined benefits elsewhere, through the offer of an enhancement to the standard transfer value. The amount offered could be increased well above the transfer value to which individual members might normally be entitled under legislation *(see Section 13)* and is usually only available for a limited period. In the past, some offers included direct cash payments instead of, or in addition to, an enhancement to the transfer value itself. However, cash incentives are now less likely to be offered, following the publication of the industry Code of Good Practice on Incentive Exercises *(see below)*.

These exercises are typically proposed by sponsoring employers as a way of reducing exposure to investment and longevity risk. The employer might also benefit from an improvement in the scheme's funding position and/or their accounting figures. This is because the value placed on benefits for funding or accounting purposes can significantly exceed the statutory minimum transfer value, which is broadly equal to the expected cost of providing the benefit within the scheme. This means there is usually scope to pay a higher transfer value, sometimes significantly higher than the statutory minimum, whilst still remaining below the prudent reserves targeted for scheme funding. This enhanced transfer value may also be attractive to some members.

An industry Code of Good Practice on Incentive Exercises was published in June 2012, and is now a benchmark for such exercises. The Code is voluntary and has no legal standing, but there is an expectation that employers, trustees and their advisers will not look for creative ways to work around it. The Pensions Bill 2013 enables legislation to be passed that would prohibit transfer incentive exercises if a voluntary approach proves ineffective.

The key objectives of the Code are to help ensure that all incentive exercises enable members to make informed decisions and better choices, whilst permitting exercises and options to be offered in a responsible manner. The Code sets out seven principles which employers should follow:

(1) Cash incentives that are contingent on the member's decision to accept the offer are not permitted.

(2) Advice must be provided to members.

(3) Communications with members must be fair, clear, unbiased and straightforward.

(4) Records should be retained so that an audit trail can be maintained and examined in future.

(5) Members should have sufficient time to decide, with no undue pressure applied.

(6) Incentive exercises should only be offered to those over age 80 on an 'opt-in' basis. Special care should be taken when advising 'vulnerable clients'.

(7) All parties should be aware of their roles and responsibilities, and should act in good faith.

The Regulator has also published guidance on incentive exercises that sits alongside the Code. This highlights the role of trustees, and says that trustees should start from the presumption that such exercises are not in most members' best interests. It sets out five principles to which employers should adhere:

- the offer should be clear, fair and not misleading
- the offer should be open and transparent
- conflicts of interest should be identified and managed appropriately
- trustees should be involved from the start of the process, *and*
- independent financial advice should be made available and promoted to members.

The Code states that discussions are ongoing with the Regulator on how incentive exercises might be reported within its scheme return.

PENSION INCREASE CONVERSION EXERCISES

Under a pension increase conversion exercise:

- an offer could be made to existing pensioners to exchange future (non-statutory) increases on part of their pension for a higher immediate, but non-increasing, pension, *and/or*
- a new option could be introduced for non-pensioner members to exchange the (non-statutory) increases on part of their pension when it comes into payment for a higher, level pension at retirement.

These exercises are also typically proposed by sponsoring employers, as a way of reducing exposure to inflation and longevity risk. Depending on the terms of the conversion, the employer might also benefit from an improvement in the scheme's funding position and/or their accounting figures. Some members may find the immediate increase to their pension more attractive than the protection against the impact of inflation provided by future increases.

There can be significant legal issues depending on the terms of the conversion *(see comments under* Scheme Modifications *in Section 3)*. Some elements of pension will need to continue to be increased to meet statutory requirements (e.g. pension relating to post-5 April 1997 service) and scheme amendment powers would also need detailed consideration. There are also potential tax issues to consider as an increase in annual pension may trigger an annual allowance and/or lifetime allowance charge *(see Section 10)*.

The Code of Good Practice on Incentive Exercises *(described above)* also applies to pension increase conversion exercises in which an offer is made to existing pensioners. It does not apply to the introduction of new benefit options for non-pensioner members at retirement, although consideration of the Code is encouraged in such circumstances.

The principles of the Code *(as set out above)* apply equally to pension increase conversion exercises, except that if the exercise meets a 'value requirement', guidance (rather than advice) can be provided (with no need to give a recommendation). The 'value requirement' is met if the value of the additional pension granted is at least equal to the value of the future increases given up across the membership as a whole, and calculated on a basis consistent with the scheme's transfer value basis.

The Regulator's guidance outlined above is also applicable to pension increase conversion exercises.

TRANSFERS AT RETIREMENT

It is also possible to offer members the ability to transfer either all or part of their benefits out of the scheme at the point of retirement:

- Flexible retirement options allow members to transfer all of their benefits out of the scheme and purchase an annuity – typically in order to take a higher level of non-increasing pension (also known as a total pension increase exchange) or a pension that better suits their circumstances, such as health and marital status.
- Flexible drawdown – offering members a partial transfer, whilst retaining sufficient benefits in the scheme to meet the Minimum Income Requirement, can allow members to take advantage of the 'flexible drawdown' rules *(see Section 10)* in respect of the benefits transferred.

Under both options, the transferred liabilities – and associated risks – are removed from the scheme and, depending on the terms of the transfer, the funding position can also be improved.

OTHER WAYS OF AMENDING LIABILITIES

There are a number of other ways in which the level or nature of liabilities can potentially be controlled or amended. Examples include:

- ceasing future accrual *(see Section 21)*
- capping future increases in pensionable salary
- commutation of small pensions, *and*
- encouraging early retirements.

INVESTMENT SOLUTIONS TO MANAGE LIABILITIES

Various forms of liability management have been developed over recent years that focus on the investment of assets to manage liability risks. Two increasingly common options, liability-driven investment (LDI) and longevity swaps, are described below.

These two options can be combined to form a 'Synthetic' or 'DIY' buy-in – significantly reducing risk by effectively replicating the effect of a bulk annuity policy *(see Section 23)*. This may be at a lower cost and provide more flexibility than paying a one-off insurance premium.

Liability-driven investment

For many years, financial institutions – primarily investment banks and insurance companies – have provided protection against interest rate and inflation risks through the issue of 'swaps'. These require the purchaser to pay a series of cashflows (often fixed) over a period of time in return for a series of different cashflows that more closely reflect their own liabilities over that period (e.g. cashflows that increase in line with inflation).

For pension schemes, the use of these swaps is similar to investment in bonds. However, they can be structured much more flexibly to meet the estimated cashflows of a scheme, significantly reducing interest rate and inflation risks. Many pension schemes of all sizes are now making use of such strategies. However, the introduction of Consumer Price Indexation for some pension liabilities has added some complexity in this area as there is no developed market in CPI swaps.

Longevity swaps

Removing interest rate and inflation risks (e.g. by using swaps) leaves increasing longevity as the main risk remaining for a typical defined benefit pension scheme. 'Longevity swaps' can be used to reduce this risk. These allow the scheme to pay cashflows over a fixed period of time based on the expected longevity of a group of individuals, and receive cashflows over a period of time related to the actual longevity of that group. There are two main types of longevity swap for pension schemes:

(1) A *bespoke longevity swap* is based on the life expectancy of the actual members of a scheme. The provider agrees to meet the actual payments to members and the trustees pay a fixed schedule of payments to the provider. This removes the risk to the scheme from members living longer than expected. Until recently, bespoke hedges have only been available for large deals – typically large schemes with a high proportion of pensioner members. However, smaller deals have recently been transacted, indicating that the market is opening to medium-sized schemes. Bespoke longevity swaps now range from £400 million (Bentley Pension Fund, May 2013) to £3.2 billion (BAE Systems, February 2013), both in respect of pensioner liabilities only.

(2) An *index-based longevity swap* provides protection based on the general population rather than the scheme's membership. Therefore the trustees retain a risk that members' longevity is greater than that of the index population.

INSURANCE APPROACHES

In addition to the relatively recent innovations outlined above for managing a scheme's liabilities, insurance policies are often used to help protect the scheme from adverse death-in-service experience. Examples include:

- fully insuring the lump sum and, in some cases, the dependant's pension payable on death (although the insurance of dependants' pensions is becoming more expensive)
- insuring higher lump sums than those specified in the rules, to help offset the cost of any dependant's pension payable on death, *and*
- some form of partial insurance, for example insuring benefits in excess of a predetermined limit (e.g. benefits in excess of £1 million, or benefits in relation to a specific group of employees, such as an executive group).

Due to the very competitive insurance market, advantageous terms can often be secured which, in the long run, can be broadly equivalent to the actual underlying death claims experience for larger schemes. This can be an extremely cost-effective way to reduce risk to a pension scheme.

CEASING ACCRUAL

This section sets out the issues that employers and trustees need to consider before stopping any further benefits building up in a final salary arrangement.

In recent years, many final salary arrangements have been closed to new members, with new employees instead being offered membership of a defined contribution (DC) arrangement or a defined benefit (DB) arrangement with lower costs and/or risks to the employer (e.g. Career Average Revalued Earnings (CARE) or cash balance: *see Section 3*). Current employees had generally continued to build up final salary benefits with these new benefit arrangements typically applying to new joiners only.

However, it is becoming more common for employers to go further and stop final salary benefits for all their employees. This is referred to as 'ceasing accrual'. A scheme with no further benefits accruing is known as a 'frozen scheme'.

Ceasing accrual is not a simple exercise. There are a number of actions that have to be carried out by law, and others that employers may want to go through in order to maintain good employee relations. The process will require a significant amount of planning and involve a number of functions within the employer as well as other parties. Careful due diligence and good project management are important in order to identify potential issues and to set a realistic timeframe.

CONSIDERATIONS FOR EMPLOYERS

Business case

The main reason for ceasing accrual is usually to reduce the significant cost of pension benefits. However, employers may need to be able to justify the need for these cost savings to affected employees and other parties such as trade unions and the pension scheme trustees. These parties will often want to ensure that the employer has considered a range of possible options and be satisfied that ceasing accrual is a reasonable solution in the relevant circumstances. Many employers propose moving members to a DC scheme to achieve these cost savings. But it may be possible to arrive at similar cost savings by retaining a DB structure, and making a combination of changes to the benefits that are offered (e.g. moving from final salary to CARE, reducing the accrual rate or other benefit design changes, or increasing member contributions).

Immediate financial savings may not be the only consideration. Employers may want to reduce the risk that the costs turn out to be higher than expected over the longer term. This would involve passing some or all of the risk inherent in a pension arrangement on to members.

Employers may also want to ensure that all employees are treated equally irrespective of their length of service. If a final salary arrangement closed to new members a few years ago, the overall cost of a DC arrangement set up for new employees may have been designed to be similar to the cost of the final salary arrangement at that time. Now, because of increases in longevity and reduced gilt yields, the expected cost of benefits still accruing in the final salary arrangement is likely to be significantly higher than the cost of the DC scheme. This means that the overall employment cost of two employees in identical jobs and on otherwise identical terms can be significantly different depending on when they joined the employer. This can lead to claims of a 'two-tier workforce'.

In proposing changes, employers should always bear in mind that they have a legal obligation to act in good faith in dealings with employees.

Design of future benefits

Employers will need to consider what pension benefits they will offer to members to replace their final salary benefits. If an employer has already set up a new arrangement for employees who joined after a certain date, then it may want to move all employees to this arrangement. However, the employer will want to ensure that this arrangement continues to be appropriate.

In many cases, employees are moved into a DC arrangement. However, this can be seen as moving from one extreme to the other (with the member, rather than the employer, bearing all the risks). Some employers may consider that sharing risks to some extent is a more desirable outcome. The Government is seeking to encourage such an approach via its 'Defined Ambition' proposals *(see Section 3)*.

The accounting impact of both ceasing accrual in the DB arrangement, and the new benefit structure, will need to be considered *(see Section 25)*. The savings in cash terms are unlikely to be the same as the savings in accounting terms, and in some cases there could actually be an adverse effect on the employer's profit and loss account.

There are a number of other issues in changing benefit structures, particularly if moving from final salary to DC:

- employers should consider whether the proposed new arrangement will meet the minimum requirements for auto-enrolment *(see Section 5)*

- whether the new arrangement should be under the same trust as the final salary arrangement: this approach can involve complex issues including implications for funding cross-subsidies, contracting out and winding up

- benefits payable on death or ill health cannot be funded in a DC arrangement in the same way that they can in a DB arrangement: advice on appropriate insurance arrangements will be needed and the costs should be considered

- final salary arrangements have more flexibility to provide extra benefits in cases of redundancy and other workforce management exercises: DC arrangements are less flexible, and employers will need to consider how to provide such benefits, particularly if these are contractual entitlements

- the investment options, including the default investment option, will need to be carefully designed, monitored and communicated

- there are additional considerations for higher earners:
  - whether the new arrangement will provide appropriate remuneration for senior employees or whether additional benefits need to be provided through a separate arrangement (bearing in mind the disguised remuneration requirements introduced in April 2011 – *see Section 11*), *and*
  - the tax implications for those who may be affected by the reductions in the Annual Allowance from April 2011 and the Lifetime Allowance from April 2012 and similarly in relation to the further reductions in the Annual and Lifetime Allowances from April 2014 *(see Section 10)*. Setting up a new arrangement may in itself cause members to lose protection and provision of life cover may impact on exemptions from the Annual Allowance. This may also create additional administration for the scheme.

Design of accrued benefits

There may also be various ways in which active members' benefits in respect of past service can be calculated. For example, depending on scheme rules, the employer may have the following options for increasing pension between date of implementation and retirement:

- statutory minimum increases in line with leaving service benefits
- increases in line with price inflation, *or*
- maintaining full salary linking.

This is also an area in which legal advice is particularly important – *see below*.

If the scheme is contracted-out immediately before benefit accrual ceases, contracting-out legislation requires that a 'Protection Rule' is added to the scheme rules to ensure that any contracted-out benefits retained within the scheme (GMPs and post-1997 contracted-out rights) are protected at normal pension age and on death from being franked against benefits accrued during periods of non-contracted-out pensionable service. Separate anti-franking legislation requires GMPs to be protected at and after the age at which GMP becomes payable (65 for men and 60 for women), and possibly where service continues in the same scheme after contracting out ceases. Based on the current proposals in the Pensions Bill on abolition of contracting out from April 2016 *(see Section 2)*, these requirements may partly fall away for schemes that are forced to cease contracting out at that time.

Consultation and communication with employees

Ceasing accrual is a 'listed change' under the Pensions Act 2004 consultation requirements *(see Section 3)*. Employers will therefore have to carry out a 60 day consultation with affected members or their representatives and consider any representations made during the consultation before they can implement any changes. This process could take significantly longer than 60 days particularly if member representative groups need to be set up.

Many employers will want to do more than the legal minimum, and put in place a detailed communication strategy to ensure members understand the reasons for change, the effect on their final salary benefits built up to date, and the likely benefits they will receive from the new arrangement. For many members, the headline is likely to be a significant reduction in their projected benefits at retirement. However the detailed implications will affect individual members in different ways.

In the case of a new DC arrangement, employers may wish to encourage former DB members to take more responsibility than they have in the past for ensuring their benefits will meet their needs at retirement. This is likely to involve taking decisions relating to the level of contributions paid and their investment options. Employers may want to provide a range of information to employees about this, reflecting the level of financial literacy of the workforce.

Legal issues

There are a number of areas where employers will need to take legal advice.

Members' employment contracts will need to be reviewed. This is to check how membership of the pension scheme is described. For example, some contracts give the right to membership of a final salary pension scheme. Some contracts may also contain individual pension promises.

The scheme's trust deed and rules should be consulted and may need amendment. They should be checked to ensure that the scheme does not restrict the types of amendment that can be made, and to confirm which employers will remain liable for future contributions, either under the scheme rules or as 'statutory employers' *(see Section 8)*. If trustee consent is required for any amendment, the trustees may see this as an opportunity for negotiation *(see below)*.

One specific issue may arise if the employer wishes to break the link to final salary for accrued benefits. Case law has suggested that the wording of some trust deeds and rules may require members' benefits to be calculated by reference to their salary when they leave or retire from the employer, and in the case of *Bradbury v BBC (see Section 29)* it was suggested that attempting to break this link is inconsistent with the employer's 'implied duties', for example the duty of good faith contained in any contract of employment (although this suggestion has not yet been resolved by the courts). In such cases it would not be possible to calculate benefits using the member's salary at the date accrual ceases in the scheme. This may reduce the cost savings the employer would otherwise make.

In some cases, amending the scheme rules or members leaving the scheme as a result of ceasing accrual may trigger a wind-up *(see Section 22)* or a debt on the employer *(see Section 24)*. This could have significant financial implications, and the employer will usually want to ensure that the changes are carried out in such a way as to avoid this.

Contracting out

If the current arrangement is contracted out of S2P but the new arrangement is not, the scheme employer will need to carry out the necessary actions in order to cease to contract out *(see Section 2)*. In particular, this requires the employer to give members, trustees and trade unions at least one month's notice of the intention to cease contracting out (or three months if there are trade unions involved who do not agree to a shorter period). Such a notice must include certain prescribed items of information.

Other protections for employees

There are additional considerations if the scheme has any ex-public sector workers, or if the employer might consider bidding for public sector outsourcing contracts in the future. Employers may be required to offer a certain level of DB pensions to ex-public sector workers. It is not always easy to identify ex-public sector workers, particularly if they have joined the scheme as a result of subsequent transactions between private sector companies.

Some rights (for example redundancy or early retirement enhancements) may need to be protected by the new employer. This applies particularly for former public sector workers but employers who have taken on private sector employees may also find that they need to protect such benefits and may seek indemnities from the seller.

CONSIDERATIONS FOR TRUSTEES

Trustees' duty

The conventionally accepted view is that trustees' primary duty is to safeguard accrued rights, and that it is the employer's role to decide the basis of pension benefits it wishes to provide to its employees for future service.

However, as well as protecting members' existing benefits, trustees will want to satisfy themselves that the employer's business case for any proposal to cease accrual is properly reasoned, the proposals are workable in practice, and that they do not breach any legal obligations. Trustees should also bear in mind that they need to consider the interests of all members of the scheme, not just the active members who will be directly affected by the ceasing of future accrual.

As noted above, if trustee consent is required in order to amend the scheme to allow the ceasing of future accrual, the trustees may use this as an opportunity for negotiation with the employer over funding, security of benefits, and even benefits themselves. The trustees may need to take legal advice, particularly where their trust deed and rules provides them with a power to veto changes to future benefits.

Safeguarding accrued rights

The issue of ceasing accrual may be raised during the valuation process *(see Section 17)*. The scheme funding regulations allow trustees to modify future accrual if it appears to them that it is not otherwise possible to obtain the employer's agreement. Alternatively, the issue may be raised by the employer during funding negotiations.

The trustees will need to consider whether a proposal to cease accrual and the background to such a proposal, reflects a weakening in the employer's covenant – its ability and willingness to continue to fund the scheme *(see Section 17)*. This could have implications for the level of technical provisions the trustees consider necessary to safeguard accrued rights.

Even if the proposal is not made as part of the valuation process, the trustees will need to consider the effect of ceasing accrual on the funding position of the scheme *(see Section 17)*. This will include considering whether the current funding plan remains appropriate. The Trustees should also confirm which employers will remain liable for future contributions, either under the scheme rules or as 'statutory employers' *(see Section 8)*.

Trustees and employers are likely to pay closer attention to the risks remaining in the scheme, and look for ways to manage these *(see Section 20)*. This may include buying out portions of the liabilities over time *(see Section 23)*. Ceasing accrual will also require ongoing review of cashflow requirements, and the disinvestment of assets, as the proportion of the scheme's liabilities that relates to pension in payment rises.

Any changes to the adopted funding principles are likely to require a review of actuarial factors, such as commutation and early retirement terms, as well as transfer value assumptions. The employer's consent may be required to change some factors.

Benefit changes

As part of any negotiation with the employer, trustees may decide it is appropriate to suggest alternative future benefits. As the employer's proposals are likely to be aimed at cutting costs, the scope for alternative approaches may be limited. Trade unions and representations from members may also suggest approaches which partially offset the ending of accrual.

Administration and communication

If the new pension arrangement is being set up under the same trust, the trustees will need to consider how the administration of two separate benefit structures for the same members will work, and ensure that administration systems can cope with both the new benefits and the past service benefits (including consideration of any residual contracting-out requirements). Trustees will need training to understand their responsibilities and the features of the new benefits with which they are not familiar.

Trustees may want to be involved in the employer's communication process, to ensure that the employer is explaining the issues clearly and properly. Once any changes have been implemented, trustees may want to review how they communicate with members more generally.

SCHEME CLOSURE AND WIND-UP

The winding up of occupational pension schemes can raise complex legal and practical issues. The process can take several years, although legislation exists that is intended to speed it up. The trustees of a scheme that is being wound up need to understand their continuing responsibilities under the relevant provisions of the trust deed and rules. It is important for the trustees to take legal and actuarial advice both before wind-up commences and throughout the wind-up period.

Commencement of wind-up

The events that can trigger wind-up are normally set out in the scheme trust deed and rules. These can include the employer ceasing to contribute (or not being prepared to contribute at a rate the trustees consider adequate for funding the scheme), or becoming insolvent. However, the scheme rules may allow the alternative of postponing wind-up, and instead continuing to operate on a 'frozen scheme' basis with no further accrual of benefits. The trustees have an overriding power under the Pensions Act 1995 to choose to follow this route if the employer has gone into liquidation and they consider it appropriate. Continuing as a frozen scheme would be subject to neither the Pensions Regulator nor, if the employer is insolvent and a Pension Protection Fund (PPF) assessment period (*see Section 19*) has been completed, the PPF requiring the scheme to be wound up. During a PPF assessment period, various restrictions apply, including that benefit payments must be restricted to PPF compensation levels.

It is important for the date on which wind-up is treated as having commenced to be clearly identified and recorded. This can vary depending on the circumstances, but for most purposes can be taken as the earliest date when there are no members in pensionable service and either (i) the scheme rules provide that wind-up should commence or (ii) the power to wind up is exercised by the trustees (or by any other person or body, such as the Pensions Regulator or a court, having the authority to do so).

Winding-up procedure

Trustees of an underfunded occupational scheme that enters wind-up during a recovery period (*see Section 17*) must as soon as practicable prepare a 'winding-up procedure'. This procedure includes details of the action that will be taken to establish the liabilities and the method that will be used to discharge them, an indication of any accrued rights or benefits that are likely to be affected by a reduction in actuarial value, and an estimate of the amount of time that will be taken to complete these steps. The procedure must be submitted to the Pensions Regulator.

Schemes in wind-up are generally exempt from the scheme funding requirements (*see Section 17*).

Appointment of an independent trustee and role of the Pensions Regulator

If the employer has become insolvent, the insolvency practitioner (or, if applicable, official receiver) must notify the Pensions Regulator. The Regulator then has the power to appoint an independent trustee although it does not have to do this (e.g. if one has already been appointed).

Subject to various safeguards relating to members' rights, the Regulator may modify a scheme with a view to ensuring that it is properly wound up following an application from the trustees (which must include specified information and documents). The Regulator may also order a scheme to be wound up, or give legally binding directions to trustees, administrators and others if it considers that these are necessary to speed up the process. In June 2008, the Regulator, the PPF and the Department for Work and Pensions (DWP) (on behalf of the Financial Assistance Scheme) published a joint statement saying that the important parts of a wind-up should generally be completed within a two-year period. The Regulator also maintains guidance, last updated in October 2012, that sets out examples of good practice in order to help schemes through the winding-up process.

Debt on the employer

Where a defined benefit scheme has insufficient assets to cover the scheme liabilities, the employer may have a legal obligation to make up the shortfall. For wind-ups starting on or after 15 February 2005, the liabilities for this purpose must be based on an estimate of the actual cost of buying out benefits and meeting the expenses of wind-up.

If the wind-up was triggered by an 'insolvency event' of the sponsoring employer, any 'debt on the employer' must be treated by the trustees as having arisen immediately before this occurred. Otherwise, the debt can be treated by the trustees as having arisen at *any* time after the commencement of wind-up and before the employer goes into liquidation.

The Regulator has highlighted the importance of trustees being able to identify a scheme's statutory employer(s) who would be liable for any such debt *(see Section 8)*.

Discharging scheme liabilities

In order to wind up a scheme, its assets must be applied to discharge its liabilities. This can be done by transfer to another occupational scheme or to personal pensions, by purchasing insurance company annuities *(see Section 23)*, by assigning existing annuity contracts to members or, in certain cases where the entitlement is small, by the payment of a 'winding-up lump sum' *(see Section 10)*.

Priority order

Because of the possibility that the assets will be insufficient to fully discharge all liabilities in this way, scheme rules normally contain a 'priority order' setting out the order in which the different liability classes (e.g. pensions already in payment, accrued pensions of active members) are to be dealt with. However, the Pensions Act 1995 introduced a statutory priority order with effect from 6 April 1997, modified by subsequent legislation, which generally overrides 'scheme-specific' priority orders. For the purpose of assigning them to appropriate priority classes, scheme liabilities are normally treated as having 'crystallised' according to their status at the date when wind-up commenced.

For wind-ups commencing on or after 6 April 2005, the statutory priority order is as follows:

(1) benefits under certain contracts of insurance

(2) benefits corresponding to those that would be provided if the scheme entered the PPF *(see Section 19)*

(3) benefits from AVCs, to the extent that these are not included in the categories above

(4) all other liabilities.

Any money purchase assets and liabilities are generally excluded from the above calculations. Such benefits would normally be expected to have priority over non-money purchase benefits, but this is dependent on the scheme rules. The classification of certain benefits as money purchase or non-money purchase has also been the subject of much legal debate; some clarification will be provided by changes (expected to come into force on 6 April 2014) made by the Pensions Act 2011 to the legislative definition of money purchase benefits.

The liabilities set out in the statutory priority order must be valued by the scheme actuary using a specified basis. If the wind-up commenced on or after 15 February 2005, the basis used is the actual cost of securing the benefits, for example by means of an annuity buy-out. For earlier wind-ups, the basis used may differ, depending on when the wind-up commenced and whether or not the employer was insolvent.

Deficiency

Where the full buy-out debt basis *(see above)* does not apply, or such a debt cannot be collected, the assets of the scheme may be insufficient to discharge all of the scheme's liabilities. In this event, the benefits provided for the lowest priority class(es) will have to be cut back accordingly. Legislation now allows schemes in wind-up to reduce pensions already in payment, due to underfunding, without giving rise to unauthorised payments charges *(see Section 10)*.

The PPF *(see Section 19)* was established with effect from 6 April 2005. It provides some protection for eligible schemes with employers that become insolvent on or after that date. The Financial Assistance Scheme *(see Section 19)* was established to provide some support for workers who have lost pensions through underfunding in certain schemes that went into wind-up after 1996 and are not covered by the PPF.

Surplus

If a surplus of assets remains after all of the scheme liabilities have been discharged, this must also be dealt with in accordance with the scheme rules and relevant legislative requirements. As well as providing for the augmentation of benefits, either at the sole discretion of the trustees, or in consultation with (or with the consent of) the employer, there may be provision for payment of a refund to the employer. Before this can be done, a number of requirements under the Pensions Act 1995 (as amended by the 2004 Act) must be satisfied. These requirements include sending written notices to members inviting them to make representations in respect of the proposal.

Disclosure and reporting requirements

A notice must be given to members within one month of the commencement of wind-up, followed by annual progress reports. For defined benefit schemes, members must also be provided with details of the trustees' proposals for discharging liabilities before they are implemented. In all cases, once the assets have been applied to provide benefits, members must be given full details within three months.

Periodic progress reports must also be given to the Pensions Regulator. Where wind-up commenced between 1 April 2003 and 30 September 2007, the first such report had to be filed within three months of the third anniversary of commencement of wind-up. Where wind-up commences on or after 1 October 2007, the report must be filed within three months of the second anniversary of the commencement of wind-up. *(See also Section 14.)*

Scheme operation during wind-up

The process of winding up can take several years. During this period, no new members will be admitted and no further benefits will accrue. The trustees may pay provisional benefits to members on retirement, with final benefits to be confirmed when winding up is complete. DWP legislation specifically provides for benefits paid during the winding-up period to be reduced in line with what the priority order will ultimately require *(see above)*. Trustees should also review the terms for member options and the scheme's investment strategy to ensure they remain appropriate, particularly if the employer has become insolvent. It is possible to apply to the Pensions Regulator for permission to delay paying cash equivalent transfer values.

Operating as a frozen scheme

Schemes also sometimes operate as 'frozen schemes' (with no further accrual of benefits) *without* having started a winding-up process. For example, this may happen where a scheme's sponsoring employer has decided to cease accrual *(see Section 21)* but can still fund the scheme. Alternatively, if the sponsoring employer has become insolvent but the scheme is too well funded to be taken on by the PPF *(see Section 19)*, it may be unable to wind up and purchase insurance company annuities, perhaps because it is too large.

BULK ANNUITIES

Under a bulk annuity contract, a pension scheme pays a premium to an insurer and the insurer writes annuities in respect of a number of the scheme's members. In *Section 22*, scheme closure and wind-up is described. It is in such situations that schemes typically enter into bulk annuity contracts – as a means of discharging liabilities prior to wind-up. However, in recent years the bulk annuity market has expanded to offer more products to ongoing schemes.

Increased competition in the bulk annuity market led to the development of options such as partial buy-outs and 'buy-ins'. Prices have fluctuated over time, making the timing of a transaction significant. Many schemes have carried out preparatory work, such as data cleansing, so that they are well placed to transact when financial conditions are favourable.

These developments have arisen as a result of employers becoming increasingly sensitive to the risks associated with defined benefit schemes, the potential impact on their financial statements *(see Section 25)* and the increasing maturity of these arrangements. There is increasing focus on managing these risks, including interest rate, inflation and longevity risks. *Section 20 outlines options that may be alternatives to or precursors of bulk annuity exercises.*

As more final salary schemes cease accrual *(see Section 21)*, liability transfer becomes a long-term objective for many, often forming part of a 'flight-plan' strategy *(see Section 17)*. The capacity of the bulk annuity market is a factor in the number of schemes that can transact, as it is currently a small fraction of the total liabilities in defined benefit pension schemes. The volume of business written since 2007 has shown a perceivable trend of around £5–10 billion a year, which compares with overall scheme liabilities of around £1,500 billion.

BUY-OUT OPTIONS

The following describes buy-out options available for pension schemes. Under the broad descriptions below there are a number of products that continue to be developed to give schemes more flexibility.

Full buy-out

In the past, full buy-out was associated with the wind-up of a pension scheme. Annuities would be purchased from an insurance company for current pensioners and deferred annuities for other members.

The completion of a wind-up after securing a bulk annuity can take a significant time, as historic issues, such as incomplete data and any inadequacies in past equalisation measures *(see Section 15)*, need to be resolved.

Once these issues have been addressed, a final balancing premium is normally payable to secure the confirmed benefits under the bulk annuity, and the liabilities are discharged by the scheme – the buy-out process results in individual annuities being purchased in members' names. This allows employers to achieve a 'clean break' from their pension schemes.

Buy-out products with full risk transfer have also been used since 2007, which expedite the transfer of liability from the sponsoring employer. The insurer takes on additional liabilities, which may include wind-up costs, GMP equalisation, trustee indemnification and potential data changes, so that the employer's financial exposure to the scheme can cease on the day of the bulk annuity transaction. The additional cover carries an additional insurance premium, and is only available after a due diligence exercise on the scheme has been conducted by the insurer's advisers. In some cases, the transaction has included a replacement of the scheme sponsor, to aid the clean break from the original employer.

Partial buy-out

A partial buy-out allows for the discharge of some of the liabilities of a pension scheme. As with a full buy-out, annuity policies are purchased from an insurance company in the names of scheme members. They become policyholders of the insurer, ceasing to be members of the scheme. Again, there may be a significant period between the transaction and the finalisation of the insured benefits during which issues such as incomplete data have to be resolved.

A partial buy-out may be difficult to achieve if the rules of a scheme do not give an adequate discharge of liabilities where the scheme is not winding up, and so a buy-in *(see below)* can be a more practical option.

Also, the trustees need to consider the security of all members' benefits. Buying out the liabilities of current pensioners (for example) will generally increase the security of those benefits. Trustees will need to ensure that this is not to the detriment of non-pensioners.

Buy-in

As an alternative to buy-outs, an increasing number of pension schemes have used 'buy-ins' to insure some of their liabilities. Typically, pensioner liabilities are insured as the cost relative to the value of the liabilities for scheme funding *(see Section 17)* tends to be much lower than for other members, and there are fewer operational implications.

The trustees purchase an insurance policy which is intended to match a specific part of the scheme's liabilities closely, but not necessarily exactly. For example, where there are issues with data quality or where discretionary pension increases may be given, the buy-in policy may not exactly match the scheme's liabilities, but the contract may include scope to amend the benefits covered over time. There are many variations in contract terms, for example, to phase insurance premiums over time, or to add cover for future retirees.

Such transactions present fewer legal obstacles. The membership of the scheme is not affected – the individuals remain scheme members and the liability to pay their benefits remains with the scheme's trustees. The insurance policy can be regarded as an investment, which matches the corresponding liabilities more closely than alternative assets.

A buy-in may be used as a step towards full or partial buy-out at a later date.

Buy-in with additional security

Bulk annuity products are subject to the solvency and monitoring regime applicable to insurance companies, and are protected under the Financial Services Compensation Scheme *(see Section 26)*. Some larger buy-ins have included a bespoke layer of additional security, such as collateralisation, or the depositing in a ring-fenced account of backing assets that become accessible to the pension scheme in the event of certain trigger events occurring, such as a downgrade of the insurer.

Medically underwritten bulk annuities

Medically underwritten bulk annuities are priced using information provided by members regarding their health as well as the information to which a pension scheme normally has access. This can refine and, in some cases, lower the pricing of longevity risk. These annuities have been available from some providers since 2012.

Non-insured buy-out

Alternative models have been structured that allow the transfer of pension liabilities and assets by corporate transaction, which may or may not be followed by full buy-out. For example, a company (perhaps the parent company of an insurer) may take on an organisation's pension liabilities by purchasing that organisation, retaining the pension scheme and selling on the majority of the purchased entity.

However, the Pensions Act 2008 increased the Regulator's power to appoint trustees, and to issue Contribution Notices and Financial Support Directions where there is a materially detrimental effect on the security of members' benefits *(see Section 9)*. The government stated that the new powers were particularly aimed at non-insured buy-outs to ensure that members are protected in a changing environment without inhibiting innovation.

This form of buy-out has not occurred subsequently, although some organisations have considered other means to transfer liabilities within the occupational pensions (as opposed to insurance) regulatory environment, with a particular focus on their acceptability to trustees.

Synthetic buy-in

'Synthetic' or 'DIY' buy-ins can be constructed by the trustees or obtained as a bespoke product, arranged by an investment bank. These use a combination of swap contracts, including a longevity swap, to provide the same close liability matching that would be achieved with an annuity contract. This may be an attractive option for very large schemes in particular, given the scope to surrender or alter such investments over time, and the more gradual change in investment strategy that may be adopted under this approach. For smaller schemes, the substantial effort involved in constructing (and then maintaining) a portfolio of assets to closely match liabilities, and the possible inefficiencies in running a pension scheme indefinitely as it matures and shrinks, can make annuities more attractive. *Section 20 provides further detail on investment solutions to manage liabilities.*

SALES, PURCHASES & CORPORATE ACTIVITY

The pension aspects of corporate sales and acquisitions require careful consideration, particularly where defined benefit schemes are involved. All parties will need to take expert legal and actuarial advice.

PRICING PENSIONS IN THE DEAL

The cost of pension provision will have a significant impact on the pricing of most deals.

Where manpower represents a material business cost and the deal is priced on the basis of future income, the purchaser should consider the future pension costs, which might be different from the equivalent costs for the vendor.

If the purchaser is taking on accrued defined benefit pension liabilities, for example by acquiring an entire pension scheme or accepting a 'bulk transfer' *(see below)*, actuarial advice will be required on the net cost to the purchaser. The net cost could be material and will need to be considered as part of pricing the offer.

The cost of any debt on the employer may also have to be allowed for *(see below)* although it is not uncommon to seek an indemnity for any such debt.

ACQUISITION OF WHOLE SCHEME

If the company being acquired has its own pension scheme and this will be acquired as part of the deal, then the scheme liabilities and funding will need to be carefully examined. The current financial position on the accounting basis is unlikely to be a suitable basis for pricing purposes in isolation.

The ongoing costs of benefits, and any possible changes in the trustees' funding or investment strategies as a result of the sale or of the subsequent restructuring, should be considered. These may have a substantial impact on the future profitability, and even perhaps viability, of the business.

BULK TRANSFER ARRANGEMENTS

If the transferring employees are members of the vendor's group scheme (and the scheme will be retained by the vendor), the employees may simply become deferred pensioners in the vendor's scheme but it is often desirable, in the interest of good employee relations, for a 'bulk transfer' to be arranged. The risks associated with such a transfer need to be compared against its benefits.

Under a bulk transfer, employees exchange their accrued benefits in the vendor's scheme for benefits in the purchaser's scheme and a transfer payment is made. In some circumstances there may exist a legal or contractual obligation to arrange a bulk transfer. The bulk transfer terms are a matter of commercial negotiation between the purchaser and the vendor. These will normally be set out in the 'pensions clause' of (or 'schedule' to) the legal agreement governing the transaction. This agreement may be accompanied by a side letter between the actuaries advising both parties, setting out the actuarial basis in detail. The amount transferred may not be equal to the value placed on the liabilities for pricing purposes and so there might also need to be a pricing adjustment.

As well as specifying the basis for calculating the amount of the bulk transfer payment, the pensions clause will usually also specify the terms for the benefits in the new scheme, the treatment of any excess or shortfall in the trustee transfer payment *(see* Trustee considerations, *below)*, the communications, and the transfer process.

Trustee considerations

The commercially agreed bulk transfer terms will not normally be binding on the trustees of the vendor's scheme. The trustees will need to consider, having regard to their Trust Deed and Rules and the interests of *all* scheme members and beneficiaries, whether it is appropriate to pay a bulk transfer and, if so, the basis on which it should be calculated. If they decide that the payment should be calculated on a basis different to the commercial bulk transfer terms, then the shortfall or excess payment clause (if any) in the sale agreement may be triggered between the vendor and purchaser.

Similarly, the trustees of the purchaser's scheme are not obliged to accept the proposed bulk transfer payment or provide the commercially agreed level of benefits, and may seek additional funding from the purchaser before complying.

Member consent or actuarial certificate

For a bulk transfer to be paid from the vendor's scheme, *either* the transfer must be restricted to only those members who give their consent, *or* the trustees may decide that a transfer without consent is appropriate in which case they will need to obtain a certificate from their scheme actuary confirming that the past service benefits of each transferring member will be 'broadly no less favourable' after the transfer.

Where individual consents are sought, the trustees will need to ensure that members are provided with the information necessary to understand all of the options open to them and make an informed choice. Similarly, where a 'without-consent' transfer is anticipated, the members must be provided with appropriate information on the proposed transfer.

EMPLOYER COVENANT

The sale, or any subsequent transfer of assets, could have a material impact on the employer covenant provided to the scheme.

Whether or not a bulk transfer of pension assets and liabilities takes place, both the purchaser's and the vendor's scheme trustees will need to consider the impact on their employer's covenant and the subsequent impact on their scheme. They may request additional funding in mitigation and/or review the investment and funding strategies if they believe the impact is detrimental.

The impact on security can be complex and so the trustees may seek specialist covenant, legal and actuarial advice.

POTENTIAL 'DEBT ON EMPLOYER'

If the sale results in a participating employer ceasing to have any active members in the scheme, then a section 75 debt on the employer would be triggered. This might arise at the time of the sale, or at the end of a participation period, or on any subsequent restructuring. The debt can be significant and is calculated on a similar approach to that which applies on a wind-up *(see Section 22)*.

The debt arises in respect of the benefits accrued whilst in service with the employer and covers both the current and the ex-employees. The debt also includes a proportion relating to any 'orphan' members. Orphan members are current or deferred pensioners with no currently participating employer. Depending on the previous corporate activity of the group, these orphan members can represent a high percentage of the total membership and therefore can substantially increase the debt for which a participating employer is liable.

The debt is payable by the participating employer involved and so can effectively fall to either the purchaser or the vendor depending on the terms of the deal. If the purchaser acquires one or more whole companies, then the debt would fall to the purchaser but the purchaser is likely to seek either a price reduction or an indemnity from the vendor. If business assets are being sold and a shell company is being retained by the vendor, and this shell ceases to have eligible active employees, then a debt effectively falls to the vendor.

There are a number of ways in which the level of a debt might be reduced. These include:

- a Scheme Apportionment Arrangement – the company and trustees can agree that some or all of the debt is reapportioned to other participating employers
- a Withdrawal Arrangement – the trustees can agree that the ceasing employer pays a lower amount, at least equal to its share of any deficit relative to technical provisions *(see Section 17)*, and that a contingent guarantor will stand behind the remaining debt
- an Approved Withdrawal Arrangement – this is similar to a Withdrawal Arrangement but Regulator approval is required and applies when the proposed immediate payment is less than the employer's share of the technical provisions deficit
- a Flexible Apportionment Arrangement allows the company to agree with the trustees to apportion its whole pension liability to one or more other participating employers without triggering a section 75 debt, *or*
- transferring the accrued liabilities to the purchaser's scheme – this can reduce the debt, potentially down to nil, although the impact depends heavily on the terms of the transfer and the position of the vendor's scheme.

THE PENSIONS REGULATOR, MORAL HAZARD AND CLEARANCE

The Pensions Regulator can impact on a transaction through the 'moral hazard' provisions. These are designed to prevent employers avoiding their obligations and give the Pensions Regulator sweeping powers, including the power to issue Contribution Notices, Financial Support Directions and Restoration Orders *(see also Section 9)*. For example, a Contribution Notice can be issued if the effect of an act, regardless of the employer's intent, is materially detrimental to the security of members' benefits. Contribution Notices may be issued in relation to a variety of events, including (but not limited to) sale or acquisition of a business, group restructuring and capital restructuring. A statutory defence prevents the Regulator acting in this way where the employer reasonably concluded that there was no material detriment and certain other conditions are met. The Regulator's powers are not limited to the current employer of the scheme.

A company or individual can avoid the risk of the Regulator later taking action by applying for clearance. Once given, clearance is binding on the Regulator unless the actual circumstances were different from those disclosed at the time.

The Regulator has issued guidance on clearance applications and this can be found at *www.thepensionsregulator.gov.uk*. The guidance includes:

- a pension scheme in deficit should be treated like any other material creditor
- the Regulator wishes to know about all events having a materially detrimental effect on a pension scheme's ability to meet liabilities, *and*
- trustees and employers should work together in relation to potentially detrimental events, communicating and sharing appropriate information.

The 'notifiable events' framework also requires the trustees of an underfunded scheme to notify the Regulator if a bulk or individual transfer payment exceeding £1.5 million (or, if lower, 5% of scheme assets) is made.

TUPE

The TUPE requirements protect the terms and conditions relating to future benefits for employees who are transferred as part of a deal. (Accrued pension rights are also protected under preservation legislation.)

Transferring employees currently entitled to occupational scheme benefits have to be provided with pension benefits by the new employer. Where the new employer offers defined contribution benefits (including a stakeholder scheme) it must match the employee's contributions, up to a maximum of 6% of basic pay. This requirement is expected to be amended in 2014, for consistency with the automatic enrolment provisions, to allow the new employer to choose instead to match the old employer's contributions.

If the new employer offers a defined benefit scheme, it must *either*:

- satisfy the Reference Scheme Test (whether or not it is contracted-out), *or*
- provide for members to be entitled to benefits of a value equal to, or more than, the sum of 6% of pensionable pay for each year of employment and the total amount of contributions paid by the member

Transferring employees with rights to pension schemes established under contract (such as group personal pension or stakeholder arrangements) may also have their current pension rights preserved by TUPE, depending on the terms of their contracts.

In some circumstances, early retirement and redundancy terms and benefits in respect of accrued service may be preserved by TUPE requirements. Actuarial and legal advice should be taken on the issue and, in general, purchasers should seek appropriate indemnities against hidden liability.

PENSION COSTS IN COMPANY ACCOUNTS

Companies must show the cost of pension benefits in their accounts in accordance with relevant accounting standards. In the UK, International Accounting Standard IAS 19 is mandatory for listed companies' consolidated group accounts. Individual company accounts and the consolidated group accounts of unlisted companies may use either IAS 19 or the UK standard, FRS17. This section describes the requirements of both standards.

Additional disclosure requirements also apply to benefits, including pensions, paid to company directors. These are also summarised below.

ACCOUNTING FOR PENSION COSTS UNDER FRS 17

Coverage

FRS 17 covers companies registered in the UK or in the Republic of Ireland, and their subsidiaries. It covers all retirement benefits (including medical care during retirement) that the employer is committed to providing, wherever they arise world-wide. Reporting entities applying the Financial Reporting Standard for Smaller Entities (FRSSE) are exempt from FRS 17, although FRSSE itself imposes requirements that are essentially a simplified version of FRS 17.

A new standard, FRS 102 (Section 28), will replace FRS 17 from 1 January 2015, with reporting requirements similar to IAS 19. Further details are set out below.

Application to Multi-employer Schemes

Where a number of companies participate in a multi-employer DB scheme, individual companies may not be able to identify 'their' assets and liabilities, or may be obliged only to contribute for benefits currently being earned. In such cases, the individual companies should account for the scheme on a cash basis (cost equals contributions paid), as in DC schemes, but must make appropriate disclosures. However, for the purposes of group accounts, multi-employer schemes are accounted for on a DB basis.

A: DEFINED CONTRIBUTION SCHEMES

Summary

For DC schemes, the charge against profits must be the amount of contributions due in respect of the accounting period.

A DC scheme is defined as one 'into which an employer pays regular contributions fixed as an amount or as a percentage of pay' without a 'legal or constructive obligation to pay further contributions if the scheme does not have sufficient assets to pay all employee benefits relating to employee service in the current and prior periods'. A scheme may be taken to be a DC scheme for the purposes of this definition, even where salary-related death-in-service benefits are provided.

Disclosure

The following disclosures should be made:

- the nature of the scheme (i.e. defined contribution; funded or unfunded

- the pension cost charge for the period, *and*
- any outstanding or prepaid contributions at the balance sheet date.

B: DEFINED BENEFIT SCHEMES

Overview

A DB scheme is defined as a 'pension or other retirement benefit scheme other than a defined contribution scheme'. Financial statements should reflect pension assets and liabilities, measured at fair values. Retirement benefit-related operating costs, financing costs and any other changes in value of assets and scheme liabilities should be recognised in the period in which the benefit is earned or in which they arise, with no smoothing or spreading.

Benefits to Value

Benefits promised under the formal terms of the scheme must be valued. Benefits should be attributed to periods of service according to the scheme's benefit formula, except that uniform accrual should be assumed where the benefit formula is rear-end loaded.

Discretionary benefits are to be included only where the employer has a constructive obligation to provide them. Favourable early retirement terms should be reflected where there is an established practice of allowing retirement at the employee's request on these terms. No allowance should be made for future retirements at the employer's initiative.

Actuarial Assumptions and Methodology

Full actuarial valuations by a professionally qualified actuary are needed at least every three years; they should be updated to each intervening balance sheet date.

Pension scheme assets must be measured at fair value (bid price for quoted securities).

Scheme liabilities are measured using the projected unit method, which reflects the benefits the employer is committed to provide for service up to the valuation date and, where applicable, allows for projected increases to those benefits in line with pensionable earnings after the valuation date.

The expected costs of death-in-service or incapacity benefits should be charged on an insurance cost basis, to the extent they are insured. Any such benefits that are uninsured are to be charged on a projected unit method that reflects the proportion of the full benefits ultimately payable attributable to the accounting period.

The actuarial assumptions for projecting future outgoings in respect of the scheme liabilities are ultimately the responsibility of the directors (or equivalent), but should be set upon advice given by an actuary and must reflect market expectations at the valuation date, for consistency with the asset value. They should be mutually compatible and should lead to the best estimate of the future cashflows that will arise under the scheme liabilities. The projected outgoings must then be discounted. The discount rate to be used is the redemption yield at the valuation date on AA (or equivalent) rated corporate bonds of equivalent term and currency to the scheme liabilities.

Balance Sheet

Any surplus at the balance sheet date of assets over scheme liabilities calculated as above should be recognised in the balance sheet but is limited to the amount that the employer can recover through reduced employer's contributions in future and refunds which have already been agreed by the trustees at the balance sheet date.

A deficit (on the FRS basis) should be recognised as a liability to the extent of the employer's legal or constructive obligation to fund it. If the scheme rules require members' contributions to be increased to help fund a deficit, the liability should be reduced appropriately.

The net pension asset/liability shown in the balance sheet may differ from the above, due to deferred tax.

Pension Cost

The full cost of benefits, including actuarial gains and losses, is recognised in the performance statements in the accounting period in which the cost arises. The Profit and Loss account is protected from excessive volatility by the recognition of actuarial gains and losses in the Statement of Total Recognised Gains and Losses (STRGL) and the facility to vary the expected return on assets.

The different components making up the pension cost are shown in the table *on the next page*, along with definitions, details of where they should be recognised in the performance statements, and brief comments.

Disclosure

The disclosure requirements under FRS 17 were brought into line with those of the previous (pre-2013) version of IAS 19. The following disclosures are mandatory:

- a general description of the type of scheme (for example, flat-rate or final salary pension scheme, or retirement healthcare plan)
- a reconciliation of the scheme assets and liabilities to the net asset or liability recognised in the balance sheet, showing at least:
  o the present value of scheme liabilities that are wholly unfunded
  o the present value (before deducting the fair value of the scheme assets) of scheme liabilities that are wholly or partly funded
  o the fair value of any scheme assets
  o the past service cost not yet recognised in the balance sheet
  o any amounts which would, apart from the limits laid down by FRS 17, be recognised as an asset, *and*
  o the other amounts recognised in the balance sheet
- any self-investment included in the fair value of scheme assets
- reconciliations showing the movements over the period of the scheme assets and liabilities
- the total expense recognised in the profit and loss account for each of the following:
  o current service cost

FRS 17: SUMMARY OF CALCULATION OF PENSION COST

	Component	Where recognised	Description and Notes
	Current service cost	Staff cost section of operating cost in P&L[1]	The increase in the scheme liabilities expected to arise from employees' service in the accounting period, calculated using financial assumptions based on conditions at the beginning of the period. Includes insurance cost, for the accounting period, of insured death-in-service and incapacity benefits, and a charge calculated using a 'projected unit' method for their uninsured counterparts. Expected employees' contributions are offset from the gross cost.
+	Interest cost	Financing section of P&L	Expected increase during the period in the present value of the scheme liabilities because the benefits are one period closer to settlement.
−	Expected return on assets	Combined with interest cost (above) to give a net entry in financing section of P&L	Based on actual assets held by the scheme at the beginning of the accounting period and the expected rate of return on those assets as follows: – for bonds, current redemption yields at start of period – for equities and other assets, the rate of total return expected over the long term at start of period in either case averaged over the remaining term of the related liabilities and net of scheme expenses. Appropriate allowance should be made for expected cashflows into and out of the fund during the year. May be restricted if there is an irrecoverable surplus.
+	Actuarial loss (gain)	STRGL[2]	Changes in actuarial surpluses or deficits that arise because events have not coincided with the actuarial assumptions made for the last valuation or because the actuarial assumptions have changed. An adjustment may be required where there is an irrecoverable surplus.
+	Past service cost, offset by surplus otherwise treated as irrecoverable	Staff cost section of operating cost in P&L	A past service cost (PSC) is any increase in the scheme liabilities related to employees' service in prior periods, arising in the current period as a result of the introduction of, or improvement to, retirement benefits. PSCs are required to be recognised on a straight-line basis over the period in which the additional benefits vest. Where these vest immediately, the PSC should be recognised immediately.
+	Loss (gain) on settlement/ curtailment, offset by surplus otherwise treated as irrecoverable	Staff cost section of operating cost in P&L, unless it attaches to an exceptional item immediately after operating profit in the P&L	Settlement occurs where the responsibility for, and risk attaching to, a pension obligation is irrevocably transferred to another party, e.g. by buying matching annuities or by paying a bulk transfer value. Curtailment is where defined benefit liabilities cease to accrue or current members' future service benefits are reduced, e.g. on termination of a final salary scheme and replacing it with a money purchase scheme, or due to a redundancy exercise. Losses or gains arising as a result of settlements and curtailments instigated by the employer and falling outside the scope of the actuarial assumptions are included in this component of pension cost.

Notes: [1] Profit and loss account.   [2] Statement of Total Recognised Gains and Losses.
Where the surplus recognised in the balance sheet has to be restricted (as described under the heading 'Balance Sheet'), FRS 17 sets out details of the adjustments required to the performance statements.

- ○ interest cost
- ○ expected return on scheme assets
- ○ past service cost
- ○ any curtailment or settlement costs, *and*
- ○ the effect of any limit on the balance sheet asset (where recognised through the profit and loss account)
- the actual return on scheme assets
- the principal actuarial assumptions
- the amount recognised in the Statement of Total Recognised Gains and Losses, separately showing actuarial gains and losses and the effect of any limit on the balance sheet asset (where recognised outside the profit and loss account)
- cumulative gains and losses recognised outside the profit and loss account
- assets, showing the amount or percentage in each major asset category
- explanation of how expected return is derived, referring to the impact of each major asset category, but no requirement to disclose expected returns separately for each category
- five-year history of asset value, liabilities, surplus/deficit and experience gains and losses (there is no requirement to construct these retrospectively)
- expected contributions over the coming year, *and*
- explanation of any constructive obligations (e.g. to provide regular pension increases).

Where several DB schemes are involved, disclosure can be combined in the way felt to be most useful.

A Reporting Statement applies to UK companies using FRS 17 (or IAS 19) and recommends additional best practice disclosures. These are not mandatory but are intended to give a clear view of the risks and rewards arising from schemes, and are complementary to the disclosures required under those standards.

The recommended disclosures include:

- information on the relationship between the company and the scheme trustees/managers, including how the investment strategy and funding principles are determined, and any significant and unusual trustee power
- information on and sensitivity analysis for each of the principal assumptions, including mortality
- the buy-out cost of the liabilities, if available
- information on contributions agreed with the trustees, *and*
- other information that will enable the user to evaluate risks and rewards including on the expected rate of return of each of the major asset classes

New standard FRS 102

FRS 102 (Section 28) will replace FRS 17 from 1 January 2015. Entities that currently report under full UK FRS (i.e. not required by EU legislation to use IFRS and not small enough to use FRSSE) will move to the new standard, unless they elect instead for full International Financial Reporting Standards (IFRS, including IAS 19 for pension arrangements. FRS 102 is derived from the IASB

IFRS for SME (IFRS for Small and Medium-sized Entities), but adapted to reflect UK legislation. Early adoption has been possible since 1 January 2013.

The main implications of moving to FRS 102 are:

- Financing cost under the new standard will be calculated as the net interest on the defined benefit liability over the accounting period, allowing for contributions paid over the period. Effectively this means that the return on assets will be calculated using the discount rate rather than allowance being made for asset outperformance. This will significantly increase the annual pension cost for many entities.

- Changes to surplus restrictions which, depending on scheme rules, could either:
  - ○ facilitate the recognition of surplus that is restricted under FRS 17; *or*
  - ○ lead to further restrictions on the recognisable surplus reflecting the promise of future contributions to the scheme.

- Changes to the treatment of group schemes where all participating companies currently account as if they were DC arrangements. Under FRS 102 the principal company will need to account for the scheme in full with the other participating companies accounting as if DC.

These latter two differences may have implications for calculating realised profits, and hence for the payment of dividends.

ACCOUNTING FOR PENSION COSTS UNDER IAS 19

An amended version of IAS 19 applies for accounting periods beginning on or after 1 January 2013.

Requirement to Use International Standards

Companies governed by the law of an EU Member State, whose securities are admitted to trading on a regulated market in any EU Member State, are generally required to prepare their consolidated accounts in compliance with International Accounting Standards. For the UK, this covers companies listed on AIM (Alternative Investment Market) as well as those with a full London Stock Exchange (LSE) listing.

In December 2007, the US Securities and Exchange Commission (SEC) ruled that non-US companies reporting under International Financial Reporting Standards (IFRS) would no longer have to reconcile to US accounting standards in order to obtain a listing in the USA. The SEC is continuing deliberations on whether US companies will be required to transition to IFRS; however, any transition is likely to be some years away.

Coverage

IAS 19 covers four categories of employee benefits, with separate requirements for each:

- short-term employee benefits, such as salaries and social security contributions
- post-employment benefits, such as pensions and post-employment medical care

- other long-term employee benefits, including long-service leave (which are now largely treated in the same way as post-employment benefits, although gains/losses are recognised through profit and loss) *and*
- termination benefits.

Equity compensation benefits, including share options, which were previously covered by IAS 19, are now covered by IFRS 2.

Application to Multi-employer Schemes

Under IAS 19, only plans that are operated by companies which *are not under common control* are 'multi-employer' plans. If participants in a DB multi-employer plan are unable to identify separately the assets and liabilities, they can account for the plan on a cash contribution basis.

Where a DB plan is operated by a group of companies which *are under common control*, the principal sponsoring employer is required to account for the plan on a DB basis and other participating employers are allowed to use a cash contribution basis, unless there is a contractual agreement on the sharing of future pension costs, in which case each company should recognise its share of the DB cost.

A: DEFINED CONTRIBUTION SCHEMES

The treatment of DC schemes under IAS 19 is essentially the same as under FRS 17. The only disclosure required by IAS 19 is the amount of expense recognised for the period.

B: DEFINED BENEFIT SCHEMES

Benefits to Value

The benefits to be valued under IAS 19 are basically the same as those required to be valued under FRS 17, although IAS 19 is not specific about what allowance should be made for future early retirements.

Actuarial Assumptions and Methodology

IAS 19 requires assets and liabilities to be valued regularly enough that the amounts recognised in the accounts are not materially different from the amounts that would be determined from an up-to-date valuation. The involvement of a qualified actuary is encouraged but not required.

Assets must be measured at fair value. Auditors may require fair value to be taken as bid value rather than mid-market. Liabilities are measured using the projected unit method.

IAS 19 is silent on the treatment of risk benefits. We understand that most auditors expect the 'attribution method' to be used. For benefits that are no service-related, this method allocates benefits in proportion to the ratio of completed years of service to either the vesting period or, if the benefit is unvested, total projected years of service.

The actuarial assumptions are the responsibility of the directors and must be unbiased and mutually compatible, being best estimates of the variables determining the ultimate cost of the benefits. The discount rate to be used should be determined by reference to market yields at the valuation date on high quality corporate bonds of consistent term and currency. The market yields on government bonds should be used if there is no deep market in corporate bonds.

Balance Sheet

The amount recognised in the balance sheet should be calculated as:

	The present value of the DB obligation
+	Actuarial gains (or minus any losses) not yet recognised in pension cost
−	Any outstanding past service costs not yet recognised in pension cost
−	The fair value of scheme assets.

If the result is an asset, then it should be limited to the present value of:

	The available future refunds of surplus
+	The available reduction in future contributions
+	Any outstanding actuarial losses or past service costs not yet recognised in pension cost.

IFRIC 14, published by the Interpretation Committee of the IASB, addresses the impact of minimum funding requirements, the limit on an asset for a DB scheme and the interaction of these. IFRIC 14 explains that a refund or a reduction in future contributions may be considered available even if it cannot be realised at the balance sheet date. The company must have a right to any refund, without recourse to the trustees. The available reduction in future contributions must be restricted to allow for any contributions payable under any 'minimum funding requirement' that may apply. The balance sheet asset or liability must also be adjusted to reflect any irrecoverable surplus (on the accounting basis) that will be created in future by the payment of minimum contributions in respect of a past service deficit on the minimum funding basis.

Pension Cost

The components of pension cost are similar to those for FRS 17, with the exception of:

- A single net interest income (or expense) item replaces the interest cost and expected return on assets, and is calculated as the discount rate applied to the net balance sheet position. This effectively requires the expected return on assets component of pension cost to be calculated using the discount rate instead of an expected return based on scheme assets.
- Following removal of the alternative corridor approach, actuarial gains and losses are now always recognised in full immediately through Other Comprehensive Income (OCI). This is analogous to recognition through the STRGL under FRS17, rather than through the profit and loss account.

Administration expenses (except investment expenses) are recognised as operating costs in the profit and loss account in the year in which they occur. Investment expenses continue to be offset from actual investment returns and therefore from investment gains recognised in OCI.

Disclosure

Following the amendments to IAS 19, the disclosures required in respect of defined benefit schemes are as follows:

- a general description of the characteristics of the scheme, including the nature of the benefits provided, the regulatory framework and its impact and responsibilities for governance (including trustee powers)
- a description of the risks associated with the scheme
- a description of any amendments, curtailments and settlements
- a reconciliation of the scheme assets and liabilities to the net asset or liability recognised in the balance sheet, showing separate reconciliations for the scheme assets, the present value of the defined benefit obligation and the effect of any asset ceiling, where each reconciliation shows at least:
  o current service cost
  o interest income or expense
  o remeasurements of the net defined benefit liability or asset, showing separately:
    – the return on scheme assets
    – actuarial gains and losses arising from changes in demographic assumptions
    – actuarial gains and losses arising from changes in financial assumptions
    – changes in the effect of any asset ceiling
  o past service cost and gains or losses from settlements
  o the effect of any changes in foreign exchange rates
  o contributions to the scheme, split between employer and employee
  o payments from the scheme, with the amounts paid in respect of any settlement shown separately
  o the effect of any business mergers, acquisitions or disposals
- a disaggregation of the scheme assets according to nature and risks, and split between those that have a quoted price and those that do not
- the fair value of the employer-related investments, including property occupied by the employer
- the significant actuarial assumptions used to determine the defined benefit obligation
- a sensitivity analysis for each of the significant actuarial assumptions
- a description of any asset–liability matching strategies to manage risk
- an indication of the effect of the scheme on the employer's cashflow, including a description of the funding arrangements and policy, the expected contributions to the scheme over the following year and information on the maturity profile of the scheme
- additional disclosures for multi-employer schemes, such as information on funding arrangements, liability for the obligations of other participating employers, allocation of surplus or deficit *and*
- additional disclosures for schemes where risk is shared between participating employers.

Future developments

The IASB has, for the time being, deferred its proposed project for fundamental review of IAS 19. However, IFRIC intends to look again at the accounting for contribution-based promises, as previously considered in Draft

Interpretation D9: *Employee Benefit Plans with a Promised Return on Contributions or Notional Contributions*. IFRIC is also considering the definition of 'high quality corporate bonds', which is used in setting the discount rate under IAS 19. In addition, the IASB has published an exposure draft that proposes to clarify the treatment of employee contributions, which can be allowed for as a reduction to service cost only in the period to which they relate.

RELATED PARTY DISCLOSURES (IAS 24)

Companies complying with IAS 19 also have to provide disclosure figures under IAS 24 – *Related Party Disclosures*. This Standard requires information to be disclosed for key management personnel (in aggregate) for each of the following categories:

- short-term employee benefits
- post-employment benefits
- other long-term benefits
- termination benefits *and*
- share-based payment.

IAS 24 defines key management personnel as persons having authority and responsibility for planning, directing and controlling the activities of the entity, directly or indirectly. This includes (but is not limited to) directors.

For each category, only a single figure is required. For some benefits this one figure is easy to access (for example, actual contributions paid to a DC plan). Our understanding is that, in the case of DB plans and other long-term benefit plans, the IAS 19 service cost for each relevant individual should be used rather than a proportion of the whole profit and loss charge.

DISCLOSURE OF DIRECTORS' PENSIONS

New Companies Act disclosure requirements apply to quoted companies for years ending on or after 30 September 2013 in relation to directors' pensions. Listed company accounts are also subject to disclosure requirements in relation to directors' pensions imposed by the FCA's Listing Rules, although the FCA is expected to remove these requirements for years ending on or after 1 January 2014, as it considers that the new Companies Act requirements require sufficient disclosure.

The legislative and FCA requirements apply in addition to the requirements of IAS 24 – *Related Party Disclosures* where applicable. A summary of the current legislative disclosure requirements relating to directors' pensions is given below.

Unquoted company disclosures

Unquoted companies are required to make the following disclosures in the notes to their accounts:

- the aggregate value of company contributions paid or treated as paid to a pension scheme to provide money purchase benefits in respect of directors' service
- the number of directors accruing retirement benefits under money purchase schemes and the number accruing benefits under DB schemes

- except where, broadly, aggregate directors' pay and other specified emoluments fall below a specified threshold, the following must be disclosed in respect of the highest-paid director: company contributions in respect of money purchase benefits, and accrued DB pension and lump sum (both excluding benefits from AVCs) at year-end, *and*

- the aggregate amount by which directors' retirement benefits in payment exceeded the amount they were entitled to at 31 March 1997, or the date the benefits became payable, if later. This does not apply if the benefits were sufficiently funded without recourse to additional contributions and benefits were paid to all pensioner members of the scheme on the same basis.

Quoted company disclosures

Under the new regulations, the directors' remuneration report must show a single total remuneration figure for all types of reward received by each director over the year, including pension benefits. Defined benefit pensions are valued using similar methodology to that for calculating the annual allowance, but with a factor of 20 rather than 16 for valuing pension accrual.

In addition to the single figure, companies also need to provide details of any defined benefit or cash balance pension rights at the end of the year including the director's normal retirement date, plus a description of any additional benefit that will be receivable on early retirement (split between different types of benefit).

Other disclosures are also required, including the link between company performance and pay for the reporting period and scenarios for what directors will be paid for performance at minimum, maximum or on-target levels.

To meet the FCA's requirements (for years ending before 1 January 2014) in relation to defined benefits, details of the amount of the increase in accrued benefit during the year (excluding inflation) must also be included, and either

(i) the transfer value (less director's contributions, and with no reduction for underfunding) of the increase in accrued benefit net of inflation; *or*

(ii) so much of the following information as is necessary to make a reasonable assessment of the transfer value in respect of each director:

- current age
- normal retirement age
- the amount of any contributions paid or payable by the director during the period
- details of spouse's and dependants' benefits
- early retirement rights and options, expectations of pension increase after retirement (whether guaranteed or discretionary), *and*
- discretionary benefits for which allowance is made in transfer values, and any other relevant information which will significantly affect the value of the benefits.

FINANCIAL SERVICES LEGISLATION AND PENSION SCHEMES

Following the financial crisis that began in 2007, the Government believed that the 'tripartite' regulatory system – with the Bank of England, the Financial Services Authority and the Treasury collectively responsible for financial stability – had failed in a number of ways. A formal restructuring of financial regulation followed in 2013.

From 1 April 2013, the Financial Services Authority (FSA) was renamed the Financial Conduct Authority (FCA). It is responsible for the conduct supervision of all regulated financial firms. Some responsibilities in relation to deposit-taking institutions, insurers and investment banks were transferred to a new Prudential Regulation Authority (PRA) – the FCA is also responsible for the prudential supervision of those institutions not supervised by the PRA.

The Financial Services and Markets Act 2000 (FSMA) is the principal legislation for the regulation of the financial services market. It specifies that 'regulated activities' may only be carried out as a business in the UK by persons who are either authorised or exempt. Regulated activities include dealing in investments, managing investments, arranging deals in investments, offering investment advice, taking custody of investments and establishing collective investment schemes and certain pension schemes. Authorisation is granted by the FCA or the PRA. The Pensions Regulator also has a regulatory role in respect of workplace contract-based pension arrangements.

Professional firms may be licensed by 'Designated Professional Bodies', such as the Institute and Faculty of Actuaries, to carry out a limited range of 'exempt' regulated activities that are incidental to their main business without FCA authorisation. Firms that are managed or controlled by suitably qualified professionals and fall within the FCA's definition of 'Authorised Professional Firms' may also be able to avail themselves of corresponding exemptions when carrying out similar, non-mainstream, regulated activities.

Implications for pension schemes

Pension scheme trustees and administrators are clearly concerned with investments in various ways. They may be:

- responsible for the management of the scheme's assets (whether in insurance policies or directly invested)
- involved in giving advice to scheme members and prospective members, *and/or*
- involved in arranging investments for individual members, such as DC fund choices, additional voluntary contributions, purchase of annuities and insurance company buy-outs.

Each of the above can be a 'regulated activity' requiring authorisation by the FCA, for which stringent requirements must be met, unless covered by an exemption. Establishing whether authorisation is required for a particular action can be complicated, particularly when considering relationships between trustees and individual members. The FCA has formal 'perimeter guidance' setting out the circumstances in which authorisation is or is not required.

Definition of investments

Under the FSMA, the definition of investments includes cash deposits (and also mortgages and general insurance contracts), shares, debentures, Government and public securities, options and futures, units in unit trust schemes and long-term insurance contracts. However, the provisions relating to managing, dealing in and advising on investments do not apply to cash deposits.

Generally, a scheme member's interests under the trusts of an occupational pension scheme are not classed as investments. However, rights under a stakeholder scheme are specifically included (even if it is an occupational scheme), as are rights under a personal pension scheme (including a Self-Invested Personal Pension).

Management of investments

The FSMA specifically provides that those engaged in the activity of managing the assets of occupational pension schemes must be authorised or exempt, even if (as is the case with many trustees) they would not normally be regarded as doing so as a business. However, the Act goes on to provide that authorisation will not be required if all day-to-day decisions about the management of investments are taken on their behalf by a person who is himself authorised or exempt. Trustees are also permitted to make 'day-to-day' decisions on pooled investment products and insurance contracts, provided that they have first obtained and considered advice from an appropriate authorised or exempt person.

The Pensions Act 1995 also imposes a requirement on pension schemes for trustees to appoint a competent and experienced fund manager who has the necessary authorisation or exemption. It identifies certain matters on which trustees are required to obtain investment advice and also sets out a requirement for a written statement of investment principles to govern the investment of the scheme's assets.

The Myners principles, guidance from the Investment Governance Group and the FRC Stewardship Code set out best practice for pension scheme (and wider institutional) investment activity *(see Section 8 for further details)*. These remain voluntary, although the Government has suggested that legislation will be introduced if pension schemes do not comply with the Myners principles.

In 2011, the DWP issued guidance on standards for default investment options in DC schemes used for automatic enrolment.

Communication with members

To reflect the requirements of the EU Distance Marketing Directive, UK legislation prevents an employee from being supplied with financial services without a 'prior request'. This means that any information given to employees offering membership of a stakeholder or group personal pension arrangement will need to include a reply slip, unless consent is obtained and recorded by some other means.

However, from 2012 employers are not prevented from auto-enrolling employees into workplace pension arrangements, including group personal pension and stakeholder schemes, as an alternative to NEST *(see Sections 4 to 6)*

Although these are regulated, contract-based schemes, FCA rules now confirm that automatic enrolment for the purpose of complying with the employer's statutory duty does not count as a 'distance contract'.

The FSMA also places restrictions on financial promotion, prohibiting the communication of any 'invitation or inducement to engage in investment activity', unless it is issued or approved by an authorised person. There are certain exemptions set out in secondary legislation, covering some (but not all) communications involving trustees, beneficiaries and trust settlors (generally, employers in a pension scheme context), but these are generally relevant only to occupational schemes. However, employers offering stakeholder or group personal pension arrangements to their employees can avoid the restrictions, provided certain conditions are met. These include requirements that the employer must contribute and must not receive any direct financial benefit. This exemption also applies to promotions by third-party administrators on behalf of such employers.

Ahead of automatic enrolment in 2012, the Pensions Regulator and the then FSA produced a joint guide for employers, to help build their confidence in talking to employees about pensions without breaching the rules on financial advice.

The Retail Distribution Review

Following the Retail Distribution Review, from the start of 2013 new rules from the then FSA came into effect. These aim to make the sale of investment products – including pensions – more fair and transparent to consumers.

The new rules require the cost of financial advice to be clearly set out and agreed with the client in advance. In addition, advisers must make clear the scope of their advice services.

Other activities of the Financial Conduct Authority

The FCA's strategic objective is to ensure that the financial markets function well. It has three operational objectives: securing consumer protection, protecting and enhancing the integrity of the financial system and promoting effective competition. As part of this, the FCA regulates the marketing and promotion of all personal pension and stakeholder pension schemes, the authorisation of such schemes' managers, and the activities of pension scheme investment managers.

Since 2012 the then FSA, HMRC and the Pensions Regulator have issued warnings about 'early pension release' or 'pension liberation' schemes, which claim to allow members to unlock or transfer cash tax free before they are entitled to receive their funds.

Other publications of relevance to pensions include guidance on product projections and pension transfer value analysis.

Role of the Pensions Regulator

See Section 8 for details of the Regulator's guidance and Section 9 for more information on the Regulator itself.

The regulation of workplace contract-based pension schemes (such as group personal pension arrangements) is shared between the Pensions Regulator and the FCA. In April 2013 the two parties issued a Memorandum of Understanding explaining their respective roles.

From 2012, the Pensions Regulator is responsible for maximising employers' compliance with their automatic enrolment duties. The Regulator's role also includes dealing with late payment of contributions and other breaches of legislation, promoting good administration, and providing information and education. As part of this, in order to support employers the Regulator has published guidance on selecting a good-quality scheme for automatic enrolment, including a guide to management committees for employers who choose to be more closely involved in the running of a group personal pension or master trust scheme. In 2013 it consulted on, and started to release, a package of measures to establish its approach to the regulation of workplace defined contribution schemes. These included a strategy document for regulating workplace defined contribution schemes and a consultation on its compliance and enforcement policy. The stategy document emphasises the Regulator's commitment to work with the FCA and relevant government departments with the aim of ensuring that the regulation of occupational and other workplace pensions is joined up, quality standards are consistent and the regulatory framework offers similar levels of member protection. The document also highlights areas of formal interaction with the FCA, including the sharing of information, sharing and aligning of risks, and joint thematic review or enforcement. At the time of writing the Regulator was expected to release a regulatory approach document that will set out how it will work with the FCA in relation to personal pension schemes.

The Financial Services Compensation Scheme (FSCS)

The FSCS is a safety net for customers of financial services firms, dealing with all financial-services-related claims. It was created under the FSMA and became operational on 1 December 2001.

The FSCS was set up to pay compensation where an authorised firm is unable or unlikely to be able, to pay claims against it. This is generally when a firm i insolvent or has gone out of business. It covers deposit-related claims, insurance- and investment-related claims and claims related to mortgage advice and arranging Stakeholder and group personal pension arrangements are covered, as are small self-administered schemes; larger companies' trust-based occupational schemes are not

The FSCS can also be called upon by the government to contribute to the costs associated with the exercise of a 'stabilisation power', for example, when it intervenes to ensure the continued existence of a bank or building society, or to make payments on behalf of another compensation scheme.

The Office of Fair Trading (OFT)

In September 2013, the OFT published a study on the defined contribution workplace pension market. It makes several recommendations, including:

- the Government should introduce minimum governance standards for all pension schemes
- improvements should be made on transparency of pension costs and charges
- actions should be taken to protect savers' money in contract and bundled trust schemes, and assets in small and medium-sized trust-based schemes which are at risk of providing poor value for money, *and*
- additional protection should be provided for individuals who are automatically enrolled.

RECENT DEVELOPMENTS

22 Nov 2012	The Government published a strategy document, *Reinvigorating Workplace Pensions*, including options for 'defined ambition' schemes.
1 Jan 2013	An amended version of IAS 19 took effect, removing the option of deferring the recognition of gains and losses and introducing more detailed disclosure requirements.
10 Jan 2013	Following a consultation on possible changes, the National Statistician announced that the existing formulation of the Retail Prices Index would continue (but a new geometric index, RPIJ, would be introduced).
14 Jan 2013	The DWP published a White Paper setting out proposals for a new, single-tier State pension (later included in Pensions Bill 2013). It was subsequently announced that the new pension would be introduced from 6 April 2016.
1 Mar 2013	The ABI's Code of Conduct on Retirement Choices was implemented, to help annuity purchasers make informed choices.
7 Mar 2013	The Court of Justice of the European Union (CJEU) ruled in *Wheels Common Investment Fund v HMRC* that DB pension schemes are not exempt from paying VAT on third-party investment management charges.
14 Mar 2013	FRS 102 was issued, which will replace FRS 17 from 1 January 2015.
20 Mar 2013	Chancellor George Osborne delivered the 2013 Budget. This announced a new statutory objective for the Pensions Regulator on scheme funding, to minimise any adverse impact on the sustainable growth of an employer (wording to be agreed).
6 Apr 2013	Real Time Information (RTI) for PAYE came into force, requiring employers and pension providers to report tax and other deductions to HMRC in 'real time'.
6 Apr 2013	Reduced projection rates (investment return assumptions) for personal pension schemes can be used from this date; use of the reduced rates will become compulsory from 6 April 2014.
1 Apr 2013	The Financial Conduct Authority (FCA) and the Prudential Regulation Authority replaced the Financial Services Authority.
8 May 2013	The Pensions Regulator published its second annual statement on funding, setting out its views on acceptable approaches to valuations in the prevailing economic environment.
9 May 2013	The Supreme Court ruled in *Futter v HMRC*, largely upholding the decision in *Pitt v Holt* that a trustee decision may be set aside only if made in breach of the trustees' duties or if there was a mistake of sufficient gravity.

20 May 2013	The Takeover Code was extended to cover pension scheme trustee issues.
23 May 2013	The European Commission announced that proposals for a revised Pensions Directive will not cover solvency funding requirements, but will still include proposals to improve the governance and transparency of occupational pension schemes.
10 Jun 2013	HMRC started consultation on Individual Protection (IP14), a new type of transitional protection to be available when the standard lifetime allowance reduces in 2014.
25 Jun 2013	Pensions Minister Steve Webb announced that the PPF compensation cap will be increased for longer-serving members.
4 Jul 2013	The DWP published a call for evidence on introducing legislative quality standards in work-based DC pension schemes.
11 Jul 2013	The Regulator published a new Code of Practice on the governance and administration of trust-based DC pension schemes, which is due to come into force in autumn 2013.
17 Jul 2013	The Finance Act 2013 received Royal Assent. It reduces the annual allowance to £40,000 and the standard lifetime allowance to £1.25 million from 6 April 2014, subject to transitional provisions.
17 Jul 2013	The Marriage (Same Sex Couples) Act 2013 received Royal Assent, although the main provisions are expected to come into force during 2014.
24 July 2013	In the *Nortel Companies* case, the Supreme Court ruled that a Financial Support Direction issued during the course of an administration ranks as a provable debt rather than an expense, therefore ranking alongside the claims of other unsecured creditors.
13 Sep 2013	A new Industry Code of Conduct on DC pension charges came fully into force, to ensure that employers are provided with information that is clear and comparable when selecting a scheme for automatic enrolment.
14 Sept 2013	Legislation banning consultancy charging in automatic enrolment schemes came into effect.
20 Sep 2013	The Regulator's revised Codes of Practice on reporting late payment of contributions to DC schemes came into effect. Revised guidance was also published.
25 Sep 2013	The DWP published updated versions of its guidance on certifying DB and DC schemes for automatic enrolment purposes.
1 Oct 2013	Revised regulations on the disclosure of directors' remuneration took effect, requiring disclosure of a single total remuneration figure including pensions.

SIGNIFICANT PENSION DATES

AUTO-ENROLMENT

05.07.10	NEST Corporation established.
01.07.12	Earliest date to which large employers could bring forward their staging date for auto-enrolment.
01.10.12	(i) Employer auto-enrolment obligations start, with employers being brought in at staging dates over a period of some five years dependent on employer payroll size. *(Details of the dates are given at the end of Section 4.)*
	(ii) Minimum contribution of 2% (including minimum 1% employer) of qualifying earnings where DC scheme used to meet obligations.
01.10.17	Minimum contribution of 5% (including minimum 2% employer) of qualifying earnings where DC scheme used to meet auto-enrolment obligations.
01.10.18	Minimum contribution of 8% (including minimum 3% employer) of qualifying earnings where DC scheme used to meet auto-enrolment obligations.

DISCLOSURE AND ACCOUNTING

01.11.86	Pension scheme disclosure requirements introduced.
28.09.92	Time limits for disclosure introduced.
06.04.97	New disclosure requirements introduced by Pensions Act 1995.
22.06.01	FRS 17 accounting procedures gradually introduced.
31.12.02	New directors' remuneration reporting standards introduced.
06.04.03	Statutory money purchase illustrations (SMPIs) to be provided to pension scheme members with money purchase benefits.
01.01.05	Consolidated group accounts of companies listed and regulated in EU Member States generally required to comply with International Accounting Standards (IAS). Full implementation of FRS 17 required by UK companies not adopting IAS.
30.12.05	New requirement for trustees to provide defined benefit members with an annual summary funding statement.
06.04.07	FRS 17 disclosure requirements brought into line with those of IAS 19.
01.12.10	Pension schemes permitted to meet disclosure requirements by providing some information electronically.
01.01.13	Revised IAS 19 to apply for reporting years beginning on or after this date.

30.09.13	New directors' remuneration reporting standards for reporting years ending on or after this date.
01.01.14	FCA consulting on removing the 'Greenbury' Listing Rules requirements relating to directors' remuneration disclosures on pensions for financial years ending on or after this date.
01.01.15	FRS 102 will replace FRS 17. Early adoption allowed for years ending on or after 31.12.12.

DIVORCE

01.07.96	Courts in England and Wales required to take pension rights into account when making financial provision orders on petitions for divorce filed on or after this date.
19.08.96	Courts in Scotland required to take pension rights into account when making financial provision orders on actions for divorce filed on or after this date.
01.12.00	Pension sharing provisions in force.
05.12.05	Revised forms and procedures for pension sharing and earmarking introduced.
06.04.09	Legislative restrictions on safeguarded rights abolished.
06.04.11	PPF compensation can be shared on divorce or dissolution of a civil partnership.

EQUAL TREATMENT

08.04.76	*Defrenne* judgment in ECJ established (after later clarification) the right of men and women to equal access to pension schemes.
07.11.87	Sex Discrimination Act 1986 came into force: compulsory retirement ages must be the same for men and women.
06.04.88	Protected Rights annuities must be on unisex basis.
17.05.90	*Barber* judgment (as clarified by later cases): occupational pensions are pay, and benefits in respect of service after 17.05.90 must be equal (unless claims lodged before this date).
23.06.94	Maternity and family leave provisions of Social Security Act 1989 brought into effect. Benefits during periods of paid maternity absence must continue to accrue based on notional full salary.
16.10.94	All employment rights (other than pay) to be maintained during statutory ordinary maternity leave.
02.12.96	Parts of Disability Discrimination Act 1995 dealing with employment and the supply of services effective.
01.07.00	Discrimination against part-timers illegal under the terms of Employment Relations Act 1999 unless objectively justified.

01.10.02	Discrimination against fixed-term workers became illegal unless objectively justified.
01.12.03	Legislation against discrimination by sexual orientation in force.
02.12.03	Legislation against discrimination by religion or belief in force.
01.10.04	Revised disability discrimination legislation in force.
05.12.05	Civil Partnership Act 2004 came into force. Civil partners must be given the same benefits, for future service, as those who are married.
01.12.06	Legislation against discrimination by age in force.
01.04.07	Statutory maternity and adoption pay periods increased from 26 to 39 weeks.
08.04.10	Equality Act 2010 received Royal Assent, harmonising, and in some respects extending, existing discrimination laws.
01.10.11	Default retirement age of 65 abolished.
21.12.12	Insurance premiums based on gender not permitted from this date, as a result of the *Test-Achats* CJEU judgment.
17.07.13	Marriage (Same Sex Couples) Act 2013 enacted (but main provisions not yet in force). It will extend marriage to same-sex couples and allow the conversion of civil partnerships.

PROTECTING MEMBERS

06.04.88	Compulsory membership of occupational schemes prohibited.
17.08.90	No surplus refund to employer unless LPI given.
12.11.90	Requirement to appoint independent trustee on employer insolvency.
02.04.91	Pensions Ombudsman in operation.
09.03.92	Self-investment restrictions effective.
29.06.92	Debt on employer on winding up of pension scheme.
06.10.96	Member-nominated trustees legislation commenced (and became fully effective from 06.04.97).
06.04.97	(i) Minimum Funding Requirement (MFR) and Statement of Investment Principles introduced.
	(ii) LPI increases became compulsory for future benefit accrual.
	(iii) Appointments of scheme actuary and auditor required.
	(iv) Internal Dispute Resolution Procedures required.
	(v) Pensions Compensation Board powers commenced.
	(vi) Opra could remove or suspend trustees and impose civil penalties.
9.05.00	Protection of pension rights on bankruptcy under approved pension schemes introduced.

06.04.01   Requirement for monitoring contributions to personal pensions introduced.

19.03.02   Interim MFR changes: lengthened deficit correction periods; partial abolition of annual recertification; changes to wind-up asset allocation priority calculations and debt-on-employer calculations where employer solvent.

15.03.04   For calculation effective dates from this date debt on employer increased for solvent employer scheme wind-ups beginning after 10.06.03, from MFR to full buy-out shortfall.

06.04.05   First provisions of Pensions Act 2004 came into force, including Pension Protection Fund, new Pensions Regulator and:
   (i) introduction of pension protection on transfer of employment to which TUPE regulations apply, *and*
   (ii) changes to LPI cap from 5% p.a. to 2.5% p.a. for future service. Money purchase benefits exempt from LPI.

01.09.05   Financial Assistance Scheme came into operation.

02.09.05   Debt on employer when leaving multi-employer schemes increases to share of full buy-out deficiency, unless approved withdrawal arrangement put in place.

30.12.05   (i) Introduction of new scheme-specific funding requirement contained in Pensions Act 2004 replacing the MFR.
   (ii) New requirements in force for schemes operating as 'cross-border' within the EEA.

06.04.06   Remaining Pensions Act 2004 provisions in force, including:
   (i)   new regulations on scheme modifications (section 67)
   (ii) new requirements for member-nominated trustees, including removal of the facility to opt out, *and*
   (iii) new requirements placed on trustees to have specific knowledge and understanding of pension issues.

06.04.08   Revised debt-on-employer provisions give more flexibility in multi-employer schemes.

06.04.10   Corporate restructuring permitted without triggering an employer debt provided certain conditions are satisfied.

06.04.12   Further amendments to debt-on-employer provisions provide more flexibility in multi-employer schemes.

01.07.12   Time limits for employers to pay over member contributions to schemes changed.

01.04.13   The Financial Services Authority is replaced by two bodies, the Prudential Regulation Authority and the Financial Conduct Authority.

STAKEHOLDER SCHEMES

01.10.00	Stakeholder schemes may be established.
06.04.05	Maximum annual management charge increased from 1% p.a. to 1.5% p.a. for the first ten years and 1% p.a. thereafter.
01.10.12	Employers are no longer required to provide access to a stakeholder scheme.

STATE SCHEMES AND CONTRACTING OUT

06.04.75   Benefits under Graduated Scheme cease to accrue.

06.04.78   Start of SERPS and contracting out.

01.01.85   Anti-franking introduced for leavers on or after this date.

01.11.86   Contracting-out quality test removed.

06.04.87   (i)   Contracting out via personal pension could be backdated to this date.
           (ii)   Trustees liable for CEPs/LRPs.

06.04.88   (i)   SERPS benefits reduced for individuals retiring after 2000.
           (ii)   GMP accrual rates reduced.
           (iii) GMPs accrued after this date must receive increases of up to 3% p.a. from scheme.
           (iv)   Fixed rate GMP revaluation for future leavers reduced from 8.5% to 7.5%.
           (v)   Widowers' GMPs introduced.
           (vi)   Money purchase contracting out introduced.
           (vii) 2% incentive payments introduced.

17.05.90   Protected rights under COMPs may commence at any age between 60 and 65.

06.04.93   (i)   Fixed rate GMP revaluation for future leavers reduced to 7%.
           (ii)   2% incentive payments ceased; 1% incentive payments introduced for personal pension contributors aged 30 or over.

06.04.96   Protected rights from COMPs can be secured on winding up by means of appropriate insurance policies.

06.04.97   (i)   1% incentive payments paid to personal pension contributors aged 30 or over ceased.
           (ii)   Age-related rebates introduced for COMPs and APPs.
           (iii) Link with SERPS broken.
           (iv)   GMP accruals cease and Reference Scheme Test introduced for COSRs.
           (v)   Limited Revaluation and State Scheme premium options (other than CEPs) removed.
           (vi)   Fixed rate GMP revaluation for future leavers reduced to 6.25%.

	(vii) COMBs permitted.
	(viii) Annuities purchased with post-April 1997 protected rights must in all cases have LPI, fixed 5% p.a. or full RPI increases, but need not include a widow(er)'s pension for single retirees.
01.01.01	Members' protected rights may be commuted in cases of serious ill-health.
06.04.02	(i) State Second Pension (S2P) replaces SERPS. (ii) New table of rebates effective from 2002 to 2007, with different levels of rebates applying to different tranches of earnings for personal pensions (but not occupational pensions) for the first time. (iii) Fixed rate GMP revaluation for future leavers reduced to 4.5%. (iv) New pre-97 protected rights annuities need not include a contingent widow(er)'s pension for retirees who are single. (v) Removal of requirement for automatic periodic certification of adequacy of assets of COSRs for contracting out.
06.10.02	Inherited SERPS pension reduced from 100% to 50%, subject to age-related transitional provisions.
06.10.03	Introduction of State Pension Credits, which replace Minimum Income Guarantee.
06.04.05	Higher increases given to individuals deferring State benefits beyond State pension age, and introduction of a new lump sum option.
28.11.05	An amendment to regulations allows the bulk transfer of protected rights from one COMP to another without the consent of the member.
06.04.07	(i) New table of rebates effective for 2007 to 2012. (ii) Fixed rate GMP revaluation for future leavers reduced to 4%.
06.04.09	Trustees, with employer consent, able to convert GMPs into 'normal' scheme pensions.
06.04.10	State pension age for women starts to increase from 60 to 65 over a transitional period now due to last until December 2018.
06.04.10	Pensions Act 2007 introduces extensive changes to State pensions including: (i) reduction in the number of contributory years needed to qualify for full Basic State Pension (BSP) to 30 for both men and women, *and* (ii) phasing-in of reforms to S2P to make it a flat-rate top-up to BSP.
06.04.11	(i) BSP to increase each year in line with the highest of earnings increases, price increases and 2.5%. (ii) First GMP increase order based on CPI rather than RPI effective.

06.04.12	(i) Abolition of contracting out on a money purchase basis and removal of all restrictions applying to protected rights funds.
	(ii) New rebates for COSRs effective for 2012 to 2017.
	(iii) Transfers of COSR rights to non-COSRs permitted.
	(iv) Fixed rate GMP revaluation for future leavers increased to 4.75%.
06.04.16	(i) New single-tier State pension for those reaching State pension age on or after this date.
	(ii) Salary-related contracting out to be abolished.
06.12.18	State pension age for men and women to start increasing from 65 to 66 over a transitional period to October 2020.
06.04.26	State pension age for men and women to start increasing from 66 to 67 over a transitional period to April 2028.

TAXATION

17.03.87	Revised limits for new members on or after this date.
06.04.87	Controls on surplus.
01.07.88	Personal pensions available.
14.03.89 & 01.06.89	1989 Revenue limits regime introduced for members joining newly established schemes on or after 14.03.89 and existing schemes on or after 01.06.89.
27.07.89	Concurrent membership of approved and unapproved schemes permissible.
30.06.95	Annuity purchase deferral and income withdrawal permitted for personal pensions.
01.01.97	Reinstatement to pension schemes permitted on special terms for those mis-sold personal pensions.
02.07.97	Tax credits on UK dividend income can no longer be claimed by pension schemes.
30.06.99	Annuity purchase deferral and income drawdown introduced for money purchase occupational schemes and buy-out contracts.
06.04.01	Changes to personal pension tax regime:
	(i) Contributions of up to £3,600 p.a. permitted irrespective of earnings.
	(ii) 'Carry forward' facility removed.
	(iii) 'Carry back' facility radically reduced.
	(iv) Contributions for risk benefits, for new entrants, limited to 10% of total contribution paid for year.
	(v) Concurrent membership of occupational and personal pension schemes permitted for those earning under £30,000 p.a.

11.05.01	Rate of tax on refund of surplus reduced from 40% to 35%.
06.04.06	(i) New tax regime replaces former contribution and benefit limits, permitting all individuals lifetime tax-privileged pension savings up to a standard limit.
	(ii) Requirement for occupational pension schemes to offer an AVC facility removed.
22.04.09	Special annual allowance charge introduced for 2009/10 and 2010/11.
01.12.09	Additional authorised payments permitted, including *de minimis* commutation payments of up to £2,000.
06.04.10	(i) Increase in the normal minimum pension age from 50 to 55.
	(ii) 50% additional rate of income tax introduced.
06.04.11	(i) Annual allowance reduced to £50,000.
	(ii) Requirement to annuitise before age 75 removed; flexible drawdown introduced.
	(iii) Lump sum death benefits paid after age 75 authorised but, along with certain other lump sum death benefits, taxed at 55%.
06.04.12	Lifetime allowance reduced to £1.5 million.
06.10.13	Deadline for all employers to have moved to Real Time Information (i.e. sending PAYE information to HMRC every time an employee is paid).
06.04.14	Lifetime allowance will be reduced to £1,250,000 and the annual allowance will be reduced to £40,000.
06.04.16	Scotland Act 2012 will empower the Scottish Parliament to set income tax at a different rate in Scotland.

TRANSFERS, PRESERVATION AND REVALUATION

06.04.75	Leavers on or after this date aged at least 26 and with 5 years' qualifying service entitled to preserved benefits.
01.01.86	(i) Statutory right to cash equivalent for leavers on or after this date. Non-GMP deferred pensions of such leavers accrued from 01.01.85 to be revalued, broadly at lower of 5% p.a. or price inflation.
	(ii) Age 26 requirement for preservation dropped.
06.04.88	Minimum period of qualifying service for entitlement to preserved benefits amended to two years, for leavers on or after this date.
01.01.91	Leavers on or after this date receive revaluations on whole non GMP deferred pension.
29.07.94	Protected rights may be transferred to a contracted-out occupational scheme of which the individual has previously been a member.

19.03.97	Occupational pension scheme members permitted to transfer personal pension benefits into a FSAVC.
06.04.97	(i) Rights to cash equivalent extended to pre-01.01.86 leavers. (ii) Three-month guarantee on cash equivalent quotations for salary-related benefits introduced. (iii) Cash equivalents subjected to a minimum of the MFR value.
01.12.00	Investment-linked annuity allowed as an alternative to LPI increase for non-protected rights under a money purchase scheme.
04.08.03	Trustees permitted to cut back individual transfer values where scheme is underfunded.
06.04.06	Leavers with between 3 and 24 months' pensionable service entitled to a cash transfer sum as an option.
01.10.08	Transfer values to be set by trustees (on at least a 'best estimate' basis after taking actuarial advice).
06.04.09	Minimum revaluation of non-GMP deferred pensions accrued from this date reduced to the lower of 2.5% p.a. or price inflation.
01.01.11	First statutory revaluation order based on CPI rather than RPI effective.

UNAPPROVED BENEFITS/EFRBS

27.07.89	Membership of unapproved schemes permitted to provide benefits on top of those from approved schemes.
01.12.93	Taxation of lump sum benefits from certain offshore Funded Unapproved Retirement Benefit Schemes (FURBS).
06.04.98	National Insurance contributions payable on contributions to money purchase FURBS.
06.04.99	National Insurance contributions payable on contributions to final salary FURBS.
06.04.06	Special tax treatment of unapproved pension arrangements removed (subject to transitional provisions). Unapproved schemes become Employer-Financed Retirement Benefit Schemes (EFRBS).
06.04.11	New Finance Act 2011 provisions apply, amending the taxation of funded and certain unfunded secured EFRBS.

UK PENSIONS CASE LAW

This section lists a number of legal cases that we feel are of significance in the development and understanding of pensions. We have included summaries of cases heard in courts of law and tribunals, and Pensions Ombudsman cases. Determinations, and other regulatory intervention, by the Pensions Regulator are covered in sections pertaining to the issues arising.

The list is not intended to be exhaustive and the comments given are merely an indication of the case content. No reliance should be placed on these summary comments. Legal advice should always be sought for guidance as to the applicability of case law.

The year quoted below for each case usually, but not always, refers to the year of appearance in a published law report. This may be a later year than that in which the judgment was given.

TRUSTEESHIP

Re Whiteley (Court of Appeal) [1886]
The duty of a trustee is to take such care as an ordinary prudent man would take if he were minded to make investment for the benefit of other people for whom he felt bound to provide.

Learoyd v Whiteley (House of Lords) [1887]
A trustee must use ordinary care and caution and is entitled to rely upon skilled persons.

Re Skeats' Settlement (High Court) [1889]
The power of appointment of trustees is fiduciary. The person in whom the power is vested cannot appoint themselves as a trustee.

Re Hastings-Bass (Court of Appeal) [1975]
Concerns the ability of trustees to have their past mistakes corrected by the courts. Subsequent cases (see in particular *Futter v HMRC*, 2013) have limited the application of the 'rule in *Hastings-Bass*', which broadly states that where trustees have acted without taking relevant considerations into account, resulting in an effect that had not been intended, the court may intervene to correct the error.

Cowan v Scargill (High Court) [1984]
The duty of trustees to act in the best interests of the present and future beneficiaries of the trust is paramount. This almost certainly means best *financial* interests.

Martin v City of Edinburgh District Council (Court of Session, Scotland) [1989]
Whilst trustees cannot be expected to set aside completely all personal preferences and conscientiously held principles, they must exercise fair and impartial judgement on the merits of the issues before them. The investment duty of a trustee is not merely to rubber-stamp the professional advice of financial advisers.

Wilson v Law Debenture (High Court) [1995]

Courts will not compel trustees to disclose the reasons for the exercise of a discretion.

Elliott v Pensions Ombudsman (High Court) [1998]

Trustees can exercise discretion to favour certain categories of members over other categories.

Harding and Others (Trustees of Joy Manufacturing Holdings Ltd Pension and Life Assurance Scheme), petitioners (Court of Session, Inner House, Scotland) [1999]

Trustees in Scotland may not surrender the exercise of their discretion to the Court.

Edge v Pensions Ombudsman (Court of Appeal) [2000]

The main purpose of a pension scheme is not served by putting an employer out of business, nor by setting contributions or benefits at levels that deter employees from joining. Trustees are not obliged to put forward proposals on use of surplus that they do not think are fair to the employers.

When exercising discretions, trustees must give proper consideration to all relevant matters, and may reach a decision that appears to favour one interest over others. However, any explanation given may be evaluated critically, and appropriate inferences drawn from a failure to give an explanation when called for.

Allen v TKM Group Pension Scheme (Pensions Ombudsman) [2002]

Trustees may find themselves judged to have acted with maladministration even where they have not acted unlawfully. It is good administrative practice for trustees to provide reasons for their decisions to those with a legitimate interest in the matter, and they should generally make the minutes of their meetings available to scheme members.

The Ombudsman's ruling appears to contradict an established trust law principle that trustees are not obliged to reveal the reasons for their decisions when exercising discretions. An Ombudsman's ruling is, however, not a binding precedent on schemes generally and it may be that a Court would take a different view from the Ombudsman.

Lawrence Graham Trust Corporation v Trustees of Greenup and Thompson Limited Pension Scheme (Pensions Ombudsman) [2008]

The trustees made a loan to the principal employer, in breach of section 40 of the Pensions Act 1995. The Ombudsman determined that, when the employer went into liquidation, the loan had not been repaid. The trustees were guilty of breach of trust and personally liable for the outstanding amount.

Gregson v HAE Trustees (High Court) [2008]

Beneficiaries cannot bring indirect 'dog-leg' claims against directors of a corporate trustee, as this would circumvent the principle that no direct duty is owed by the directors to the beneficiaries. Although this appears to conflict with a 1997 ruling that an indirect claim could be brought, the difference seems to hinge on the specific circumstances of the case, in particular that the trustee company in the earlier case was the trustee of only one trust and had no other business interest.

Independent Trustee Services Limited v Hope (High Court) [2009]

Trustees cannot take account of the PPF in making certain decisions. Although this 'Ilford' case related specifically to the purchase of annuities to secure certain benefits, similar principles can be expected to apply in other situations.

Futter v HMRC (Supreme Court) [2013]

The rule in *Hastings-Bass* (1975 – *see above*) may only be applied where the error made by the trustees amounted to a breach of their fiduciary duty (such breach would not normally be the case where they have relied in good faith on incorrect professional advice). However, in the case of *Futter,* the court was able to use the legal rule of mistake to correct the error.

EMPLOYERS

Re Courage Group's Pension Schemes, Ryan v Imperial Brewing (High Court) [1987]

The ability to substitute a principal employer is dependent on the purpose for which the intended substitution would be made. A rule-amending power could not be used to change the principal employer to a holding company that had no connection with the previous principal employer and whose purpose was to retain control of a surplus contributed by companies that the holding company had bought.

Imperial Group Pension Trust v Imperial Tobacco (High Court) [1991]

Pension benefits are part of the consideration received by employees for their services. The employer owes his employees a duty of good faith in relation to a pension scheme, and should not act so as to destroy or seriously damage their relationship of confidence and trust.

Hillsdown v Pensions Ombudsman (High Court) [1997]

Under the scheme, the trustees had sole power to deal with a surplus. The employer threatened to bring in employees of new employers to run down the surplus, and persuaded the trustees to agree to an amendment enabling a transfer to another scheme from which a refund to the employer could be made. The Court ruled that the amendment and transfer were for an improper purpose and ordered the refunded surplus to be returned to the scheme. It further ruled that the employer's implied obligation of trust and confidence prevented it from using a power to suspend contributions, whilst at the same time using a power to adhere further employers.

Air Jamaica v Charlton (Privy Council) [1999]

Bearing in mind the employer's obligation to exercise powers in good faith, it was difficult to see how the scheme could be amended in any significant respect once it had discontinued and wind-up was anticipated.

University of Nottingham v Eyett (High Court) [1999]

Where all the relevant information is available to the employee to make his own informed choice, the employer's implied obligation of good faith does not require it to draw the member's attention to the fact that he might have done better financially by changing the timing of his choice.

BENEFITS AND CONTRIBUTIONS

Packwood v APS (Pensions Ombudsman) [1995]

Where trustees failed to consider the use of a power of amendment to increase benefits, this was held to be a breach of trust and maladministration. However, the employer did not breach his implied obligation of good faith by preferring his own interests, having first considered the interests of pensioners.

Barclays Bank v Holmes (High Court) [2000]

Where a defined contribution section has been added to a defined benefit scheme, the surplus in the defined benefit section may (provided that this is not contrary to the trust deed) be used to meet the defined contributions.

Merchant Navy Ratings Pension Fund Trustees v Chambers (High Court) [2001]

An amendment that allows a pensioner's benefits to be transferred without consent is not automatically prohibited. It is for the actuary to consider whether to give a 'section 67' certificate.

Royal Masonic Hospital v Pensions Ombudsman (High Court) [2001]

Unfunded pension schemes are not subject to the preservation requirements.

Hagen v ICI Chemicals and Polymers Ltd (High Court) [2001]

The Court ruled that the employer had misrepresented the position to employees, when informing them that they would receive broadly similar benefits on transfer to a new scheme following a business transfer. In fact, some individuals' benefits under the new scheme were as much as 5% worse than under the old scheme.

Beckmann v Dynamco Whicheloe Macfarlane Ltd (European Court of Justice) [2002]

Benefits payable from an occupational pension scheme on redundancy, being benefits payable before normal pension age, do not fall under the exemption for occupational pension scheme rights under the TUPE legislation. The 2003 ruling in *Martin and Others v South Bank University* built on this decision, extending it to some other early retirement situations.

The 2012 High Court ruling in *Procter & Gamble v SCA* provided further clarification and confirmed that the principles applied to private sector schemes. Although the High Court granted the defendants leave to appeal, it has been reported that the parties subsequently settled out of court.

Aon Trust Corporation Ltd v KPMG (Court of Appeal) [2005]

The exercise of an express power in the scheme rules (to reduce benefits when the scheme was in deficit) was a power to modify the scheme, coming within the ambit of section 67 of the Pensions Act 1995. Consequently, the power could not be exercised (without member consent) if it would adversely affect accrued rights or entitlements.

The judgment also placed limitations on what could be regarded as a 'money purchase scheme'. The judge ruled that the scheme in question was not such a scheme because it provided 'average salary benefits', and hence it was subject to the funding and debt-on-the-employer legislation.

Pinsent Curtis v Capital Cranfield Trustees Ltd (Court of Appeal) [2005]

Under a scheme rule which empowered the trustees to determine 'appropriate' contributions, the trustees could seek a lump sum contribution equal to the buy-out deficit during the period for which notice had been given by the employer that he would terminate the scheme.

PNPF Trust Co Ltd v Taylor & Others (High Court) [2010]

The rules of the Pilots' National Pension Fund, an industry-wide scheme, gave the trustees the power to set contributions subject to certain conditions. The scheme funding legislation could be used to set contributions in excess of those allowable under the rules, although this would require the employer's agreement.

IMG v German (Court of Appeal) [2010]

Section 91 of the Pensions Act 1995 does not prevent the bona fide compromise of disputed or doubtful entitlements or rights under an occupational pension scheme.

Prudential Staff Pensions v Prudential Assurance (High Court) [2011]

In 2006, after granting discretionary pension increases broadly in line with the Retail Prices Index (RPI) for a number of years, the employer revised its policy by capping annual increases at 2.5%. The Court ruled that, in doing so, the employer had not breached its duty of good faith.

Houldsworth v Bridge Trustees (Court of Appeal) [2010], (Supreme Court) [2011] (commonly referred to as the *Imperial Home Décor* case)

Pensions deriving from money purchase assets but paid directly by the scheme, DC funds with notional investment returns, and money purchase benefits subject to a GMP underpin all remain money purchase benefits for the purposes of the statutory winding-up provisions (and, by implication, other areas of legislation where the same definition is used). The judgment meant that a scheme considered to be a money purchase scheme could have a deficit (or surplus) on winding up, but not be covered by the PPF, and it therefore raised doubts about the UK's compliance with EU legislation protecting pension schemes. As a result the legislative definition of money purchase benefits is to be amended – including, for the purposes of scheme funding, employer debts and PPF protection.

Raithatha v Williamson (High Court) [2012]

The Court ruled that a pension that had not yet started, but which a bankrupt could have drawn because the relevant age requirements had been met, could be made subject to an Income Payments Order. Previously a bankrupt's undrawn pension benefits had not been considered as income for this purpose. An appeal was due to be heard: however, the parties settled out of court so the initial judgment remains unchallenged.

QinetiQ Trustees v QinetiQ Holdings (High Court) [2012]

The rules of the QinetiQ scheme related indexation and revaluation to the RPI 'or any other suitable cost-of-living index selected by the Trustees'. The Court ruled that the particular scheme rules gave the trustees the power to switch to using the Consumer Prices Index (CPI) to calculate future pension increases and revaluation in respect of all service.

Bradbury v BBC (High Court) [2012]

In 2011, Mr Bradbury was offered a pay rise, on condition of acceptance of a split in salary between pensionable and non-pensionable salary. The judge ruled that the employer's conduct was not contrary to the scheme rules and there would have been no alienation of an entitlement or right under section 91 of the Pensions Act 1995. However, the judge did not rule on whether it was a breach of the implied duties contained in Mr Bradbury's contract.

WINDING UP AND INSOLVENCY

Robins and others v Secretary of State for Work and Pensions (European Court of Justice) [2007] (commonly referred to as the *Allied Steel Workers (ASW)* case)

The ECJ ruled that the UK government had not adequately protected the rights of workers in occupational schemes in the event of insolvency (in particular, an insolvency occurring in April 2003), under the 1980 European Insolvency Directive.

In a related case, shortly afterwards, the UK High Court found in *Bradley and others v Secretary of State* that the UK government was guilty of maladministration because it had provided misleading official information on the security of occupational pension schemes.

Bainbridge v Quarters Trustees Ltd (High Court) [2008]

Unless they are specifically ring-fenced under the rules, money purchase assets will not be ring-fenced on wind-up. The extent to which this applies to schemes entering wind-up after 5 April 2005 is unclear.

NBPF Pension Trustees Ltd v Warnock-Smith (High Court) [2008]

Trustees may use scheme assets on wind-up to purchase insurance to protect themselves against 'run-off' liabilities and claims from overlooked beneficiaries.

MCP v Aon (High Court) [2009]

Trustees are not discharged from liabilities in a scheme wind-up despite giving notice under section 27 of the Trustee Act 1925 to which beneficiaries failed to respond, as the trustees should have been aware of those beneficiaries' interests.

Bonas UK (Upper Tribunal) [2011]

The purpose of a Contribution Notice should be to compensate the scheme for the detriment suffered, rather than to actively penalise the company.

Hogan v Ireland (Court of Justice of the European Union) [2012]

The CJEU has given a preliminary ruling that the 1980 European Insolvency Directive applied to the entitlement of former employees to old-age benefits under a supplementary pension scheme set up by their employer which they were obliged to join. As a result the Irish Government had not complied with its obligation under that Directive to protect the rights of workers in that scheme in the event of insolvency of the employer. The matter was referred back to the High Court of Ireland to determine the compensation the affected members should receive.

Nortel & Lehman Brothers v The Pensions Regulator (Supreme Court) [2013]

A Financial Support Direction can be issued after the insolvency of the employer. However, the debt arising would rank as a 'provable debt' (not an expense of liquidating the company) and so the trustees trying to enforce the debt would be unsecured, non-preferential creditors. This overturns the rulings from inferior courts giving FSDs a 'super-priority'.

Olympic Airlines Pension Scheme v Olympic Airlines (Court of Appeal) [2013]

In some circumstances, the High Court has jurisdiction to wind up a company in England (which might then result in its scheme being eligible to enter the PPF) as a secondary proceeding under European insolvency legislation, even though the company is already in liquidation abroad. In this case, however, the Court of Appeal overturned the High Court's decision on the grounds that Olympic did not have an 'establishment', as defined in the EC insolvency regulation.

SURPLUS AND DEFICITS

British Coal Corporation v British Coal Staff Superannuation Scheme Trustees (High Court) [1995]

An employer's liability to pay future standard contributions may be set against any scheme surplus.

National Grid Co plc v Laws (Court of Appeal) [1999]

Members have no rights in a surplus, only a reasonable expectation that any dealings with that surplus will pay a fair regard to their interests.

Wrightson Ltd v Fletcher Challenge Nominees Ltd (Privy Council) [2001]

In a balance of cost scheme, any surplus on a final dissolution is generally to be considered as resulting from past overfunding by the employer.

EQUAL TREATMENT

Defrenne v Sabena (No. 2) (European Court of Justice) [1976]

The principle of equal pay, under Article 119 (now Article 141) of the Treaty of Rome, may be relied upon by the national courts. However, this cannot be applied to claims for periods prior to 8 April 1976. (This case has been taken to indicate that *access* to pension schemes should be equal for men and women from 8 April 1976.)

Bilka-Kaufhaus GmbH v Weber von Hartz (European Court of Justice) [1986]

Where the exclusion of part-timers affected a far greater number of women than men, the equal pay requirements of the Treaty of Rome were infringed unless the employer could show that the exclusion was objectively justified.

Barber v GRE (European Court of Justice) [1990]

Benefits under a pension scheme are deferred pay and therefore subject to equal treatment between men and women.

Roberts v Birds Eye Walls (European Court of Justice) [1993]

The principle of equal treatment presupposes that men and women are in identical situations. Therefore, where a 'bridging pension' is paid only to a male member to offset the fact that a woman's State pension starts earlier, this is not direct sex discrimination. [Note: a later case in the ECJ, *Bestuur van het Algemeen Burgerlijk Pensioenfonds v Beune*, seemingly contradicts this conclusion, although some arguments have been advanced, distinguishing the circumstances and reconciling the results.]

Ten Oever v Stichting Bedrijfspensioenfonds voor het Glazenwassers (European Court of Justice) [1993]

A survivor's pension falls within the scope of the equal pay requirements. However, equal benefits only had to be provided in respect of benefits earned from 17 May 1990 (the date of the *Barber* judgment), unless a claim had already been started before then.

Coloroll Pension Trustees v Russell (European Court of Justice) [1994]

Equal pension benefits for men and women need only be provided for service from 17 May 1990, except where a claim had been initiated earlier. Unequal benefits must be levelled up for any service after 17 May 1990, but schemes can, in principle, change benefit structures to level down for any subsequent service after the date of change. Additional benefits stemming from contributions paid by employees on a purely voluntary basis are not pay and therefore not subject to the same equal treatment requirements.

Preston v Wolverhampton (European Court of Justice) [2000]

Part-timers whose exclusion from membership of an occupational pension scheme amounts to indirect sex discrimination can claim retrospective membership as far back as 8 April 1976. However, national courts may impose a time limit on lodging claims after leaving service. The House of Lords later confirmed that, for the UK, this time limit is six months.

Uppingham School v Shillcock (High Court) [2002]

Offsets from pensionable salary without pro-rating for part-timers are not discriminatory where applied equally to all members. The approach adopted was in any case objectively justifiable as a reasonable method of implementing the legitimate objective of integration with the State scheme.

Allonby v Accrington & Rossendale College (European Court of Justice) [2004]

The female claimant did not have to identify a male comparator with the same employer, where the indirect sex discrimination arose from a wider 'single source'. (In this case, the single source was the entry rules to a particular statutory pension scheme.)

Bloxham v Freshfields (Employment Tribunal) [2007]

The tribunal held that the treatment suffered by Mr Bloxham when Freshfields introduced new pension arrangements was potentially discriminatory on grounds of age, but that Freshfields' actions were objectively justified as no less discriminatory means were available to them.

Foster Wheeler v Hanley (Court of Appeal) [2009]

To give effect to rights to equal treatment, the modification of a scheme should be the minimum substantive change and should not give rise to windfall benefits. In the context of the scheme rules, here minimal interference was to prohibit consent to retirement from age 60 from being withheld from members with service in the *Barber* window (with a normal retirement age of 60). The scheme was also modified so that an early retirement reduction could be applied for any part of the benefit due from age 65.

Rosenbladt v Oellerking (Court of Justice of the European Union) [2010]

A collective agreement providing for the automatic retirement of employees at age 65 constituted age discrimination, but was justified as a proportionate means of achieving legitimate aims. The Supreme Court judgment in *Seldon v Clarkson Wright and Jakes (see below)* provides further help in defining the criteria employers will need to meet to objectively justify a compulsory retirement age.

Test-Achats (Court of Justice of the European Union) [2011]

The Court found that the use of insurance premiums based on gender is incompatible with the principle of equal treatment for men and women, and decided that the use of gender-based premiums would be unlawful from 21 December 2012.

Seldon v Clarkson Wright and Jakes (Supreme Court) [2012]

The retirement clause in the partnership deed applying to Mr Seldon provided for the mandatory retirement of partners at age 65. The Court found that the aims cited by the firm were legitimate justification for age discrimination but sent the case back to the Employment Tribunal to consider the question of whether a mandatory retirement age of 65 was a proportionate means of achieving the stated aims (which had not previously been considered). The tribunal ruled that the means were proportionate but made the decision on the basis that, at the relevant time, 65 was the default retirement age. The judgment specifically leaves open the question of what is proportionate now that there is no default retirement age and in view of the planned changes in the state pension age.

ADVISERS AND PROFESSIONALS

Re George Newnes Group Pension Fund (High Court) [1969]

An actuary is an expert. If an actuary acts honestly and does not make an objective mistake, the decision is not open to challenge.

Bartlett v Barclays Trust Co Ltd (No. 1) (High Court) [1980]

A higher duty of care is expected from professional trustees.

Auty v National Coal Board (Court of Appeal) [1985]

Actuarial evidence (relating to loss of value dependent on future economic trends) can be rejected by courts on the grounds that it is based on hearsay and speculative in nature.

Re Imperial Foods Ltd Pension Scheme (High Court) [1986]

An actuarial certificate (relating to a bulk transfer payment) could not be successfully challenged in the absence of a cardinal error of principle or a mathematical error.

Re the Minworth Limited Pension Scheme, Anderson v William M Mercer (Pensions Ombudsman) [1999]

A professional trustee who had failed to give proper thought to risks associated with investment mismatching during a wind-up was 'recklessly indifferent' to the fact that it was in breach of its duties, and was therefore not entitled to be exonerated by a clause exempting trustees from liability other than arising from wilful default or fraud. In addition, the Ombudsman ruled that an actuary was inherently 'concerned with the administration' of the scheme, and so a complaint against the actuary came within his jurisdiction.

Wirral BC v Evans (Court of Appeal) [2000]

Administrators have no general duty to advise present or intending members of the scheme.

Gleave v PPF (High Court) [2008]

Insolvency practitioners cannot dispute section 75 debt claims as calculated by the scheme actuary. The companies went into administration in 2001. The insolvency practitioners had argued that the actuary had overestimated the claim, exercisable by the PPF, by using later mortality tables.

TAXATION

Hillsdown v Commissioners of Inland Revenue (High Court) [1999]

The employer had been obliged to repay a refund of surplus on which tax had been paid. The Inland Revenue had originally refused to reimburse this tax. The Court ruled that a repayment of surplus in which no beneficial interest passed was not a payment for the purposes of section 601 ICTA 1988.

JP Morgan Fleming Claverhouse Investment Trust plc and the Association of Investment Trust Companies v Commissioners of HM Revenue & Customs (European Court of Justice) [2007]

The ECJ suggested that Investment Trust Companies (ITC) should be exempt from paying VAT in respect of investment management charges. The NAPF and the Wheels Common Investment Fund launched a joint challenge against HMRC in the ECJ (now CJEU) on the grounds that the exemption should also apply to pension schemes. The CJEU ruled that UK workplace defined benefit pension funds are not 'special investment funds' and are therefore not exempt.

Re PPG Holding BV (Court of Justice of the European Union) [2013]

In a Dutch case involving a defined benefit scheme, the CJEU ruled that both the day-to-day management costs and the investment management fees paid by a sponsor (as opposed to those paid by the scheme as in the *Wheels* case) should be exempt from VAT as long as the investment services provided to the scheme have a direct and immediate link with the employer's taxable activities.

The decision appears out of line with HMRC's historic policy of regarding investment services and advice to be purely the trustees' responsibility.

ERRORS AND DISPUTES

Bradstock v Nabarro Nathanson (High Court) [1996]

In negligence claims, time runs from the date when damage occurred, not from when the negligence of the advice first became known.

Armitage v Nurse (Court of Appeal) [1997]

Trustees can be indemnified under an exoneration clause, even where they have been grossly negligent, provided that they were not reckless.

Hogg Robinson v Pensions Ombudsman (High Court) [1998]

The trustees were not guilty of maladministration by refusing to extend a guarantee period where the member had had problems because of an incorrect quotation. (But the Court's implication, and the Ombudsman's subsequent determination when he revisited the case, was that the failure to produce an accurate quotation in good time was maladministration.)

Derby v Scottish Equitable (Court of Appeal) [2001]

A member who had received a substantial overpayment from a personal pension was obliged to give up the overpayment after the insurer had realised its mistake, except to the limited extent to which he had spent the money irreversibly and could claim a 'change of position'.

Steria v Hutchison (Court of Appeal) [2006]

The appeal judges ruled, against the High Court judgment, that a caveat in the booklet that it did not override the trust deed and rules was adequate to prevent an override provided it was clear and 'not tucked away in tiny print in a footnote'. However, a letter to the member that did not contain a caveat could be overriding, but was irrelevant to the outcome of the case.

Tyler v Robert Fleming Benefit Consultants and Minet Benefit Consultancy (Pensions Ombudsman) [2008]

The Ombudsman held that Minet (the former administrators) were responsible for the disappearance of data in respect of Mr Tyler. He directed Minet to put Mr Tyler in the position he would have been in had he been included in the subsequent bulk buy-out by purchasing a deferred annuity for him.

Colorcon v Huckell (High Court) [2009]

The Court granted an order for rectification of the scheme rules. Evidence showed that the rules relating to the revaluation of deferred pensioners had been amended incorrectly and contrary to the common intention of the employer and trustees.

IBM UK Pensions Trust v IBM UK Holdings (High Court) [2012]

Evidence showed that a rule requiring employer consent for retirement at 60 from active service had been unintentionally introduced in 1983. The trustee successfully argued for the removal of the requirement for consent. The Court granted an order for rectification of the scheme rules.

GENERAL AND MISCELLANEOUS

Mettoy Pension Trustees v Evans (High Court) [1991]

Interpretation of pension scheme documents should be practical and purposive, rather than detailed and literal.

Nuthall v Merrill Lynch (UK) Final Salary Plan trustees (Pensions Ombudsman) [1999]

Trustees can be guilty of maladministration for unnecessary delays in transferring money to individual members' accounts, even if the payments have been made within the maximum timescales permitted by the Pensions Act 1995. In *Bonner v NHS Pension Scheme* (2004), the Ombudsman essentially extended its 1999 determination to other types of pension scheme transaction – ruling that the scheme's inability to deal quickly with a transfer payment was maladministration.

Hoover Ltd v Hetherington (High Court) [2002]

The word 'retires' signifies final withdrawal from some office, without prejudicing the individual's entitlement to work for another office or business. The Court also held that retirement from service by reason of incapacity included retirement in circumstances where the member was in fact capable of full-time work, albeit not of the kind normally undertaken by him or her.

Durant v Financial Services Authority (Court of Appeal) [2003]

Personal data is information that affects an individual's privacy. Two questions can assist in determining the nature of the information: is the information 'biographical', and who is the focus of the information? The fact that an individual's name appears in a document does not mean it will necessarily be personal data about that individual.

The Data Protection Act applies to manual data held in a 'relevant filing system'. A filing system will only be such if it is of sufficient sophistication to provide 'ready accessibility' broadly equivalent to a computerised filing system.

Jones v Tyco Holding (UK) Ltd CARE Pension Scheme (Pensions Ombudsman) [2011]

Administrators should take no more than five working days to raise and issue a cheque for a transfer value once they have all the necessary documentation; and to take longer than that is maladministration, even if the payment is made within the statutory timescale.

INTERNATIONAL

Introduction

The summaries below have been derived from Aon Hewitt's online eGuides. Necessarily, much detail has been omitted. For example, the 'Recent developments' section contains a single item that we hope will be of interest. Readers interested in seeing the fully detailed eGuides should e-mail *InternationalBenefits@aonhewitt.com*.

Countries covered:

- Americas:
  - Brazil
  - Canada
  - United States of America
- Europe:
  - Notes on the European Union
  - Belgium
  - France
  - Germany
  - The Netherlands
  - Russia
  - Spain
  - Switzerland
- Asia Pacific:
  - Australia
  - China
  - India
  - Japan.

The economic indicators and social security information for selected countries *on pages 191 to 196* have been obtained by Economic and Financial Publishing Ltd from the sources indicated.

ECONOMIC INDICATORS AND SOCIAL SECURITY INFORMATION FOR SELECTED COUNTRIES

Notes to the Following Table

(a) Gradually being raised to 67 m&f by 2023 (Australia), 2025 (The Netherlands), 2027 (Denmark, Spain and USA), 2029 (Canada and Germany), 2040 (Poland). German state pension age is currently (2013) 65 years 2 months (m&f).

(b) 60 (m), 55 (f) for rural workers.

(c) Flexible retirement age. Gradually being increased:
- France: to 62–67 (m&f) by 2017, *and*
- Italy: to 66 (m&f) by 2015.

(d) Gradually being equalised at 65 (m&f) by 2015 (Hungary), 2018 (UK). UK age will rise to 66 by 2020, 67 by 2028 and 68 by 2046.

(e) Under the New Pensions System. A flat-rate National Old Age pension is also provided for poor people aged 65 and over.

(f) Mostly funded through general taxation.

(g) On all earnings (in some countries above a minimum amount).

(h) Up to earnings ceiling.

(i)
- Australia: Employer contribution rising to 12% by 2019.
- Japan: Employer contribution rising to 9.15% by 2017.
- UK: Up to earnings limit, but no contributions are paid on earnings below £7,696. Employee contributes an additional 2% on earnings above the ceiling.
- USA: 6.2% on earnings up to the ceiling plus 1.45% on all earnings.

(j)
- Brazil: Employee contribution variable depending on employee level of earnings.
- Japan: Employee contribution rising to 9.15% by 2017.
- Nigeria: Administrative fees paid in addition to employee contribution.

(k) Small, flat-rate (Denmark: employer DDK2,160, employee DDK1,080).

(l)
- China: Three times the average wage for the district, city or province.
- France: Figure shown is the TA ceiling for contributions towards old-age benefits.
- Italy: There is no earnings ceiling on employee contributions for those entering the social security system before 1 January 1996.
- Netherlands: Earnings limit for employer contributions is €49,297.

(m) China's first national law on social insurance came into force in July 2011. It mostly unifies existing schemes.

State pension formula:
- A: not related to earnings
- B: related to earnings below a fixed ceiling
- C: effectively related to all earnings
- D: individual capitalisation system

Sources: *2013 World Population Data Sheet*, Population Reference Bureau; *World Development Indicators*, World Bank; *OECD iLibrary*, Organisation for Economic Co-operation and Development; TradingEconomics.com; and *Social Security Programs Throughout the World: Europe 2012, Africa 2013, Asia and the Pacific 2012* and *The Americas 2011*, US Social Security Administration and International Social Security Association, August 2012, August 2013, March 2013 and February 2012.

	Australia	Belgium	Brazil		Canada		China (exc. HK/Macau)
1. Economic indicators							
Population (2013, million)	23.1	11.2	195.5		35.3		1,357.4
Percentage of population aged 15–64	67	66	68		69		75
Percentage of total population aged 65+	14	17	7		15		9
GDP (2012, local currency bn)	1,474.6	376.2	4,402.5		1,820.0		52,760.8
GDP per capita, local currency	65,009	33,766	22,162		52,177		39,062
GDP per capita, £ equivalent	38,033	28,487	6,208		31,421		3,967
Price inflation (2012, % pa)	2.2	2.2	5.8		0.8		2.4
Money market/Treasury bill rate (October 2013, % pa)	2.70	0.04	8.90		0.92		1.00
Government bond yield (October 2013, % pa)	4.04	2.61	11.73		2.59		4.05
Exchange rate (£1 as at 7 October 2013)	1.7093	1.1853	3.5698		1.6606		9.847
2. Social Security information							
Current at	2012	2012	2011		2011		2012
State pension age	65m 64f *(a)*	65 m&f	65m 60f *(b)*		65 m&f *(a)* 60m 50–60f		20 *(h,m)*
Contribution to State pension (employer, %)	9 *(h,i)*	8.86 *(g)*	20 *(h)*		4.95 *(h)*		20 *(h,m)*
Contribution to State pension (employee, %)	0 *(f)*	7.5 *(g)*	*(i)*		4.95 *(h)*		8 *(h,m)*
Earnings ceiling (local currency)	183,000	n/a	44,300.88		48,300		*(l)*
Earnings ceiling (approx £ equivalent)	107,061	n/a	12,410		29,086		–
Social Security pension type	A	B	C or D		A+B		A+D

Note: In some countries (notably France) the total social security contributions payable are considerably higher than the figures shown ... usually because separate contributions are levied for old-age and other social security and/or regional programmes.

	Denmark	France	Germany	Hungary	India
1. Economic indicators					
Population (2013, million)	5.6	63.9	80.6	9.9	1,276.5
Percentage of population aged 15–64	65	64	66	68	64
Percentage of population aged 65+	18	17	21	17	6
GDP (2012, local currency billion)	1,820.2	2,032.3	2,644.2	28,252.2	100,206.2
GDP per capita, local currency	325,598	30,935	32,290	2,841,205	81,028
GDP per capita, £ equivalent	36,825	26,099	27,242	8,082	815
Price inflation (2012, % pa)	1.9	1.3	2.1	5.0	11.1
Money market/Treasury bill rate (October 2013, %)	0.05	0.04	0.04	3.90	10.90
Government bond yield (October 2013, %)	2.00	2.37	1.83	5.90	8.62
Exchange rate (£1 as at 7 October 2013)	8.8418	1.1853	1.1853	351.5412	99.3954
2. Social Security information					
Current at	2012	2012	2012	2012	2012
State pension ages	65 m&f *(a)*	60–65 m&f *(c)*	65+ m&f *(a)*	62.5 m&f *(d)*	58 m&f *(e)*
Contribution to State pension (employer, %)	*(k)*	9.9 *(f,h)*	9.8 *(h)*	27 *(g)*	17.61 *(h)*
Contribution to State pension (employee, %)	*(k)*	6.75 *(h)*	9.8 *(h)*	10 *(g)*	12 *(h)*
Earnings ceiling (local currency)	n/a	36,372 *(l)*	67,200	n/a	78,000
Earnings ceiling (approx £ equivalent)	n/a	30,686	56,695	n/a	785
Social Security pension type(s)	A	B	B	C	B+D

Note: In some countries (notably France) the total social security contributions payable are considerably higher than the figures shown above, usually because separate contributions are levied for old-age and other social security and/or regional programmes.

	Indonesia	Italy	Japan	Mexico	Netherlands
1. Economic indicators					
Population (2013, million)	248.5	59.8	127.3	117.6	16.8
Percentage of population aged 15–64	65	65	62	64	67
Percentage of population aged 65+	5	21	25	6	16
GDP (2012, local currency billion)	8,243,270.9	1,565.9	475,528.9	15,503.4	600.6
GDP per capita, local currency	33,391,926	25,705	3,727,841	128,289	35,821
GDP per capita, £ equivalent	1,800	21,686	23,923	6,068	30,221
Price inflation (2012, % pa)	4.3	2.3	-0.1	3.6	3.0
Money market/Treasury bill rate (October 2013, %)	13.50	0.04	0.00	2.90	0.04
Government bond yield (October 2013, %)	8.12	4.32	0.66	5.83	2.22
Exchange rate (£1 as at 7 October 2013)	18,548.34	1.1853	155.8251	21.1406	1.1853
2. Social Security information					
Current at	2012	2012	2012	2011	2012
State pension ages	55 m&f	62-66 m&f (c)	65 m&f	65 m&f	65 m&f (a)
Contribution to State pension (employer, %)	4 (g)	23.81 (g)	7.852 (h,i)	6.9 (h)	5.7 (h)
Contribution to State pension (employee, %)	2 (g)	9.19 (l)	8.338 (h,j)	1.75 (h)	19 (h)
Earnings ceiling (local currency)	n/a	93,622	7,440,000	32,901	33,436 (l)
Earnings ceiling (approx £ equivalent)	n/a	78,986	47,746	1,556	28,209
Social Security pension type(s)	D	B+D	A+B	D	A
			(A underpin)		

Note: In some countries (notably France) the total social security contributions payable are considerably higher than the figures shown above, usually because separate contributions are levied for old-age and other social security and/or regional programmes.

	Nigeria	Poland	Russia	South Africa	Spain
1. Economic indicators					
Population (2013, million)	173.6	38.5	143.5	53.0	46.6
Percentage of population aged 15–64	53	71	71	65	67
Percentage of population aged 65+	3	14	13	5	18
GDP (2012, local currency billion)	41,179.1	1,595.3	62,599.1	3,155.2	1,049.5
GDP per capita, local currency	243,904	41,389	436,130	61,638	22,708
GDP per capita, £ equivalent	945	8,318	8,390	3,822	19,158
Price inflation (2012, % pa)	12.0	2.3	6.5	5.7	2.9
Money market/Treasury bill rate (October 2013, %)	11.30	2.50	6.40	5.30	0.04
Government bond yield (October 2013, %)	13.54	4.42	7.26	7.68	4.22
Exchange rate (£1 as at 7 October 2013)	258.0673	4.9756	51.9839	16.1278	1.1853
2. Social Security information					
Current at	2013	2012	2012	2013	2012
State pension ages	50 m&f	65m 60f (a)	60m, 55f	60 m&f	65 m&f (a)
Contribution to State pension (employer, %)	7.5 (g)	14.26 (h)	34 (h)	0	23.6 (h)
Contribution to State pension (employee, %)	7.5 (g,i)	11.26 (h)	0	0	4.7 (h)
Earnings ceiling (local currency)	n/a	102,480	512,000	n/a	39,149
Earnings ceiling (approx £ equivalent)	n/a	20,597	9,849	n/a	33,029
Social Security pension type(s)	C+D	C+D	A+B+D	A (means tested)	B

Note: In some countries (notably France) the total social security contributions payable are considerably higher than the figures shown above, usually because separate contributions are levied for old-age and other social security and/or regional programmes.

	Sweden	Switzerland	UK	USA
1. Economic indicators				
Population (2013, million)	9.6	8.1	64.1	316.2
Percentage of population aged 15–64	64	68	66	67
Percentage of population aged 65+	19	17	16	14
GDP (2012, local currency billion)	3,561.9	592.8	1,541.5	15,684.8
GDP per capita, local currency	374,282	74,127	24,380	49,965
GDP per capita, £ equivalent	36,120	51,002	24,380	31,061
Price inflation (2012, % pa)	–0.1	–0.4	2.7	1.7
Money market/Treasury bill rate (October 2013, %)	1.10	–0.10	0.40	0.10
Government bond yield (October 2013, %)	2.53	1.04	2.73	2.65
Exchange rate (£1 as at 7 October 2013)	10.3621	1.4534	1	1.6086
2. Social Security information				
Current at	2012	2012	2013	2011
State pension ages	65 m&f	65m, 64f	65m 61f (d)	66 m&f (a)
Contribution to State pension (employer, %)	10.21 (g)	4.2 (g)	13.8 (i)	6.2 (i)
Contribution to State pension (employee, %)	7 (h)	4.2 (g)	12 (i)	4.2
Earnings ceiling (local currency)	440,622	n/a	41,444	110,100
Earnings ceiling (approx £ equivalent)	42,522	n/a	41,444	68,445
Social Security pension type(s)	A+B+D	A+C	A+B	B

Note: In some countries (notably France) the total social security contributions payable are considerably higher than the figures shown above, usually because separate contributions are levied for old-age and other social security and/or regional programmes.

AUSTRALIA

Economy and Government

Australia is a constitutional monarchy with a parliamentary government. The Queen is represented in Australia by a governor-general and six state governors.

The national (federal) Parliament consists of the Queen (through the governor-general), the House of Representatives and the Senate. The 150 members of the House of Representatives (each representing an electoral district) are elected for three-year terms. The majority party or group forms the government, selecting a prime minister and the cabinet from its ranks. The current Prime Minister is Tony Abbott of the Australian Liberal Party.

Labour relations

From 1 July 2009, Fair Work Australia (FWA) and the Fair Work Ombudsman subsumed or replaced much of the WorkChoices industrial relations system. FWA is responsible for facilitating collective bargaining; approving enterprise agreements; reviewing minimum wage levels and award conditions; addressing unfair dismissal claims; dealing with industrial action; and settling workplace disputes. The Fair Work Ombudsman provides advice, assistance and education to employers and employees, monitors compliance and takes legal action if necessary.

Cost of employment

The social security system is financed from general tax revenues. For workers' compensation, employers contribute varying percentages of payroll, depending on the risk category and the state.

Employment terms and conditions

FWA has updated and consolidated existing awards under new modern awards. Employers and employees, or their union representatives, may engage in enterprise-level collective bargaining within a single workplace or across multiple employers. FWA applies the Better Off Overall Test (BOOT) to ensure that employees are better off overall in comparison to the relevant modern award. There is no legislative provision for individual agreements. Existing Australian Workplace Agreements (AWAs) and Individual Transitional Employment Agreements (ITEAs), which were permitted until 31 December 2009, may remain in effect for up to five years. Existing workplace agreements must conform with the National Employment Standards (NES).

From 1 January 2013, 'Dad and Partner Pay' is available to eligible fathers and partners, including same-sex partners. They may claim two-week leave, during which the government pays a benefit that equals the national minimum wage and is the same amount as is payable for parental leave.

Social security and other required benefits

The social security system is a combination of universal and social assistance programmes financed from general tax revenues. Benefit payments and customer service are coordinated through Centrelink, which centralises the many services provided by the Departments of Family and Community Services; Education, Training, and Youth Affairs; Health and Ageing; Primary Industries and Energy; and Transport and Regional Services.

Healthcare system

Healthcare is administered at the Commonwealth (federal), state and local levels and is delivered through a combination of public and private resources.

At the Commonwealth level, the Department of Health and Ageing is responsible for overall health policy (especially in the areas of public health, research, and information management) and is involved in the coordination of healthcare primarily through the national health insurance system known as Medicare. The Commonwealth government also maintains the Medicare fee schedules – the Medicare Benefits Schedule Book and the Schedule of Pharmaceutical Benefits for Approved Pharmacists and Medical Practitioners. Medicare Australia administers Medicare, the Pharmaceutical Benefits Scheme (the national prescription drug programme) and an immunisation programme for children, and acts as both claims payer and auditor.

Taxation of compensation and benefits

Australia has a federal tax on personal income, but no state or local income taxes. Residents are taxed on income from all foreign and domestic sources. If tax has been withheld on foreign-source income by the foreign country, a tax credit is granted equal to the lesser of Australian tax or the foreign tax. Tax on employment income is withheld at source. Non-residents are taxed on Australian-source income only. The tax year (like the fiscal year) runs from 1 July to 30 June. Tax returns based on self assessments generally must be filed by the following 31 August.

Recent developments

Employers' superannuation contributions will progressively increase over the next eight years under the Superannuation Guarantee (Administration) Amendment Act 2012. From 1 July 2013, the employer contribution rate increased from 9.0% to 9.25%, and from 1 July 2014 it will increase to 9.5%. The rate will increase by 0.5% on 1 July of every year thereafter, until it reaches 12% in 2019. The superannuation guarantee age limit (age 70) has been abolished as of 1 July 2013, and employers are required to make contributions for employees aged 70 and over. Also, from 1 July 2013 superannuation funds are permitted to offer a new type of account, 'MySuper' From 1 January 2014 employers will be required to deposit contributions in a fund that offers a MySuper account for employees who have not selected a fund.

The Trans-Tasmanian Retirement Savings Portability Scheme is effective from 1 July 2013. Individuals are permitted to transfer their retirement savings between the pension systems in each country (superannuation in Australia and KiwiSaver in New Zealand) without additional taxation. In Australia, transfers may not be made to a self-managed superannuation fund. For the purpose of taxation, transfers are subject to the nonconcessional contribution cap.

In health care news, the government will increase the Medicare levy rate from 1.5% to 2.0% of taxable income beginning with the 2014/15 income year. The increase will be used to finance the DisabilityCare Australia Fund for ten years.

BELGIUM

Economy and Government

Belgium is a constitutional monarchy with a parliamentary democracy. The current king, Philippe, is the head of state. The government is led by the prime minister (appointed by the king on the basis of majority support in the House of Representatives) and the Council of Ministers. Parliament consists of a House of Representatives with 150 members elected through a system of proportional representation and a Senate with 71 members (40 popularly elected, 31 appointed by the Regional Councils). Members of both houses stand for election every four years. The House is the dominant legislative body; the Senate's responsibilities include oversight of constitutional revisions, treaties and relations between the linguistic communities.

Labour relations

Terms of employment and labour relations are governed by statute and through collective agreements signed at the national and inter-industry level, at the industry level, by regions or groups of companies, and at the company level. They are hierarchical – agreements signed at a lower level build on those signed at a higher level – and cumulative – they amend or add to earlier agreements.

Cost of employment

The social security system is comprehensive in scope and coverage and involves substantial cost, approximately 75% of which is borne by the employer. Contributions are based on the employee's gross salary plus any bonuses and benefits in kind, with no earnings ceiling (except for workers' compensation). All employees and firms employing ten or more persons pay full social security contributions on the vacation bonus.

Employment terms and conditions

Historically, employment law distinguished between blue- and white-collar workers. While the classifications were ambiguous – blue-collar as 'manual' and white-collar as 'intellectual' – distinct provisions applied to each classification as regards termination procedures, probationary periods, payment intervals and non-competition agreements. In 2011, the Constitutional Court ruled that Parliament had two years to harmonise the employment terms and conditions for white- and blue-collar employees. In July 2013, the social partners (unions and employers' associations) announced that they had reached an agreement to end the distinctions. Legislation transposing the agreement must still be drafted and passed by Parliament.

The 1978 Law on Contracts of Employment, as amended, governs contracts for blue- and white-collar workers, commercial representatives, domestic workers and students. Employment contracts may be written or verbal; however, fixed-term, part-time, temporary, replacement and student contracts must be written. In practice, almost all employment contracts are in writing.

Social security and other required benefits

Separate but closely related programmes exist for wage earners, salaried employees, the self-employed, miners and seamen. The first two programmes cover all employees in private industry and commerce, except for some company directors considered self-employed for social security purposes. Benefits for the self-employed are significantly lower than those under the other programmes. Other separately financed and administered statutory systems cover national and local government employees and railway workers.

Healthcare system

The extensive healthcare system, which covers all Belgian residents, includes hospital care, visits to doctors (both general practitioners (GPs) and specialists), dental care, pharmaceuticals and home care. The system includes both private and public elements and is highly regulated. The Ministry of Social Affairs and the Ministry of Public Health share responsibility for health insurance, hospital costs, drugs, medical practice and vaccinations. Some responsibility for public health, institutions and home care has devolved to the regional governments.

The National Institute for Sickness and Invalidity Insurance (INAMI/RIZIV) oversees health insurance. Government-approved 'mutuelle' (sickness fund) groups administer the system. All Belgians must enrol with a *mutuelle* of their choice. The *mutuelles* developed from self-funded, self-help community organisations, although now primarily funded by employee and employer (and self-employed) payroll contributions through the federal government. There are six networks of government-approved *mutuelles*, although the affiliation may not be apparent to the *mutuelle* member.

Taxation of compensation and benefits

A resident is subject to Belgian income taxes on worldwide income. An individual is resident if he or she is living in or has a 'centre of economic interest' in Belgium. Non-residents are taxed only on income produced or received in Belgium. Special rules may apply to expatriates. Income taxes are imposed at the national level. Municipalities may levy a surtax, which varies from 0% to 8.9%. There is no wealth tax in Belgium and the capital gains tax varies according to the type of property held and the length of time it is held. The tax year is the calendar year. Individuals must file a tax return by 30 June following the tax year.

Recent developments

Employees who retire early and continue to work will have their old age/survivors' pensions reduced if annual gross earnings exceed €7,570.00 (€11,355.02 for pensioners with dependants), based on the percentage in excess of the ceiling. If gross earnings exceed the threshold by more than 25%, the pension is suspended. Employees who have reached the normal retirement age, have at least 42 years of service and continue to work will have their old age/survivors' pensions reduced if annual gross earnings exceed €21,865.23 (€26,596.50 with dependants), also based on the percentage in excess of the ceiling. If gross earnings exceed the threshold by more than 25%, the pension is suspended. Lower thresholds apply to fully or partially self-employed individuals. Higher thresholds apply to individuals under age 65 receiving only a survivor's pension. These changes, included in the Program Law of 28 June 2013, are retroactive to 1 January 2013.

The Program Law also includes provisions creating a new pension bonus for employees who defer their retirement for at least one year from the time they qualify for early retirement. During the first 12 months, a bonus is not paid. During the second year, employees receive a bonus equal to €1.50 per day. Thereafter, this amount increases by €0.20 per year, up to an additional €2.50 for employees who continue to work 72 months after reaching the early retirement age. The bonus continues to accrue even after the employee reaches normal retirement age.

BRAZIL

Economy and Government

Brazil is a democratic republic with a presidential government. The president serves as chief of state and head of government. The president and vice president are elected by direct popular vote for a four-year term and may be re-elected once.

Labour relations

The constitution protects employees' and employers' rights of association and prohibits government intervention in the organisation or administration of unions or employers' associations. Most employer–union negotiations occur at the industry or professional level or at the level of the enterprise. National-level negotiations between the social partners (employers, unions and government) are infrequent, generally addressing macropolitical or economic stabilisation issues.

Cost of employment

Employee social security contributions are levied on total earnings according to salary brackets, up to an earnings ceiling of R4,159.00 per month as of 1 January 2013. The employee's contribution is based on 12 months' pay only.

The employer's contribution is levied on total payroll with no ceiling. Employer contributions may vary slightly according to the nature of the business.

Employment terms and conditions

Terms of employment and labour relations are governed by the constitution and legislation. Most employment and labour laws have been consolidated in the CLT – Consolidação das Leis do Trabalho (the labour code).

Employment conditions and labour relations may also be regulated by collective agreement and individual contract. Employees may not waive rights granted to them by law. Employment contracts may be written or oral. In practice, most employment contracts are in writing. A Superior Labor Court recently ruled that Brazilian employment laws apply to employees who are transferred outside the country.

Social security and other required benefits

The National Institute of Social Security (INSS) administers social security benefits for insured persons and their dependants, including the self-employed and foreign residents. Civil servants, military personnel, politicians and rural workers are covered by special legislation.

Social security benefits include old-age pensions, special early retirement pensions for working in a hazardous environment, survivors' pensions, long-term disability pensions, cash sickness benefits, medical care benefits, maternity leave and family allowances. Professional rehabilitation after work-related accidents is also provided under social security. Employers are responsible for prefunding severance obligations through a government-administered savings fund and must contribute to government-run training and apprenticeship programmes.

Healthcare system

The Ministry of Health is responsible for national policy, regulating the public healthcare system (Sistema Unificado de Saude, SUS), and providing technical and financial assistance to states and municipalities. State ministries of health control regional healthcare networks and provide technical and financial assistance to the municipalities. The municipalities have primary responsibility for local healthcare planning and delivery. Health councils assist the government at all three levels.

In addition to the SUS, there is a large private sector, whose growth has been stimulated by reductions in public services and the provision of employer and employee tax deductions for private health insurance. An estimated 24% of the population is covered by private health insurance or group medical plans, most of which are employer-sponsored.

Taxation of compensation and benefits

Residents are subject to a graduated federal income tax on worldwide income. An individual is considered resident if he or she has a permanent residence permit, an employment contract in Brazil (even if he or she has a temporary work visa), or lives in Brazil for more than 183 days in a 12-month period. Non-residents pay a flat 15% withholding tax on Brazilian-source income. Income source is established by the location of the payer regardless of where work is performed. A resident absent from Brazil for 12 months is taxed as a non-resident.

Recent developments

Debate over replacing the 'Fator Previdencíario' (social security factor law) continues within both the Ministry of Social Welfare and Congress. Individuals who first enrolled in the social security system after 29 November 1999 may opt to have their benefits calculated according to the Fator Previdencíario, which is based on contribution rate, contribution period, age and life expectancy. The monthly benefit equals the Fator Previdencíario times 70% of the benefit wage. Alternatives include a new minimum retirement age and a new total of age and service.

In other mandatory benefit news, the tax treatment of profit-sharing payments has changed. Payments up to R6,000 are exempt from tax. Payments exceeding this amount are subject to a 7.5%, 15%, 22.5%, or 27.5% tax. Profit-sharing payments are taxed at source and separate from other income.

CANADA

Economy and Government

Canada is a constitutional monarchy. The Queen is represented by a governor-general (appointed on the advice of the prime minister) who convenes and dissolves Parliament, assents to bills and exercises other executive functions. Canada is structured as a confederation of ten provinces and three territories. The federal government consists of an elected House of Commons and an appointed Senate.

Labour relations

Employment standards and human rights legislation in each of the federal, provincial and territorial jurisdictions set the minimum age for industrial employment, maximum work hours, overtime rates of pay, minimum wage rates and statutory vacations with pay. They also regulate employment practices and termination procedures, prohibit discrimination and regulate apprenticeships. Provincial and territorial legislation covers employees working within their borders, except those under federal jurisdiction (generally employees engaged in any work of an interprovincial, national or international nature). Terms of employment are also governed by collective agreements, which cannot establish terms less favourable than those provided by legislation.

Cost of employment
Retirement, death and disability benefits under the Old Age Security Act (flat-rate benefit and means-tested supplements) are financed through general revenues. In addition, there are employer and employee payroll deductions to cover the Canada Pension Plan (earnings-related benefits), employment insurance (including cash on sickness and maternity), hospital/medical benefits and workers' compensation. (In Quebec, employees are covered by the Quebec Pension Plan.)

Employment terms and conditions
Full- and part-time permanent employees are not usually covered by a contract other than a collective agreement. However, it is strongly recommended that employers require all employees to enter into written employment contracts. All employees, whether or not they are party to a written employment contract, are protected under employment standards legislation at the federal, provincial or territorial level. Employment contracts are subject to all applicable employment and tax law in the contract's jurisdiction. If a self-employed person invoices for work done, he or she is treated as an agency or separate company for tax and employment law purposes and is normally liable for income tax, employment insurance, health insurance premiums and other employment costs.

Social security and other required benefits
The social security system is a combination of federal, provincial or territorial, and federal provincial programmes, which provide benefits in all the categories generally found in European social security systems. Virtually all residents are covered by social security. Foreign nationals employed in Canada and paid from a Canadian payroll may also be covered. Under specified circumstances, Canadian nationals employed outside Canada may continue to contribute to the Canada Pension Plan.

Healthcare system
Healthcare falls under provincial and territorial rather than federal control. Each province and territory administers a healthcare plan meeting criteria set out in the (federal) Canada Health Act. Healthcare represents a major expenditure and is a highly visible government concern. The ministry of health in each province or territory is responsible for negotiating the pay of health professionals, the distribution and management of hospitals and their services, setting education policies, standards and quotas for health practitioners, and funding and oversight of the agency that pays for services.

In general, provincial governments prohibit private plans from covering the services offered under the provincial plan. Supplemental plans cannot be used to purchase enhanced care for government-provided services. In June 2005, the Supreme Court of Canada ruled that individuals in Quebec have the right to obtain private health insurance for services already available under the public health care system, and in 2006 the Quebec government passed legislation allowing the purchase of private insurance for three surgical procedures (knee- and hip-replacement surgery and cataract surgery).

Taxation of compensation and benefits

Residents pay personal income tax on worldwide income. Non-residents are taxed only on Canadian-source income. Canadian income taxes are imposed by the federal government and the provincial and territorial governments. In all provinces and territories, except Quebec, provincial and territorial personal income taxes are a fixed percentage of the federal tax, collected by the federal government. Quebec assesses and collects income tax separately. Starting in 2000, the other jurisdictions delinked the provincial or territorial and federal tax calculations and moved to a separate tax on income, although individuals (other than Quebec residents) continue to file a single tax return.

Recent developments

Canada's 2013 federal budget includes provisions relating to pensions. Specifically, it addresses over-contributions to registered pension plans (RPPs). If an over-contribution is made by a plan member or an employer as a result of a reasonable error, the plan administrator would be allowed to refund the over-contribution to the member or employer without obtaining prior approval from the Canada Revenue Agency (CRA). The refund would have to be made no later than 31 December of the year following the year in which the over-contribution was made. Otherwise, authorisation to make the refund must be sought from the CRA. A refund made to a member would be included as income in the year it is received, and the deduction claimed by the member for the year in which the over-contribution was made would not be adjusted. With regard to a refund made to an employer, this would generally reduce the RPP contribution expense for the year to which it related. The proposed change applies to RPP contributions made on or after the later of 1 January 2014 and the day the legislation receives Royal Assent.

Also, the Canadian Accounting Standards Board released its final standard for accounting for employee benefits by private enterprises using CICA 3461. For fiscal years beginning on or after 1 January 2014, private enterprises are no longer able to smooth gains and losses over a number of years in their income statements nor use an early measurement date, similar to the recently revised IAS 19 *(see Section 25)*. Plan sponsors now need to recognise all gains and losses in the fiscal year in which they occur. Unlike under IAS 19, this recognition must be through the profit and loss account, as there is not an 'Other Comprehensive Income' option. With regard to the finance cost/credit in the income statement, the new standard requires the interest cost and the expected return on assets on the liability or asset to be combined, using one interest rate. The concept of 'expected rate of return on plan assets' is eliminated. With regard to remeasurement, the standard eliminates gain and loss amortisation as well as past service cost amortisation. It also eliminates deferred recognition. The balance sheet must reflect the actual surplus or deficit of the plan.

CHINA

Economy and Government

Formally, the government and the Communist Party are separate, complementary institutions; however, there is considerable cross-membership Xi Jinping is currently head of state, General Secretary of the Party and Chairman of the Central Military Commission.

Labour relations

Employment terms are mainly established by the Labour Law, which applies to all types of company. The Labour Contracts Law substantially changed a number of terms of employment covered by the Labour Law. Pre-2008 Regulations for Labour Management in Foreign-Invested Enterprises apply only to joint ventures, wholly foreign-owned enterprises and Chinese–foreign joint stock companies. Some areas of the Labour Law and the Regulations may be unclear and subject to interpretation. Local labour authorities should be consulted.

Cost of employment

Contribution rates for social security and other mandatory programmes vary according to city or province. Many cities and provinces have established contribution rates which vary from the national guidelines. City or provincial regulations supersede national guidelines.

Employment terms and conditions

Employers are required to register the following employment details at the labour and social security bureau where the business is registered: the name, legal representative, economic type and enterprise code of the employer; and the name, gender and national identification number of the employee, along with the date the contract was signed and its expiry date. Employers are required to file the required information within 30 days of hiring an employee and 7 days after termination of the employment.

With effect from 1 July 2013 'dispatch workers' (workers hired through a temporary agency) are entitled to the same employment terms and conditions as comparable full-time employees hired directly by the employer. Dispatch workers may be used only for temporary, ancillary or alternative jobs. A temporary position is one that lasts no longer than six months. An ancillary position provides services for those serving the main business in the enterprise. An alternative position is one in which an employee substitutes for another employee who is unavailable due to leave or full-time study.

Social security and other required benefits

The social security system includes pensions, housing and medical care. Each person is assigned a social security number. Social security and other mandatory programmes are financed through contributions by employers and employees which (as mentioned above) vary by city or province.

Healthcare system

The healthcare system was made more complex by the move from a planned to a market economy. Between 1983 and 2003, government and social insurance expenditures fell, respectively, from 37.43% and 31.12% to 16.96% and 27.16%. Government expenditures have begun to increase in recent years. Total healthcare expenditures are projected to equal 5.15% of GDP in 2013 (approximately US$336 per capita). Of the expenditures, 54.5% are expected to be public expenditures, with private expenditures accounting for the remaining 45.5%. The government is undertaking reforms to reduce the service gap between rural and urban regions and high- and low-income employees. It introduced health insurance portability from 1 July 2011. Under the reform, workers are able to enrol in the health insurance system of the province or municipality in which they are working. This reform generally benefits migrant workers from rural areas. The government also plans to establish an independent system for the production, procurement and distribution of prescription drugs and a national drug formulary. It wants to reduce hospitals' involvement in the sale of prescription drugs in order to cut prices.

Taxation of compensation and benefits

Individual income tax rates for Chinese citizens and for foreign-national residents are the same, but different monthly allowances apply. Residence is principally based on physical presence, domicile or (in certain cases) the right to reside in China. The length of stay establishing residence is not explicitly defined; however, in practice, individuals who are in China for one full tax year or more are considered to be resident and are subject to tax on worldwide income. Temporary absences not exceeding 30 days at a time or 90 days (in aggregate) over a tax year are included in calculating the period of stay. Chinese nationals who have a domicile in China are considered resident for tax purposes. Foreign individuals resident in China for between one and five years can, with the approval of the tax authorities, be taxed only on China-sourced income. Non-residents are taxed only on China-sourced income.

Recent developments

The China Insurance Regulatory Commission, the tax authority and the Shanghai municipal government have reached agreement on a pilot programme for a third-pillar pension. Contributions to the third-pillar pension would be tax-deferred, and the ceiling on contributions would be ¥1,000. Employees and employers could participate. The plan must be submitted to the State Council for review. It is not yet known when the pilot programme will be launched. Also, employers in Tianjin may ask employees to postpone retirement for business reasons. According to the city's human resources and social security authority, the move is temporary, to relieve the shortage of skilled employees.

With regard to healthcare, China's Ministry of Health announced that 20 provinces are piloting a 'pay after' healthcare treatment system. Currently, citizens must pay for medical services before receiving them and apply for reimbursement from their medical plan. Following widespread criticism of delays in urgent care, the government rolled out the pilot programme in local hospitals. The Ministry cautions that the pay-after system will not be instituted nationwide in the near future. Instead, local government will be permitted to determine its feasibility.

EUROPEAN UNION
Economy and Government

The 28 Member Countries of the EU are: Austria, Belgium, Bulgaria, Croatia, Cyprus, Czech Republic, Denmark, Estonia, Finland, France, Germany, Greece, Hungary, Ireland, Italy, Latvia, Lithuania, Luxembourg, Malta, Netherlands, Poland, Portugal, Romania, Slovak Republic, Slovenia, Spain, Sweden and the UK. Candidate countries include Macedonia, Iceland and Turkey.

The 31 countries of the EEA are the 28 Member Countries of the EU plus Iceland, Liechtenstein and Norway. The three additional countries in the EEA do not participate in the development of EU legislation and have no vote on EU matters. Also, the EEA is not a customs union and border controls with Iceland, Liechtenstein and Norway remain.

Labour relations

All EEA members, including Iceland, Liechtenstein and Norway, must observe the labour requirements of the EU, including Directive 93/104 on Working Time, and their nationals have the right of freedom of movement of employees within the EEA. The Directive applies to all public- and private-sector employees, with no exceptions for small firms, but there are numerous exceptions to the provisions for certain types of work. There are also extended transition periods for the provisions on vacation and length of the working week. The EU has also adopted directives on employee representation (works councils), information and consultation of employees.

Cost of employment

Social security benefits are provided by the programmes of each EEA Member Country. The EU itself provides no social security system. There is no obligation upon Member Countries to have a similar level of contributions or benefits under their social security programmes. However, Resolution 94/C 368/03 on EU Social Policy Objectives notes that the objectives of EU social policy include improving competitiveness, protecting workers' rights through minimum standards, convergence of social security systems rather than the imposition of uniform rules, and reinforcing dialogue among Member Countries. The United Kingdom did not agree to the Resolution, however.

Employment terms and conditions

EU directives provide the framework for national legislation on certain employment terms and conditions. EU Member Countries may pass legislation that is more favourable to employees than the terms provided by a directive.

Social security and other required benefits

The EU social security totalisation agreement now extends to the nationals and social security institutions of Iceland, Liechtenstein and Norway. The agreement allows nationals of EEA countries to combine their years of participation under the social security systems of all EEA countries to establish eligibility for benefits. Each country then pays benefits proportionate to the years of coverage under its own social security system. All EU requirements for statutory benefits are extended to Iceland, Liechtenstein and Norway, as EEA members.

In June 2010, the Council of Ministers agreed on a regulation designed to ensure that third-country nationals who are legally resident in the EU and in a cross-border situation are subject to the same rules for coordinating social security entitlements as EU citizens.

Healthcare system

Following several European Court of Justice judgments covering patient reimbursement for healthcare received in another Member Country, the long-awaited directive on cross-border care 'aims to clarify how patients can exercise their rights to cross-border health care, while at the same time providing legal certainty for Member States and health care providers'. Among the directive's major provisions:

- patients will have the right to seek healthcare within the European Union and be reimbursed up to what they would have received at home
- Member Countries will be responsible for providing healthcare in their territory, *and*
- the development of European reference networks would be facilitated, that is, specialised centres in different Member Countries. The directive also seeks to promote activities in e-health and health technology assessment.

The directive was approved on 28 February 2011. Member states have 30 months to transpose the directive's provisions into national legislation.

Taxation of compensation and benefits

Income tax is levied by each Member Country of the EEA. The EU itself does not levy any taxes, but collects revenues from a percentage of value added taxes levied in each Member Country. There is no obligation to harmonise the income tax systems at present.

Recent developments

The European Council for Employment, Social Policy, Health and Consumer Affairs has reached an agreement on the European Commission's proposal for a directive to improve the portability of supplementary pensions. Under the directive, Member States would be required to implement minimum requirements for the acquisition and preservation of pension rights for individuals who go to work in other Member States. Member States would remain responsible for the conditions under which individuals changed jobs within the same country; but the Commission expects that they would apply the directive's standards to internal mobility.

In May 2013, the European Commission announced that in autumn 2013 it would put forward proposals for a directive to improve the governance and transparency of occupational pension funds. The directive will not cover the issue of solvency capital requirements.

FRANCE

Economy and Government

France has a 'mixed' system of presidential and parliamentary government. The president is the head of state and commander in chief. He or she names the prime minister, formally presides over the cabinet (and may name members) concludes treaties, and can dissolve the parliament and call for national referenda. The prime minister is the head of government; he or she is usually the leader of the majority party in parliament and nominates cabinet members. The parliament consists of the National Assembly and the Senate. Representatives to the National Assembly are directly elected for five-year terms. Senators are elected by an electoral college and serve nine-year terms; one-third of the Senate is elected every three years. Two other institutions – the Economic and Social Council and the Constitutional Council – play important roles. The Economic and Social Council (representatives from the trade union confederations employers' associations, social welfare groups and consumers' organisations) is consulted on long-range economic plans and various bills. The Constitutional

Council reviews acts of parliament to determine their constitutionality. It consists of nine members: three are appointed by the president, three by the speaker of the National Assembly and three by the speaker of the Senate.

Labour relations

Labour relations and the terms of employment are determined by statute, case law and collective agreement. At the national level, trade union confederations and employers' associations meet to study and seek solutions for labour market problems, such as skill development and training and unemployment. Despite collaboration between the 'social partners' (government, labour and employers), workplace conflict persists. Strikes are often called during periods of corporate restructuring, especially if the unions and management cannot reach agreement on a 'job protection plan'. They are also used as a political tool – to protest governmental or EU policies.

Cost of employment

Salary *tranches* are used to determine both contributions and benefits under social security and to express premiums and costs under employer-sponsored benefit plans. The *tranches* are adjusted once a year (in January) in relation to wage and price changes.

Employment terms and conditions

In France, employees may be classified as:

- non-*cadres*: blue-collar and lower-level, white-collar employees
- *cadres*: employees who are primarily managerial or who have special academic qualifications
- *cadres assimilés*: technicians, foremen and senior white-collar employees, *and*
- *cadres supérieurs, cadres dirigeants*: executives, top management.

Employees' rights are established primarily through statute and collective agreement. However, a benefit granted repeatedly over time may become a right, unless the employer explicitly stipulates that the benefit is granted at its discretion.

Social security and other required benefits

Coverage under the social security system is mandatory for all employees in commerce, industry and public works. Pensions are payable in any country with which France has diplomatic relations. The Ministry of Employment and Social Affairs, assisted by a Secretary of State for Health, is responsible for the general supervision of the social security system. Compulsory employee and employer contributions are collected by a joint collection agency and distributed to the National Sickness Insurance Fund, the National Old Age Insurance Fund and the National Family Allowance Fund, from which benefits are paid. The government funds additional pension benefits and allowances, certain health and social services and, under certain circumstances, unemployment benefits.

Healthcare system

Membership in a health insurance fund is compulsory for any person working in France (excluding the overseas *départements* and territories), regardless of nationality, provided that an employment relationship exists and the work is paid.

Dependants are covered through the employee's insurance. Coverage is now almost universal. The majority of the population is covered through CNAMTS (the programme for salaried employees).

Taxation of compensation and benefits

Residents are subject to national income tax on worldwide income. In addition to a local property tax which is levied on the occupants of all types of accommodation, taxpayers are also subject to three social taxes – the general social contribution (CSG), the social debt reimbursement (CRDS) and the social levy. Individuals who are physically present for more than 183 days a year, who have a home or primary abode in France, or whose main occupation or centre of economic activities is in France, are considered resident for tax purposes. Non-residents are subject to tax only on France-sourced income. The tax year is the calendar year. Tax returns must generally be filed by the following 1 March. Income tax is not withheld from employee pay for individuals domiciled in France. Income taxes are paid in advance (based on pre-assessments of tax liability) in two instalments equal to one-third of the total liability from the previous year or via monthly instalments. Final settlement is due in September/October or November/December, respectively, based on final assessments issued by the tax authorities.

Recent developments

The French Government is expected to undertake another round of social security pension reforms following the publication of a report by an independent advisory board – the Moreau Commission – that concluded that the pension reform introduced in 2010 was not sufficient to address the system's deficit. The Commission's recommendations include:

(1) a gradual increase in contribution years from 41.5 years, to 43 years for individuals born in 1962 and to 44 years for those born in or after 1966

(2) a 0.1% increase in pension contributions per year for four years for employees exceeding a specified salary cap; the increase would be equally divided between employers and employees, *and*

(3) a limit on the indexation of pensions for wealthy retirees. Wealthy pensioners would receive fewer tax rebates and pay higher social security contributions.

President Hollande indicated that the social partners (government, unions and employers' associations) are not wedded to the recommendations of the Moreau Commission. The Cabinet was expected to review draft legislation in 2013, after which it will be presented to the parliament. A vote on the reforms will take place before the end of the year.

In January 2013, the social partners signed a new Accord National Interprofessionnel (ANI), which requires all employers to provide supplementary health care to their employees. Unions have until 1 June 2013 to launch industry negotiations and until 1 July 2014 to have an industry-wide collective agreement signed. Employers will have 18 months from the date the agreement is signed to comply with its terms. If no industry-wide agreement is signed by 1 July 2014, employers must negotiate a company collective agreement, which includes the details of a required health insurance plan. In the absence of a company collective agreement, employers must offer their employees a minimum health insurance plan, as stipulated by law, by 1 January 2016.

GERMANY

Economy and Government

Germany is a parliamentary democracy with a federal system of government. It has a bicameral legislature and an independent judiciary. The president may be elected to two five-year terms, but his or her duties are largely ceremonial; executive power is exercised by the chancellor.

The Bundestag has 620 deputies, who are elected every four years; one-half of the deputies are elected directly from single-member districts, while the remainder are elected through proportional representation. It is responsible for electing the chancellor and controls the executive branch through its power to call for a vote of no confidence. The Bundesrat (upper house or Federal Council) has 69 members who are delegates of the 16 *Länder* (state governments). Their terms vary in length. The Bundesrat represents the interests of the states at the national level.

Labour relations

Labour relations and terms of employment are determined by statutes, case law and collective bargaining. Traditionally, collective bargaining has been centralised at the industry level. During the past decade, however, some decentralisation has occurred; and the number of agreements signed at the company level has increased. Labour relations in Germany are cooperative. Employees enjoy a dual system of representation: at the industry level they are represented by trade unions and at the company level by works councils.

Cost of employment

Annual earnings ceilings applicable in the western and eastern *Länder* for sickness, maternity and medical benefits, as well as long-term care insurance, were equalised in 2001. Two different earnings ceilings still exist for contribution to old age, survivors' and disability pensions, as well as employment promotion. As income levels become uniform, these ceiling levels will also be made uniform.

Employment terms and conditions

Employers must provide employees with specified terms of their employment within one month of the start of the employment relationship. Fixed-term contracts may not run for more than two years.

Social security and other required benefits

The social security system covers all German employees and provides old age, survivors' and long-term disability pensions, as well as unemployment insurance. Medical care (routine and long-term) and cash sickness and maternity benefits are administered through health funds. Workers' compensation is maintained through a variety of funds administered by employers' associations, or *Land* or local municipalities. When the West German social security system replaced the East German system on 1 January 1992, transitional regulations and grandfathering provisions were implemented, some of which are still in effect.

Healthcare system

The healthcare system is a hybrid of the managed care model and a centralised system in which the government can intervene. The Law to Strengthen GKV Competition (GKV Wettbewerbsstärkungsgesetz) created a split-revenue system, in which insurers can charge additional contributions, payable by employees, to make up any shortfall in revenue.

Taxation of compensation and benefits

Residents are taxed on worldwide income. In general, residents are defined as persons living in Germany for more than 183 days per year. Non-residents are taxed only on German-source income at the same rates as German residents. Taxable income is always assessed by calendar year. Married couples who are residents may file separately or jointly.

Recent developments

New tax laws have made pension asset pooling possible in Germany. In 2013 the federal government passed legislation transposing the European Union Directive on Alternative Investment Fund Managers (Directive 2011/61/EU) and drafted amendments to tax laws that correspond to the new legislation. Under the new law, a limited partnership company may be established to offer tax-transparent options for pension pooling.

In 2013 the German Corporate Governance Code Commission made amendments to the German Corporate Governance Code, which included changes to management board compensation. The Commission recommended that a cap be placed on individual management board compensation, both fixed and variable. Variable compensation elements must be based on a multi-year assessment and related to 'demanding, relevant comparison parameters'. Retroactive changes to performance targets or comparison parameters are prohibited. Payments made to a management board member for premature termination of the contract cannot exceed two years' compensation, including fringe benefits, and cannot provide the compensation that would have been paid for the remainder of the contract. If the contract is terminated for cause, the management board member is not entitled to compensation. Payments made due to a change in control cannot exceed 150% of the severance pay cap. For pension plans, the Supervisory Board must establish the level of provision in each case, considering the length of time an individual has been a management board member as well as the annual and long-term expense to the company.

INDIA

Economy and Government

India is a federal republic with a parliamentary government. The 'union executive' consists of a president, vice president, prime minister and the council of ministers. The president serves as head of state while the prime minister serves as head of government. The president and vice president are elected to a five-year term by an electoral college that is composed of members of the national parliament and the state legislative assemblies. The president is empowered to declare a 'state of emergency' if he or she believes the country faces an external threat, and to assume control over state governments if there is a constitutional crisis in a state.

Labour relations

Labour relations and terms of employment are determined primarily by statute. National laws are applicable, except where states have passed amending acts to address local circumstances. At both the national and state levels, employers and employees must comply with omnibus acts, as well as 'sectoral' acts. The most important sectoral acts regulating the terms of employment are the Factories Act, which is a national law covering factories, and various shops and establishments acts, passed by the states and covering shops, offices and commercial establishments that are not regulated by the Factories Act. Case law and custom also play an important role in guiding labour–management relations and employment issues. The Supreme Court regularly hears appeals of decisions made by industrial tribunals; it has ruled on labour–management disputes, employee terminations, conditions of employment and wages and benefits. Custom and local practice are significant factors in the establishment of acquired rights.

Cost of employment

Contributions for old age, survivors', disability, cash sickness and maternity benefits are based on monthly basic salary plus 'dearness' allowance (cost of living) and retaining allowance (if any), (both employer and employee contributions) up to a specified ceiling. Employees whose earnings exceed the ceilings are excluded from these programmes.

Employment terms and conditions

Employment contracts can be written or oral. Typically, employers issue an 'appointment letter' that outlines the general terms and conditions of employment. A 'letter of confirmation' is sent to the employee within 30 days of hire. The contents of an appointment letter are not determined by statute, except for employees covered by the Sales Promotion Employees (Conditions of Services) Act. This act requires that the job title, date of appointment, probation period, wage scale, rate of wage increases, total wages and conditions of service be delineated in the appointment letter. The Industrial Employment (Standing Orders) Act requires employers to create a written document, known as 'standing orders', that establishes the terms of employment, and provides a 'model standing orders' for any employer to use. If an employer wishes to develop its own standing orders, it must be certified by the relevant authorities, and the orders cannot contain terms and conditions that do not meet the standards outlined in the model document.

Social security and other required benefits

The social security system consists of programmes at the national and state levels, including compulsory savings (provident fund), pensions, and insured welfare benefits in the event of sickness, maternity, death and work-related accident or illness. Indemnities are payable by the employer upon termination of employment for any reason except just cause (with some exceptions). Employees covered by Employees' State Insurance are entitled to unemployment and medical benefits in the event of layoffs. Several states have their own unemployment programmes, which are financed from general revenue.

Healthcare system

The states are responsible for the delivery of most healthcare services. The federal (union) government responsibilities include population control, medical education, family welfare and food and drug regulation. Nationally, the Ministry of Health and Family Welfare oversees all aspects of healthcare policy and delivery through the Department of Health and Family Welfare (DHFW) and the Department of Ayurveda, Yoga and Naturopathy, Unani, Siddha and Homeopathy (AYUSH). The DHFW regulates the manufacture or import, distribution and sale of drugs and oversees medical education, training and research standards as well as numerous educational institutions. The Central Government Health Scheme (CGHS), under the DHFW, operates medical facilities for certain groups including active and retired national government employees and members of parliament. The second department (AYUSH) was created in 1995 to develop the Indian Systems of Medicine and integrate them into the general healthcare system.

Taxation of compensation and benefits

Residents are taxed on worldwide income. Non-residents are taxed on Indian-source income only. A person is a resident if he or she spent at least 182 days in the previous tax year in India, or 60 days in the previous tax year plus at least 365 days in the preceding four years. However, an Indian national who leaves India to work abroad is not considered a resident unless he or she has been in India for at least 182 days in that year. Income payable for services rendered in India is considered Indian-source income, irrespective of its place of accrual or payment. Persons 'resident but not ordinarily resident' in India – someone who has not been a resident in India in nine of the ten previous years or who has not been in India a total of 730 days or more during the preceding seven years – generally do not pay tax on income earned outside India, unless it is derived from a business controlled in India. Taxable income includes wages, salaries, allowances, fees, commissions, benefits in kind, annuities or pensions, gratuities in excess of the tax-free portion, dividends, interest and discounts, rent, royalties, technical service fees and lottery or contest winnings. The tax year begins on 1 April and ends on 31 March.

Recent developments

In March 2013 the Pension Fund Regulatory and Development Authority announced that deferred withdrawals would replace phased withdrawals from the New Pension Scheme (NPS) with immediate effect. The change affected Tier 1 accounts, which allow contributors to save for retirement with restricted access to savings prior to reaching retirement age. Under the deferred withdrawal facility, subscribers have the option to defer the withdrawal of their lump sum beyond age 60 and remain invested in the NPS. No new contributions can be accepted, and partial withdrawals are not permitted during the period of deferment. However, the subscriber is allowed to withdraw the deferred lump sum before age 70 with written application or notice.

At the end of November 2012, the Employee Provident Fund Organization (EPFO) issued guidelines intended to clarify the definition of 'basic wages' on which contributions to the EPF are calculated. Basic wages were defined as all income earned by employees according to the terms and conditions of employment that i payable in cash. The cash value of food concessions, the dearness allowance and gifts made by the employer would be excluded. All other allowances ordinarily paid to employees would be considered basic wages. The Ministry of Labor is seeking further clarification as to whether special, transportation, medical and other allowances, that were previously not considered part of the basic wage, should now be subject to EPF contributions. Additional guidance is pending.

JAPAN

Economy and Government

Japan is a constitutional monarchy with a parliamentary government. The emperor serves as the symbolic head of state; the prime minister is the head of government and leads the executive branch. The prime minister is elected by the parliament or Diet and must be a member of the Diet at the time of his or her election to the executive branch. The prime minister appoints cabinet members, a majority of whom must also be members of the Diet. The Diet consists of the House of Representatives and the House of Councillors. The House of Representatives has 480 members who are elected to four-year terms. The 242 members of the House of Councillors are elected for six-year terms. Of the two houses, the House of Representatives is more powerful.

Labour relations

Employment terms are defined primarily by employers. The Labour Standards Law stipulates minimum conditions. Wages, on the other hand, are often established through the 'spring labour offensive' or *Shunto*, a system of annual industrial collective bargaining. Given Japan's recent economic difficulties, the impact of the *Shunto* on wage increases has been negligible during the past few years. Historically, labour relations have been cooperative, though recent circumstances have created some distrust between employers and workers. The 2001 Law for Promoting the Resolution of Individual Labour Disputes, aiming to facilitate the prompt resolution of labour disputes by rapid intermediation through 300 general labour consultation desks, has had somewhat limited success, however, so the 2004 Labour Tribunal Law provides a venue for the speedy resolution of labour disputes.

Cost of employment

Social security combines a universal programme providing flat-rate benefits through the National Pension Plan (NPP), with an employment-related programme providing benefits based on earnings through the Employees' Pension Insurance Plan (EPIP). Contributions to the EPIP are based on monthly covered earnings, with 30 earnings grades. Contributions to the Employee Health Insurance System (EHI) are based on monthly covered earnings, with 47 earnings grades. Contributions to unemployment insurance, workers' compensation insurance and family allowances are based on total payroll.

Employment terms and conditions

Traditionally, employment law and practices have emphasised homogeneous groups of employees, who are long-serving and receive seniority-based wages. Given this focus, employment law stipulates that employers with ten or more employees must establish a set of work rules that specify the terms of employment. These work rules generally substitute for contracts and collective agreements, even though they are not subject to negotiation.

Social security and other required benefits

The NPP provides flat-rate benefits for all residents. The EPIP provides pay-related benefits that supplement the NPP. The EPIP also provides limited flat-rate benefits. Employers and sole proprietors with five or more full-time employees, and all corporations, including employers (legal directors and auditors) and employees, must participate in the EPIP and the EHI. This includes branches and sales offices of foreign companies which are treated as incorporated businesses and representative offices which are treated as sole proprietorships. Employers with at least 1,000 employees may contract out of the EPIP under certain conditions, and employers with at least 700 employees may contract out of the EHI. Workers' compensation insurance, unemployment insurance and family allowances are provided under separate programmes.

Healthcare system

The Ministry of Health, Labour and Welfare (MHLW) develops healthcare policy and coordinates overall health and welfare administration. In the MHLW, the Department of National Hospitals manages and administers national medical facilities including hospitals, sanatoriums and specialised medical centres. The Health Insurance Bureau handles policy planning and coordination of the health insurance systems which the MHLW oversees. The Social Insurance Agency manages and administers the various health, welfare and pension plans. While the government administers and/or coordinates health insurance coverage, healthcare providers are almost exclusively private. More than 80% of hospitals and 90% of physicians, dentists, clinics and nursing homes operate on a for-profit basis.

Taxation of compensation and benefits

Japan levies national, prefectural and municipal income taxes on individuals. Permanent residents are taxed on worldwide income. Individuals who are domiciled in Japan or who are present in Japan for one year or more are considered to be resident for tax purposes; domicile is defined as the place in which an individual's life is centred. Individuals who have been resident in Japan for fewer than five of the past ten years are considered to be non-permanent residents and are taxed only on Japanese-source income and on income received in Japan from overseas. Non-residents are taxed on income from services in Japan, even if paid overseas, at a flat 20% rate (without residents' deductions). Individuals present in Japan for fewer than 183 days in a 12-month period are generally exempt from income tax on foreign-sourced income. The tax year is based on the calendar year. Employers are required to withhold taxes from salaries, wages and bonuses paid to resident employees. Withholding tables are adjusted for the employee's personal and family situation.

Recent developments

Under the amended Act for the Stabilisation of Employment of Older Persons from 1 April 2013 employers must continue to provide employment to any employee who wants to remain employed until he or she reaches age 65. It is no longer possible to screen employees for continued employment by certain conditions such as performance, attendance or health. Employers are not required to offer continued employment if an employee meets conditions for dismissal as specified in the work rules (e.g. disabled and unable to work). While employment must be continued upon request, employers are not required to offer employees the same position or under the same terms and conditions. If a labour–management agreement already specifies a retirement age of age 65, no action is needed. If the agreement specifies a retirement age of age 60 to age 64, the agreement must be reviewed, and the employer and employee representatives must reach agreement on a new 'extended employment policy' or 'rehire policy'. The work rules must be amended to align with the new policy, and the revised work rules must be submitted to government authorities. Firm-wide communications must be prepared to explain the changes. During a 12-year transition period (to 31 March 2025), employers with an existing extended employment or rehire policy are permitted to impose the stipulated conditions for rehire only if the employee is eligible to receive a pension from the Employee Pension Insurance scheme.

Also, Employer Pension Funds (EPFs) with assets that fall short of the liability for contracted-out benefits ('minimum reserve') must be dissolved within five years. The establishment of new EPFs will not be permitted. Participating employers must make up for the funding shortfall in the minimum reserve. Assets equal to the minimum reserve must be returned to the government. A special dissolution rule will be applied to accelerate the dissolution of funds. EPFs with assets that exceed the minimum reserve may continue. They will be subject to two annual funding tests – assets must equal or exceed 1.5 times the minimum reserve, and must equal or exceed liabilities on a discontinuance basis. These tests will begin in 2019. If an EPF does not meet the tests, the government may require its dissolution. The legislation is scheduled to be effective from 1 April 2014; the government is expected to issue additional guidance. Employers should confirm whether or not they participate in an EPF and if so, explore the implications of remaining in the EPF.

THE NETHERLANDS

Economy and Government

The Netherlands is a constitutional monarchy with King Willem-Alexander as the reigning head of state. Formally, the government is divided into the Crown; the legislature, represented by the States General (parliament); and the judiciary. The States General has two houses: the Upper Chamber with 75 members and the Lower Chamber with 150 members. General elections for both chambers are held at least every four years. Members of both chambers are elected by proportional representation. Members of the Upper Chamber are elected by the members of the provincial governing bodies not more than three months after the election of the members of the provincial councils. Members of the Lower Chamber are elected directly by all Dutch nationals aged 18 and over.

Labour relations

Employment terms are determined through national labour laws, collective bargaining and individual employment contracts. Labour–management relations are cooperative. The government has a statutory obligation to consult with the Social and Economic Council (SER) over proposed changes in labour and employment laws and general decisions affecting employment. SER functions primarily as an advisory board on macro-economic issues. Additionally, the Labour Foundation (STAR), a bipartite body representing employers and unions, is a central forum for consultation and negotiation.

Cost of employment

Employers and employees pay social security contributions to two programmes based on total earnings up to specified ceilings. Rates and ceilings are normally revised in January and July. Cash sickness and maternity benefits (ZW) are funded in full by the government. There is no separate workers' compensation programme. Benefits for work-related accidents are paid under the medical, disability and survivors' benefit plans of social security. Employees contribute to the health insurance fund (ZVW) for healthcare.

Employment terms and conditions

Employment contracts are required and, unless otherwise stated, are indefinite. The maximum term for a probationary period is two months if the contract is indefinite or for a fixed term exceeding two years. For fixed-term contracts that do not exceed two years, the maximum probationary period is one month. During a probationary period, the contract may be terminated without notice by either party. Only within a Collective Labour Agreement (CAO) can there be different probation periods. If the employer terminates the employment contract during the probation period, the employer must state the reasons for the termination in writing, upon the employee's request.

Social security and other required benefits

The comprehensive social security system provides benefits through the National Insurance System and the Employed Persons Insurance System. Social security programmes do not distinguish between blue- and white-collar employees. The basic National Insurance System is financed through employee contributions and provides flat-rate old age pensions and survivors' benefits, family allowances and special health insurance for the entire population, as well as disability benefits for the self-employed. The Employed Persons Insurance System is financed by employer and employee contributions and provides additional health insurance for lower-paid persons, and disability, cash sickness, maternity and unemployment benefits.

Healthcare system

There is no national health service. Health insurance in the Netherlands is a three-tiered system based on a combination of private insurance companies (either independently or under contract to the government) and public entities. Prior to 2006, about 64% of the population was covered for basic healthcare services by the first tier of the system (Ziekenfondswet (ZFW)), which was compulsory for persons with income below €33,000. That portion of the population earning above the ceiling were supposed to have private health insurance, typically as a result of their employment. Due to rising national healthcare costs as well as concerns regarding equitable access to and choices for healthcare, the government passed the Health Insurance Act (Zorgverzekeringswet (ZVW)) t replace the ZFW for basic medical care and hospitalisation, effective from 1 January 2006. The second tier of insurance is the AWBZ, which covers long-term care and high-cost treatment. The AWBZ is compulsory for residents and non-residents employed in the Netherlands independent of their income. It is run by state-appointed insurers. The third tier is voluntary health insurance, which covers treatments not covered under the first two, including dental care.

Taxation of compensation and benefits

Residents are taxed on worldwide income. Non-residents are subject to tax only on Dutch-source income. Dutch tax law does not define residence, which is determined on individual circumstances such as where a person lives regularly, the length of stay in the Netherlands and the taxpayer's centre of interests. The tax year for individuals is the calendar year. Tax returns must generally be filed by 1 April of the following year. Taxes are collected via withholding or advance payment.

Recent developments

The Pension Governance Act was passed by both houses of parliament. All pension funds must establish a permanent supervisory board after three years. Company pension funds must have a 'visitation committee' for internal supervision. The number of pensioners serving on the pension fund board will be capped at 25%. The new Act on pension governance will be effective from 1 July 2014.

In April 2013, legislation modifying pension build-up provisions was introduced to parliament. Maximum pensionable income would be capped at €100,000 in 2015. This amount would be pro-rated for part-time employees. A transitional regime would be established for employees with pensionable income that exceeded €100,000 prior to 2015; excess income would be treated as a voluntary pension. The pension build-up period would increase from 35 to 40 years; after this time employees would be entitled to an old age pension equal to 70% of the average wage. Also, the deduction for annuity premiums paid to cover a shortage in pension contributions would be reduced from 17% to 12.7% of the calculation base.

RUSSIA

Economy and Government

The Russian Federation comprises Russia plus 21 autonomous republics and numerous other autonomous territories and regions. The president has extensive powers, nominates the highest governmental officials, including the 'chairman of the government' (prime minister) who must be approved by the legislature, and can pass decrees without consent from the legislature. Presidents are elected for four-year terms and cannot serve more than two consecutive terms. The legislative body has two chambers – the State Duma (lower house) and the Federation Council (upper house). The State Duma consists of 225 members elected from single member districts and 225 members elected from party lists. The Federation Council consists of 178 members – two representatives from each of the country's regions, one from the legislative body and one from the executive body of the region.

Labour relations

An amended Russian Federation Code of Labour Laws (KZOT) came into effect in October 2006. The 2006 amendments primarily affect employment contracts, wage payment, severance and vacation pay. The Ministry of Health and Social Development's Federal Labour Inspectorate and regional and local government inspectorates have the responsibility to enforce the labour and safety laws. These inspectors have free access to all enterprises and companies to conduct inspections and have the power to levy fines for infractions. In 2013, the Labour Code was amended to permit the establishment of works councils.

Cost of employment

From 1 January 2010, Russia abolished the Unified Social Tax and replaced it with separate contributions to the federal Pension Fund, the Social Insurance Fund, and federal and regional Compulsory Medical Insurance Funds. Unemployment benefits are now financed through general income tax revenues.

Employment terms and conditions

All employment relationships in Russia, regardless of the location of the employee's legal employer, are subject to the Labour Code. The Code defines 'employer' to include individual entrepreneurs and domestic employers and requires that all employees have a written employment contract (a labour contract). Self-employed persons may be hired under civil law agreements, provided they are registered as entrepreneurs. Civil law agreements are regulated by the Civil Code instead of the Labour Code.

Social security and other required benefits

The administration and assets of the social security system are separated into the Pension Fund and the Social Insurance Fund. Contributions to these funds are collected locally, and the assets are managed by local officials. The Pension Fund administers the old age, survivors', and long-term disability pensions, plus child care allowances. The Fund is an independent body reporting to the State Duma. Cash sickness and maternity benefits, workers' compensation benefits and other social welfare benefits are paid through the Social Insurance Fund. The Fund is run by the government and guarantees benefits to all employees. A workers' compensation system, with risk-related premiums paid by employers, is managed by the Social Insurance Fund. Previously, work injuries were treated as regular death and disability (i.e. Pension Fund) events.

Healthcare system

The healthcare system is still highly inefficient and needs continued reforms. The Ministry of Health and Social Development formulates federal policies and controls their execution. Below the national level the *oblast*, autonomous, or *kra* health departments govern regional healthcare. The degree of independence from the ministry varies for each regional unit. District or *rayon* health authorities have an executive role at the local level. Health insurance foundations administer medical insurance funds. Health insurance foundations have not been established in all parts of the country. The district health authorities manage the public-sector hospitals and clinics in areas without the foundations' presence.

Taxation of compensation and benefits

The Ministry of Taxes and Collections regulates tax matters and issues numerous 'instructions', 'orders' and 'letters' to expand on, clarify or reverse earlier documents, and occasionally they appear to conflict with the tax or other laws. Individuals who have been in Russia more than 183 days in a consecutive 12-month period are considered resident for tax purposes. Residents are taxable on worldwide income. Foreign nationals who are resident are taxed in the same manner as local nationals. Non-residents are taxed on income from Russian sources only; payment from offshore companies for work in Russia is counted as Russian-source income. The tax year is the calendar year. Procedures for registration with the tax authorities and filing tax returns, due dates for returns and penalties for non-compliance change frequently. Therefore, professional tax advice is necessary to ensure up-to-date information and compliance.

Recent developments

Debate over pension reform continues. Under the latest government proposal, pensions would be calculated using points based on a total of three coefficients – pay at retirement, work history and actual retirement age. The insurance portion of the pension would increase every year an employee deferred retirement beyond the normal retirement age. If retirement were deferred for five years, the pension benefit would increase by 1.5 times. The points would be adjusted for inflation; however, the mechanism for adjustment is still pending. Government officials reiterated that pension reform would not include an increase in the normal retirement age. However, the number of contribution years would increase from five to fifteen years.

In related developments, the Ministry of Labour and Social Security drafted a bill on corporate pensions. Employers would be permitted to sponsor pension plans to provide employees with additional funds for retirement. The plan could be administered by the employer, without the use of a nongovernmental pension fund or an insurance company. Employers and employees could contribute to the plan; contributions up to two times the minimum living wage would not be subject to tax. To receive tax-favourable treatment, the employer would be required to register the plan with the government; information requirements would include payment terms, eligibility, changes to pension rights, rights of employees who are terminated and the rights of survivors. It is not known when action will be taken on the draft legislation.

SPAIN

Economy and Government

Spain is a parliamentary monarchy; the president of the government is nominated by the monarch and subject to approval by the Congress of Deputies (lower house). The Spanish legislature is bicameral: Senators are elected in each of the provinces, and members of the Congress are elected via proportional representation. The structure of governance is semi-federal, with the powers of the national government shared with 17 'autonomous communities'. Each of these communities, or regional governments, has its own president, parliament and court system. The Basque Country and Catalonia have the strongest regional traditions, marked by their history and separate languages.

Labour relations

Employment terms and labour relations are governed by statute, national framework agreements and collective agreements. There are mechanisms at the national level and regional or provincial levels – the Economic Social Councils – to promote social dialogue among employers, trade unions, government officials and political parties. Employees have the right to affiliate with the labour union of their choice, elect union representatives and take industrial action.

Cost of employment

The social security system has been subject to several revisions in contribution rates and ceilings in recent years in an attempt to base the contributions on an amount closer to actual salary for each of the applicable wage classes (11 in all). However, the current ceilings are still too low to compensate executives effectively. All social security contributions are paid on earnings within the applicable class's wage range. Contributions are based on 12 monthly salaries (bonuses are spread *pro rata*). A minimum contribution wage base applies to each occupational group (or wage class). The maximum contribution wage base has been the same for all wage groups since 1 January 2002. The minimum wage base for the employer's workers' compensation tax is the same as for wage classes 4–11.

Employment terms and conditions

All employment contracts must be in writing. Spain has implemented the EU directive on proof of employment, which requires an employer to confirm in writing the terms and conditions of employment. There are different types of employment contract in Spain – indefinite-term contracts, temporary contracts, 'special relationship' contracts and the partial retirement contract. The growth in type and number of temporary contracts is a consequence of government policies designed to encourage job creation. Provided there are no collective agreements to the contrary, employers may stipulate a limited trial period during which the employer or the employee may unilaterally terminate the employment contract without notice, cause or compensation.

Social security and other required benefits

The social security system is a comprehensive programme covering a significant portion of the population and providing a wide range of protection. It is based on a combination of employment-related (contributory) and universal (non-contributory) plans. The General System (*Régimen General*) is compulsory for all employees aged 16 and over, including foreign nationals working for companies that are registered in Spain. Under the *Régimen General*, there are special programmes for employees of specific industries (for example, certain types of employment in market research/public opinion firms and in the hotel and food industries). There are special systems for the self-employed, maritime workers, mining, homemakers and agricultural workers.

Healthcare system

During the 20th century, healthcare services evolved into a true system of national healthcare provision, and almost 100% of the population is covered. A responsibility for purchasing and delivery of healthcare rests with Spain's 1 autonomous regions, aided by the National Institute of Public Health (INGS). The Ministry of Health and Consumer Affairs has overall responsibility for health policy, including establishing minimum healthcare standards and ensuring that national policies are implemented at the regional level. It has direct responsibility for public health policy, immunisations and inspection of meat and animal products imported from other countries (*sanidad exterior*), and legislation on pharmaceutical products.

Taxation of compensation and benefits

Individual income tax (IRPF – *Impuesto sobre la Renta de las Personas Físicas*) is levied by three tiers of government: the central government, the autonomous regional governments and local municipal governments. Central government taxes are administered by the Ministry of Economy and Taxation and are collected at provincial branches across the country. The laws applicable to individual taxpayers were consolidated in Law 40/1998 effective for income and capital gains (or losses).

Recent developments

From 1 January 2013, the normal retirement age increased from age 65 to age 67 and the number of years of contributions required for a full retirement benefit increased from 35 years to 38.5 years. In March 2013, the government published Royal Decree 5/2013, which increases restrictions on early retirement, both for involuntary and voluntary reasons. For involuntary early retirement, the retirement age will increase from age 61 to age 63 and the number of years of contributions required will increase from 31 years to 33 years. For voluntary early retirement, the retirement age will increase from age 63 to age 65 and the number of years of contributions required will increase from 33 years to 35 years.

SWITZERLAND

Economy and Government

Switzerland has a federal system of government with both parliamentary and direct systems of democracy. The federal government (whose official name is the Helvetic Confederation) is composed of 26 cantons (20 of which are 'full' cantons and 6 are 'half' cantons). The federal government is responsible for matters that affect the entire country, for example foreign policy, national defence, customs and monetary controls. The cantons implement federal laws, and can pass their own legislation on local issues. Each canton has its own parliament and government. In three half cantons, members of the federal government are elected by assemblies of the citizens. In the other cantons, federal and cantonal government members are elected by ballot.

Labour relations

Labour relations and terms of employment are determined by the Federal Constitution, statutes and collective agreements. The cantons are responsible for administering federal laws and providing arbitration courts, labour courts and appeal processes. Labour–management relations are cooperative. The government regularly consults with union confederations and employers' associations over proposed changes in labour and employment laws.

Cost of employment

Contributions to the federal social security system are required of all employed persons over age 17 and of residents aged 20 and older who are not part of a direct employer–employee relationship. Widows/widowers receiving a widow's/widower's pension and spouses who do not reach normal retirement age at the same time are required to contribute to social security during the years prior to reaching normal retirement age. Contribution rates are applied to total earnings, including bonuses, severance pay and income replacement benefits. For individuals with no earned income, the contribution is based on the individual's assets. Contributions are not required on workers' compensation benefits, special bonuses or awards, or employer-paid insurance premiums.

Employment terms and conditions

Employment contracts may be written or oral. Contracts for special categories of employees – apprentices, 'commercial travellers' and home workers – must be in writing. Employment law does not specify the contents of the employment contract. However, some provisions must be in writing to be valid (for example, non-competition provisions). Employees' rights are established through laws and collective agreements. However, a benefit granted repeatedly over time may become a right unless the employer specifically states that the benefit is granted at its discretion.

Social security and other required benefits

The retirement system is based on the 'three pillars'. The federal social security system is the first pillar, a basic universal pension financed on a pay-as-you-go basis. Mandatory occupational pension plans under federal law (BVG/LPP) form the second pillar and individual savings and insurance constitute the third. The federal social security system provides old-age and survivors' pensions (AHV/AVS) and long-term disability benefits (IV/AI) as well as short-term income replacement benefits (EO/APG). Workers' compensation, unemployment insurance and family allowances are provided under separate legislation. Medical care benefits are not provided by social security.

Healthcare system

The role of the federal government is limited to matters such as control of food and drugs, control of communicable diseases, poison control, etc. Healthcare delivery is managed at the level of the 26 cantons. Each canton decides the type and scope of healthcare services to be provided to residents. Services can range from government-run hospitals (at canton or community level) to financial support for services provided by private facilities to purchasing services from facilities in other cantons. About half of the cost of these services is covered by the cantons through general revenues and half by patient insurance.

Taxation of compensation and benefits

Taxes are levied by federal, cantonal and municipal authorities on the worldwide income of residents, exclusive of income from foreign real estate and foreign permanent establishments. Criteria for residence, which vary for federal, cantonal and municipal tax purposes, are based on length of domicile, economic activity or ownership of property. The rates of federal tax are common to all cantons, but each canton sets its own basic tax rates and allowances for cantonal and municipal tax purposes. The cantonal and municipal taxes payable in any year are calculated by applying multiples to the basic rates. All cantons levy a wage withholding tax for foreigners who do not have a permit to stay permanently in Switzerland. Each cantonal authority is responsible for the assessment and collection not only of cantonal tax but also of federal and municipal taxes. For federal and cantonal tax purposes, the tax year is the current income year. In general, cantonal tax is payable in instalments. Federal tax bills must be settled by the end of March of the following year. The income of husband and wife is assessed jointly. Different tax tables apply to single and married persons.

Recent developments

The government has published its comprehensive plans for pension reform, 'Retirement Provision 2020'. Formal proposals are expected to be introduced to the parliament in 2014, but the proposed reforms include:

- increasing the retirement age for women from age 64 to age 65
- allowing individuals with lower average income and who began making social security contributions at age 18, 19 or 20 to retire early without a loss in benefits
- allowing individuals aged 62 and older to work part-time without a loss in benefits
- increasing the Value Added Tax, *and*
- reducing the minimum conversion rate for the mandatory occupational pension (BVG/LPP) by 0.2% each year for four years.

In addition, in a national referendum the Swiss voted to impose strict controls on executive pay, giving shareholders the ultimate say on compensation.

UNITED STATES OF AMERICA

Economy and Government

The United States is a federal republic with powers shared by the national and state governments. The tension between the rights of states and the rights of the federal government plays a crucial role in US politics.

Labour relations

Legal mechanisms exist to impose settlements in disputes in workplaces deemed to be essential to the public good. In addition, minimum wage and maximum work hours are established by law. In general, however, the terms of employment are determined by employers or through collective bargaining. Employers are subject to extensive labour law rules. The Department of Labor is responsible for overseeing employer practices in such areas as hiring, employee benefits and overtime pay. The National Labor Relations Board oversees collective bargaining. In addition, most states also have their own labour laws, which are often different from those of the federal government.

Cost of employment

Social security benefits are financed through contributions paid by employers, employees and the self-employed under the Federal Insurance Contributions

Act (FICA) and the Self-Employment Contributions Act (SECA). Employers and employees both contribute an equal percentage of pay up to an annual earnings limit (the taxable wage base).

Employment terms and conditions

The Fair Labor Standards Act (FLSA) governs maximum hours worked and overtime pay. It divides employees into two categories: 'exempt' (salaried employees including executive, professional and administrative [as defined by law]) employees and 'non-exempt' (hourly-paid) employees. The latter are covered by FLSA rules. From 23 August 2004, the determination of employees as exempt or non-exempt under the FLSA changed. Notably, the minimum salary level to qualify for the exemption from the FLSA minimum wage and overtime pay requirements increased to a minimum of US$455 per week (US$23,660 annually). For certain computer-related occupations, employees who earn at least US$27.63 per hour are eligible for the exemption even if they are not paid on a salary basis. In addition, employees must generally meet one of the duties tests to qualify for exemption.

Social security and other required benefits

There are three main programmes in the social security system: old age and survivors' insurance (OASI), disability insurance (DI) and Medicare. Sometimes, they are grouped together and known as OASDHI, or old age, survivors', disability and hospital insurance. Workers' compensation and unemployment insurance are provided under separate laws. The social security system covers most employees and the self-employed. However, various classes of employee are exempt from coverage, including, for example, certain agricultural, domestic and casual workers as well as certain employees of the federal or state governments. Financing is through contributions (taxes) paid by employers, employees and the self-employed.

Healthcare system

The USA does not have a comprehensive national health insurance programme. The majority of US families rely on group health insurance plans provided by employers or on insurance that they have purchased individually.

The two existing national insurance programmes, Medicare and Medicaid, provide healthcare benefits only to certain segments of the population. Medicare, as a part of the federal social security system, provides medical benefits only for individuals aged 65 or older and for the disabled, while Medicaid helps finance medical care for people with low incomes. Medicaid is primarily funded at the federal level and administered at the state level.

Taxation of compensation and benefits

Citizens and permanent residents are subject to federal income tax on worldwide foreign and domestic income. However, tax relief may be available in the form of unilateral tax credits, double income tax treaty benefits and certain exclusions for specified foreign income. As a result, citizens and permanent residents must file annual tax returns even if they are non-resident for tax purposes for the year in question. Non-resident aliens are taxed only on certain income from sources or businesses in the USA. Most citizens and residents pay federal, state and sometimes local income taxes.

Recent developments

Two issues dominated US employee benefits in 2012 – the Supreme Court decision that struck down a key section of the Defense of Marriage Act (DOMA) and the rollout of the Patient Protection and Affordable Care Act (Affordable Care Act).

In its decision, the Supreme Court ruled that the definition of marriage as the union of one man and one woman for purposes of federal law is unconstitutional. The Court addressed the impact on spousal entitlement to benefit programs sponsored by the federal government and private employers. It stated that its opinion applied only to 'lawful marriages'. As a result, federal law will now defer to state law in determining whether a couple is legally married for purposes of federal laws defining terms such as 'marriage' and 'spouse'. Guidance from government agencies is due shortly.

The Obama Administration announced that the employer mandate under the Affordable Care Act will be delayed, giving employers an extra year to comply with the law's complicated hours-tracking and related reporting rules. Under the Affordable Care Act, an employer with 50 or more full-time equivalent employees is liable for monetary penalties if the employer does not offer affordable, minimum-value healthcare coverage to a full-time employee and that employee obtains subsidised healthcare coverage from a health insurance exchange. Those penalties, along with the insurance reporting requirements imposed on employers under the Affordable Care Act, will not be enforced against employers until 2015. The delay means that employers will have an additional year to offer health insurance coverage to their full-time employees before the Inland Revenue Service (IRS) will assess penalties, known as the employer shared-responsibility payment. Employers will also have an additional year to comply with the information reporting provisions that require them to provide information to the IRS regarding the health insurance coverage offered to their full-time employees. That information will, in part, determine whether employees are entitled to subsidised health insurance and whether employers are liable for an employer shared responsibility payment. Proposed rules on these reporting requirements are expected to be published in 2013. It should be noted that the transition relief does not delay the effective date for other provisions of the Affordable Care Act, such as the requirement that individuals purchase health insurance or pay a penalty.

In benefits administration, forward thinking is the future.

The latest Aon Hewitt Benefits Administration Survey reveals that in today demanding business environment, forward thinking employers and trust boards are seeking smarter ways of managing their benefits.

Progressive, efficient administration services allow organisations to meet benefits requirements, as well as overcome wider business challenges.

Innovative technology, a client focused approach and an ability to stay ahead of the market's ever-evolving needs, mean that our pensions and administration solutions deliver exceptional value, whatever the future h

For a copy of the survey or for more information, call 0800 279 558 or email enquiries@aonhewitt.com

aonhewitt.co.uk/administration

Follow us on **twitter** @aonhewittuk

ECONOMIC & DEMOGRAPHIC DATA

RETAIL PRICES INDEX (RPI)

Index based on January 1987 = 100

	Jan.	Feb.	Mar.	Apr.	May	Jun.	Jul.	Aug.	Sep.	Oct.	Nov.	Dec.
2009	210.1	211.4	211.3	211.5	212.8	213.4	213.4	214.4	215.3	216.0	216.6	218.0
2010	217.9	219.2	220.7	222.8	223.6	224.1	223.6	224.5	225.3	225.8	226.8	228.4
2011	229.0	231.3	232.5	234.4	235.2	235.2	234.7	236.1	237.9	238.0	238.5	239.4
2012	238.0	239.9	240.8	242.5	242.4	241.8	242.1	243.0	244.2	245.6	245.6	246.8
2013	245.8	247.6	248.7	249.5	250.0	249.7	249.7	251.0	251.9	251.9		

Source: *World Economics*, compiled from government information.

RPI INFLATION

Percentage increase in the Retail Prices Index over previous 12 months

	Jan. %	Feb. %	Mar. %	Apr. %	May %	Jun. %	Jul. %	Aug. %	Sep. %	Oct. %	Nov. %	Dec. %
2009	0.1	0.0	-0.4	-1.2	-1.1	-1.6	-1.4	-1.3	-1.4	-0.8	0.3	2.4
2010	3.7	3.7	4.4	5.3	5.1	5.0	4.8	4.7	4.6	4.5	4.7	4.8
2011	5.1	5.5	5.3	5.2	5.2	5.0	5.0	5.2	5.6	5.4	5.2	4.8
2012	3.9	3.7	3.6	3.5	3.1	2.8	3.2	2.9	2.6	3.2	3.0	3.1
2013	3.3	3.2	3.3	2.9	3.1	3.3	3.1	3.3	3.2	2.6		

Source: *World Economics*, compiled from government information.

CONSUMER PRICES INDEX (CPI)

Index based on June 2005 = 100

	Jan.	Feb.	Mar.	Apr.	May	Jun.	Jul.	Aug.	Sep.	Oct.	Nov.	Dec.
2009	108.7	109.6	109.8	110.1	110.7	111.0	110.9	111.4	111.5	111.7	112.0	112.6
2010	112.4	112.9	113.5	114.2	114.4	114.6	114.3	114.9	114.9	115.2	115.6	116.8
2011	116.9	117.8	118.1	119.3	119.5	119.4	119.4	120.1	120.9	121.0	121.2	121.7
2012	121.1	121.8	122.2	122.9	122.8	122.3	122.5	123.1	123.5	124.2	124.4	125.0
2013	124.4	125.2	125.6	125.9	126.1	125.9	125.8	126.4	126.8	126.9		

Source: *World Economics*, compiled from government information.

CPI INFLATION

Percentage increase in the Consumer Prices Index over previous 12 months

	Jan. %	Feb. %	Mar. %	Apr. %	May %	Jun. %	Jul. %	Aug. %	Sep. %	Oct. %	Nov. %	Dec. %
2009	3.0	3.2	2.9	2.3	2.2	1.8	1.8	1.6	1.1	1.5	1.9	2.9
2010	3.5	3.0	3.4	3.7	3.4	3.2	3.1	3.1	3.1	3.2	3.3	3.7
2011	4.0	4.4	4.0	4.5	4.5	4.2	4.4	4.5	5.2	5.0	4.8	4.2
2012	3.6	3.4	3.5	3.0	2.8	2.4	2.6	2.5	2.2	2.7	2.7	2.7
2013	2.7	2.8	2.8	2.4	2.7	2.9	2.8	2.7	2.7	2.2		

Source: *World Economics*, compiled from government information.

TRENDS IN AVERAGE EARNINGS PER PERSON
PER WEEK AND THE HOUSEHOLDS' SAVINGS RATIO

	at Current Prices		at Constant 2012 Prices		Households' Savings Ratio (%)
	Average Earnings (£pw)	Annual Change (%)	Average Earnings (£pw)	Annual Change (%)	
1972	34.26	9.0	382.23	1.4	7.3
1973	37.38	9.1	382.14	0.0	8.2
1974	44.74	19.7	394.51	3.2	8.4
1975	59.04	32.0	419.66	6.4	9.2
1976	64.81	9.8	394.87	−5.9	8.7
1977	70.62	9.0	371.39	−5.9	7.6
1978	79.69	12.8	387.13	4.2	9.4
1979	92.00	15.4	394.08	1.8	10.9
1980	111.15	20.8	403.62	2.4	12.3
1981	125.35	12.8	406.86	0.8	12.0
1982	137.15	9.4	409.91	0.8	10.8
1983	148.77	8.5	425.05	3.7	9.0
1984	157.67	6.0	429.19	1.0	10.2
1985	171.00	8.5	438.79	2.2	9.7
1986	184.80	8.1	458.51	4.5	8.1
1987	198.90	7.6	473.87	3.4	5.2
1988	218.70	10.0	496.67	4.8	3.5
1989	239.80	9.6	505.18	1.7	5.3
1990	263.20	9.8	506.50	0.3	7.5
1991	284.70	8.2	517.58	2.2	9.6
1992	304.80	7.1	534.18	3.2	10.9
1993	317.30	4.1	547.52	2.5	9.9
1994	326.10	2.8	549.11	0.3	8.3
1995	337.60	3.5	549.72	0.1	9.2
1996	351.50	4.1	558.85	1.7	8.4
1997	367.60	4.6	566.65	1.4	8.0
1998	392.50	6.8	584.98	3.2	6.5
1999	407.80	3.9	598.60	2.3	4.7
2000	425.10	4.2	606.04	1.2	4.6
2001	449.70	5.8	630.03	4.0	5.9
2002	472.10	5.0	650.51	3.3	4.7
2003	487.10	3.2	652.27	0.3	4.3
2004	498.20	2.3	647.84	−0.7	3.8
2005	516.40	3.7	652.97	0.8	2.9
2006	534.90	3.6	655.56	0.4	3.4
2007	550.30	2.9	646.68	−1.4	2.1
2008	575.60	4.6	650.58	0.6	2.2
2009	587.20	2.0	667.10	2.5	7.0
2010	598.60	1.9	649.97	−2.6	7.3
2011	602.90	0.7	622.17	−4.3	6.7
2012	607.10	0.7	607.10	−2.4	6.8

Notes: **Constant 2012 Prices:** Deflated by the Retail Prices Index (2012 = 100). **Earnings:** Wages and salaries of those in employment, excluding those whose pay is affected by absence. Data are derived from the earnings index of all adults in employment. **Households' Savings Ratio:** Households' saving as % Total Resources; the latter is the sum of Gross Household Disposable Income and the Adjustment for the net equity of the households in pension funds.

Sources: ASHE and *UK Economic Accounts*, National Statistics © Crown Copyright 2013; *World Economic*

POPULATION DATA, MID-2012

By Nation   Thousands

	Total	Males	Females
England	53,107	26,133	26,974
Wales	3,064	1,505	1,559
Scotland	5,300	2,570	2,730
Great Britain	**61,471**	**30,208**	**31,263**
Northern Ireland	1,814	889	925
United Kingdom	**63,705**	**31,315**	**32,390**

By Sex and Age, UK

	Total		Males		Females	
Age	'000s	%	'000s	%	'000s	%
0–4	3,996	6.3	2,045	3.2	1,951	3.1
5–9	3,641	5.7	1,864	2.9	1,777	2.8
10–14	3,576	5.6	1,831	2.9	1,745	2.7
15–19	3,927	6.2	2,013	3.2	1,913	3.0
20–24	4,332	6.8	2,192	3.4	2,141	3.4
25–29	4,318	6.8	2,152	3.4	2,166	3.4
30–34	4,240	6.7	2,109	3.3	2,131	3.3
35–39	4,036	6.3	2,009	3.2	2,028	3.2
40–44	4,567	7.2	2,254	3.5	2,314	3.6
45–49	4,686	7.4	2,313	3.6	2,373	3.7
50–54	4,236	6.6	2,098	3.3	2,138	3.4
55–59	3,684	5.8	1,820	2.9	1,864	2.9
60–64	3,624	5.7	1,776	2.8	1,848	2.9
65–69	3,345	5.3	1,626	2.6	1,719	2.7
70–74	2,476	3.9	1,170	1.8	1,306	2.0
75–79	2,047	3.2	929	1.5	1,118	1.8
80–84	1,534	2.4	638	1.0	896	1.4
85–89	926	1.5	336	0.5	590	0.9
90+	513	0.8	141	0.2	372	0.6
Total	**63,705**	**100.0**	**31,315**	**49.2**	**32,390**	**50.8**

Population Projections, UK   Thousands

	2012 (2010 base)	Projections			
		2017	2022	2027	2032
0–14	11,058	11,847	12,390	12,419	12,193
15–44	25,185	25,097	25,704	26,537	27,069
45–64	16,142	16,753	16,881	16,751	16,719
65–74	5,777	6,476	6,522	6,918	7,784
75+	5,082	5,580	6,596	7,601	8,367
Total	**63,244**	**65,755**	**68,092**	**70,226**	**72,133**

Sources: *Mid-2012 Population Estimates,* National Statistics © Crown Copyright 2013; General Register Office for Scotland; Northern Ireland Statistics and Research Agency; Government Actuary's Department.

EXPECTATIONS OF LIFE

Age x	Males Expectation	Females Expectation	Age x	Males Expectation	Females Expectation
0	78.66	82.64			
1	78.05	81.97	51	29.94	33.16
2	77.08	80.99	52	29.04	32.24
3	76.09	80.01	53	28.16	31.32
4	75.10	79.02	54	27.28	30.41
5	74.11	78.02	55	26.40	29.51
6	73.12	77.03	56	25.54	28.61
7	72.12	76.04	57	24.69	27.72
8	71.13	75.04	58	23.84	26.83
9	70.14	74.05	59	23.01	25.95
10	69.14	73.05	60	22.17	25.07
11	68.15	72.06	61	21.36	24.21
12	67.16	71.07	62	20.54	23.35
13	66.16	70.07	63	19.74	22.49
14	65.17	69.08	64	18.94	21.64
15	64.18	68.09	65	18.16	20.80
16	63.19	67.10	66	17.38	19.97
17	62.21	66.11	67	16.63	19.14
18	61.23	65.12	68	15.88	18.33
19	60.26	64.13	69	15.15	17.52
20	59.29	63.15	70	14.43	16.73
21	58.32	62.16	71	13.74	15.96
22	57.35	61.17	72	13.05	15.19
23	56.38	60.18	73	12.38	14.44
24	55.42	59.20	74	11.72	13.70
25	54.45	58.21	75	11.08	12.97
26	53.48	57.23	76	10.45	12.26
27	52.51	56.24	77	9.85	11.57
28	51.55	55.26	78	9.26	10.90
29	50.58	54.28	79	8.70	10.25
30	49.62	53.30	80	8.15	9.62
31	48.66	52.32	81	7.63	9.02
32	47.69	51.34	82	7.14	8.43
33	46.73	50.36	83	6.67	7.88
34	45.77	49.38	84	6.23	7.35
35	44.82	48.41	85	5.81	6.85
36	43.87	47.44	86	5.42	6.37
37	42.92	46.47	87	5.04	5.93
38	41.97	45.50	88	4.70	5.50
39	41.02	44.53	89	4.39	5.10
40	40.08	43.57	90	4.14	4.74
41	39.14	42.60	91	3.86	4.41
42	38.21	41.65	92	3.59	4.08
43	37.28	40.69	93	3.31	3.76
44	36.34	39.74	94	3.08	3.48
45	35.42	38.79	95	2.89	3.24
46	34.50	37.84	96	2.71	3.03
47	33.58	36.90	97	2.55	2.83
48	32.66	35.96	98	2.41	2.64
49	31.75	35.02	99	2.29	2.47
50	30.84	34.09	100	2.15	2.30

Note: The table above shows the 'period' expectation of life at various ages, that is, the average numbe of additional years a person would live if he or she experienced the age-specific mortality rates 2009–2011 for the rest of their life. No allowance is made for future improvements in mortality

Source: Interim Life Tables 2009–11 for England and Wales, Office for National Statistics © Crown copyright 20

WORKING POPULATION – UNITED KINGDOM

	June 1993		June 2012		June 2013	
	'000s	%	'000s	%	'000s	%
Employees in employment:						
– Male	11,052	39.1	12,745	40.8	12,897	41.1
– Female	10,356	36.6	12,327	39.5	12,496	39.8
All employees	21,407	75.7	25,071	80.3	25,392	80.9
Self-employed persons	3,387	12.0	4,223	13.5	4,173	13.3
HM Forces	250	0.9	186	0.6	175	0.6
Government-supported trainees	348	1.2	152	0.5	164	0.5
Total employed labour force	25,392	89.7	29,633	94.9	29,905	95.3
Claimant unemployment	2,902	10.3	1,597	5.1	1,471	4.7
Total	28,294	100.0	31,230	100.0	31,376	100.0
Index (June 1993=100)	100.0		110.4		110.9	

Notes: [1] Seasonally adjusted.

[2] Totals might differ from sum of preceding figures owing to rounding.

Source: *Labour Market Statistics*, Office for National Statistics © Crown Copyright 2013.

INVESTMENT DATA

UK ANNUAL INFLATION

UK INVESTMENT YIELDS AND INFLATION

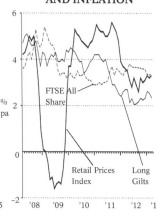

UK INTEREST RATES AND INFLATION

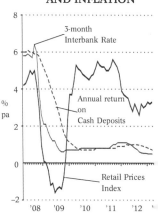

Notes:

[1] Base for Retail Prices Index (RPI) is 1987, and base for Average Weekly Earnings index (AWE) is 2000.

[2] Index for Long Gilts is based on all issues with a term of 15 years.

[3] The 3-month interbank rate shown is the mid-rate.

[4] Annual return on cash deposits is calculated using the 3-month interbank mid-rate.

Sources:

RPI and AWE data derived from information published by Office for National Statistics. AWE figures are based on the 2007 Standard Industrial Classification (SIC 2007) using the not-seasonally-adjusted index for the whole economy, including bonuses and arrears. All other figures collated by Aon Hewitt.

UK INVESTMENT HISTORY (1)

One year returns to end of:	Annual increase:[1]			Corresponding annual rate of return on investments:			
	RPI[2] %	CPI[3] %	AWE[4] %	Cash Deposits %	Long Gilts %	Index-linked Gilts %	U.K. Equities %
2003	2.8	1.3	3.8	3.7	1.2	6.6	20.9
2004	3.5	1.7	4.2	4.6	8.4	8.5	12.8
2005	2.2	1.9	4.4	4.7	11.0	9.0	22.0
2006	4.4	3.0	5.8	4.8	0.0	2.9	16.8
2007	4.0	2.1	3.4	6.0	2.7	8.5	5.3
2008	0.9	3.1	2.5	5.5	13.7	3.7	−29.9
2009	2.4	2.9	0.7	1.2	−4.8	6.5	30.1
2010	4.8	3.7	1.3	0.7	8.8	8.9	14.5
2011	4.8	4.2	2.0	0.9	26.3	19.9	−3.5
2012	3.1	2.7	1.3	0.9	2.9	0.6	12.3

Length of period:	Average annual increases and rates of return for different periods to end of 2012:						
10 years	3.3	2.6	2.9	3.3	6.7	7.4	8.8
9 years	3.3	2.8	2.8	3.2	7.3	7.5	7.5
8 years	3.3	2.9	2.6	3.1	7.2	7.4	6.8
7 years	3.5	3.1	2.4	2.8	6.7	7.1	4.8
6 years	3.3	3.1	1.8	2.5	7.8	7.8	3.0
5 years	3.2	3.3	1.5	1.8	8.9	7.7	2.5
4 years	3.8	3.4	1.3	0.9	7.7	8.8	12.7
3 years	4.2	3.5	1.5	0.8	12.2	9.5	7.5
2 years	4.0	3.5	1.6	0.9	14.0	9.9	4.1

Notes: [1] The increase shown is measured over the calendar year(s) from December to December.

   [2] Retail Prices Index, all items.

   [3] Consumer Prices Index, all items.

   [4] Average Weekly Earnings, whole economy, not seasonally adjusted, including bonuses and arrears. AWE figures are based on the 2007 Standard Industrial Classification (SIC 2007).

Source: Annual increases in indices and annual rates of return collated, and averages calculated, by Aon Hewitt.

UK INVESTMENT HISTORY (2)

Historic yields and returns (% p.a.)

		UK assets: real rates of return		
5 years to end of:	Retail Prices Index	Equities	Government Bonds	Treasury Bills
1967	3.3	6.6	–0.9	1.8
1972	6.6	8.9	–2.4	–0.1
1977	16.3	–8.5	–3.9	–4.8
1982	12.0	6.6	1.9	1.2
1987	4.6	17.6	7.2	5.6
1992	6.3	8.0	5.0	6.0
1997	2.6	13.0	8.8	3.3
2002	2.3	–4.3	5.6	3.6
2007	3.2	11.2	1.0	1.4
2012	3.3	–0.9	5.9	–1.7
10 years to end of:				
1967	2.9	11.4	0.8	–
1972	4.9	7.7	–1.7	0.8
1977	11.3	–0.2	–3.2	–2.5
1982	14.1	–1.2	–1.0	–1.9
1987	8.2	12	4.5	3.4
1992	5.5	12.7	6.1	5.8
1997	4.5	10.4	6.9	4.6
2002	2.4	3.9	7.2	3.4
2007	2.7	3.1	3.3	2.5
2012	3.3	5.0	3.4	–0.2

Sources: Office for National Statistics and Barclays Equity Gilt Study 2013.

UK INVESTMENT RETURNS AND INFLATION

Notes: [1] WM All Funds represents around two-thirds of UK defined benefit pension funds by value.
[2] Average Weekly Earnings data: whole economy, not seasonally adjusted, including bonuses and arrears. AWE figures are based on the 2007 Standard Industrial Classification (SIC 2007).
Returns shown are to March 2013.

Sources: The WM Company, data to 31 March 2013. Aon Hewitt, compiled from government information.

CUMULATIVE INDEX RETURNS TO 31 MARCH 2013

Annualised Returns	Last 12 months %	Last 3 years %	Last 5 years %	Last 10 years %
FTSE All Share	16.8	8.8	6.7	10.7
FTSE World North America	**19.3**	**11.8**	**11.5**	9.5
FTSE World Europe ex UK	18.0	4.0	2.9	11.4
FTSE World Japan	14.3	3.5	5.1	7.3
FTSE Pacific ex Japan	18.1	8.9	10.7	16.4
FTSE All Emerging	7.4	3.2	7.2	**18.2**
FTSE All World ex UK*	17.2	8.2	8.6	10.6
FTSE All World*	17.1	8.2	8.4	10.6
FTSE UK Gilts All Stocks	5.2	8.2	7.1	5.8
ML Corporate Bonds	12.0	8.8	8.1	5.9
JP Morgan ex UK (Hedged)	4.8	4.8	5.0	5.4
FTSE UK I/L All Stocks	10.2	11.5	8.6	7.9

Notes: * FTSE World Index until December 2006
        The best performing sector over each period is highlighted in **bold** typeface.

Source: The WM Company.

PENSION FUND ASSET DISTRIBUTION

This table shows the average distribution of pension fund assets between the major market sectors at 31 March each year between 2009 and 2013.

	2009	2010	2011	2012	2013
WM All Funds					
Universe value (£bn)	376	467	480	488	512
Asset Mix	(%)	(%)	(%)	(%)	(%)
Total Equities	47.8	50.9	48.9	43.5	45.2
Global Pooled (inc UK)	1.9	5.1	3.6	3.8	3.9
UK Equities	19.9	20.1	18.8	15.9	16.5
Overseas Equities	26.0	25.7	26.5	23.8	24.9
North America	9.0	8.3	8.8	8.1	8.5
Europe	7.0	6.5	6.8	5.5	5.8
Japan	3.2	3.0	3.0	2.7	2.3
Pacific (ex Japan)	2.8	2.6	2.9	2.4	2.9
Emerging Markets	2.5	4.8	4.6	4.2	4.8
Global ex UK	1.5	0.6	0.5	1.0	0.6
Total Bonds	35.6	34.4	34.7	37.4	36.0
UK Bonds	17.2	16.1	15.3	15.4	14.9
Overseas Bonds	3.6	4.4	3.8	5.0	4.5
Index-linked	13.0	11.2	12.5	13.2	11.8
Pooled Bonds	1.8	2.6	3.0	3.8	4.8
Total Cash	2.6	2.2	1.1	3.3	3.1
Alternatives	7.5	6.7	8.8	8.8	8.7
Private Equity	3.5	3.1	4.2	4.2	4.5
Hedge Funds	2.3	2.0	2.8	3.0	2.8
Other Alternatives	1.6	1.6	1.8	1.6	1.4
Pooled Multi-Asset	–	–	–	0.3	0.8
Total Assets (ex Property)	93.6	94.1	92.9	93.5	93.7
Total Property	6.4	5.9	6.3	6.5	6.3
Total Assets	100.0	100.0	100.0	100.0	100.0

Source: The WM Company.

LONG-TERM PERFORMANCE ON WM ALL FUNDS
OVER CUMULATIVE PERIODS ENDING 31 MARCH 2013

	% p.a.			
	1 year %	3 years %	5 years %	10 years %
WM UK Equities	17.5	9.3	6.9	10.7
WM North America	19.0	11.8	10.6	8.7
WM Europe	19.4	5.2	3.7	11.3
WM Japan	14.9	3.8	4.5	6.5
WM Pacific	**19.7**	9.6	10.4	16.7
WM Emerging Markets	11.5	4.6	7.4	**17.6**
WM Overseas	17.2	7.7	7.5	11.2
WM Equity	17.2	8.4	7.2	11.0
WM UK Government Bonds	7.9	9.6	7.6	–
WM UK Corporate Bonds	12.8	9.0	7.7	–
WM Overseas Bonds	13.0	9.0	**11.5**	7.5
WM Index-linked	11.8	**12.9**	10.1	8.6

Note: This table highlights (in **bold**) the best-performing asset class in each period.

Source: The WM Company.

CHANGES TO ASSET ALLOCATION

	2008 (%)	2009 (%)	2010 (%)	2011 (%)	2012 (%)
Equities	51	45	44	43	37
Fixed interest securities	33	38	38	40	40
Other	16	17	19	19	23

Note: The above data represent simple or unweighted averages of asset allocation for private and 'other public sector' schemes (funded schemes, such as those of universities).

Source: NAPF Annual Survey, 2012.

PENSION STATISTICS

NOTES ON SOURCES USED

This section provides a snapshot of selected features of occupational pension schemes in the UK. The charts and tables on pages 240 to 245 are based on data from the following sources:

- **Occupational Pension Schemes Survey, 2011** and **2012**: this survey, produced by National Statistics, covers a sample of some 1,600 private and public sector schemes registered in the UK. The survey covers a range of topics, including scheme membership, contribution rates and benefits.

- **The NAPF Annual Survey, 2012**: the extract from this survey is based on 217 responses from NAPF fund members, mainly in the private sector.

- **The Association of Consulting Actuaries' (ACA) 2011 Pension trends survey**: this survey covers 468 employers of all sizes.

- **The Pensions Regulator's Annual Report and Accounts, 2012–13** summarises membership data for occupational private and public sector schemes taken from the Regulator's Score database.

- **Pension Funds Online**: a database maintained by Wilmington Publishing & Information that includes information on some 3,600 major UK pension funds. Data current as at September 2013.

- **The General Lifestyle Survey, 2011** (formerly known as the General Household Survey): a survey by National Statistics through field work, which started in 1971 and is normally carried out annually.

- **The Purple Book 2012, DB pensions universe risk profile**: a joint study by the Pensions Regulator and the Pension Protection Fund focusing mainly on private sector defined benefit schemes. Most of the analysis is based on a sample of some 6,300 schemes, with much of the basic information coming from scheme returns provided to the Pensions Regulator.

- **Pension Trends,** produced by National Statistics from the **Annual Survey of Hours and Earnings (ASHE) 2012**. ASHE replaced the New Earnings Survey (NES) in 2004 and is based on a sample of some 280,000 jobs, giving information about the levels, distribution and make-up of earnings and paid hours worked.

It should be noted that, as some of the questions were multiple-response, percentages shown in some tables may total more than 100% and so care is needed in interpreting the figures. Figures throughout may not total due to rounding.

PERCENTAGE OF EMPLOYEES WITH A WORKPLACE PENSION
By size of employer

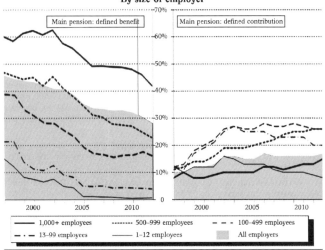

Note: Excludes membership where pension type is unknown.

Source: Pension Trends 2013, Office for National Statistics. (*See note on page 239 concerning this source.*)

PERCENTAGE OF PRIVATE SECTOR EMPLOYEES WITH A WORKPLACE PENSION
By main pension type

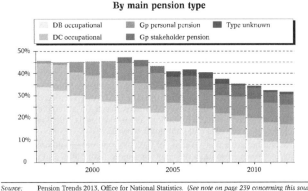

Source: Pension Trends 2013, Office for National Statistics. (*See note on page 239 concerning this source.*)

NORMAL PENSION AGE
% Private sector defined benefit schemes

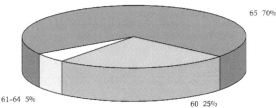

65 70%

61–64 5%

60 25%

Source: Based on data from the National Statistics *Occupational Pension Schemes Survey, 2011.*
(*See note on page 239 concerning this source.*)

ACCRUAL RATES
Accrual rate used in private sector defined benefit schemes (% schemes)

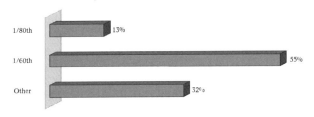

1/80th — 13%

1/60th — 55%

Other — 32%

Note: 'Other' is mainly a combination of differing accrual rates for different accrual periods, or for different grades or job categories.
Source: Based on data from the NAPF *Annual Survey,* 2012. (*See note on page 239 concerning this source.*)

CONTRIBUTION RATES
Average contributions paid into pension schemes (% total earnings)

% by benefit type	Member contributions	Employer contributions
Defined benefit occupational schemes	6.0	21.4
Defined contribution occupational schemes	4.5	6.9
Group personal pension arrangements	4.4	5.8
Stakeholder schemes *(see note)*	3.8	4.3

Note: Stakeholder figures exclude nil employer contributions, which is the level for 28% of stakeholder schemes.
Source: Data from the Association of Consulting Actuaries' *2011 Pension trends survey.*
(*See note on page 239 concerning this source.*)

PRIVATE SECTOR OCCUPATIONAL SCHEME STATUS

	2007	2008	2009	2010	2011	2012
Open	30,460	34,030	24,930	21,730	22,690	22,700
Closed	20,110	10,080	16,480	12,990	12,520	11,620
Frozen	4,550	6,870	4,050	8,400	6,940	8,370
Winding up	1,890	3,130	3,110	1,250	2,040	1,750
Total	57,010	54,110	48,580	44,380	44,190	44,440

Source: ONS *Occupational Pension Schemes Survey.* (See note on page 239 concerning this source.)

PENSION SCHEME MEMBERSHIP BY BENEFIT TYPE

Private sector schemes

Status of scheme	Number of members ('000)			Number of schemes		
	DC	DB	Hybrid	DC	DB	Hybrid
Open	1,086	1,944	2,955	29,344	861	591
Closed	156	4,409	2,567	3,881	2,522	552
Paid up	75	1,186	473	4,365	1,621	306
Winding up	66	140	68	1,154	506	114
Total	**1,382**	**7,679**	**6,063**	**38,744**	**5,510**	**1,563**

Source: Data taken from the Pensions Regulator's Annual Report and Accounts, 2012–13.
(See note on page 239 concerning this source.)

PENSION SCHEME MEMBERSHIP BY AGE AND SEX, 2011

	Percentage of employees who are members, by age group					
Scheme members in Great Britain	18–24	25–34	35–44	45–54	55+	**Total**
Men full time						
Occupational pension*	29	47	57	63	54	**53**
Personal pension	6	14	23	30	30	**22**
Any pension	29	51	64	74	66	**60**
Women full time						
Occupational pension*	28	56	61	69	61	**58**
Personal pension	2	13	14	22	26	**15**
Any pension	28	58	64	75	66	**61**
Women part time						
Occupational pension*	5	34	49	50	34	**38**
Personal pension	n/a	7	17	16	11	**12**
Any pension	5	36	54	57	37	**41**

Note: * The data include a few people who were not sure if they were in a scheme, but thought it possible.

Source: General Lifestyle Survey, 2011. (See note on page 239 concerning this source.)

THE LARGEST UK PENSION FUNDS

£ million		£ million	
38,783	BT Pension Scheme	6,186	Marks & Spencer Group plc DB Scheme
34,235	Universities Superannuation Scheme	6,169	Tesco plc Pension Scheme
30,683	Royal Mail Pension Plan	6,027	Transport for London Pension Fund
23,541	Electricity Supply Pension Scheme	5,841	Unilever UK Pension Fund
22,845	Barclays Bank UK Retirement Fund	5,570	Lloyds TSB Group Pension Scheme No. 2 DB Section
22,758	Royal Bank of Scotland Pension Fund	5,547	British American Tobacco, DB Section
18,898	Railways Pension Scheme	5,492	IBM Pension Plan – DB Section
18,018	HSBC Bank plc DB Scheme	5,200	Merseyside Pension Fund
16,687	BP plc Pension Fund	5,192	J Sainsbury plc Staff and Executive Pension Schemes
16,611	BAE Systems 2000 Pension Plan	5,133	Centrica Combined Common Investment Fund Limited
14,431	National Grid UK Pension Scheme DB	5,037	Pensions Trust DB Scheme
13,052	Shell Contributory Pension Fund	4,911	Diageo plc Pension Scheme
12,281	AVIVA Staff Pension Scheme – Final Salary	4,841	Tyne & Wear Pension Fund
12,152	Lloyds TSB Group Pension Scheme No. 1 DB Section	4,707	Jaguar Land Rover Pension Plan
11,993	British Steel Pension Scheme	4,667	South Yorkshire Pension Fund
11,451	Strathclyde Pension Fund	4,539	Alliance Boots plc DB Scheme
11,143	Greater Manchester Pension Fund	4,451	RWE npower Group DB Scheme
11,055	Pension Protection Fund	4,445	Zurich Financial Services DB Section
10,960	Mineworkers' Pension Scheme	4,380	Lancashire County Council Pension Fund
9,981	GSK Pension Scheme	4,331	BMW Operations Pension Scheme
9,734	Rolls-Royce Pension Fund		
9,615	New (British) Airways Pension Scheme	4,283	Invensys Pension Scheme
9,284	BBC Pension Scheme	4,236	AstraZeneca UK Ltd
9,223	HBOS Final Salary Pension Scheme	4,214	London Pensions Fund Authority Pension Fund
8,834	West Midlands Metropolitan Authorities Pension Fund	4,052	Local Government Pension Scheme for Northern Ireland
8,784	West Yorkshire Pension Fund	3,821	E.ON UK plc Electricity Supply Pension Scheme
8,754	British Coal Staff Superannuation Scheme	3,806	Reed Elsevier (UK) Pension Scheme
8,536	ICI Pension Fund	3,787	MMC UK Pension Fund
7,503	Santander Pension Scheme	3,777	Hampshire County Council Pension Fund
7,315	(British) Airways Pension Scheme	3,723	Vodafone Pension Scheme
6,721	Co-operative Group Pension (Average Career Earnings) Scheme	3,683	The Railways Pension Scheme, Network Rail Section
6,465	Ford Motor Co Pension Funds	3,669	Exxon Mobil Pensions Scheme
6,231	Prudential plc DB Scheme	3,620	Sun Alliance Pension Scheme

THE LARGEST UK PENSION FUNDS (continued)

£ million		£ million	
3,584	Lothian Pension Fund	3,377	Civil Aviation Authority Pension
3,520	Essex County Council Pension		Scheme (NATS Section)
	Fund	3,311	Kent County Council
3,470	TRW Pension Scheme		Superannuation Fund
3,377	Mars UK Ltd Pension Plan		

Notes: 1. Certain figures relate to the total of several funds within a group; however in some cases the data available treat separate sections under the same trust as separate schemes.
2. Certain figures are estimates not necessarily supplied by the fund.

Source: Based on information derived from *Pension Funds Online*, Wilmington Publishing & Information. (*See note on page 239 concerning this source.*)

AVERAGE ASSET ALLOCATION IN RETURNS MADE TO REGULATOR
(all figures are in percentages)

	Year of return						
	2006	2007	2008	2009	2010	2011	2012
Equities	61.1	59.5	53.6	46.4	42.0	41.1	38.5
Gilts and fixed interest	28.3	29.6	32.9	37.1	40.4	40.1	43.2
Insurance policies	0.9	0.8	1.1	1.4	1.4	1.6	0.2
Cash and deposits	2.3	2.3	3.0	3.9	3.9	4.1	5.1
Property	4.3	5.2	5.6	5.2	4.6	4.4	4.9
Hedge funds	N/A	N/A	N/A	1.5	2.2	2.4	4.5
Other investments	3.1	2.5	3.8	4.5	5.4	6.3	3.6

Notes: [1]   Due to rounding, figures may not add up to 100%.
[2]   There can be a significant gap between the date of the return and the date at which the asset allocation was taken. For 2012 returns, 60% of schemes gave asset allocations as at a date in 2011; 33% at a date in 2010; and the remainder at some earlier date.

Source: *The Purple Book*, DB pensions universe risk profile, the Pensions Regulator/PPF, 2012. (*See note on page 239 concerning this source.*)

OVERALL FUNDING LEVELS

	Section 179 (£bn)	Full buy-out (£bn)
Total assets	1,026.8	1,026.8
Total liabilities	1,231.0	1,702.6
Total balance	−204.2	−675.8
Total balance (for schemes in deficit)	−231.3	−677.3
Total balance (for schemes in surplus)	27.1	1.5

Note: Shows estimated figures for a total of 6,316 schemes as at 31 March 2012.

Source: *The Purple Book*, DB pensions universe risk profile, the Pensions Regulator/PPF, 2012. (*See note on page 239 concerning this source.*)

SECTION 179 FUNDING LEVELS BY SCHEME SIZE

Scheme membership	Schemes in sample	Market value of assets (£bn)	Total s179 liabilities (£bn)	Weighted average funding level (%)	Simple average funding level (%)
5–99	2,260	11.6	12.6	92	90
100–999	2,829	89.6	111.9	80	78
1,000–4,999	823	151.9	194.0	78	77
5,000–9,999	192	121.7	149.6	81	79
10,000+	212	652.0	762.9	85	85
Total	**6,316**	**1,026.8**	**1,231.0**	**83**	**82**

Note: Data as at 31 March 2012.

Source: *The Purple Book, DB pensions universe risk profile*, the Pensions Regulator/PPF, 2012. (*See note on page 239 concerning this source.*)

SECTION 179 FUNDING LEVELS BY SCHEME MATURITY

Pensions in payment as % liabilities	Schemes in sample	Market value of assets (£bn)	Total s179 liabilities (£bn)	Weighted average funding level (%)	Simple average funding level (%)
25% and less	2,529	160.4	233.5	69	75
26%–50%	2,735	599.3	731.0	82	82
51%–75%	879	244.6	247.1	99	100
76%–100%	173	22.5	19.4	116	120
Total	**6,316**	**1,026.8**	**1,231.0**	**83**	**82**

Note: Data as at 31 March 2012.

Source: *The Purple Book, DB pensions universe risk profile*, the Pensions Regulator/PPF, 2012. (*See note on page 239 concerning this source.*)

SOCIAL SECURITY BENEFITS AND TAX RATES

INTRODUCTION

Social Security benefits, and tax allowances and rates, that may be relevant when considering private sector pension provision are outlined in this section. Further information, including details of other State benefits, can be found at *www.gov.uk*. This section sets out rates for State pensions; *further detail is set out in Section 1.*

SOCIAL SECURITY BENEFIT RATES AND ELIGIBILITY RULES

This table gives the rates for 2013/2014 and sets out the main eligibility rules. Receipt of some benefits affects entitlement to other benefits. **Eligibility conditions are not necessarily comprehensive and may also be subject to change.** Further information on benefits can be found at *www.gov.uk*. Information is correct as at 19 November 2013, at which date the Government had not announced certain benefit and tax rates for 2014/2015. Spaces have been provided for these figures, which will be published at *www.pensionspocketbook.com.*

Between April and September 2013, a cap was introduced on the total amount of benefit that working age people can receive. The cap is £500 per week for couples and single parent households and £350 per week for single adult households without children, but will not apply where someone in the household (claimant, partner or any children they are responsible for and who live with them) is entitled to Working Tax Credit or is in receipt of one of the following benefits: Disability Living Allowance, Personal Independence Payment, Attendance Allowance, the support component of Employment Support Allowance, Industrial Injuries Benefits (and War Disablement Pension and equivalent payments under the Armed Forces Compensation Scheme), War Widow's Pension or War Widower's Pension. Benefits subject to cap are noted in the table.

All rates are weekly unless otherwise specified

Benefit	Rates, 2013/14	2014/15	Eligibility

RETIREMENT BENEFITS

The Basic State Pension and Additional Pension will be replaced by a single-tier pension from April 2016 *(see Section 1)*.

Benefit	Rates, 2013/14	2014/15	Eligibility
Basic State Pension	Based on own or late spouse's NICs: £110.15 Based on spouse's NICs: £66.00	£_____ * £_____ *	(i) Reached State Pension Age *and* (ii) NIC record sufficient.
	Over 80 pension: £66.00 Over 80 addition: £0.25	£_____ * £_____ *	The Over 80 pension is non-contributory and subject to residence conditions. Payable to individuals who receive little/no other State pension.
	taxable		

All rates are weekly unless otherwise specified

Benefit	Rates, 2013/14	2014/15	Eligibility

RETIREMENT BENEFITS (continued)

Benefit	Rates, 2013/14	2014/15	Eligibility
Additional Pension	SERPS/State Second Pension (S2P) – *see Section 1.* *taxable*		(i) Reached State Pension Age *and* (ii) paid Class 1 NICs and/or received credits.
Graduated Retirement Benefit	Per unit: 12.79p Employees may have been contracted-out and receive EPBs instead. *taxable*	____p*	Based on NICs paid between April 1961 and April 1975.
Pension Credit	Tops up weekly income to: single pensioner £145.40 (minimum) couple £222.05 (minimum) *tax free*	£____* £____*	Aged over women's State Pension Age. Lower capital limit £10,000. *means tested*

WIDOW'S/WIDOWER'S BENEFITS

Benefit	Rates, 2013/14	2014/15	Eligibility
Widow's Pension (replaced by **Bereavement Allowance** from 9 April 2001)	Standard rate: £108.30 *Plus* State Additional pension. Lower rates where widow under age 55 on benefit becoming payable. *taxable;* *subject to the benefit cap*	£____*	Woman widowed before 9 April 2001 and husband's NIC record sufficient, *and either*: (i) 45 or over when husband died and **Widowed Mother's Allowance** is not payable *or* (ii) 45 or over when **Widowed Mother's Allowance** ceased.

Widowed Mother's Allowance (replaced by **Widowed Parent's Allowance** from 9 April 2001)	Allowance: £108.30
	Additional child allowance:
	  first child: £8.10
	  each other child: £11.35
	Plus
	State Additional pension.
	taxable but child allowance tax free;
	subject to the benefit cap
		£____*
		
		£____*
		£____*
			(i) Woman widowed before 9 April 2001
			and
			(ii) has dependent child in respect of whom she is entitled to Child Benefit
			and
			(iii) husband's NIC record sufficient.

Bereavement Payment	Lump sum: £2,000 *tax free*	£____*	Husband's, wife's or civil partner's NIC record sufficient or their death was work-related *and either*: (i) he or she was not entitled to State retirement pension *or* (ii) claimant was under State Pension Age when husband, wife or civil partner died.

All rates are weekly unless otherwise specified

Benefit	Rates, 2013/14	2014/15	Eligibility

WIDOW'S/WIDOWER'S BENEFITS (continued)

Benefit	Rates, 2013/14	2014/15	Eligibility
Bereavement Allowance	Standard rate: £108.30 Lower rates where widow, widower or surviving civil partner was under age 55 when benefit became payable. *taxable* *subject to the benefit cap*	£____ *	Husband's, wife's or civil partner's NIC record sufficient or their death was work-related *and*: (i) claimant is under State Pension Age and was 45 or over when husband, wife or civil partner died *and* (ii) **Widowed Parent's Allowance** is not payable.

Widowed Parent's Allowance	Allowance: £108.30
	Additional child allowance:
	  first child: £8.10
	  each other child: £11.35
	Plus
	State Additional pension.
	taxable but child allowance tax free;
	subject to the benefit cap
		£____ *
		
		£____ *
		£____ *
			Husband's, wife's or civil partner's NIC record sufficient or their death was work-related *and*:
			(i) has child for whom entitled to Child Benefit *and*
			(ii) claimant is under State Pension Age.

MATERNITY

Benefit	Rates, 2013/14	2014/15	Eligibility
Maternity Allowance	For up to 39 weeks: Lesser of (a) 90% of average earnings, *and* (b) £136.78. *tax free* *subject to the benefit cap*	Lesser of (a) 90% of average earnings, *and* (b) £____ *	(i) Not eligible for **Statutory Maternity Pay** *and* (ii) employed/self-employed *and* (iii) must have been employed/ self-employed for at least 26 of the 66 weeks before baby is due, and average earnings at least £30.00 per week (the Maternity Allowance Threshold).
Statutory Maternity Pay	First 6 weeks: 90% of average earnings After 6 weeks, and up to week 39: Lesser of: (a) 90% of average earnings, *and* (b) £136.78. *taxable subject to NICs*	90% of average earnings Lesser of (a) 90% of average earnings, *and* (b) £____ *	In the qualifying week (15th week before the baby is due): (i) employed with same employer for at least 26 weeks, 15 weeks before the baby is due *and* (ii) average earnings above Lower Earnings Limit in that week.

All rates are weekly unless otherwise specified

Benefit	Rates, 2013/14	2014/15	Eligibility

MATERNITY (continued)

Benefit	Rates, 2013/14	2014/15	Eligibility
Statutory Paternity Pay	For up to 2 weeks: Lesser of: (a) 90% of average earnings, *and* (b) £136.78. *taxable subject to NICs*	Lesser of (a) 90% of average earnings, *and* (b) £___ *	As for **Statutory Maternity Pay**. Additional Statutory Paternity Pay may be payable for up to 26 weeks where partner does not take **Statutory Maternity Pay**, etc.
Statutory Adoption Pay	For up to 39 weeks: Amount as for **Statutory Paternity Pay**. *taxable subject to NICs*	Amount as for **Statutory Paternity Pay**.	(i) Employed with same employer for at least 26 weeks before adoption agency informed that matched with child *and* (ii) earning above Lower Earnings Limit.

SICKNESS

Benefit	Rates, 2013/14	2014/15	Eligibility
Statutory Sick Pay	Standard rate: £86.70 (up to 28 weeks) *taxable subject to NICs*	£___ *	(i) Earnings at least equal to Lower Earnings Limit *and* (ii) has been sick for at least 4 consecutive days.

Note: * As at 19 November 2013 the Government had not announced benefit rates for 2013/2014. These figures can be found at *www.pensionspocketbook.com*.

SOCIAL FUND

Benefit	Rates, 2013/14	2014/15	Eligibility
Funeral Payments	Necessary fees, other specified expenses *and up to* £700 for any other funeral expenses. *tax free*	£___ *	(i) Specified relationship with deceased *and* (ii) is in receipt of certain benefits or tax credits.

OTHER SOCIAL SECURITY BENEFITS

Other Social Security benefits that may have some relevance when considering private sector pension provision include the following; *for details, see www.gov.uk.*

Disability	Disability Living Allowance
	Attendance Allowance
	Severe Disablement Allowance
	Employment and Support Allowance
	   (replaced Severe Disablement Allowance
	   for new claims)
	Carer's Allowance

Industrial Injuries and Disease	Industrial Injuries Disablement Benefit Reduced Earnings Allowance Retirement Allowance Constant Attendance Allowance Exceptionally Severe Disablement Allowance
Sickness	Incapacity Benefit Employment and Support Allowance (replaced Incapacity Benefit)
Social Fund	Sure Start Maternity Grant Budget Loan Cold Weather Payment Winter Fuel Payment

BASIC STATE RETIREMENT PENSIONS

	Single person		Married couple	
From	£ per week	£ per year	£ per week	£ per year
10.04.2000	67.50	3,510.00	107.90	5,610.80
09.04.2001	72.50	3,770.00	115.90	6,026.80
08.04.2002	75.50	3,926.00	120.70	6,276.40
07.04.2003	77.45	4,027.40	123.80	6,437.60
12.04.2004	79.60	4,139.20	127.25	6,617.00
11.04.2005	82.05	4,266.60	131.20	6,822.40
10.04.2006	84.25	4,381.00	134.75	7,007.00
09.04.2007	87.30	4,539.60	139.60	7,259.20
07.04.2008	90.70	4,716.40	145.05	7,542.60
06.04.2009	95.25	4,953.00	152.30	7,919.60
12.04.2010	97.65	5,077.80	156.15	8,119.80
11.04.2011	102.15	5,311.80	163.35	8,494.20
09.04.2012	107.45	5,587.40	171.85	8,936.20
08.04.2013	110.15	5,727.80	176.15	9,159.80

Note: For Basic State pensions in years from 1948 to 1999 inclusive, see *www.pensionspocketbook.com.*

NATIONAL INSURANCE CONTRIBUTION RATES AND STATE SCHEME EARNINGS LIMITS

| Tax Year | National Insurance Contribution Rates | | | | | | National Insurance Earnings Limits | | | | State Scheme Limits | | |
| | Full rate | | Contracted-out Rebate | | | | LEL² | | UEL² | | LET | UAP¹,² | |
Earnings per week (£)	Employer (%)	Employee (%)	Earnings	Employer COSR¹ (%)	COMP¹ (%)	Employee (%)	Per week (£)	Per month (£)	Per week (£)	Per month (£)	Per annum (£)	Per week (£)	Per month (£)
2010/11													
£110.01³–UEL	12.80	11.00	LEL–UAP	3.70	1.40	1.60	97	421	844	3,656	14,100	770	3,337
Above UEL	12.80	1.00											
2011/12													
£136.01³–£139³	13.80	0.00	LEL–UAP	3.70	1.40	1.60	102	442	817	3,540	14,400	770	3,337
£139.01³–UEL	13.80	12.00											
Above UEL	13.80	2.00											
2012/13													
£144.01³–£146³	13.80	0.00	LEL–UAP	3.40	n/a	1.40	107	464	817	3,540	14,700	770	3,337
£146.01³–UEL	13.80	12.00											
Above UEL	13.80	2.00											
2013/14													
£148.01³–£149³	13.80	0.00	LEL–UAP	3.40	n/a	1.40	109	473	797	3,454	15,000	770	3,337
£149.01³–UEL	13.80	12.00											
Above UEL	13.80	2.00											

Notes:

* As at 19 November 2013 the Government had not announced rates for 2014/15. These figures can be found at *www.pensionspocketbook.com*. **UAP**: Upper Accrual Point. **LET**: Low Earnings Threshold

1 **COSR**: Contracted-Out Salary Related scheme. **COMP**: Contracted-Out Money Purchase scheme.

2 The National Insurance Earnings Limits and the UAP depend on the employee's earnings period. Weekly- and monthly-paid figures are shown above.

3 The Primary and Secondary Thresholds (above which, respectively, employee and employer contributions are payable) also depend on the employee's earnings period. The figures shown above (e.g. £148, the Secondary Threshold for 2013/14) are for weekly-paid employees. In 2010/2011, the Primary and Secondary Thresholds were equal.

TAX ON PENSION SCHEMES
(See Section 10 for further details)

Registered Pension Schemes

Tax Charge	Tax Rate
Lifetime allowance charge	25% if benefits taken as pension 55% if benefits taken as lump sum
Annual allowance charge[1]	Between 20% and 45% depending on total taxable income[2]
Unauthorised payments charge	40%
Unauthorised payments surcharge	15%
Scheme sanction charge	40%, but may be reduced to as low as 15% where the unauthorised payments charge has been paid
Authorised surplus payments charge	35%
Short service refund lump sum charge	20% on first £20,000 50% on balance
Charge on trivial commutation and winding-up lump sums	25% of uncrystallised rights tax free, balance taxed as the top slice of income
Special lump sum death benefits charge[3]	55%
Serious ill-health lump sum charge[4]	55%

Notes:
[1] In addition to the annual allowance charge, a 'special annual allowance charge' applied for tax years 2009/10 and 2010/11.

[2] The rates given are those applicable to 2013/14. From 6 April 2011, the taxable input is treated as the individual's top slice of taxable income and taxed as such. Before then, the taxable input was taxed at 40%.

[3] This applies to pension protection, annuity protection and drawdown pension fund lump sum death benefits. The tax was 35% for deaths before 6 April 2011. From 6 April 2011, the charge also applies to defined benefits and uncrystallised funds lump sum death benefits paid where the member was aged 75 or over at death.

[4] This applies to serious ill-health lump sums paid to members aged 75 or over.

TAX ALLOWANCES AND RATES

Tax	2013/14	2014/15
Income Tax		
Allowances		
Personal allowance[1,2]	£9,440	£10,000
Age-related allowances[2,3]		
– born 1938–1948[4]	£10,500	£10,500
– born before 1938[5]	£10,660	£10,660
Married couple's allowance[3,6]		
– maximum amount	£7,915	£_____ *
– minimum amount	£3,040	£_____ *
Income limit for higher allowances[3]	£26,100	£_____ *

TAX ALLOWANCES AND RATES (continued)

Tax		2013/14	2014/15
Income Tax			
Bands and Rates			
Starting rate for savings[7]	10%	£0–2,790	£0–_____ *
Basic rate[8]	20%	£0–32,010	£0–31,865
Higher rate[8]	40%	£32,011–150,000	£31,866–150,000
Additional rate[8]		45% over £150,000	45% over £150,000
Capital Gains Tax			
Exempt amount		£10,900	£11,000
Standard rate[9]		18%	___%*
Higher rate[10]		28%	___%*
Inheritance Tax			
Nil rate band		£325,000[11]	£325,000
Rate (above nil rate band)[12]		40%	___%*
Corporation Tax		Main rate 23%	Main rate 21%
Value Added Tax (VAT)			
Registration level		£79,000	£_____ *
Standard rate		20%	___%*
Insurance Premium Tax (IPT)			
Standard rate		6% of gross premium	___% of gross premium*
Higher rate[13]		20% of gross premium	___% of gross premium*

Notes:

*   As at 19 November 2013 the Government had not announced many tax rates for 2014/15. These figures can be found at *www.pensionspocketbook.com*.

1   Applies to individuals born after 5 April 1948.

2   Allowance is reduced by £1 for every £2 above an income of £100,000.

3   Age-related allowance is reduced by £1 for every £2 above the income limit until the level of the standard personal allowance is reached. Once the age-related allowance has been reduced to the level of the standard personal allowance, any excess income serves to reduce the level of any married couple's allowance *(see note 6)*.

4   Applies to individuals born after 5 April 1938 but before 6 April 1948.

5   Applies to individuals born before 6 April 1938.

6   Tax relief restricted to 10%. One spouse/civil partner must have been born before 6 April 1935. Amount depends on husband's income if married prior to 5 December 2005, and on person with the higher income if married on or after 5 December 2005 or in a civil partnership. Once the age-related allowance has been reduced to the level of the standard personal allowance *(see note 3)*, for each further £2 of income the married couple's allowance reduces from the maximum amount by £1 (but is subject to the minimum amount).

7   Applies only if non-savings income is below this limit. (Non-savings income is taxed first, then savings income, then dividends.)

8   The corresponding tax rates on dividends are 10%, 32.5% and 37.5%.

9   'Entrepreneurs' Relief' is available for gains made on certain business disposals. A flat-rate 10% tax applies, subject to a lifetime limit of £10 million.

10   Where total income and gains exceed the higher-rate Income Tax threshold.

11   Any unused nil-rate band can be transferred to the surviving spouse or civil partner.

12   A lower rate of 36% may apply if at least 10% of the estate is left to charity. A sliding scale of 'Taper Relief' applies on certain gifts (known as Potentially Exempt Transfers) made between three and seven years of death.

13   Higher rate applies to travel insurance, breakdown insurance and insurance sold in relation to goods subject to VAT.

ABBREVIATIONS IN COMMON USE

AA	Annual Allowance
ABI	Association of British Insurers
ACA	Association of Consulting Actuaries
ACT	Advance Corporation Tax
AE	Automatic Enrolment
APP	Appropriate Personal Pension
ARR	Age-related Rebate
AVCs	Additional Voluntary Contributions
AWE	Average Weekly Earnings
BCE	Benefit Crystallisation Event
BIS	Department for Business, Innovation and Skills
BSP	Basic State Pension
CA	Certified Amount *or* Companies Act
CARE	Career Average Revalued Earnings
CB	Cash Balance
CEP	Contributions Equivalent Premium
CETV	Cash Equivalent Transfer Value
CGT	Capital Gains Tax
CIMPS	Contracted-in Money Purchase Scheme
CMI	Continuous Mortality Investigation
COMBS	Contracted-out Mixed Benefit Scheme
COMPS	Contracted-out Money Purchase Scheme
CoP	Code of Practice
COSRS	Contracted-out Salary-related Scheme
CPA	Compulsory Purchase Annuity
CPI	Consumer Prices Index
CPS	Combined Pension Statement
DA	Defined Ambition
DB	Defined Benefit
DC	Defined Contribution
DPA	Data Protection Act
DWP	Department for Work and Pensions
ECJ	European Court of Justice
ECON	Employer's Contracting-out Number
EEA	European Economic Area

EFRBS	Employer-financed Retirement Benefit Scheme
EIOPA	The European Insurance and Occupational Pensions Authority
EPB	Equivalent Pension Benefit
EPP	Executive Pension Plan
ERF	Early Retirement Factor
ETV	Enhanced Transfer Value
EU	European Union
FA	Finance Act
FAS	Financial Assistance Scheme *or* Financial Accounting Standard
FASB	Financial Accounting Standards Board
FCA	Financial Conduct Authority
FCF	Fraud Compensation Fund
FRC	Financial Reporting Council
FRS	Financial Reporting Standard
FSA	Financial Services Authority
FSCS	Financial Services Compensation Scheme
FSD	Financial Support Direction
FSMA	Financial Services and Markets Act
GAD	Government Actuary's Department
GMP	Guaranteed Minimum Pension
GN	Guidance Notes
GPP	Group Personal Pension
GSIPP	Group Self-invested Personal Pension
HMRC	Her Majesty's Revenue & Customs
HMT	Her Majesty's Treasury
IAS	International Accounting Standard
IASB/IASC	International Accounting Standards Board/Committee
ICTA	Income & Corporation Taxes Act
IDR/IDRP	Internal Dispute Resolution (Procedure)
IFRS	International Financial Reporting Standard
IGG	Investment Governance Group
IHT	Inheritance Tax
IORP	Institutions for Occupational Retirement Provision (especially IORP Directive)
ISA	Individual Savings Account
ITEPA	Income Tax (Earnings and Pensions) Act
JWG	Occupational Pension Schemes Joint Working Group

LDI	Liability-driven Investment
LEL	Lower Earnings Limit
LET	Low Earnings Threshold
LPI	Limited Price Indexation
LRF	Late Retirement Factor
LTA	Lifetime Allowance
MIR	Minimum Income Requirement
MND	Member-nominated Director
MNT	Member-nominated Trustee
MPP	Maximum Permitted Pension
NAPF	National Association of Pension Funds
NEST	National Employment Savings Trust
NI	National Insurance
NICO	National Insurance Contributions Office
NISPI	National Insurance Services to Pensions Industry
NMPA	Normal Minimum Pension Age
NPA/NPD	Normal Pension Age/Normal Pension Date
NRA/NRD	Normal Retirement Age/Normal Retirement Date
OEIC	Open-ended Investment Company
OMO	Open Market Option
ONS	Office for National Statistics
OPS	Occupational Pension Scheme
PA	Pensions Act
PAYE	Pay As You Earn
PAYG	Pay As You Go
PCLS	Pension Commencement Lump Sum
PIA	Pension Input Amount
PIE	Pension Increase Exchange
PIP	Pension Input Period
PLA	Purchased Life Annuity *or* Personal Lifetime Allowance
PMI	Pensions Management Institute
PPF	Pension Protection Fund
PPP/PPS	Personal Pension Plan/Scheme
PR	Protected Rights
PRA	Prudential Regulation Authority
PRAG	Pensions Research Accountants Group
PSA	Pension Schemes Act
PUP	Paid-up Pension/Pensioner
QROPS	Qualifying Recognised Overseas Pension Scheme

RAC	Retirement Annuity Contract
RPI	Retail Prices Index
RPSM	Registered Pension Schemes Manual
RST	Reference Scheme Test
S2P	State Second Pension
SCON	Scheme Contracted-out Number
SERPS	State Earnings-related Pension Scheme
SFO	Statutory Funding Objective
SFP	Statement of Funding Principles
SFS	Summary Funding Statement
SI	Statutory Instrument
SIP	Statement of Investment Principles
SIPP	Self-invested Personal Pension
SLA	Standard Lifetime Allowance
SMPI	Statutory Money Purchase Illustration
SoC	Schedule of Contributions
SORP	Statement of Recommended Practice
SPA	State Pension Age
SPC	Society of Pension Consultants
SRI	Socially Responsible Investment
SSA	Social Security Act
SSAS	Small Self-administered Scheme
SSB	Short Service Benefit
SSPA	Social Security Pensions Act
TAS	Technical Actuarial Standard
TKU	Trustee Knowledge and Understanding
TPAS	The Pensions Advisory Service
TPR	The Pensions Regulator
TUPE	Transfer of Undertakings (Protection of Employment) Regulations
TV	Transfer Value
UAP	Upper Accrual Point
UEL	Upper Earnings Limit
WGMP	Widow's/Widower's Guaranteed Minimum Pension
WR&PA	Welfare Reform and Pensions Act

Source: Aon Hewitt.

GLOSSARY OF TERMS

Bold Text:	Cross references that it is felt might improve the understanding of the term concerned.
Italicised Text:	Terms which, whilst not forming part of the basic definition, provide the reader with additional guidance.

DEFINITIONS

The definitions in this Glossary are current at the time of going to print.

ACCRUAL RATE   The rate at which rights build up for each year of **pensionable service** in a **DB scheme**.

ACCRUED BENEFITS   The benefits for service up to a given point in time, whether **vested rights** or not. They may be calculated in relation to current earnings or projected earnings.

Allowance may also be made for **revaluation** *and/or* **pension increases** *required by the scheme rules or legislation.*

ACCRUED RIGHTS   The benefits to which a member is entitled, as of right, under an **occupational pension scheme**. These include **accrued benefits**. Depending on the context, accrued rights for an **active member** can be based on benefits as if the member had left service or could include a right to have benefits linked to future salary changes.

The term is given various specific definitions in PSA 1993 for the purposes of **preservation**, **contracting out** *and in the Disclosure Regulations. It is also given a specific meaning in PA 1995, e.g. in relation to scheme amendments.*

ACTIVE MEMBER   A member of an **occupational pension scheme** who is at present accruing benefits under that scheme in respect of current service.

ACTUARIAL EQUIVALENCE   A test of actuarial value which compares benefits, in particular, immediately before and after a modification. For the test to be satisfied, the total value of the member's subsisting rights immediately after the modification must be no less than the value of those rights immediately before the modification. This term is used in connection with **section 67** of PA 1995.

ACTUARIAL REDUCTION   A reduction made to a member's **accrued benefits** in order to offset any additional cost arising from their payment in advance of the **normal pension date**.

ACTUARIAL REPORT A written report, prepared and signed by the **scheme actuary**, on the developments affecting the scheme's **technical provisions** since the last **actuarial valuation** was prepared.

ACTUARIAL VALUATION

(1) Commonly refers to an investigation by an actuary into the ability of a **DB scheme** to meet its liabilities. This is usually to assess the **funding level** and a recommended contribution rate based on comparing the value of the assets and the actuarial liability.

(2) Under PA 2004, specifically refers to a written report, prepared and signed by the **scheme actuary**, valuing the scheme's assets and calculating its **technical provisions**.

ADDED YEARS The provision of extra benefits by reference to an additional period of **pensionable service** in a **DB scheme**, arising from the receipt of a **transfer payment**, the paying of **AVCs** or by way of **augmentation**.

ADDITIONAL VOLUNTARY CONTRIBUTIONS (AVCs)

Contributions over and above a member's normal contributions if any, which the member elects to pay to an **occupational pension scheme** in order to secure additional benefits.

ADMINISTRATOR

(1) The person or persons notified to HMRC as being responsible for the management of a pension scheme.

(2) The person who is responsible for the day-to-day administration of the pension scheme.

(3) A type of insolvency practitioner in relation to companies under the Insolvency Act 1986.

AGE-RELATED REBATE Payments made by NICO to a contracted-out **occupational money purchase scheme** or an appropriate **personal pension scheme**, for members who were **contracted out**. These increased with the age of the member.

Contracting out on a money purchase basis was abolished from 6 April 2012.

ANNUAL ALLOWANCE The maximum amount of pension savings that can be built up in any one tax year before liability to an **annual allowance charge** arises.

ANNUAL ALLOWANCE CHARGE The tax charge levied on an individual who is a member of one or more **registered pension schemes** in respect of the amount by which the **total pension input amount** for a tax year exceeds the **annual allowance**.

ANNUAL REPORT The means by which the **trustees** of an **occupational pension scheme** communicate financial and other information about the scheme to the members, the employer and other interested parties.

The term is used to describe the specific information that is required to be made available by trustees in relation to each scheme year under the Disclosure Regulations. Subject to certain exemptions, this must include a copy of the audited accounts and other information specified, including an investment report. The detailed content of the audited accounts is described in the Pension Scheme **SORP**.

Trustees often publish a simplified annual report for members containing the above material suitably summarised.

ANNUITY A series of payments, which may be subject to increases, made at stated intervals until a particular event occurs. This event is most commonly the end of a specified period or the death of the person receiving the annuity.

An annuity may take one of a number of different forms including **compulsory purchase annuity**, *deferred annuity,* **purchased life annuity** *and* **short-term annuity**.

ANTI-FRANKING REQUIREMENTS The requirements which ban the process whereby statutory increases in **GMP** e.g. between termination of **contracted-out** employment and **State pensionable age** are offset against other scheme benefits, rather than being added to a member's total benefits.

The requirements are covered in Chapter III of Part IV PSA 1993.

ARRANGEMENT Under FA 2004, a contractual or **trust**-based arrangement made by or on behalf of a member of a pension scheme under that scheme. A member may have more than one arrangement under a scheme.

ASSESSMENT PERIOD The period of time when a scheme is being assessed to determine whether the **Pension Protection Fund** can assume responsibility for it.

ASSET ALLOCATION STRATEGY The splitting of the assets of a pension scheme between the various **asset classes** such as equities, bonds and cash. This will primarily reflect the long-term needs of the fund, the 'strategic view', but may be adjusted to favour particular asset classes or markets which look attractive in the short term, the 'tactical view'.

ASSET AND LIABILITY MATCHING A process of selecting assets which are likely to generate proceeds broadly equal to the cashflow needed to meet the liabilities as they occur under different economic scenarios.

An example of this would be the matching of a level pension with fixed interest securities.

ASSET AND LIABILITY MODELLING A technique used to test the effect of different economic scenarios on the assets and liabilities of an **occupational pension scheme**, the inter-relationship between them, the **funding level** and the contribution rates.

ASSET-BACKED PENSION CONTRIBUTION A non-cash business asset used by an employer to underpin regular cash contributions to a pension scheme.

ASSET CLASS A collective term for investments of a similar type. The main asset classes are equities (shares), bonds, cash and property.

ATTAINED AGE METHOD A funding method in which the actuarial liability makes allowance for projected earnings. The contribution rate is that necessary to cover the cost of all benefits which will accrue to existing members after the valuation date by reference to total earnings throughout their future working lifetimes projected to the dates on which benefits become payable.

AUGMENTATION The provision of additional benefits in respect of particular members of an **occupational pension scheme**, normally where the cost is borne by the scheme and/or employer.

AUTHORISED PAYMENT A payment made by a **registered pension scheme** to an employer or member which is permitted under the provisions of FA 2004.

AUTOMATIC ENROLMENT The process whereby employers must automatically enrol workers that meet specified eligibility conditions into a **qualifying pension scheme**. Workers can subsequently opt out by giving notice within a prescribed period.

Employers without their own qualifying scheme may use NEST.

AUTOMATIC TRANSFER The process whereby a member's small DC pot is transferred automatically to the **DC scheme** of their new employer. This is due to be introduced following the abolition of **short service refund lump sums** and **cash transfer sums** from DC **occupational pension schemes.**

BASIC PENSION The flat-rate (not earnings-related) State pension paid to all who have met the minimum NI contribution requirements. The amount paid is increased if the recipient is married and a spouse or widow(er) may claim on the record of his/her spouse.

*Due to be replaced by the **single-tier pension** from 6 April 2016.*

BENEFICIARY   A person entitled to benefit under a pension scheme or who will become entitled on the happening of a specific event.

BENEFIT CRYSTALLISATION EVENT   One of eleven events defined in FA 2004 that triggers a test of benefits 'crystallising' at that point against the individual's available **lifetime allowance**.

BRIDGING PENSION   An additional pension paid from a scheme between retirement and **State pensionable age**, which is usually replaced by the State pension payable from that age.

BULK TRANSFER   The transfer of a group of members from one **occupational pension scheme** to another, sometimes with a **transfer payment** that is enhanced in comparison with an individual's **cash equivalent**.

BUY-IN   The purchase by **trustees** of an **occupational pension scheme** of an insurance policy in the name of the trustees. This remains an asset of the trustees.

BUY-OUT   The purchase by **trustees** of an **occupational pension scheme** of an insurance policy in the name of a member or other **beneficiary**, in lieu of entitlement to benefit from the scheme, following termination of the member's **pensionable service**.

CAPPED DRAWDOWN   A form of **drawdown pension**. The maximum income is capped at the level of an equivalent single life level **annuity** that could be provided from the drawdown pension fund. The cap is checked at the outset and periodically after that. There is no minimum level of drawdown pension.

CAREER AVERAGE REVALUED EARNINGS (CARE) SCHEME

A **DB scheme** in which the benefit for each year of membership is related to that year's **pensionable earnings**, revalued in line with an appropriate index during and after **pensionable service**.

CASH BALANCE SCHEME   A scheme in which a guaranteed cash sum is built up on the basis of a formula directly related to the employee's **pensionable earnings** in each year of membership. The resulting 'cash balance' can be used either to purchase an **annuity** or to make other arrangements for retirement.

CASH EQUIVALENT   The amount which a member of a pension scheme may, under section 94 PSA 1993, require to be applied as a **transfer payment**.

CASH TRANSFER SUM   The amount that a leaver with between 3 and 24 months' **pensionable service** may require to be applied as a **transfer payment**, as an alternative to a refund of contributions.

CERTIFICATION   In the context of **automatic enrolment**, the formal confirmation by the employer or **scheme actuary** that a scheme meets the quality requirements necessary to be a **qualifying scheme**.

CLOSED SCHEME   A scheme that does not admit new members.

CODES OF PRACTICE   The **Pensions Regulator** issues various codes of practice providing practical guidance on compliance with the requirements of relevant pensions legislation.

COMMUTATION   The forgoing of a part or all of the pension payable from retirement for an immediate lump sum benefit.

COMPULSORY PURCHASE ANNUITY   The term used to describe an **annuity** purchased on retirement for a member of a **registered pension scheme**.

CONTINGENT ASSETS   Assets that produce cash for a scheme contingent on certain events, in particular when an insolvency event occurs to the employer. These include charges over assets, group company guarantees and bank letters of credit.

CONTRACTED OUT/CONTRACTED IN   A pension scheme is contracted out where it provides benefits (**GMPs** or **section 9(2B) rights**) in place of **SERPS** or **S2P** and has been given a **contracting-out certificate** by HMRC. Members are contracted out if they are in employment which is contracted out by reference to an **occupational pension scheme**.

A pension scheme is commonly called contracted in where it is not contracted out, i.e. it provides benefits in addition to S2P. The term 'contracted in' is not referred to in legislation.

Contracting out on a money purchase basis was abolished from 6 April 2012. Contracting out on a salary-related basis is due to be abolished from 6 April 2016.

CONTRACTED-OUT REBATE   The amount by which the employer's and the employee's NI contributions are reduced or rebated in respect of employees who are **contracted out** by virtue of their membership of an appropriate **personal pension scheme** or an **occupational pension scheme**.

The contracted-out rebate consists of a flat-rate rebate and (for contracted-out **money purchase schemes** *and appropriate personal pension schemes, up to 5 April 2012) an* **age-related rebate**.

CONTRACTING-OUT CERTIFICATE   The certificate issued by HMRC, in respect of an **occupational pension scheme** which satisfies the conditions for contracting out, confirming that the employees in the employments named in the certificate are to be treated as being in **contracted-out** employment.

CONTRACTUAL ENROLMENT An alternative to **automatic enrolment**, whereby an employer fulfils its duties under PA 2008 *(see Section 4)* by enrolling all workers into a suitable pension scheme when they start work with the employer.

CONTRIBUTION NOTICE A direction by the **Pensions Regulator** to a company or individual that is, or is connected to, an employer, to pay a contribution to that employer's scheme. The Regulator must be of the opinion that they have acted in order to prevent recovery of a **section 75 debt** or that a 'material detriment' test is met.

CONTROLLING DIRECTOR A director who, on his own or with associates, owns or controls 20% or more of the ordinary shares of the employing company.

CROSS-BORDER SCHEME If a UK scheme has members working in another EEA state, who are not **seconded employees**, the scheme is operating as a cross-border scheme. Such schemes require regulatory approval to accept contributions in respect of cross-border operations and are subject to additional regulations, for example in relation to the **statutory funding objective**.

DEFERRED MEMBER/DEFERRED PENSIONER A member entitled to **preserved benefits**.

DEFINED BENEFIT SCHEME (DB Scheme) A scheme where the scheme rules define the benefits independently of the contributions payable, and benefits are not directly related to the investments of the scheme. The scheme may be funded or unfunded.

DEFINED CONTRIBUTION SCHEME (DC Scheme) A scheme which determines the individual member's benefits by reference to contributions paid into the scheme in respect of that member, usually increased by an amount based on the investment return on those contributions. Sometimes referred to as a **money purchase scheme**.

DEPENDANT For HMRC purposes:

(1) a person who was married to, civil partner of or financially dependent on the member, or dependent on the member because of physical or mental impairment, at the date of the member's death, is a dependant of the member, *and*

(2) a child of the member is a dependant of the member if the child has not reached the age of 23, or has reached age 23 and, in the opinion of the scheme **administrator**, was at the

date of the member's death dependent on the member because of physical or mental impairment.

DISCLOSURE

(1) A requirement introduced by PSA 1993 (formerly SSPA 1975) and strengthened by PA 1995 for pension schemes to disclose information about the scheme and benefits to interested parties.

(2) Rules introduced by regulatory bodies to disclose product and commission information to the purchasers of life assurance and insured pension products.

DISCONTINUANCE   The cessation of the liability of the sponsoring employer to pay contributions to a pension scheme.

DISCRETIONARY INCREASE   An increase to a pension in payment or to a **preserved benefit** arising on a discretionary basis, i.e. other than from a system of **escalation** or **indexation**. Such an increase may be of a regular or an ad hoc nature.

DRAWDOWN PENSION   Pension paid in the form of **income withdrawal** and/or **short-term annuity**, avoiding the need to purchase a **scheme pension** or **lifetime annuity**.

ELIGIBLE JOBHOLDER   For the purposes of **automatic enrolment**, this means a **jobholder** who is at least age 22, has not reached **State pensionable age** and earns more than the 'earnings trigger' *(see Section 4)*. A worker must be auto-enrolled into a **qualifying pension scheme** within a month of becoming an eligible jobholder.

EMPLOYER COVENANT   The employer's legal obligation, willingness and ability to fund its pension scheme now and in the future.

EMPLOYER-FINANCED RETIREMENT BENEFIT SCHEME

A scheme which is neither a **registered pension scheme** nor a section 615(3) scheme.

ENHANCED LIFETIME ALLOWANCE   This is where the **standard lifetime allowance** has been increased as a result of **primary protection**, **pension credits** or transfers from **overseas schemes**, or where the member has not always had taxable UK earnings or been resident in the UK. This results in a **personal lifetime allowance**.

ENHANCED PROTECTION   A form of protection from the **lifetime allowance charge** available for all members who registered for it under the FA 2004 tax regime, regardless of the amount of their benefits pre-6 April 2006.

ENTITLED WORKER   For the purposes of **automatic enrolment**, this means a worker who ordinarily works in the UK, is aged at least 16 and under 75 and is in receipt of earnings of no more than the lower limit for **qualifying earnings**. Entitled workers are entitled to join a pension scheme but it need not be a **qualifying pension scheme** and the employer is not obliged to contribute.

ESCALATION   A system whereby pensions in payment and/or **preserved benefits** are automatically increased at regular intervals and at a defined percentage rate.

The percentage may be restricted to the increase in a specified index.

EXPRESSION OF WISH   A means by which a member can indicate a preference as to who should receive any lump sum death benefit.

*The choice is not binding on the **trustees**, and, as a result, inheritance tax is normally avoided.*

FINAL PENSIONABLE EARNINGS/PAY/SALARY   The **pensionable earnings** on which the benefits are calculated in a **DB scheme**. The earnings may be based on the average over a number of consecutive years prior to retirement, death or leaving **pensionable service**.

FINANCIAL ASSISTANCE SCHEME   A scheme introduced by the government to help workers who have lost pension rights through company insolvency but do not qualify for the **Pension Protection Fund**.

FINANCIAL SUPPORT DIRECTION   A direction by the **Pensions Regulator**, requiring a company that is, or is connected to, an employer in relation to the scheme to put in place financial support arrangements where the effect of the corporate structure is that the employer is 'insufficiently resourced'.

FIXED RATE REVALUATION   A method used by a COSR to revalue **GMP** between termination of **contracted-out** employment and age 65 (men), 60 (women) as one of the alternatives to applying **section 148 orders**.

The rate is reviewed periodically.

FIXED PROTECTION   A form of protection from the **lifetime allowance charge** available to individuals with benefits in **registered pension schemes**, who do not have **enhanced** or **primary protection**, who registered for it before 6 April 2012 and do not accrue further benefits. It was introduced to coincide with the reduction in the **lifetime allowance** from £1.8 million to £1.5 million from 6 April 2012.

FIXED PROTECTION 2014   A form of protection from the **lifetime allowance charge**, with conditions similar to those for **fixed protection.** It will coincide with the reduction in the **lifetime allowance** from £1.5 million to £1.25 million from 6 April 2014.

FLEXIBLE DRAWDOWN   A form of **drawdown pension** available to individuals who meet the **minimum income requirement**. Individuals who satisfy certain criteria can take unlimited amounts as income and are not subject to **capped drawdown**.

FLEXIBLE RETIREMENT   The option available from 6 April 2006 under FA 2004 to take benefits in stages. The member can also remain in employment with the same employer.

FRAUD COMPENSATION FUND   Payments can be made from the fund in cases where the assets of a scheme have been reduced since 6 April 1997 as a result of an offence involving dishonesty, including an intent to defraud.

FROZEN SCHEME   A scheme with no further benefits accruing.

FUNDING LEVEL   The relationship at a specified date between the value of the assets and the actuarial liability. Normally expressed as a percentage.

GMP CONVERSION   The conversion of **GMPs** into 'normal' scheme benefits of equal actuarial value, permitted from 6 April 2009.

GUARANTEED MINIMUM PENSION (GMP)   The minimum pension which an **occupational pension scheme** must provide as one of the conditions of contracting out for pre-6 April 1997 service (unless it was **contracted out** through the provision of **protected rights**).

HYBRID ARRANGEMENT   Under FA 2004, an **arrangement** where only one type of benefit will ultimately be provided, but the type of benefit that will be provided is not known in advance because it will depend on certain circumstances at the point benefits are drawn.

HYBRID SCHEME

(1)   An **occupational pension scheme** in which the benefit is calculated as the better of two alternatives, for example on a final salary and a money purchase basis.

(2)   An occupational pension scheme which offers both **defined benefit** and **defined contribution** benefits.

INCOME WITHDRAWAL   An alternative to buying a **lifetime annuity**. It allows a member of a **money purchase arrangement** to draw an income from their **drawdown pension** fund while the fund remains invested.

INDEPENDENT TRUSTEE   An independent trustee must be registered and an 'independent person in relation to the scheme'. This requirement will be satisfied if he or she has no interests in the assets of the employer or scheme and is not connected with the employer, insolvency practitioner or official receiver.

INDEXATION

(1)   A system whereby pensions in payment and/or **preserved benefits** are automatically increased at regular intervals by reference to a specified index of prices or earnings.

(2)   An investment strategy designed to produce a rate of return in line with a particular index, either by replicating the constituents or by sufficient sampling to give a proxy.

INDIVIDUAL PROTECTION   A form of protection from the **lifetime allowance charge**, to be introduced when the **lifetime allowance** reduces to £1.25 million from 6 April 2014.

INTERNAL DISPUTE RESOLUTION PROCEDURE (IDRP)

Occupational pension schemes (subject to exceptions) are required by section 50 PA 1995 to have a procedure to deal with disputes between **trustees** on the one hand and members and **beneficiaries** on the other hand.

JOBHOLDER   For the purposes of **automatic enrolment** this means a worker who ordinarily works in the UK, is aged at least 16 and under 75 and to whom **qualifying earnings** are payable.

LEVY

(1)   The general levy meets the expenditure of the **Pensions Ombudsman** (and PPF Ombudsman), the **Pensions Regulator** and grants made by the Pensions Regulator (e.g. to TPAS). It is payable by registrable **occupational pension schemes** and **personal pension schemes**.

(2)   The Fraud Compensation Levy is payable by occupational pension schemes to fund the **Fraud Compensation Fund**.

(3)   Schemes that are eligible for future entry to the **PPF** pay a Pension Protection Levy to the PPF. A PPF Administration Levy is also payable.

LIFESTYLING   An **asset allocation strategy** used mainly in **DC schemes** whereby a member's investments are adjusted depending on age and term to retirement. Typically assets are switched from equities into bonds and cash as retirement approaches.

LIFETIME ALLOWANCE   The lifetime allowance is an overall ceiling on the amount of tax-privileged savings that any one individual can draw. The exact figure will be the same as the **standard lifetime allowance** for the tax year concerned, or a (higher) proportion where certain circumstances apply.

LIFETIME ALLOWANCE CHARGE   The tax charge levied on excess funds, following a **benefit crystallisation event**, for any individual with a benefit value more than their **lifetime allowance** (unless they have **enhanced protection**).

LIFETIME ANNUITY   Under FA 2004, an **annuity** contract purchased from an insurance company of the member's choosing that provides the member with an income for life.

LIMITED PRICE INDEXATION (LPI)   The requirement under PA 1995 to increase pensions in payment under an **occupational pension scheme** (excluding **AVCs** and money purchase benefits) by a minimum amount. The minimum is in line with price inflation or, if lower, 5% p.a. for benefits accrued between 6 April 1997 and 5 April 2005 and 2.5% p.a. for benefits accrued after 5 April 2005.

LOWER EARNINGS LIMIT (LEL)   The minimum amount (historically approximately equivalent to the single person's **basic pension**) which must be earned in any period in order for an individual to accrue State pension benefits.

MINIMUM CONTRIBUTIONS   Contributions payable to an appropriate scheme by NICO in respect of a member who had elected to contract out. The contributions consisted of the **age-related rebate** and, where payment was to an APP or **stakeholder pension**, basic rate tax relief on the employee's share of the rebate.

Contracting out on a money purchase basis was abolished from 6 April 2012. There are transitional arrangements for minimum contributions.

MINIMUM INCOME REQUIREMENT (MIR)   The level of secure lifetime income that is required to qualify for **flexible drawdown**. The intention is that individuals must demonstrate a sufficient level of income to prevent them exhausting their savings and falling back on the state. Only certain sources of income – such as **annuities**, **scheme pensions** and State pensions – count towards the MIR. The Treasury will review this limit at least every five years.

MINIMUM PAYMENTS   The minimum amount that an employer had to pay into a **contracted-out money purchase scheme**. *(...continues)*

MINIMUM PAYMENTS *(continued)*
> This consisted of the flat-rate rebate of NI contributions in respect of employees who were contracted out.

> *Contracting out on a money purchase basis was abolished from 6 April 2012.*

MONEY PURCHASE ARRANGEMENT Under FA 2004, this is an **arrangement** under which the member is entitled to money purchase benefits. A **cash balance** arrangement is one type of money purchase arrangement.

MONEY PURCHASE SCHEME A **DC scheme** where the benefit is provided from contributions to the scheme, increased by the amount of investment return on those contributions.

> *When the relevant provision is commenced, the Pensions Act 2011 will amend the definition of money purchase benefits (and hence schemes) for certain purposes.*

NET PAY ARRANGEMENT The procedure whereby contributions to an **occupational pension scheme** are deducted from the member's pay before tax is calculated under PAYE, giving immediate tax relief at the highest applicable rate.

> *In some cases, relief at source may be used instead, or relief claimed via self-assessment.*

NON-ELIGIBLE JOBHOLDER A **jobholder** who is not an **eligible jobholder**. A non-eligible jobholder is not eligible for **automatic enrolment** but can opt into a **qualifying pension scheme**.

NORMAL MINIMUM PENSION AGE The earliest age, currently 55, at which a member is allowed to draw benefits from a **registered pension scheme**, other than in ill health. Prior to 6 April 2010 normal minimum pension age was 50. There are transitional provisions allowing members to protect existing rights at 5 April 2006 to receive their benefits from an earlier age.

NORMAL PENSION AGE (NPA)

(1) Commonly the age by reference to which the **normal pension date** is determined.

(2) The statutory definition (relevant for **preservation** and **contracting-out** purposes) is generally the earliest age at which a member is entitled to receive benefits (other than **GMP**) on his/her retirement from employment to which the scheme relates, ignoring any special provisions as to early retirement on grounds of ill health or otherwise (section 180 PSA 1993). This is commonly interpreted to mean the

earliest age at which a member has the right to take benefits without reduction.

This may be different from definition (1) above or **normal retirement age**.

NORMAL PENSION DATE (NPD)   The date at which a member of a pension scheme normally becomes entitled to receive his/her retirement benefits.

NORMAL RETIREMENT AGE (NRA)

(1)   For employment purposes the age at which the employees holding a particular position normally retire from service.

This is often (but not always) the same as **normal pension age** *or definition (2) below.*

(2)   The age of a member of an **occupational pension scheme** at the **normal retirement date** as specified in the scheme rules.

NORMAL RETIREMENT DATE (NRD)   The date (usually the date of reaching a particular age) specified in the rules of an **occupational pension scheme** at which a member would normally retire.

NOTIFIABLE EVENTS   Certain specified events to be automatically notified to the **Pensions Regulator** under section 69 of PA 2004.

OCCUPATIONAL PENSION SCHEME   A scheme established by an employer or on behalf of a group of employers to provide pensions and/or other benefits for or in respect of one or more employees on leaving service or on death or on retirement. An occupational pension scheme can be registered with the **Pensions Regulator** as a **stakeholder pension scheme** if the necessary conditions are met.

The statutory definitions are in section 1 PSA 1993 and section 150 FA 2004.

OPEN MARKET OPTION   The option to apply the proceeds of an insurance or investment contract to buy an **annuity** at a current market rate from the same or another insurance company.

OVERSEAS PENSION SCHEME   A pension scheme established outside the UK for local residents of that country or employees of an international organisation, which is subject to local pension scheme and taxation regulations.

PARTICIPATING EMPLOYER   An employer, some or all of whose employees have the right to become members of an **occupational pension scheme**.

Usually applied where more than one employer participates in a single scheme.

PAYMENT SCHEDULE   A schedule, required under section 87 PA 1995 for **money purchase occupational pension schemes**, specifying contribution rates to be paid and the due dates for such payments.

PENSION COMMENCEMENT LUMP SUM   Under FA 2004, the term for the tax-free cash sum that may be paid to a member on taking pension benefits.

PENSION CREDIT

(1)   The amount of benefit rights that an ex-spouse of a scheme member becomes entitled to following a **pension sharing order**.

(2)   An income-related (means-tested) benefit that boosts a pensioner's State pension to ensure they have a minimum level of income.

PENSION DEBIT   The amount of benefit rights given up by a scheme member when a **pension sharing order** is made in respect of that member.

PENSION GUARANTEE   An arrangement whereby, on the early death of a pensioner, the pension scheme pays a further sum or sums to meet a guaranteed total.

This total may be established by relation to, for instance, a multiple of the annual rate of pension or the accumulated contributions of the late member.

PENSION INCREASE   An increase to a pension in payment.

Such an increase may arise as a result of **escalation** *or* **indexation** *or may be a* **discretionary increase**.

PENSION INCREASE CONVERSION/EXCHANGE EXERCISE   An offer to members to exchange future, non-statutory increases on their pension for a higher fixed pension.

PENSION INPUT AMOUNT   The amount of contributions paid or increase in value of a member's benefits in an **arrangement** measured for **annual allowance** purposes.

PENSION INPUT PERIOD   The period over which the **pension input amount** for an **arrangement** is measured.

PENSION LIBERATION   The transfer of members' pension savings to an **arrangement** that will allow them to access their funds before they are properly entitled or to exceed the allowable lump sum.

PENSION PROTECTION FUND (PPF)   A fund set up under PA 2004 to provide benefits to members of **DB schemes** that **wind up** due to the employer's insolvency with insufficient assets to pay benefits.

PENSION SCHEMES REGISTRY   The register of **occupational pension schemes** and **personal pension schemes**, maintained by the **Pensions Regulator**.

The registry enables members to trace schemes with which they have lost touch and collects the **levy***.*

PENSION SHARING ORDER   An order made in accordance with the provisions of Chapter I of Part IV of WR&PA 1999 which makes provision for the pension rights of a scheme member to be split on divorce.

PENSIONABLE EARNINGS/PAY/SALARY   The earnings on which contributions and/or benefits are calculated under the rules of an **occupational pension scheme**.

PENSIONABLE SERVICE   The period of service which is taken into account in calculating benefits.

PSA 1993 gives the term a statutory definition for the purposes of the **preservation**, **revaluation** *and* **transfer payment** *requirements of the Act. PA 1995 gives a further statutory definition.*

PENSIONS OMBUDSMAN   The Pensions Ombudsman deals with disputes about entitlement and complaints of maladministration from members of **occupational pension schemes** and **personal pension schemes**. The Ombudsman's role also includes investigating complaints or disputes between **trustees** of occupational pension schemes and employers, and between trustees of different occupational pension schemes or between trustees of the same scheme.

PENSIONS REGULATOR, THE (The Regulator, TPR)   An independent body set up under PA 2004 to regulate **occupational pension schemes** from 6 April 2005. Its role is to protect members of work-based pension schemes, to promote good administration of schemes, to reduce the risk of situations arising that may give rise to a claim on the **Pension Protection Fund** and to maximise employers' compliance with their **automatic enrolment** duties. It has the power to impose orders and fines on **trustees** and employers.

PERSONAL LIFETIME ALLOWANCE   The **lifetime allowance** applicable to individuals who have registered for **primary protection**. It is indexed in line with changes in the **standard lifetime allowance** but taking that allowance to be at least £1.8m for tax years following 5 April 2012.

See also **enhanced lifetime allowance**.

PERSONAL PENSION SCHEME   A scheme provided by an insurance company (or another financial institution) to enable individuals to save for a private retirement income.   *(...continues)*

PERSONAL PENSION SCHEME *(continued)*

A personal pension scheme can be registered with the **Pensions Regulator** as a **stakeholder pension scheme** if the necessary conditions are met.

The statutory definition is in section 1 PSA 1993.

POSTPONEMENT   In the context of **automatic enrolment**, the use by an employer of a waiting period, of up to three months, to defer the obligation to auto-enrol a worker.

PRESERVATION   The granting by a scheme of **preserved benefits** to a member leaving **pensionable service** before **normal pension age** under an **occupational pension scheme**, in particular in accordance with minimum requirements specified by PSA 1993.

PRESERVED BENEFITS   Benefits arising on an individual ceasing to be an **active member** of an **occupational pension scheme**, payable at a later date.

PRIMARY PROTECTION   A mechanism by which individuals could register pre-6 April 2006 rights of more than £1.5m and obtain an increased **personal lifetime allowance**.

PRINCIPAL EMPLOYER   Commonly used in scheme documentation for the particular **participating employer** in which is vested special powers or duties in relation to such matters as the appointment of the **trustees**, amendments and **winding up**. Usually this will be the employer which established the scheme or its successor in business.

PRIORITY RULE   The provisions contained within the scheme documentation setting out the order of precedence of liabilities to be followed if the scheme is wound up.

Section 73 PA 1995 introduced an overriding statutory order of priorities, which was amended by PA 2004 with effect from 6 April 2005.

PROJECTED UNIT METHOD   A funding method in which the actuarial liability makes allowance for projected earnings. The contribution rate is that necessary to cover the cost of all benefits which will accrue in the control period following the valuation date by reference to earnings projected to the dates on which the benefits become payable.

Also known as the projected unit credit method.

PROSPECTIVE MEMBER   An individual, not currently a member of the pension scheme of his/her employer, who is either entitled to join or will become eligible to join in the future by virtue of continuing in employment with the employer.

PROTECTED RIGHTS   The benefits from a scheme **contracted out** on a money purchase basis deriving from at least the **minimum contributions** or **minimum payments**, provided in a specified form as a necessary condition of contracting out.

Protected rights were abolished from 6 April 2012, when contracting out of **S2P** *on a money purchase basis was abolished.*

PUBLIC SECTOR PENSION SCHEME   An **occupational pension scheme** for employees of central or local government, a nationalised industry or other statutory body.

PUBLIC SECTOR TRANSFER ARRANGEMENTS   The arrangements of the **transfer club** to which certain schemes, mainly in the public sector, belong.

PURCHASED LIFE ANNUITY   An **annuity** purchased privately by an individual. In accordance with section 717 of Income Tax (Trading and Other Income) Act 2005, instalments of the annuity are subject to tax in part only.

QUALIFYING EARNINGS   The band of gross earnings between limits set each year on which minimum contributions for the purposes of **automatic enrolment** are calculated. Qualifying earnings include a worker's salary, wages, overtime, bonuses and commission, as well as statutory sick, maternity, paternity and adoption pay.

Information on the current limits can be found in Section 4.

QUALIFYING PENSION SCHEME   For the purposes of **automatic enrolment** this means any **occupational** or **personal pension scheme** that meets statutory minimum criteria for the worker in question.

QUALIFYING RECOGNISED OVERSEAS PENSION SCHEME

A **recognised overseas pension scheme** where the scheme manager has advised HMRC of its status and undertaken to provide HMRC with certain information.

QUALIFYING SERVICE   The term defined in section 71(7) PSA 1993 denoting the service to be taken into account to entitle the member to **short service benefit**. The current condition is for a minimum of two years' qualifying service.

This minimum is due to be abolished for **DC occupational pension schemes** *in 2014.*

RECOGNISED OVERSEAS PENSION SCHEME   Under FA 2004, an **overseas pension scheme** which is established and recognised in a prescribed country and satisfies all prescribed requirements.

RECOGNISED TRANSFER   Under FA 2004, a transfer representing a member's **accrued rights** under a **registered pension scheme** to another registered pension scheme (or, in certain circumstances, to an insurance company) or a **qualifying recognised overseas pension scheme**.

RECOVERY PLAN   If an **actuarial valuation** shows that the **statutory funding objective** is not met, the **trustees** will have to prepare a 'recovery plan' setting out the steps to be taken (and over what period) to make up the shortfall.

REFERENCE SCHEME TEST   The comparison of the benefits provided by a COSR with those under the reference scheme to ensure that they are at least equal, as required under section 12B PSA 1993.

The **scheme actuary** *must certify that the scheme complies with the reference scheme test.*

REGISTERED PENSION SCHEME   A pension scheme is a registered pension scheme at any time when, either through having applied for registration and having been registered by HMRC, or through acquiring registered status by virtue of being an approved scheme on 5 April 2006, it is registered under Chapter 2 of Part 4 of FA 2004.

RELIEF AT SOURCE   The procedure whereby member contributions are paid net of basic rate tax and the scheme **administrator** claims the tax from HMRC. Any higher-rate tax is claimed under self-assessment.

For an **occupational pension scheme**, *a* **net pay arrangement** *is more likely to be used.*

RETIREMENT ANNUITY   An **annuity** contract between an insurance company or friendly society and a self-employed individual or a person not in pensionable employment, which was established before 1 July 1988.

REVALUATION

(1)   Application, particularly to **preserved benefits**, of **indexation** or **escalation** or the awarding of **discretionary increases**. PSA 1993 imposes a minimum level of revaluation in the calculation of **GMP** and of preserved benefits other than GMP.

(2)   An accounting term for the revision of the carrying value of an asset, usually having regard to its market value.

SALARY SACRIFICE   An agreement between the employer and employee whereby the employee forgoes part of his/her future earnings in return for a corresponding contribution by the employer to a pension scheme. Also known as 'Smart Pensions'.

This is not the same as an **AVC**.

SCHEDULE OF CONTRIBUTIONS A schedule specifying the contribution rates and payment dates (normally) agreed between the employer and the **trustees** and certified by the **scheme actuary** as being adequate to satisfy the **statutory funding objective**.

Required for most **DB schemes** *under section 227 PA 2004.*

SCHEME ACTUARY The named actuary appointed by the **trustees** or managers of an **occupational pension scheme** under section 47 PA 1995.

SCHEME ADMINISTRATION MEMBER PAYMENT Under FA 2004, payments made by a **registered pension scheme** to a member, or in respect of a member, for the purposes of administration or management of the scheme.

SCHEME AUDITOR The auditor appointed by the **trustees** or managers of an **occupational pension scheme** under section 47 PA 1995.

SCHEME PAYS Where a member's pension savings in a scheme exceed the **annual allowance** for the tax year and the **annual allowance charge** is more than £2,000, the member can oblige the scheme to pay all or part of the charge on their behalf and reduce their benefit entitlement accordingly.

SCHEME PENSION Under FA 2004, a pension entitlement provided to a member of a **registered pension scheme**, which is an absolute right to a lifetime pension payable by the scheme.

SCHEME RETURN Information submitted by schemes to the **Pensions Regulator**, which it uses to make sure the details it holds on the register of pension schemes are accurate, calculate **levies** due from pension schemes and regulate pension schemes. The information collected is also used by the **Pension Protection Fund**. Schemes with five or more members must complete an annual scheme return.

SECONDED EMPLOYEE For the purposes of the legislation on **cross-border schemes**, this is an employee who is sent, by a UK employer, to work overseas for a limited period in another EEA state, is still providing services on behalf of the UK employer and intends to return to resume work for that employer in the UK or to retire at the end of that period.

SECTION 9(2B) RIGHTS Rights to benefits (other than benefits from **AVCs**) under an **occupational pension scheme** which is **contracted out** on a salary-related basis by virtue of section 9(2B) PSA 1993 and which are attributable to contracted-out employment after 5 April 1997.

Section 9(2B) rights are benefits payable under the scheme, not just the minimum level of benefits required under the **reference scheme test***.*

SECTION 32 POLICY   Used widely to describe an insurance policy used for **buy-out** purposes.

This term came into use as a result of section 32 FA 1981, which gave prominence to the possibility of effecting such policies.

SECTION 67   Section 67 of PA 1995 requires that **trustees** obtain members' consents, or a certificate from an actuary, before making any modification to an **occupational pension scheme** which would or might affect members' entitlements or **accrued rights** in respect of service before the modification.

SECTION 75 DEBT   A debt due to a pension scheme under PA 1995 from a sponsoring employer if that employer becomes insolvent, or the scheme starts to **wind up**, when the scheme is underfunded.

SECTION 143 VALUATION   A written valuation of a scheme's assets and liabilities for the purposes of enabling the **Pension Protection Fund** to determine whether it must assume responsibility for a scheme.

SECTION 148 ORDERS   Orders issued each year in accordance with section 148 Social Security Administration Act 1992 specifying the rates of increase to be applied to the earnings factors on which **S2P** and **GMPs** are based.

*This **revaluation** is based on the increase in national average earnings. Formerly known as section 21 orders.*

SECTION 179 VALUATION   A written valuation of a scheme's assets and liabilities, prepared and signed by the **scheme actuary**, for the purposes of enabling **Pension Protection Fund levies** to be calculated.

SELF-ADMINISTERED SCHEME   An **occupational pension scheme** where the assets are invested, other than wholly by payment of insurance premiums, by the **trustees**, an in-house investment manager or an external investment manager.

Although on the face of it the term self-administered should refer to the method of administering contributions and benefits, in practice the term has become solely related to the way in which the investments are managed.

SELF-INVESTMENT   The investment of the assets of an **occupational pension scheme** in employer-related investments.

A 5% limit is imposed on employer-related investments by PA 1995 (with certain exemptions).

SERIOUS ILL HEALTH COMMUTATION   Full commutation of benefits if a member's life expectancy is less than 12 months.

SHORT SERVICE BENEFIT   The benefit that must be provided for an early leaver with a legal right under the **preservation** legislation.

SHORT SERVICE REFUND LUMP SUM   A refund of contributions available to employees who have stopped accruing benefits under the scheme and have less than two years' **qualifying service**.

Due to be abolished for **DC occupational pension schemes** *in 2014.*

SHORT-TERM ANNUITY   Under FA 2004, an **annuity** contract purchased from a member's **drawdown pension fund** held under a **money purchase arrangement** that provides that member with pension income for a term of no more than five years.

SINGLE-TIER PENSION   The new flat-rate State pension, due to replace the **basic pension** and **State Second Pension** for those reaching **State Pensionable Age** from 6 April 2016.

SOCIALLY RESPONSIBLE INVESTMENT (SRI)   Investment strategies or restrictions that take account of the environmental, social and governance (ESG) impacts that a company's activities can have on individuals and the environment.

Pension funds are required to disclose in their **Statement of Investment Principles** the extent to which they take these factors into account.

STAGING   The process of introducing employer duties for **automatic enrolment** at monthly stages on allocated dates between 2012 and 2018.

STAGING DATE   This is the first date from which an employer must comply with its **automatic enrolment** duties. It will depend on the employer's size (as measured by the number in its PAYE scheme on 1 April 2012). An employer will have a single staging date; where it operates multiple PAYE schemes, the staging date will be determined by the largest one.

STAKEHOLDER PENSION SCHEME   A **DC scheme** that, in addition to being registered with HMRC, must satisfy the CAT standards necessary to be registered with the **Pensions Regulator** as a stakeholder scheme.

STANDARD LIFETIME ALLOWANCE   The maximum amount of tax-advantaged pension savings that can be built up by an individual who has not registered for **enhanced protection** and does not have an **enhanced lifetime allowance**.

STATE EARNINGS-RELATED PENSION SCHEME (SERPS)
The additional pension provisions of the State pension scheme. This was replaced by the **State Second Pension (S2P)** from 6 April 2002.

STATE PENSIONABLE AGE (SPA)   The age from which pensions are normally payable by the State pension scheme as defined in Schedule 4 PA 1995.

STATE SECOND PENSION (S2P)   The State pension scheme introduced with effect from 6 April 2002 to replace **SERPS** and to enhance the **basic pension**.

*Due to be replaced by the **single-tier pension** from 6 April 2016.*

STATEMENT OF FUNDING PRINCIPLES   Statement by the **trustees** setting out their policy for securing that the **statutory funding objective** is met and recording the decisions as to the basis for calculating the scheme's **technical provisions** and the period within which any shortfall is to be remedied.

STATEMENT OF INVESTMENT PRINCIPLES (SIP)   A written statement of principles governing decisions about investment for an **occupational pension scheme**, which **trustees** are required to prepare and maintain. Trustees must have regard to advice from a suitably qualified person and consult with the employer.

STATEMENT OF RECOMMENDED PRACTICE (SORP)   Guidance on best accounting practice for the presentation of financial information prepared by the particular industry to which the SORP relates.

STATUTORY EMPLOYER   In a **DB scheme**, the employer legally responsible for meeting the **statutory funding objective**, paying any **section 75 debt** and triggering entry to the **PPF**.

STATUTORY FUNDING OBJECTIVE   The requirement that a **DB scheme** 'must have sufficient and appropriate assets to cover its **technical provisions**'.

STATUTORY MONEY PURCHASE ILLUSTRATION (SMPI)   An annual statement, which must be issued to members of a **money purchase scheme**, illustrating on a prescribed statutory basis the projected value of a member's pension at retirement, in today's terms.

SUMMARY FUNDING STATEMENT   A summary of the scheme's funding position. It must be issued to all scheme members and **beneficiaries** (annually except for small schemes) and is their primary source of information on funding matters. Its content is prescribed by regulations.

TECHNICAL PROVISIONS   Under the scheme funding provisions of PA 2004, the amount required on an actuarial calculation to make provision for the scheme's liabilities.

TOTAL PENSION INPUT AMOUNT   The aggregate for a tax year of the **pension input amounts** in respect of each **arrangement** relating to an individual under **registered pension schemes** of which the individual is a member.

TRANSFER CLUB   A group of employers and **occupational pension schemes** which has agreed to a common basis of **transfer payments**.

TRANSFER INCENTIVE EXERCISE   An offer of an enhanced transfer value, to encourage members to transfer their **defined benefits** elsewhere.

TRANSFER PAYMENT   A payment made from a pension scheme to another pension scheme, or to purchase a **buy-out** policy, in lieu of benefits which have accrued to the member or members concerned, to enable the receiving **arrangement** to provide alternative benefits.

The transfer payment may be made in accordance with the scheme rules or in exercise of a member's statutory rights under PSA 1993. See also **cash equivalent**.

TRUST   A legal concept whereby property is held by one or more persons (the **trustees**) for the benefit of others (the **beneficiaries**) for the purposes specified by the trust instrument. The trustees may also be beneficiaries.

TRUST DEED   A legal document, executed in the form of a deed, which establishes, regulates or amends a **trust**.

TRUSTEE   An individual or company appointed to carry out the purposes of a **trust** in accordance with the provisions of the **trust deed** (or other documents by which a trust is created and governed) and general principles of trust law.

TRUSTEE REPORT   A report by the **trustees** describing various aspects of an **occupational pension scheme**. It may form part of the **annual report**.

UPPER ACCRUAL POINT (UAP)   The maximum amount of earnings on which **S2P** and contracted-out rebates are based. It replaced the **UEL** for this purpose from 6 April 2009.

UPPER BAND EARNINGS   Earnings between the **lower earnings limit** and the **upper accrual point**.

UPPER EARNINGS LIMIT (UEL)   The upper limit to earnings on which full-rate NI contributions are payable by employees. NI contributions are payable by employees at a lower rate on earnings above this limit.

VESTED RIGHTS

(a)   For **active members**, benefits to which they would unconditionally be entitled on leaving the scheme

(b)   for **deferred pensioners**, their **preserved benefits**, *and*

(c)   for pensioners, pensions to which they are entitled including where appropriate the related benefits for spouses or other **dependants**.

WHISTLE-BLOWING   The statutory duty imposed on **trustees**, employers, **administrators** and advisers by section 70 PA 2004 to advise the **Pensions Regulator** as soon as practicable in writing if they have reasonable cause to believe there is a material problem with an **occupational pension scheme**.

WINDING UP   The process of terminating an **occupational pension scheme** (or less commonly a **personal pension scheme**), usually by applying the assets to the purchase of immediate **annuities** and deferred annuities for the **beneficiaries**, or by transferring the assets and liabilities to another pension scheme, in accordance with the scheme documentation or statute (section 74 PA 1995).

WITH-PROFITS POLICY   An insurance policy under which a share of the surpluses disclosed by **actuarial valuations** of the insurance company's life and pensions business is payable in addition to the guaranteed benefits or in reduction of future premiums.

Many of the definitions used in this Glossary of Terms originate from *Pensions Terminology* published by The Pensions Management Institute, whose kind permission to reproduce here is gratefully acknowledged. The Eighth Edition of *Pensions Terminology* is now available from the PMI.

COMPOUND INTEREST TABLES

How to use the compound interest tables to generate additional factors:

Present value of a payment of
one unit due in n years' time

$$v^n = \frac{1}{(1+i)^n}$$

Present value of an annuity of
one unit per annum payable
annually in arrears for n years

$$a_{\overline{n}|} = \frac{1-v^n}{i}$$

Present value of an annuity of
one unit per annum payable
annually in advance for n years

$$\ddot{a}_{\overline{n}|} = \frac{1-v^n}{d}$$

Present value of an annuity of
one unit per annum payable
continuously for n years

$$\bar{a}_{\overline{n}|} = \frac{1-v^n}{\delta}$$

Present value of an annuity of
one unit per annum payable
in two half-yearly instalments
in arrears for n years

$$a_{\overline{n}|}^{(2)} = \frac{i}{i^{(2)}} a_{\overline{n}|}$$

Present value of an annuity of
one unit per annum payable
in four quarterly instalments
in arrears for n years

$$a_{\overline{n}|}^{(4)} = \frac{i}{i^{(4)}} a_{\overline{n}|}$$

Present value of an annuity of
one unit per annum payable
in twelve monthly instalments
in arrears for n years

$$a_{\overline{n}|}^{(12)} = \frac{i}{i^{(12)}} a_{\overline{n}|}$$

Accumulated value after n years
of an annuity of one unit payable
annually in arrears

$$s_{\overline{n}|} = \frac{(1+i)^n - 1}{i}$$

APPENDIX 3: COMPOUND INTEREST TABLES

Accumulated value after n years of a single unit payment $[(1+i)^n]$

n	$i=1\%$	$i=2\%$	$i=3\%$	$i=4\%$	$i=5\%$
1	1.010000	1.020000	1.030000	1.040000	1.050000
2	1.020100	1.040400	1.060900	1.081600	1.102500
3	1.030301	1.061208	1.092727	1.124864	1.157625
4	1.040604	1.082432	1.125509	1.169859	1.215506
5	1.051010	1.104081	1.159274	1.216653	1.276282
6	1.061520	1.126162	1.194052	1.265319	1.340096
7	1.072135	1.148686	1.229874	1.315932	1.407100
8	1.082857	1.171659	1.266770	1.368569	1.477455
9	1.093685	1.195093	1.304773	1.423312	1.551328
10	1.104622	1.218994	1.343916	1.480244	1.628895
11	1.115668	1.243374	1.384254	1.539454	1.710339
12	1.126825	1.268242	1.425761	1.601032	1.795856
13	1.138093	1.293607	1.468534	1.665074	1.885649
14	1.149474	1.319479	1.512590	1.731676	1.979932
15	1.160969	1.345868	1.557967	1.800944	2.078928
16	1.172579	1.372786	1.604706	1.872981	2.182875
17	1.184304	1.400241	1.652848	1.947900	2.292018
18	1.196142	1.428246	1.702433	2.025817	2.406619
19	1.208109	1.456811	1.753506	2.106849	2.526950
20	1.220190	1.485947	1.806111	2.191123	2.653298
21	1.232392	1.515666	1.860295	2.278768	2.785963
22	1.244716	1.545980	1.916103	2.369919	2.925261
23	1.257163	1.576899	1.973587	2.464716	3.071524
24	1.269735	1.608437	2.032794	2.563304	3.225100
25	1.282432	1.640606	2.093778	2.665836	3.386355
26	1.295256	1.673418	2.156591	2.772470	3.555673
27	1.308209	1.706886	2.221289	2.883369	3.733456
28	1.321291	1.741024	2.287928	2.998703	3.920129
29	1.334504	1.775845	2.356566	3.118651	4.116316
30	1.347849	1.811362	2.427262	3.243398	4.321942
31	1.361327	1.847589	2.500080	3.373133	4.538039
32	1.374941	1.884541	2.575083	3.508059	4.764941
33	1.388690	1.922231	2.652335	3.648381	5.003189
34	1.402577	1.960676	2.731905	3.794316	5.253348
35	1.416603	1.999890	2.813862	3.946089	5.516015
36	1.430769	2.039887	2.898278	4.103933	5.791816
37	1.445076	2.080685	2.985227	4.268090	6.081407
38	1.459527	2.122299	3.074783	4.438813	6.385477
39	1.474123	2.164745	3.167027	4.616366	6.704751
40	1.488864	2.208040	3.262038	4.801021	7.039989

	$i=1\%$	$i=2\%$	$i=3\%$	$i=4\%$	$i=5\%$
d	0.009901	0.019608	0.029126	0.038462	0.047619
$i^{(2)}$	0.009975	0.019901	0.029778	0.039608	0.049390
$i^{(4)}$	0.009963	0.019852	0.029668	0.039414	0.049089
$i^{(12)}$	0.009954	0.019819	0.029595	0.039285	0.048889
δ	0.009950	0.019803	0.029559	0.039221	0.048790

Note: For GMP fixed rate revaluation factors *see page 11*.

Accumulated value after n years of a single unit payment $[(1+i)^n]$

n	i=6%	i=7%	i=8%	i=9%	i=10%
1	1.060000	1.070000	1.080000	1.090000	1.100000
2	1.123600	1.144900	1.166400	1.188100	1.210000
3	1.191016	1.225043	1.259712	1.295029	1.331000
4	1.262477	1.310796	1.360489	1.411582	1.464100
5	1.338226	1.402552	1.469328	1.538624	1.610510
6	1.418519	1.500730	1.586874	1.677100	1.771561
7	1.503630	1.605781	1.713824	1.828039	1.948717
8	1.593848	1.718186	1.850930	1.992563	2.143589
9	1.689479	1.838459	1.999005	2.171893	2.357948
10	1.790848	1.967151	2.158925	2.367364	2.593742
11	1.898299	2.104852	2.331639	2.580426	2.853117
12	2.012196	2.252192	2.518170	2.812665	3.138428
13	2.132928	2.409845	2.719624	3.065805	3.452271
14	2.260904	2.578534	2.937194	3.341727	3.797498
15	2.396558	2.759032	3.172169	3.642482	4.177248
16	2.540352	2.952164	3.425943	3.970306	4.594973
17	2.692773	3.158815	3.700018	4.327633	5.054470
18	2.854339	3.379932	3.996019	4.717120	5.559917
19	3.025600	3.616528	4.315701	5.141661	6.115909
20	3.207135	3.869684	4.660957	5.604411	6.727500
21	3.399564	4.140562	5.033834	6.108808	7.400250
22	3.603537	4.430402	5.436540	6.658600	8.140275
23	3.819750	4.740530	5.871464	7.257874	8.954302
24	4.048935	5.072367	6.341181	7.911083	9.849733
25	4.291871	5.427433	6.848475	8.623081	10.834706
26	4.549383	5.807353	7.396353	9.399158	11.918177
27	4.822346	6.213868	7.988061	10.245082	13.109994
28	5.111687	6.648838	8.627106	11.167140	14.420994
29	5.418388	7.114257	9.317275	12.172182	15.863093
30	5.743491	7.612255	10.062657	13.267678	17.449402
31	6.088101	8.145113	10.867669	14.461770	19.194342
32	6.453387	8.715271	11.737083	15.763329	21.113777
33	6.840590	9.325340	12.676050	17.182028	23.225154
34	7.251025	9.978114	13.690134	18.728411	25.547670
35	7.686087	10.676581	14.785344	20.413968	28.102437
36	8.147252	11.423942	15.968142	22.251225	30.912681
37	8.636087	12.223618	17.245626	24.253835	34.003949
38	9.154252	13.079271	18.625276	26.436680	37.404343
39	9.703507	13.994820	20.115298	28.815982	41.144778
40	10.285718	14.974458	21.724521	31.409420	45.259256

	i=6%	i=7%	i=8%	i=9%	i=10%
d	0.056604	0.065421	0.074074	0.082569	0.090909
$i^{(2)}$	0.059126	0.068816	0.078461	0.088061	0.097618
$i^{(4)}$	0.058695	0.068234	0.077706	0.087113	0.096455
$i^{(12)}$	0.058411	0.067850	0.077208	0.086488	0.095690
δ	0.058269	0.067659	0.076961	0.086178	0.095310

Note: For GMP fixed rate revaluation factors *see page 11.*

ANNUITY FACTORS

MALE LIFE ANNUITIES ON S1PMA (Year of Use=2014) TABLE

With future improvements in life expectancy based on the CMI_2012 Core Projections for males with a long-term rate of improvement of 1.5% p.a.

Exact age:	55	60	65	70	75
Interest					
0%	32.673	27.604	22.891	18.236	13.923
1%	27.443	23.733	20.122	16.387	12.776
2%	23.386	20.636	17.842	14.820	11.777
3%	20.194	18.132	15.948	13.483	10.902
4%	17.652	16.086	14.362	12.334	10.133
5%	15.600	14.397	13.022	11.342	9.452

Note: The columns represent the present value of a life annuity of one unit per year payable continuously to a male from the exact age given subject to the mortality experience of the S1PMA table, adjusted for use in 2014, allowing for future improvements in life expectancy based on the CMI_2012 Core Projections for males with a long-term rate of improvement of 1.5% p.a. and valued at the rates of interest shown.

FEMALE LIFE ANNUITIES ON S1PFA (Year of Use=2014) TABLE

With future improvements in life expectancy based on the CMI_2012 Core Projections for females with a long-term rate of improvement of 1.5% p.a.

Exact age:	55	60	65	70	75
Interest					
0%	35.102	30.109	25.206	20.394	15.834
1%	29.166	25.610	21.937	18.152	14.402
2%	24.621	22.059	19.278	16.276	13.168
3%	21.091	19.222	17.095	14.692	12.099
4%	18.309	16.930	15.286	13.346	11.168
5%	16.088	15.058	13.774	12.195	10.353

Note: The columns represent the present value of a life annuity of one unit per year payable continuously to a female from the exact age given subject to the mortality experience of the S1PFA table, adjusted for use in 2014, allowing for future improvements in life expectancy based on the CMI_2012 Core Projections for females with a long-term rate of improvement of 1.5% p.a. and valued at the rates of interest shown.

USEFUL WEBSITES

This chapter shows the website addresses of the main sites likely to be of relevance to readers, together with brief description of some of the sites where content may not be familiar.

Government departments

Department for Work and Pensions (DWP)	*www.gov.uk/government/organisations/ department-for-work-pensions*
Pensions	*https://www.gov.uk/browse/working/state-pension*
Welfare, including universal credit	*https://www.gov.uk/government/topics/ welfare*
Department for Business Innovation and Skills	*www.gov.uk/government/organisations/ department-for-business-innovation-skills*
HM Treasury (HMT)	*www.gov.uk/government/organisations/hm-treasury*
HM Revenue & Customs	*www.hmrc.gov.uk*
National Insurance Services to Pensions Industry	*www.hmrc.gov.uk/nic/coeg.htm*
HMRC manuals	*www.hmrc.gov.uk/thelibrary/manuals-subjectarea.htm*
Pension schemes	*www.hmrc.gov.uk/pensionschemes/index.htm*
Pension scheme forms	*http://search2.hmrc.gov.uk/kb5/hmrc/ forms/pensionschemesforms.page*
Information reporting and record keeping	*www.hmrc.gov.uk/pensionschemes/ info-records.htm*
Government Actuary's Department (GAD)	*www.gad.gov.uk*
Other Government departments and information	*www.gov.uk*

Regulators and ombudsmen

Financial Reporting Council (FRC) regulates accounting, auditing and actuarial functions	*www.frc.org.uk*
Financial Conduct Authority replaced FSA in regulating financial services industry	*www.fca.org.uk*
Information Commissioner's Office (ICO) data protection control and information	*www.ico.org.uk*
Financial Ombudsman Service financial services complaints	*www.financial-ombudsman.org.uk*
PPF Ombudsman	*www.ppfo.org.uk*
Pensions Ombudsman	*www.pensions-ombudsman.org.uk*
Pensions Regulator (TPR)	*www.thepensionsregulator.gov.uk*
Prudential Regulation Authority supervises certain financial firms	*www.bankofengland.co.uk/pra*

Other Government sites

Companies House Executive Agency	*www.companieshouse.gov.uk*
Parliament	*www.parliament.uk*
National Employment Savings Trust (NEST)	*www.nestpensions.org.uk*
Pension Protection Fund (PPF) and Financial Assistance Scheme (FAS)	*www.pensionprotectionfund.org.uk*
Financial Services Compensation Scheme	*www.fscs.org.uk*
Office for National Statistics	*www.statistics.gov.uk*

Industry and Professional Bodies

Association of British Insurers (ABI)	*www.abi.org.uk*
Association of Consulting Actuaries (ACA)	*www.aca.org.uk*
Association of Member-Directed Pension Schemes mainly represents SIPPS and SSAS	*www.ampsonline.co.uk*
Association of Pension Lawyers (APL)	*www.apl.org.uk*
Chartered Insurance Institute (CII)	*www.cii.co.uk*
Institute and Faculty of Actuaries	*www.actuaries.org.uk*
Law Society	*www.lawsociety.org.uk*
National Association of Pension Funds (NAPF)	*www.napf.co.uk*
Pensions Management Institute (PMI)	*www.pensions-pmi.org.uk*
Society of Pension Consultants (SPC)	*www.spc.uk.com*
Pensions Research Advisory Group (PRAG) principally reporting and accounting	*www.prag.org.uk*
Pensions Policy Institute (PPI) comment on, and analysis of, public pensions policy	*www.pensionspolicyinstitute.org.uk*

Sources of Information or Advice

British and Irish Legal Information Institute court judgments (including EU)	*www.bailii.org*
Government legislation service replaces the Office of Public Sector Information and the Statute Law Database	*www.legislation.gov.uk*
The Pensions Advisory Service (TPAS) advice on occupational and personal pensions	*www.pensionsadvisoryservice.org.uk*
Money Advice Service generic information on money issues	*www.moneyadviceservice.org.uk*
Unbiased links to FCA-regulated advisers	*www.unbiased.co.uk*